SETTLER CANNABIS

Indigenous Confluences

CHARLOTTE COTÉ AND COLL THRUSH *Series Editors*

KAITLIN REED

SETTLER CANNABIS

From Gold Rush to Green Rush in Indigenous Northern California

University of Washington Press   *Seattle*

A CAPELL FAMILY BOOK
Settler Cannabis was made possible in part by a grant from the Capell Family Endowed Book Fund, which supports the publication of books that deepen the understanding of social justice through historical, cultural, and environmental studies.

This book was supported by the Tulalip Tribes Charitable Fund, which provides the opportunity for a sustainable and healthy community for all.

Additional support was provided by the College of Arts, Humanities, and Social Sciences at Cal Poly Humboldt.

Copyright © 2023 by the University of Washington Press
Design by Mindy Basinger Hill
Composed in ITC Galliard Pro

All rights reserved. No part of this publication may be reproduced or transmitted in any form or by any means, electronic or mechanical, including photocopy, recording, or any information storage or retrieval system, without permission in writing from the publisher.

UNIVERSITY OF WASHINGTON PRESS   *uwapress.uw.edu*

LIBRARY OF CONGRESS CATALOGING-IN-PUBLICATION DATA
Names: Reed, Kaitlin, author.
Title: Settler cannabis : from gold rush to green rush in indigenous Northern California / Kaitlin Reed.
Other titles: Indigenous confluences.
Description: Seattle : University of Washington Press, [2023] | Series: Indigenous confluences | Includes bibliographical references and index.
Identifiers: LCCN 2023002339 | ISBN 9780295751559 (hardback) | ISBN 9780295751566 (paperback) | ISBN 9780295751573 (ebook)
Subjects: LCSH: Colonization—Environmental aspects—California, Northern. | Indians of North America—Colonization—California, Northern. | Cannabis—Irrigation—Environmental aspects—California, Northern. | Indians of North America—Crimes against—California, Northern.
Classification: LCC E78.C15 R38 2023 | DDC 979.4—dc23/eng/20230127
LC record available at https://lccn.loc.gov/2023002339

♾ This paper meets the requirements of ANSI/NISO Z39.48-1992 (Permanence of Paper).

CONTENTS

PREFACE Black Snakes *ix*

ACKNOWLEDGMENTS *xv*

NOTE ABOUT TERMS *xvii*

INTRODUCTION Settler Colonialism and Ecological Violence *1*

1 GOLD, GREED, AND GENOCIDE Settler Colonialism and Resource Extraction in the California Gold Rush *25*

2 FORESTS ON FIRE Constructing Natural Resources and Imposing Ecological Regimes *50*

3 SALMON IS EVERYTHING Controlling Rivers and Commodifying Kin *75*

4 BACK TO WHOSE LAND? Hippies, Environmentalism, and Cannabis *98*

5 WEED GREED Explosion of the California Green Rush *122*

6 NO JUSTICE ON STOLEN LAND Cannabis Cultivation and Land Dispossession *152*

7 CANNABIS AND WATER Use, Rights, and Infrastructure *181*

8 TOXIC ENVIRONMENTS Cannabis, Chemicals, and Legacy Impacts *209*

CONCLUSION Ecological Crisis and Land Back *234*

NOTES *241*

REFERENCES *251*

INDEX *281*

PREFACE

Black Snakes

The July sun was hot on the back of my neck as I struggled to find my footing on a steep mountainside along the Klamath River. Yurok ancestral territory is located here in northwestern California and has been the ground zero for cannabis production since the 1960s. At the height of the contemporary cannabis "green rush," Yurok ancestral territory was under siege by large-scale trespass cannabis cultivation. Illegal and unregulated water diversions ran our streams dry and degraded water quality with chemical pollution and human waste. My colleagues with the Yurok Tribe Environmental Program were tasked with dismantling the cannabis irrigation structures that were sucking tribal water resources dry and documenting the ecological impact of cannabis cultivation. We were looking for thin black plastic tubing—hard to see and even harder to remove. As sweat poured down my face, the quantity of tubing seemed never-ending. I ripped up as much polyethylene tubing as possible in an attempt to liberate our tributaries. Within a short time there was a gargantuan pile of black snakes ready to be removed from the landscape. However, the concern that additional black snakes remained continues to linger.

The onslaught of settler-colonial destruction is not relegated to history; it is very much a part of our present and lived experiences as Indigenous peoples in this region. Our River, the lifeblood of our people, has been under attack since settler-colonial invasion a little over a century and a half ago. The history of water development and extraction in the Klamath Basin has disproportionately impacted Indigenous peoples, water, plants, and wildlife. The Klamath Project of 1905, the first Bureau of Reclamation project, led to the construction of four deadly dams and extensive agricultural pollution of the Klamath River, effectively collapsing the possibility of future sustainable subsistence fishing economies. This has had detrimental impacts on the cultural and food sovereignty of Native peoples within the Klamath Basin, as well as on fish, wildlife, and plant species.

Within Yurok epistemology Salmon are understood as relatives and ancestors. While the word "genocide" is reserved for human beings within a Western paradigm, we conceptualize the fish kill as a genocide. In 2002 our Salmon relatives faced a genocide of cataclysmic proportions. Steward for the Many Nations Longhouse Gordon Bettles (Klamath Tribe) (2014) argues that the tragic 2002 fish kill that left seventy thousand dead Salmon rotting along the banks of the Klamath River "was caused by a collision of cultures that began when the first ships landed on the east coast of North America in 1492" (xi). Similarly, Tasha Hubbard (2014) argues that the strategic and systematic slaughter of buffalo also constitutes an act of genocide: "In other words, destroy the buffalo, and one destroys the foundation of Plains Indigenous collectivity and their very lives" (294). Given that the arrival of the first ships and the fish kill transpired 510 years apart, Bettles clearly does not mean that those aboard the first ships killed our Salmon. Rather, Bettles argues that the settler-colonial worldview that separates humans from nature and understands land as property and a source of wealth accumulation is responsible for creating the conditions that allowed a fish kill to occur. In other words, Columbus had snakes on his boats.

A century of water infrastructure development and increasing demand for water for grazing and agricultural production dramatically decreased the flows and increased the temperature of the Klamath River. This created an environment in which disease could spread rapidly—and it did. Conservative estimates suggest that in 2002 at least thirty thousand Chinook, six hundred coho, and one thousand steelhead succumbed to a deadly pathogen, known locally as "Ich" (*Ichthyophthirius multifiliis*) (Belchik, Hillemeier, and Pierce 2004).

As Salmon people we understand ourselves to be in relationship with Salmon and the Klamath. Salmon are a cultural and physical staple for Yurok people. Even our creation story instructs Yuroks on this ancient relationship. But the significance of the River and the Salmon are difficult to explain in objective Western frameworks of science and may be impossible to understand for those who measure Mother Earth's bounty in numeric values. Case in point: Salmon and the environment they depend on have been under a series of continuous assaults since settler invasion—from mining to timber harvesting to grazing and damming, and now to irrigating for cannabis. Reflecting on battles over fishing rights in western courtrooms, Susan Masten (Yurok), tribal chair of the Yurok Tribe and president of the

National Congress of the American Indians at the turn of the twenty-first century, declared: "We are salmon people. We couldn't let anyone take that from us" (quoted in Wilkinson 2005, 150). And the Yurok Tribe has held this responsibility through its consistent efforts at Salmon protection and dam removal.

Within Yurok epistemology, the Klamath River is a living being. As a Yurok person, I understand the Klamath as a vein that connects me to the Earth. It is central to our "sacred geography" (V. Deloria 1994, 199) and is often referred to as an "umbilical cord to the Earth" (Orona 2013). To describe Indigenous relationships with water, Melanie K. Yazzie (Bilagáana/Diné) and Cutcha Risling Baldy (Hupa/Yurok/Karuk) (2018) have developed an analytical framework of "radical relationality" within which water is not a "resource to be weaponized . . . to boost the capitalist economies of settler nation-states . . . [instead] water is a relative with whom we engage in social (and political) relations premised on interdependency and respect" (3). Struggles over water figure centrally in Indigenous fights for sovereignty, nationhood, and futurity. As Indigenous peoples around the globe rise up to defend and protect our waters, we are fighting for the future of the Earth, our peoples, and all living beings.

In 2016 the eyes of the world turned to watch the Standing Rock Sioux Nation and their allies spanning the globe rise up to challenge the construction of an oil pipeline. The Oceti Sakowin Nation of the Mni Sose (Missouri River) have a prophecy about Zuzeca Sapa, or Black Snake. Nick Estes (Lower Brule Sioux Tribe), in his book *Our History Is the Future: Standing Rock versus the Dakota Access Pipeline, and the Long Tradition of Indigenous Resistance* (2019), writes:

> Prophecy told of Zuzeca Sapa, the Black Snake, extending itself across the land and imperiling all life, beginning with the water. From its heads, or many heads, it would spew death and destruction. Zuzeca Sapa is DAPL—and all oil pipelines trespassing through Indigenous territory. But while the Black Snake prophecy foreshadows doom, it also foreshadows historic resistance and resurgent Indigenous histories not seen for generations, if ever. To protect Unci Maka, Grandmother Earth, Indigenous and non-Indigenous peoples will have to unite to turn back to the forces destroying the earth—capitalism and colonial-

ism. But prophets and prophecies do not predict the future, nor are they mystical, ahistorical occurrences. They are simply diagnoses of the times in which we live, and visions of what must be done to get free. (14)

I first heard this story on November 15, 2016. By then, water protectors were facing arrest; six days later law enforcement began the use of tear gas and water cannons. Safe on my college campus, I attended a Standing Rock teach-in at the University of California, Davis. Everyone was brought up to speed on what had happened to water protectors; educational resources were suggested. However, the part of this event I still think about quite frequently was an Oceti Sakowin Nation prophecy shared by my colleague Jessa Rae Growing Thunder (Dakota/Nakoda/Assiniboine). Apart from Growing Thunder being a terrific storyteller, her words captivated me. Like in Estes's telling, Zuzeca Sapa, or the Black Snake, would bring great destruction and the people would have to rise up to defeat it. Though I arrived at this teach-in prepared to think about Standing Rock and the ways I could support the activism occurring on my college campus, as I biked back to my apartment my mind was not on Cannon Ball, North Dakota, at all—no, I was thinking about the ancestral homeland of my people in northwestern California. And it dawned on me that my people, too, were fighting their own black snake.

During the summer of 2014 I was hired as an environmental technician at the Yurok Tribe Environmental Program. On the morning of July 21, I stared out the window of the commute rig as we made our way up Highway 101 to Klamath, California. I remember sitting at my desk, sipping weak coffee. After logging into my email, I saw a *Los Angeles Times* article that had been forwarded to all tribal employees: "Massive Raid to Help Yurok Tribe Combat Illegal Pot Grows" (Romney 2014). While I sat safely in that office, other tribe members and employees, accompanied by dozens of law enforcement officers clad in camouflage and carrying assault rifles, made their way upriver. Their goal that morning was to eradicate cannabis cultivation and document the resulting environmental damages, both within and beyond the boundary of the Yurok Indian Reservation. Operation Yurok was a tribe-led cannabis eradication campaign that took place from 2014 to 2017, designed to eliminate environmentally hazardous trespass cultivation. One of the primary concerns of the campaign was to address illicit water diversion used for cannabis production. But we didn't have just one clearly visible black snake to battle—there were hundreds, probably even thousands, hidden away in the hills. Our black snakes are not constructed of metal or filled with oil. Instead, our black snakes are made of polyethylene. Small and thin, and sometimes nearly invisible if you do not know where to look, our black snakes are scattered over hillsides, siphoning water from springs and streams to thirsty cannabis plants. There was (and continues to be) fear that drought conditions and climate change, with the added impact of unregulated illicit water diversion for cannabis, could result in another catastrophic fish kill. This cultural collision culminated in 2002, but it began with invasion.

As Yurok people, we cannot talk about water diversion for cannabis without talking about Salmon and the health of our River. The River is already overtaxed and overallocated—and must endure the impacts of human-caused climate change. This is true of many Rivers throughout California—all of which have significant ties and connections to Indigenous peoples of that region. When our Rivers give us a choice between Salmon or cannabis, I hope the answer is an easy one. Salmon constitute both an ecological and a cultural keystone species. People, plants, and wildlife all depend upon Salmon and the often-unacknowledged ecological labor they perform. If Salmon disappeared from the Klamath Basin, the ecosystem would collapse. Their well-being is fundamentally tied to ours. As Yurok people fight for the very survival of Salmon, they are fighting for their own right to survive—to live in a world of ecological and spiritual balance. Salmon's resilience keeps alive the hope of a better future for Yuroks and all California Indian peoples.

This book aims to connect the historical and ecological dots between the California gold rush and the contemporary green rush. The surge in cannabis production, dubbed the green rush, is an apt analogy to the gold rush–era ideology of manifest destiny, resource extraction, and wealth accumulation. For California Indians, the gold rush was an apocalypse aimed at destroying Indigenous cultural and ecological worlds. The state of California was founded on genocidal violence toward California Indians, on Indigenous land dispossession, and on resource extraction. I argue that violence against the landscape is mirrored or paralleled in violence against Indigenous bodies. Just as our Rivers are attacked by black snakes, so are our peoples, our cultures. Moreover, this violence has been fundamental for the creation and maintenance of the state of California; thus, contemporary green rush violence against Indigenous lands, waters, and bodies cannot be understood in isolation. It is part of a larger historical pattern of the violence associated with resource "rushing." While state-sponsored militias no longer commit for-profit murder of California Indians, our traditional gatherers and basketweavers have faced threats, fear of physical violence, and intimidation from trespass grow operations. More-than-human relatives have been intentionally poisoned and exposed to chemicals located at grow sites. Whether it be oil pipelines or cannabis irrigation infrastructure, these black snakes are merely symptoms of two greater foes: capitalism and colonialism. Resource rushing, guided by the rush mentality, is a violent settler-colonial pattern of resource extraction that has been repeatedly played out—first gold, then timber, then fish, and now cannabis. California Indians have watched this pattern play out over and over again. We already know how the story ends. Everywhere we look, it seems, lands and waters are being desecrated in the name of profit. But as Estes notes, the Zuzeca Sapa prophecy foretells resistance and resurgence to capitalist and colonialist forces. We are rising up.

ACKNOWLEDGMENTS

This book is the work of many and would not exist without the innumerable educators and mentors I have learned from over the years, without the continued resistance and activism of tribal peoples in the present, and of course, without our ancestors, who fought to make sure California Indians are here today.

    I am thoroughly indebted to my amazing colleagues and friends at the University of California, Davis. Thank you to my esteemed committee: Dr. Beth Rose Middleton Manning, Dr. Liza Grandia, and Dr. Cutcha Risling Baldy. Thank you for reading those early, early drafts. Your insightful comments and words of wisdom have shaped the thinker I am today. Thank you to all of my terrific colleagues in the Native American Studies Department. From seminar to happy hour, I loved intellectually developing with all of you and I eagerly wait for our paths to cross again. SimHayKin: thanks for making graduate school such a great experience. Reading by the pool, afternoons at Pho King, and marathoning episodes of *Avatar: The Last Air Bender* were the highlights of my graduate school experience. I am grateful for the financial support I have received from UC Davis, including the Provost's Fellowship for the Arts, Humanities, and Social Sciences; the Emily Schwalen Memorial Prize; the Mellon Social Justice Initiative Graduate Summer Research Fellowship; the UC Davis & Humanities Graduate Research Award; and the UC Humanities Research Institute Graduate Student Dissertation Support Award.

    Thank you to the Native American Studies Department at Dartmouth College. Even though I had to spend a year in the snow, you all made it a warm and inviting place. Thank you for reading chapters, listening to job talks, and inviting me to speak to your students about my work. I am especially grateful for receiving the Charles Eastman Dissertation Fellowship in 2018. This award made it possible to finish my dissertation and get this manuscript underway.

    For all the support I have received at Cal Poly Humboldt, thank you. I have felt so lucky to call the Native American Studies Department there my home of the past three years. I am excited to see the #dreamteam get even bigger. Thank you for the financial support I have received, including the Research, Scholarship, and Creative Activities Program Grant and the Emeritus & Retired Faculty and Staff Association Grant. Lastly, thank you to The Squad. I don't know how I would have navigated these past three years without you.

Thank you to everybody who offered feedback and suggestions on drafts of my manuscript. Thank you to my book manuscript workshop committee, Beth Rose Middleton Manning, Nick Reo, Lindsay Bear, and Kari Norgaard. Thank you so much for your insightful feedback—and I'm even more appreciative of the two-day pep talk. I needed it. Thank you for the support of the University of Washington Press. I have received nothing but kindness and patience as I've worked to bring my first book into the world. Thank you to the two anonymous peer reviewers who provided such useful feedback and kind words of support and the editorial staff that made this work possible.

I want to express my deep gratitude to the Yurok Tribe for the continued support of my academic career and research. Starting with the Yurok Tribe Higher Education grants provided to me during my undergraduate study, the Yurok Tribe has supported my educational journey from the beginning. Thank you to all the amazing staff that make up the Yurok Tribe Environmental Program. When y'all hired me as an intern in the summer of 2013, I had no idea it would lead me here. Thank you so much. Thank you to all the hardworking folks in the Planning Department, the Cannabis Task Force, and the Yurok Tribal Council. While I have been writing this book about cannabis, you are actively defending our territory from the green rush. You all make me so proud to be a Yurok tribal member.

Lastly, I reserve closing acknowledgments for my family, as this book would not exist without their support and sacrifices. I would like to thank my mother, Rachel Nelson, and my grandmother, Carol Swanson, for all that they have done to make my education possible. Thank you to my sister, Lexi, for providing laughs along the way. And, of course, thank you to my partner, Michael. Thank you for relocating across the country at the whim of an academic's ambitions, for your constant care and encouragement, and for picking up the slack around the house as I sat glued to a computer screen. I dedicate this book to my family.

NOTE ABOUT TERMS

When referencing Native American communities I employ tribal specificity where possible. Native American tribes, such as the Yurok Tribe, Hoopa Valley Tribe, Wiyot Tribe, Karuk Tribe, Blue Lake Rancheria, and so on are referred to by name. Generally I use Native American, Indian, and Indigenous interchangeably. I also use the term California Indian to refer to Native American individuals and communities throughout the state.

When referencing the plant *Cannabis sativa* or *Cannabis indica*, I use the term "cannabis." The term "marijuana" (Spanish for "Mary Jane") is tied to the racist origins of American prohibition policies and was deployed to racialize the consumption of cannabis. The term "marijuana," however, is still widely used in both speech and text, as are numerous other synonyms, including "pot" and "weed." In my own prose I have opted for the term "cannabis," but when reproducing the text or speech of others, I have been consistent in the terms they used. Thus, a variety of synonyms for cannabis are used throughout the text.

Lastly, following the completion of this manuscript, the Yurok Tribe Environmental Program, mentioned throughout, became the Yurok Tribe Environmental Department. I have referred to this entity as the Yurok Tribe Environmental Program, or YTEP, throughout.

SETTLER CANNABIS

INTRODUCTION

Settler Colonialism and Ecological Violence

Before time began, some say from time immemorial, California Indians have stewarded and cared for their places. Many of us believe that we were created in our place-worlds, that we came from the land. In his book *California through Native Eyes*, historian William Bauer Jr. (Wailaki/Concow) demonstrates the ways by which California Indian creation stories ground us in our places, provide the foundations of our identity, and help explain the differences between Peoples. Bauer (2016) suggests that "if the Creator made the land specifically for the People, then the Creator made a People expressly for that land" (14). While the many creation stories across California are diverse, they share a tendency to link Indigenous peoples to their respective lands, waters, plants, and animals. Through this process of creating place-worlds, "Indigenous people become responsible to all things of creation, including those 'inanimate objects' like rocks, mountains, rivers and trees. Each of these things is endowed with a spirit, a literal 'force of nature' that Indigenous peoples regard as creators of their world" (Risling Baldy 2015, 10). Brittani Orona (Hupa) (quoted in Jones 2019) explains: "We are a part of the land, and the land is us." This environmental ethos—far from a New Age metaphor—guides Indigenous ecological management practices. We mean it literally. When a group of people live in the same place for thousands of years, our ancestors become the soil, they become the Earth. The gifts we receive from Creator—Salmon, Elk, and Acorns—nourish us and become part of our bodies. In caring for the land, gathering the plants, dancing for the Salmon, we engage in an ancient relationship with our land bases, rooted in a connection and reciprocity that has developed over millennia.

Prior to invasion, there were over a million Indigenous peoples in what we now call California (Miranda 2010). Typically, estimates of how long California Indians have existed in California range from twelve to fifteen thousand years. However, new research that suggests California Indians have been here at least one hundred thousand years (Holen et al. 2017)—approximately the same time that scientists suggest that human beings were first leaving

Africa. Native California was the most linguistically and culturally diverse place north of Tenochtitlan (Mexico City). Tribal cultures and governance structures emerged from the land, their center of the world: "Their mores, customs, and sacred ceremonies revolved around this concept. Their society and their lands held them together" (Norton 1979, 3). The influential Native American studies scholar Jack Forbes (Powhatan-Renapé/Delaware-Lenápe) estimates that more than five hundred autonomous republics existed within the boundaries of California that were able to live in balance with both each other and the natural world. Jack Forbes (1971) asks: "Can we imagine today numerous republics without armies, living largely at peace with each other, each without police or other formal instruments of societal coercion?" (235). Prior to settler-colonial invasion, California Indian tribes operated as "cohesive socio-politico-religious units" that engaged in land tenure and stewardship, trade, and ceremony with each other, living "side by side for thousands of years in relative peace and security" (Norton 1979, 12, 9). California Indians (as well as other Native peoples throughout Turtle Island) understand themselves not as independent and autonomous individuals, but ones deeply bound together with other humans and more-than-humans in a complex interconnected web of life. Rather than property rights oriented around the individual, within Native communities the collective takes precedence over the individual. Additionally, Indigenous conceptions of the collective are not anthropocentric, but also include ecosystems and more-than-human relatives (Norgaard 2019; Whyte 2018). All parts of creation have life and agency.

From a European perspective, however, California Indians were not credited for the advanced and largely peaceful societies they had created. Instead, we were called primitive, savages, diggers. Deborah A. Miranda (Ohlone-Costanoan Esselen Nation/Chumash) (2013) writes: "All my life, I have heard only one story about California Indians: godless, dirty, stupid, primitive, ugly, passive, drunken, immoral, lazy, weak-willed people who *might* make good workers if properly trained and motivated. What kind of story is that to grow up with?" (xvi, emphasis in original). As Forbes (1971) explains, Europeans equated civilized advancement with accumulated wealth and military strength, neither of which were deemed desirable by Indigenous peoples. This stark difference between California Indians and invading Europeans—as well as the latter's desire for land—in combination with racist rhetoric, was used as justification for dispossession. However, despite European, and later American, depictions of Indian savagery, Forbes further argues that "one might well argue that democracy reached its highest stage of development not in Greece (where, after all, most of the people were slaves or excluded from decision making) but in native California" (236).[1] Much like the way California Indian societies and governance structures were not recognized for their successes, so too were California Indian land management practices. Invading settlers could not comprehend the complexity of Indigenous land management practices because they were blinded by their own rhetoric of savagery and primitiveness.

"TENDING THE WILD": TRADITIONAL ECOLOGICAL KNOWLEDGE AND CALIFORNIA INDIANS

Indigenous land and water stewardship facilitated sustainable economies and enhanced California's biodiversity. These practices—generally referred to as traditional ecological knowledge (TEK)—were based on an intimate relationship with and deep understanding of California's ecology.[2] Ecologist M. Kat Anderson (2005), a premier scholar of California Indian environmental practices, describes TEK as "a collective storehouse of knowledge about the natural world" that includes "how nature works and how to judiciously harvest and steward its plants and animals without destroying them" (4). A result of "keen observation, patience, experimentation, and long-term relationships with plants and animals," TEK must be understood as a rigorous science in its own right. While built upon knowledge developed over millennia, traditional ecological knowledge is also modern and adaptable. Out of concern that this phrase historicizes Native peoples, Jessica Hernandez (Zapotec/Maya Ch'orti') (2022) opts for the term "Indigenous science," which she defines as "Indigenous voices, perspectives and lived experiences . . . [which] embody our ways of knowing that are rooted from ancestral knowledge and valid sciences" (13). Far from the stereotypes of savage hunters and gatherers, California Indians have highly sophisticated and complex understandings of the ecology and natural resources throughout their territories. In the Klamath River Basin, for example, "long before the United States Forest Service or California Department of Fish and Game existed, the Tribes managed these resources according to a complex set of societal rules founded in Indigenous science, technology, religion, and law that produced a landscape quite different from the appearance of the Klamath River Basin today" (Bowers and Carpenter 2011, 493). Indigenous ecological management regimes successfully provided for the people and maintained biodiversity and directly refute stereotypes of Indigenous peoples as primitive hunter gatherers: to supplant Indigenous ecological management regimes, the settler state delegitimized and erased Indigenous knowledge systems by characterizing them as primitive, backward, and savage. This ultimately serves as justification to impose settler-colonial worldviews on land-use decision-making.

TEK is far more than a method, technique, or practice. It is a way of being in the world that is fundamentally different from Western conceptions of nature and environment. Nor can TEK be singularly defined, as it is place-based and not acquired through centralized educational institutions (Hernandez 2022). Within a settler-colonial worldview, responsibility for land led to the conservation-preservation paradigm, which was designed to be in contrast to the exploitation (or "wise use") paradigm. Championed by Ralph Waldo Emerson, Henry David Thoreau, and John Muir, preservation eliminates human impact; conservation, supported by Gifford Pinchot and Theodore Roosevelt, seeks to regulate and control human use. Hernandez argues that this conservation is rooted in racism and anti-Indigeneity. Far from being objective, "conservation is a Western construct that was created as a result of settlers overexploiting Indigenous lands, natural resources, and depleting entire ecosystems" (72). While thought to be antithetical to environmental exploitation, both the preservation and conservation paradigms come from the same European philosophical roots that ideologically separate human beings from nature (Pierotti and Wildcat 2000; N. Smith 1996). Western notions of conservation/preservation and exploitation are two sides of the same Eurocentric coin, because each "assume[s] that humans are autonomous from, and in control of, the natural world" (Pierotti and Wildcat 2000, 1334). TEK offers an alternative perspective that does not make this assumption. Rather, as part of a TEK framework, human beings are part of the land—not above it and not below it.

In addition to encompassing myriad localized bodies of knowledge, TEK can also be understood as an "intellectual foundation for an indigenous theory and practice of politics and ethics, centered on natural places and connection to the natural world, which is capable of generating a conservation ethic on the part of those who follow its principles" (Pierotti and Wildcat 2000, 1335). TEK as an intellectual foundation does not homogenize diverse bodies of knowledge held by distinct cultures. Rather, it helps us conceptualize an alternative way to relate to and understand our responsibilities to land. Within a TEK intellectual framework, there are commonalities across Indigenous bodies of knowledge and philosophies in Turtle Island: all things are both connected and related (a concept that has only recently begun to emerge within Western community ecology). Whereas the settler state routinely isolates a single species deemed "profitable" (by human beings, of course) and dismembers an ecosystem to maximize its production, a TEK-based approach prioritizes the well-being of the collective, the health of the whole. Nonhuman organisms (or more-than-humans) as well as the biosphere itself are recognized as relatives with agency whom human beings are obligated to treat with respect. This is fundamentally different from a Western-based environmentalist approach. Forests should remain intact not because they provide aesthetic or material value to human beings. Forests should remain intact because they are relatives with agency (who also care for hundreds of other relatives), and human beings are not overseers of or dictators over ecological systems, but rather are members and participants. In California, settler-colonial relationships to land that seek to dominate, control, and commodify have resulted in ecological crises in less than two centuries.

Our environmental issues are urgent and Indigenous knowledges can no longer be treated as a backup plan. Yet at their best they are treated as an interesting accessory to environmental sciences and at their worst are placed within a primitive-civilized binary vis-à-vis Western science. Daniel Wildcat (Yuchi/Muscogee) (2009) puts forth a two-fold argument as to why Indigenous sciences should be respected for their contributions. First, the time frame of Indigenous knowledge production is exponentially longer than the five-year or ten-year grant of a university scientist. Herbalist Sage LaPena (Nomtipom Wintu) (quoted in Yuan 2016) explains: "If you are a people, living in the same place, the same region, for a thousand years, you've watched the turn of the seasons, the migrations of animals, birds, insects, fire regimes and how they move through plant life. All of those things together, how we gather our plants, how we are able to subsist, all of that encompasses

TEK." California Indians have been here since time immemorial and we have had a lot of time to experiment, to figure out what works and what doesn't. Yet despite the literally tens of thousands of years California Indians have been studying their environments, Western scientists—who have been in California for 170 years maximum—assume they hold intellectual superiority on the functions of our ecosystems. Cutcha Risling Baldy (2021) reflects on speaking with her elders about their ongoing work with Western scientists, ethnographers, and anthropologists:

> They would often refer to them as very "young," not only in terms of their age or maturity, but also in terms of their respective discipline's knowledge of the world. "Their science is young; their knowledge is young." They would remark how the 150 years of knowledge these Western scientists and scholars were building in their academic disciplines was still in the early phases of understanding the world. The more I thought about it, the more it made sense to me. Western disciplines were just beginning to build knowledge about this place and about the more-than-human beings that we share the world with, knowledge that we had developed over many thousands of years. (172–73)

Yet stereotypes of Native people as primitive and unintelligent were used to justify land dispossession and continue to permeate contemporary understandings of Native people.[3] Indigenous contributions to the sciences are erased and delegitimized (Hernandez 2022).

Second, Wildcat (2009) argues that in addition to their length of study, Indigenous knowledges should be respected and listened to because of the spatial sacred relationship from which they emerge. Responses to climate change may incorporate new technologies, to be sure, but the most important change is a cultural climate change, a change in worldview. In other words, we need to change the way we relate to land. Chief Oren Lyons (Turtle Clan of the Onondaga Nation of the Six Nations of the Iroquois Confederacy) stated in a 2005 commencement address that "What you call resources, we call our relatives. If you can think in terms of relationships, your relatives, you are going to treat them better, aren't you?" Chief Lyons demonstrates that the framework in which you view the natural world matters. The language of Western sciences lacks what Robin Wall Kimmerer

(Potawatomi) (2015) refers to as a grammar of animacy and reduces a being to its working parts. "Saying *it* makes a living land into 'natural resources'" (57, emphasis in original). One wouldn't measure their grandmother in the monetary value of her parts (her organs, bones, or DNA), but we routinely conduct this intellectual exercise when determining whether an oil pipeline should be installed underneath a River or whether a forest should be clear-cut for a wind turbine. Settler-colonial timber extraction reduces living trees to their working parts, or the volume of timber or firewood extracted, or the potential profit margin gained.

Native peoples hold cultural, moral, and ecological obligations to care for, steward, and manage the biosphere. These responsibilities are situated within a relational kinship network wherein Native peoples are interconnected and interdependent on the natural world, and vice versa. Land has both material and metaphorical power for Native peoples because, in addition to sustaining a people, land provides identity, ancestral connection, moral responsibility, purpose, and knowledge (Teves, Smith, and Raheja 2015). Embedded within creation stories and oral histories are the "original instructions" of Creator, which Melissa Nelson (Anishinaabe) (2008) defines as "the many diverse teachings, lessons, and ethics expressed in the origin stories and oral traditions of Indigenous peoples. They are the literal and metaphorical instructions, passed on orally from generation to generation, for how to be a good human being living in reciprocal relations with all of our seen and unseen relatives" (2–3). These instructions encompass Native philosophies of being in familial and community relations to land management practices and constitute a natural law. For Indigenous peoples, land—both materially and metaphorically—is the source of the law (Black 2011). A relational connection to land, rather than a hierarchical one that asserts domination over land through law, acknowledges the needs of the entire biosphere and understands the reciprocal interconnections between all the relations.

The health of ecosystems is directly connected to the vitality of Indigenous peoples. Kyle Powys Whyte (Potawatomi) (2016) uses the concept of collective continuance to describe "both the operationalization of systems of responsibilities (and their capacity to both rely on past traditions and transform appropriately into the future) *and* the simultaneous development of social institutions that can protect the operations of these systems" (167, emphasis in original). Tribal communities' subsistence, as well as identity, is intertwined with the natural world. Our collective continuance depends upon the health and protection of our territories. For example, Yurok elders have long said that as long as our River is sick, our people will never be healthy. This includes the Salmon people swimming upriver to spawn, the Tree people dependent on the marine nutrients their Salmon relatives will deliver to the forest, and, of course, the neediest of the bunch, the human people. Our health and vitality are tied to the health and vitality of our landscapes. If the River is sick, everything that depends upon the River will not flourish. Moreover, all elements of creation possess their own agency. They do not exist within an anthropocentric hierarchy predicated on the desire for monetary wealth accumulation for human beings. When Indigenous lifeways become untenable—if we can no longer fish because the water is poisoned or the fish have died, if we can no longer weave baskets because the plants have been contaminated or dominated by invasive species, if we can no longer teach our youth how to steward the world because we spend all of our time selling our labor to survive in our homelands marked by private property and No Trespassing signs—our collective continuance is threatened.

TAMING THE WILD: SETTLER COLONIALISM AND NATURAL RESOURCES

Settler colonialism is the continuous structural elimination of Native peoples in order to gain and maintain access to land (Wolfe 2006). Gaining traction over the past two decades as a subject of academic inquiry, settler colonialism is a unique form of colonization wherein settlers create a new home on land apart from their homeland.[4] Settler-colonial theory and discourse challenges notions of postcolonialism because for contemporary Indigenous peoples living in settler states, there is nothing "post" about it (Norgaard 2019). Settler colonialism differs from external forms of colonialism wherein the colonial power seeks to extract natural resources and human bodies for wealth accumulation and labor, because within settler colonialism, settlers arrive intending to stay with an insistence on "settler sovereignty over all things in their new domain" (Tuck and Yang 2012, 5). The organizing principle of settler colonialism is what Patrick Wolfe (2006) calls the "logic of elimination": the erasure of Native peoples is a precondition and perpetual system for settler expropriation of lands and resources. While striving for the dissolution of Native societies, settler colonialism "erects a new colonial society on the expropriated land base . . . settler colonizers come to stay: invasion is a structure not an event" (388). Settler colonialism, as compared to external, internal, or postcolonialism, is the most accurate way to characterize contemporary relationships between Native Americans and the US federal government.

Settler-colonial elimination occurs in a multitude of ways and depends on violence. The logics of elimination include physical elimination that is manifested in genocidal policies of Indian-killing militias, child abductions, forced sterilization, the dissolution of Native land titles, and a wide range of assimilation projects. Settler colonialism requires violence because "people do not hand over their land, resources, children, and futures without a fight, and that fight is met with violence"; in short, settler colonialism is a genocidal policy (Dunbar-Ortiz 2014, 8). Ned Blackhawk (Te-Moak Western Shoshone) (2006) demonstrates how violence was necessary for American westward expansion, "from the use of the U.S. Army to combat and confine Indian peoples, to the state-sanctioned theft of Indian lands and resources . . . violence and American nationhood, in short, progressed hand in hand" (9). Native elimination also occurs discursively through education and media wherein a national mythology is crafted to illustrate the glory and exceptionalism of the United States while strategically and systematically erasing Native American history, knowledge, presence, and claims to land. The notion that this place was empty or that those who were here before were primitive, uncivilized, and not God's destined landowners is pervasive in mainstream society, public education, industries, and even environmental movements.

At its core, settler colonialism is fundamentally concerned with the acquisition of land and natural resources—or, as Wolfe (2006) articulates it, "territoriality is settler colonialism's specific, irreducible element" (388). Eve Tuck (Unangax) and K. Wayne Yang (2012) argue that

> within settler colonialism, the most important concern is land/water/air/subterranean earth . . . Land is what is most valuable, contested, required. This is both because the disruption of Indigenous relationships to land represents a profound epistemic, ontological, cosmological violence. This violence is not temporally contained in the arrival of

the settler but is reasserted each day of occupation. This is why Patrick Wolfe (1999) emphasizes that settler colonialism is a structure and not an event. In the process of settler colonialism, land is remade into property and human relationships to land are restricted to the relationship of the owner to his property. Epistemological, ontological, and cosmological relationships to land are interred, indeed made premodern and backward. Made savage. (5)

What separates settler colonialism from other forms of colonialism is that it revolves around land and, through eliminatory practices, constructs that land as always having belonged to the settler (i.e., manifest destiny), which is then reinforced with curricula, public history, and what Jean O'Brien (White Earth Band of Ojibwe) (2018) refers to as firsting.[5] Natsu Taylor Saito (2020) says, "Land is what allows the settlers to create and control a society of their own imagining and then, using that land and its resources, to generate the profits that enable them to consolidate and expand their sovereign prerogative" (51). Land, and its continued dispossession and destruction, is at the root of all social, environmental, and economic injustices facing Indian Country (Carroll 2015).

Justifications for settler-colonial violence depend on particular conceptions of both land and Native peoples. Land itself is a settler-colonial construct, in that "Native peoples have a spiritual relationship to the entire biosphere, not just the land. However, colonialism separates land from the rest of the creation as a marker of territorial expansion" (Teves, Smith, and Raheja 2015, 67). Kimmerer (2015) clarifies the distinction between settler and Indigenous relationships to land: "In the settler mind, land was property, real estate, capital, or natural resources. But to our people, it was everything: identity, the connection to our ancestors, the home of our nonhuman kinfolk, our pharmacy, our library, the source of all that sustained us. Our lands were where our responsibility to the world was enacted, sacred ground. It belonged to itself; it was a gift, not a commodity, so it could never be bought or sold" (17). Furthermore, as Chief Lyons articulates, relatives are transformed into resources. The term "resource" originates from Latin and implies life and a reciprocal relationship between human beings and nature. However, as Vandana Shiva (1992) argues, with colonialism came a conceptual break: the "parts of nature which were required as inputs for industrial production and colonial trade" *became* natural resources (206). There is nothing inherent or natural about conceptualizing plant and animal relatives as resources. Indeed, from an Indigenous perspective the framing of sacred relatives, such as Salmon, as an economic resource is an affront to Indigenous sensibilities, a form of cosmological or epistemological violence. The creation of natural resources, then, simultaneously "created a new dualism between nature and humans. Since nature needed to be 'developed' by humans, people had also to be developed from their primitive, backward states of embeddedness in nature" (Shiva 1992, 206–7). Humans within settler-colonial socioecological contexts orient their relationship to land as owner to property/real estate and thereby demarcate Indigenous subsistence practices as wasteful because they are not designed to generate profit.

Conceptualizing land as property—rather than as part of a complex and extended kinship network—is neither inherent nor neutral; it is a culturally specific worldview that has been imposed on Indigenous peoples by the settler state:

> Although it may first appear as a perfectly obvious, empirical object, "land" is in fact a concept, and a highly abstract one at that. We are essentially talking about taking a portion of the Earth's surface—excluding the subsurface and troposphere beyond some often vaguely formulated or unspecified distance—and bundling a complex diversity of proprietary claims within it such that a person could, in principle, acquire control over all objects and activities within that zone. As a legal and marketable object of this sort, land in this sense is a highly culturally and historically specific object in which one could invest property claims. It is not the case that all societies—even most societies—have had such a concept, let alone a set of legal and political institutions to enforce claims around it, or a market through which it could be traded. (Nichols 2020, 31)

To clarify, property such as land or a natural resource, is not the object in question, but rather is the constructed set of relations that govern its use, primarily relations of exclusion. "It is a socio-historical and racialised process of spatial production that relies on a series of mythologies that are firmly rooted in traditions of dehumanisation, exclusion, and privilege" (Nunn 2018, 1342). Within settler societies this process has been normalized to perceive the land/Earth as a material object that human beings can claim, own, fence, enclose, and exclude others from accessing. This logic is then extended to other beings (e.g., "natural resources," Trees, Fish, etc.), and for most of the United States' existence, people of color.

Property, as a set of relations, is socially constructed—and that construction is inherently racialized. Aileen Moreton-Robinson (Geonpul, Quandamooka First Nation), in her book *The White Possessive: Property, Power, and Indigenous Sovereignty*, examines how possession/dispossession is systematically entangled in whiteness and the ways in which settler states are socially and culturally constructed as white possessions. Building on Cheryl Harris's seminal work *Whiteness as Property* (1993), Moreton-Robinson (2015) argues that "white propriety rights were cemented in law through the appropriation of Native American lands and the subsequent enslavement of Africans. . . . As a form of property, whiteness accumulates capital and social appreciation as white people are recognized within the law primarily as property-owning subjects. As such, they are heavily invested in the nation being a white possession" (xix). Settler colonialism transforms land into property for white people, entrenching whiteness in property, and then uses law to protect it. Through this process "a new white property-owning subject emerged in history and possessiveness became embedded in everyday discourse" (49). The construction of property and the claim to it as a new nation-state belonging to settlers relies on a possessive logic that reproduces and reaffirms the nation-state's ownership, control, and domination over both Indigenous lands and Indigenous bodies. Within settler states, "Native American dispossession indelibly marks configurations of white national identity" (51). Throughout the green rush, we have witnessed another land use transformation to settler cultivation. Like preceding rushes, the spatial production that supports the infrastructure of the industry rests on the possessive logic of property and the assumption that the state of California and the US government have legitimate claim to this land.

This book is focused on how the project of settler colonialism claims and transforms Indigenous lands, waters, and ecosystems into property, commodities, and natural resources and the ways in which extractive violence is perpetrated simultaneously against Indigenous lands and bodies. This violence occurs in a variety of ways: through the taking/claiming/renaming of lands, the removal of Indigenous peoples, the imposition of colonial management regimes, and the ideological transformation of lands/relatives into property, commodities, and objects. The contemporary green rush—including both licit and illicit cannabis production—occurs within a context of settler-colonial land dispossession and perpetuates settler-colonial violence that maintains and reproduces settler-colonial power over Indigenous territory.

Despite the centrality of land to settler-colonial theory, scholars have paid surprisingly little attention to the ecology of settler colonialism. Kari M. Norgaard (2019) argues that while numerous scholars have emphasized the central role of land to the settler-colonial project, most have overlooked the ways in which the alteration of land and the alteration of human relationships with land contribute to settler colonialism in a critical way. Wolfe's frequently cited argument, that settler colonialism is a structure rather than an event, must also be applied to environmental degradation and land dispossession as those, too, are ongoing processes. Throughout this hemisphere, Indigenous peoples had developed methods of stewarding their lands that maintained biological diversity (see M. Anderson 2005; Lightfoot and Parrish 2009; Nelson 2008; and Norgaard 2019). Because settler-colonial tactics for territorial control, that is, Indian removal and genocide, have facilitated mass ecological transformation, settler colonialism must be understood as an ecological phenomenon (Reo and Parker 2013). The widespread lack of recognition of settler colonialism as a massive ecological transformation suggests an internalized settler-colonial logic that "this place was empty." Or that Native Americans are primitive peoples who haphazardly hunted and gathered, devoid of land management knowledge or practices. This erasure is pervasive—the vast majority of environmental activists and environmental scientists have no clue whose land they occupy, let alone the stewardship techniques Native peoples developed over millennia for that particular place. Hernandez (2022) argues that "Indigenous narratives continue to be dismissed and ignored in mainstream environmentalism.... Indigenous peoples have been the stewards and caretakers of our environments since time immemorial. Yet we are often left out from the environmental discourse and any decision-making pertaining to our environment" (13). Moreover, despite settler representations of Native peoples as primitive, the plundering of the "New World's" natural resources for obscene profit was only possible *because* of ecological abundance created through Indigenous land management (Norgaard 2019).

Settler-colonial land management regimes have always privileged settler desires and worldviews over Native survival. In what Whyte (2015) refers to as the ecological mechanics of settler-colonial domination, settlers inscribe an alternate ecology on top of existing Indigenous ecologies through "large-scale mineral and fossil fuel extraction operations to sweeping landscape-transforming regimes of commodity agriculture" (145). Indeed, "since their inception, the federal government and state of California have implemented land management policies," as Norgaard (2019) argues, "that reflect and privilege non-Native values, economic systems, cultural practices, and cosmologies" (11–12). For example, the urban water consumption projects of the Shasta Dam and Central Valley Water Project in California flooded numerous gathering sites and burial grounds (Middleton Manning 2018). Moreover, because "the wealth and power of the United States as a state is grounded in the ongoing occupation of Indigenous lands," J. M. Bacon (2019) argues that "settler colonialism—though always in connection with other forms of domination—[is] the primary force shaping eco-social relations in this country" (60). Settler colonialism structures both environmental practices and epistemologies—but because settler colonialism is intentionally invisibilized (through public education and indoctrination), so too are the ways in which settler-colonial ideology guides contemporary understandings of land and environment—reproducing and maintaining systemic violence against both Indigenous lands and bodies, or what Bacon calls "colonial ecological violence." Bacon argues that settler-colonial land management practices do "the work of eco-social disruption without the explicitly stated intent to commit violence, yet with highly destructive results for Native communities. By foreclosing the possibility of relationships with and responsibilities to ecologies, land management under settler colonialism contributes to physical, emotional, economic and cultural harms. I contend that these eco-social disruptions generate colonial ecological violence, a unique form of violence perpetrated by the settler-colonial state, private industry, and settler-colonial culture as a whole" (63). Hernandez (2022) refers to this phenomenon as "ecocolonialism" and includes the imposition of settler-colonial ecological management regimes while disregarding Indigenous sovereignty, the altering of landscapes, and the lack of resources allocated for Indigenous peoples.

My work aims to build upon this scholarship and demonstrate, through an analysis of waves of resource extraction (rushes), how colonial ecological violence has been enacted in California historically and, through an analysis of contemporary ecological and cultural impacts of cannabis cultivation associated with the green rush, in the present time. I examine the ecology of settler colonialism from a Native American/Indigenous studies perspective to demonstrate how settler-colonial relationships to land continue to enact violence against Native peoples.

It is important to clarify the meaning of two terms used here: "settler-colonial ecology" and "settler-colonial relationship." Kyle Whyte, Chris Caldwell, and Marie Schaefer (2018) define ecology as the "systematic arrangements of humans, nonhuman beings (animals, plants, etc.) and entities (spiritual, inanimate, etc.), and landscapes (climate regions, boreal zones, etc.) that are conceptualized and operate purposefully to facilitate a society's capacity to survive and flourish in a particular landscape and watershed" (159). All societies are part of and construct ecologies. What makes an ecology a settler-colonial one is when those "waves of settlement seek to incise their own ecologies required for their societies to survive and flourish in the landscapes they seek to occupy permanently" on lands already stewarded and governed by Indigenous peoples. Glen Coulthard (Yellowknives Dene) (2014), in writing about a shift in settler state politics from a paradigm of genocide/assimilation to one of recognition/accommodation, defines a settler-colonial relationship as "one that is characterized by a particular form of domination; that is, it is a relationship where power—in this case, interrelated discursive and non-discursive facets of economic, gendered, racial and state power—has been structured into a relatively secure or sedimented set of hierarchical social relations that continue to facilitate the dispossession of Indigenous peoples of their lands and self-determining authority" (6–7). In this case the settler state exerts power and domination over land use, management, and policies that continue to do the work of the settler-colonial project—and is able to perpetuate and reproduce dispossession and violence against Indigenous bodies.

In California, settlers utilized genocidal violence to acquire, commodify, and dismember Indigenous lands. California Indians experienced three distinct waves of genocide. Spanish missionization, the first, lasted from 1769 to 1820. The second ranged from 1821 to 1845, between the end of the missionization period and the Mexican-American War. The third coincided with the gold rush and lasted from 1846 to 1873 (Tolley 2006). All three waves produced disastrous results for California Indian populations, landholdings, and landscapes. Through the state-sponsored killing and enslavement of California Indian people and accompanying land theft, the settler state radically altered the ecology of California homelands. The introduction of livestock, invasive plant species, mining, deforestation, and industrial fisheries destroyed Indigenous subsistence economies, contaminated water systems, and continues to impact Native peoples in the present.

The construction of settler ecologies, from invasion to the present, continues to carry out logics of elimination by making Indigenous ecological arrangements and lifeways untenable (e.g., through fire suppression, dam construction). The central claim of this book is that settler-colonial relationships to land have always and continue to perpetuate violence against Indigenous lands and waters, and this violence is experienced in the bodies of Indigenous peoples. This violent relationship did not end with the gold rush, but is continually being reasserted, refined, normalized, and invisibilized with each wave of resource rushing. After 170 years of settler-colonial invasion, ecosystems in this region are reaching their breaking points and the repercussions of resource rushing are resulting in ecological crises via uncontrollable wildfires and unprecedented fish kills. Throughout this text I utilize the examples of various resource rushes, including gold, timber, fish, and cannabis, to dissect the ecology of settler colonialism. This argumentation builds upon the work of scholars currently examining the ecology of settler colonialism, specifically Whyte, Norgaard, and Bacon. Each wave of resource rushing illustrates a different element of what Whyte calls the "ecological mechanics of settler colonial domination." While the gold rush illustrates the interconnectedness of genocide, settler colonialism, and environmental destruction, the timber rush demonstrates how the settler state imposes ecological management regimes to achieve settler desires at the expense of Indigenous peoples' needs. The fish rush reveals how a settler-colonial worldview transforms Salmon, which for Indigenous peoples are a critical part of our kinship networks, into a commodity and economic resource. The back-to-the-land movement illustrates the continuation of Indigenous land dispossession into the twentieth century and the centrality of that dispossession within environmental protection movements and discourse. Drawing on all of these mechanics, today we find ourselves in the middle of the green rush. But this green rush would not be possible without genocidal land dispossession, imposition of ecological management regimes, and the transformation of expanded kinship networks into commodities. More than a critique of any one industry, this book is an interrogation of settler colonialism, specifically its inherently ecological character.

CANNABIS AND COLONIALISM IN CALIFORNIA

"Sustained by frontier adventurism and good old Yankee ingenuity," Martin Lee (2012) argues, "cannabis farming was as American as apple pie" (178). Cannabis was also central to the early colonization of North America, and its environmental ramifications continue to perpetuate colonial ecological violence for Native peoples. American as apple pie indeed. Historically lauded for both its psychoactive medicinal qualities and its utility as a sturdy fiber, cannabis is thought to be indigenous to Central Asia (Lee 2012). Making its way to the Western Hemisphere through the slave trade during the sixteenth century, cannabis was vital to the colonization of the Americas (Reed 2022). Without hemp, Columbus's ships would not have arrived in 1492. In fact, hemp was such an important material to incoming settlers that in 1619 in Jamestown, Virginia, the law of the land required every settler household to cultivate hemp (Lee 2012).[6] Fast forward to the early twentieth century, when cannabis prohibition policies became a new means to police and surveil people of color throughout the United States.[7] Employing racist stereotypes, "its initial association with the dregs of society—landless peasants, bandits, bootleggers, prisoners, and so on—made marijuana a convenient scapegoat for deep-rooted social inequities" (Lee 2012, 39). Cannabis prohibition has never been about *what* cannabis does but *who* does cannabis, and therefore has long been used as a tool to surveil people of color and maintain the white supremacy of the settler state.

California was the first state to both outlaw cannabis and to legalize it. In 1913 the California Legislature passed cannabis prohibition policies as a means to harass and prosecute Mexican immigrants (White and Holman 2012). This continued a pattern of racial discrimination, as opium had been outlawed in San Francisco a century prior as a pretext for harassing and incarcerating Chinese immigrants (Lee 2012). However, despite federal and state prohibition policies, unregulated cannabis production proliferated in northwestern California in the 1970s. By 1979, 35 percent of the marijuana smoked in California was produced in California primarily because, throughout the 1970s, the United States subsidized the sale of paraquat, a toxic herbicide, to the Mexican government as part of an international drug control program, thereby eliminating any competition for American black-market cannabis (Brady 2013).

California was also the first state to legalize medicinal cannabis. Medicinal-use cannabis was legalized in 1996 and by 2010, 79 percent of the marijuana smoked in the United States was grown in California (Brady 2013). Recreational cannabis was legalized in 2016. Today the scale of cannabis cultivation in California is unparalleled. Long considered the international epicenter of unpermitted cannabis production, California is now transitioning into the largest cannabis market in the world (Dillis et al. 2021). In March 2021 the California cannabis economy was valued at $3.5 billion (Yakowicz 2021). However, the same racism that has permeated cannabis prohibition policies and enforcement has also guided the nascent legal industry. Lewis (2016) argues the green rush has been whitewashed. Because Black and Brown people have a higher likelihood of being arrested on drug-related charges (though not for higher rate of use), they are disproportionately excluded from the cannabis industry because of previously existing criminal records (Lewis 2016).

The economic, social, and political tensions around cannabis create a microcosm of white supremacy. In a racial pyramid, white cannabis farmers, distributors, retailers, and investors sit at the top, collecting their green rush profits. Indigenous lands being razed, plowed, and poisoned and the incarceration of Black and Brown bodies for cannabis use form the corners that support the top. While cannabis prohibition and production are widely understood as social justice issues—especially regarding the perpetuation of systemic racism—they are rarely understood as an environmental justice issue. Cannabis prohibition and production have facilitated violence against *both* lands and bodies. Through incarceration, cannabis prohibition has subjected thousands to police violence and family separation. The cultivation of cannabis has destroyed sacred lands and waters and poisoned ecosystems. These interconnected forms of violence are rooted in a settler-colonial mentality that sees "othered" bodies as disposable and Indigenous lands as wastelands or doesn't acknowledge those homelands as Indigenous in the first place. This book examines the ecological impacts of cannabis production in Northern California using the analytical lens of settler colonialism. The relationship between cannabis production and tribal lands is relevant to the entire state, and indeed the nation, but I privilege discussions of Northern California because of its historical legacy of cultivation and the widespread cultivation in sensitive ecosystems and the concentration and magnification of ecological impacts in the region.

This work, then, situates political conflict over cannabis production as an issue of land use and access. Moreover, such a theoretical perspective blurs the boundary between environmental assaults and assaults on Indigenous peoples and their lifeways. They are one in the same (Weaver 1996). The magnitude of such assaults, however, must be contextualized within an Indigenous perspective of land and relation to place. Specifically, I aim to contribute to the future directions of Indigenous environmental studies by continuing to theorize and develop the relationship between settler colonialism and environmental justice. Traci Brynne Voyles, Kyle Powys Whyte, Dina Gilio-Whitaker (Colville Confederated Tribes), and Jessica Hernandez have all demonstrated the usefulness of this intersected assessment. Voyles (2015) argues that because settler colonialism is so intimately tied to the accumulation of natural resources, environmental injustices must always be viewed through a lens of settler colonialism. Whyte (2016) argues that settler colonialism erases the socioecological contexts in which Indigenous peoples live and nullifies the possibility of collective continuance. In *As Long as Grass Grows: The Indigenous Fight for Environmental Justice, from Colonization to Standing Rock*, Indigenous studies scholar Gilio-Whitaker (2019) argues that "the origin of environmental injustice for Indigenous peoples is dispossession of land in all its forms; injustice is continually reproduced in what is inherently a culturally genocidal structure that systematically erases Indigenous peoples' relationships and responsibilities to their ancestral places" (36). Therefore, environmental justice movements must center the Indigenous peoples of the region affected (Hernandez 2022). Settler colonialism *itself* constitutes an environmental injustice, and thus decolonization must become a central tenet of environmental justice.[8]

It was never my intention to write a book about cannabis, but here we are. My ancestral territory has become ground zero for cannabis cultivation. Looking back, I first began thinking about cannabis as a scholar in my freshman year of college. While sharing initial pleasantries with my new hallmates in upstate New York, I informed them I was born in Humboldt County, California, and their eyes lit up. Clearly they were familiar with Humboldt-grown cannabis and excited at the possibility of acquiring some. A prospective geography major at the time, I pondered, How did this plant become a commodity? How did it make its way from Yurok ancestral territory in Northern California to a college campus more than three thousand miles away? Who is benefiting from this transaction? Who is paying the price? These questions faded into the background for the next several years, only to be brought back to my attention in 2014. In response to the siege of cannabis cultivation on Yurok tribal lands, the Yurok Tribe fought to rid the reservation and ancestral territory of trespass cultivation and the numerous ecological damages it has wrought. Questions persist, including: How has cannabis cultivation become such a threat to the ecological and cultural integrity of California Indians? While many people have much to say about cannabis, it seems to me that this story has been left out.

This book is not an exposé of the cannabis industry and my intent is not to isolate it as such. Instead, my goal is to demonstrate the way that the cannabis industry is merely the predictable result of a pattern of settler-colonial resource extraction, preceded by gold, timber, and fish. The intense and urgent desire for wealth could not be met by gold alone; settlers continued to extract other resources, such as timber, fish, and oil. Today, it's cannabis. Such overlapping historical resource extraction demonstrates that "rushing" is a well-established pattern. And if the pattern tells us anything, it is that the green rush will not last forever. But, while contemporary cannabis cultivation provides ample fodder for theorizing on the ecology of settler-colonial domination, I hope to do more.

In many respects, the cannabis industry in California is still finding its footing. What if critiques of settler colonialism, an understanding of California Indian history, and the possibilities of decolonization were all entertained within these conversations? As the state transitions into a regulated cannabis market, how do we develop and regulate an industry that understands lands and waters as more than solely economic resources, but as relatives? How do we move forward within a framework of radical relationality that rejects the commodification and control of nature for wealth accumulation? We have to imagine beyond settler-colonial orientations to land; we must think outside the prescribed rush pattern of the gold rush, the fish rush, the timber rush, and now the green rush. Many cannabis advocates proclaim dedication to social and environmental justice causes. But for Native people, achieving social and environmental justice will be impossible without land return. Real justice requires decolonization. California Indians did not have a seat at the table during the gold rush. There was not a public forum or open comment period where we could submit our research and perspectives. In fact, if we had tried to sit at that table, we would have been jailed and auctioned off into slavery—thanks to the 1850 Act for the Government and "Protection" of Indians. This time around we insist on having our voices heard—until it reverberates throughout this place and our lands are returned to us.

OVERVIEW OF THE BOOK

Throughout this work I argue that the contemporary green rush cannot be disentangled from the California gold rush and the state-sponsored genocide that fueled it. Moreover, ecologically speaking, settler-colonial political economies predicated on resource extraction are unsustainable during a time of global climate change. Indigenous knowledges and perspectives on environmental issues are critically needed at a time when our Mother Earth is responding in dramatic ways to long-standing and ongoing mistreatment and disrespect. The overarching questions of the text include: How has the settler-colonial orientation to land manifested in California, and in what ways are they perpetuated today? How has settler-colonial resource extraction impacted California's ecosystems and Indigenous peoples, and what are the relationships between these impacts? How can Indigenous relationships to and knowledge of land aid in the dismantling of settler-colonial political economies and governance structures?

First, I offer a historical overview of resource rushing in California that includes gold, timber, and fish, in attempt to demonstrate how, through patterns of resource rushing, the ecological mechanics of settler-colonial domination have perpetuated violence against both Indigenous lands and bodies. This establishes critical historic context for the unfolding of the green rush and, hopefully, makes clear that the real gold has always been, and still is, the land itself. Chapter 1 examines the impact of the gold rush on California Indians, specifically how state-sponsored genocide was central to Indigenous land dispossession and environmental exploitation. Chapter 2 turns to the timber rush, with a focus on the continuation of land dispossession through the enclosure of forestlands by private corporations and state entities as well as the criminalization of traditional ecological knowledge through fire-suppression policies. Chapter 3 examines the impact of the fish rush, specifically how culturally significant species—considered relatives to many California Indians—were transformed into commodities and how infrastructure such as dams have harmed and displaced fish relatives. As fish relatives experienced genocidal violence, Native peoples were deprived of a critical cultural food staple that resulted in health disparities.

Next, I turn to the green rush. Beginning with the emergence of cannabis cultivation during the back-to-the-land movement, chapter 4 extends Laura Hurwitz's critical question: Back to whose land? This chapter situates the back-to-the-land movement within a context of settler colonialism and demonstrates how cannabis cultivation in Northern California has always been rooted in Indigenous land dispossession. Chapter 5 offers a brief historical context of cannabis cultivation in the region the transition to a legal state market, as well as tribal participation in the cannabis industry and the various challenges tribes face. This chapter concludes with an overview of the environmental concerns of legal/illegal cannabis cultivation and some of the challenges and barriers to conducting environmental research on cannabis cultivation. The next three chapters provide more in-depth analyses of the environmental and cultural concerns of cannabis cultivation, which are organized around land, water, and toxics. Chapter 6 argues that land dispossession, like settler colonialism, is ongoing and maintained through cannabis cultivation and land use in California. This dispossession occurs through land and species alteration, physically or financially preventing Indigenous peoples from accessing their ancestral territories, and violence. Chapter 7 turns to what is perhaps the most emotional and divisive point of tension between Indigenous peoples and the cannabis industry: control of water. This chapter examines cannabis-related water use—much of which is contested—but, more significantly, it contextualizes contemporary water use for cannabis and other extractive industries within a legacy of settler colonialism by situating contemporary water rights and infrastructure within the physical and cultural genocide from which they emerged. Chapter 8 concludes the main body of the book with an examination of toxicity and settler-colonial violence. Beginning with the thirteen thousand tons of mercury dumped into California's waters and the aerial spraying of chemicals over California's forests, this chapter argues that the environmental contamination associated with the cannabis industry must be contextualized within a historical trajectory of legacy and cumulative impacts that continue the work of settler colonialism by trying to sever Indigenous relationships to lands, waters, and our more-than-human relatives.

While it is my sincere hope that my work will build upon current theorization of settler-colonial resource extraction and contemporary ecological violence and ultimately contribute to scholarly discourse at the intersections of Native American/Indigenous studies and environmental studies, this ambition is not what led me here. When I began researching the environmental and cultural impacts of cannabis production, Yurok tribal lands were under siege by large-scale trespass cannabis cultivation. I witnessed the repetition of history. I understood that the colonial violence of the California gold rush was not over. In line with the goals of other Native American studies scholarship, the first and foremost goal of this research is to generate useful information for the communities affected by the issues discussed. Research in Indigenous communities has historically been aligned with a settler-colonial agenda and characterized by exploitation and extraction. Therefore research *for* and *by* Indigenous communities must decenter the settler-colonial worldviews and methodologies while centering Indigenous worldviews, knowledges, and sovereignties (L. Smith 2012). This research included participatory observation of Operation Yurok in 2016 and in-depth qualitative interviews with tribe members, tribe employees, and settler state employees (local, state, and federal) that took place primarily between June 2017 and August 2018. In an effort to broaden the geographical scope of the project to include experiences and insights of other tribal nations of Northern California, I also conducted additional interviews with members from other tribes in Northern California and gathered a collection of primary source material—including letters, hearing testimony, press releases, and so forth—produced by tribal nations in response to the green rush.

The conclusion of this book looks toward the future. A settler-colonial orientation to land is both unjust and unsustainable and cannot continue indefinitely. Major transformations will occur whether by choice or by force. Because all contemporary social problems (poverty, trauma, health disparities) can be traced back to land—its dispossession or contamination—we must engage with decolonization to heal from the violence that has occurred in this place over the past 170 years. Moreover, land return is the most strategic route for ecological restoration and must become a central component of environmental research and restoration. The future is land return. The future is decolonization. If California Indians have been able to survive the atrocities of the past centuries years, and not only survive but maintain our cultures, traditions, and knowledges, then I am confident we will see the end of capitalism and the end of settler colonialism. A decolonized future is possible.

1

GOLD, GREED, AND GENOCIDE

Settler Colonialism and Resource Extraction in the California Gold Rush

The Gold Rush was an instrumental event in the economic history of California, setting the tone, mind-set, fervor and conditions for the exploitation of other resources and the mistreatment of minorities. Gold Rush immigrants were quick to realize that gold was just one of the resources that could make one wealthy; the state was full of animal, plant, mineral, and hydrological resources waiting to be tapped, brought to market, and transformed into commodities. —M. Kat Anderson, *Tending the Wild*

In California genocide is written on the landscape. It shaped not only the way the state and federal government continued to approach Native people as a "problem" but also how generations of people would come to understand Native cultures, histories, and futures. —Cutcha Risling Baldy, *We Are Dancing for You*

On the night of February 25, 1860, Wiyot peoples—gathered at Tuluwat for the annual World Renewal Ceremonies—were attacked by local settlers in what became infamously known as the Indian Island Massacre. A month prior, in January 1860, out-of-work settlers had formed a volunteer militia under Captain Wright in southern Humboldt County. Local citizens of Hydesville supplied the "Hydesville Dragoons" with weapons and this citizen military "resolved to kill every peaceable Indian man, woman and child in Humboldt County" (quoted in Norton 1979, 81). Jack Norton (Hupa/Cherokee), in his book *Genocide in Northwestern California: When Our Worlds Cried* (1979), documents the accounts of this violence as well as editorials published in local and regional newspapers in response to the violence. The *Northern Californian*, based in Arcata, published this description four days after the massacre: "Blood stood in pools on all sides; the walls of the huts were stained and the grass colored red. Lying around were dead bodies of both sexes and all ages from the old man to the infant at the breast. Some had their heads split in twain by axes, others beaten into jelly with clubs, others pierced or cut to pieces with bowie knives. Some struck down as they mired; others had almost reached the water when overtaken and butchered" (82). The estimated death toll ranges from forty, on the conservative end, to over two hundred lives. As Norton argues, this massacre was not an aberration, but methodically and carefully planned. Neither was this massacre the only one to take place that night: "three other massacres took place simultaneously; two at the south spit of Humboldt Bay and the other at the mouth of the Eel River" (82).

Despite common knowledge of who was responsible for the massacre, no one was ever charged. The Humboldt County grand jury said: "After a strict examination of all witnesses, nothing was elicited to enlighten us as to the perpetrators" (85). As Norton (1979) argues, this is illogical, because there existed a muster roll of the volunteer militia and, a year following the massacre, Lieutenant Daniel D. Lynn included mention in a report that a local cattle rancher, referred to as Mister Larrabee, was "an accomplice and actor in the massacre at Indian Island and South Beach" (86). This massacre is but one example of genocidal violence that Indigenous peoples of California experienced at the hands of settlers. These were not unfortunate happenstances, but rather exist at the core of settler-colonial land dispossession. Genocide was carried out to claim the land and natural resources within California for the settler state.

The gold rush—fueled by a desire to transform the land and resources of California into monetary wealth accumulation—"represents one of the largest migrations in human history" (Schneider 2017, 37). Hundreds of thousands of Euro-Americans began their journey westward in the 1840s (Lindsay 2012). Approximately ten to thirteen thousand wealth seekers arrived in 1848, effectively doubling California's non-Indian population; the population of newcomers—almost exclusively young adult males—peaked at one hundred thousand in 1852 (Clay and Wright 2005). Norton (1979) describes this as a "plundering horde" (37). Despite the apocalyptic violence experienced by Indigenous peoples during the California gold rush, it is widely celebrated and memorialized, from elementary school field trips to pan for gold to "Gold Discovery" festivities across the state, where locals and tourists gather and celebrate the gold rush with tours and exhibits.[1] Young children are taught to glorify the brave and individualistic miners that risked it all for the pursuit of extreme wealth. The California Office of Tourism, in partnership with the nonprofit marketing corporation Visit

California, advertises prepackaged "family-friendly gold rush adventures" wherein tourists are "present[ed] the Gold Rush in living, breathing color ... [and can] find flecks of gold, just like the fortune-seeking pioneers" (Visit California, n.d.). At Knott's Berry Farm—visited by millions of people a year—children can "travel back in time and experience life as a prospector trying to stake their claim" (Knott's Berry Farm, n.d.). Even adults celebrate the gold rush: choose between the Gold Rush IPA or the Fool's Gold Ale, or head to one of the dozens of towns throughout California that hold annual gold rush festivals and 49er Day celebrations. Many California residents carry with them an image of a gold miner emblazoned on the state-issued driver's license. Such narratives form the basis of the "California Story" and the "California Dream."

The California Story presents a narrative of nineteenth-century California history as a heroic tale of how the West was "won" (Platt 2011). William Bauer (2016) argues that the California Story rationalizes "settler colonialism, exculpate[s] white Americans for nineteenth- and twentieth-century violence, and erase[s] Indigenous People from the historical and contemporary scene" (2016, 5). The maintenance and protection of this narrative also requires the systematic erasure of settler-colonial violence—specifically the state-sponsored genocide against California Indians—within education and the public consciousness. In *We Are the Land: A History of Native California*, Damon Akins and Bauer (2021) argue that the history of Indigenous peoples within California has become disconnected from California history—which erases Indigenous presence and undermines the sovereignty of contemporary Indigenous communities. Cutcha Risling Baldy (2018) argues that such erasure "makes the founding of the state of California benign, removes any lasting or residual trauma, and pretends that ownership or rights to land and resources in this state are settled and beyond reproach" (58). However, examining California history from a framework of settler colonialism allows us to understand the ways in which settler claims to lands, waters, and other natural resources relied on genocidal violence and have always been contested and resisted by Indigenous peoples in California.

Akins and Bauer (2021) argue that California is both a place and an idea. As a place, California has always been Indigenous land. Developed over millennia, Indigenous relationships to and understandings of place are rooted in kinship and reciprocity. Within this epistemological framework, land is alive and possesses its own agency. This is fundamentally different from settler-colonial conceptions of land as inanimate property; Indigenous peoples understand themselves as part of and in relationship with the land. In addition to California as place, Akins and Bauer emphasize that California is also an idea: "as an idea—or, as it was often described, a dream—that colonial entities brought with them, 'California' represented a natural abundance of resources to be exploited; it could not be Indigenous land" (4). The abundance of Trees, Fish, and other relatives observed by invading settlers was the result of the knowledge and land management practices of California's Indigenous peoples—practices such as harvesting, propagating, pruning, and, most importantly, burning. In other words, settler-colonial resource extraction and wealth accumulation would not have been possible without Indigenous peoples' previous management of the landscape (Norgaard 2019). However, settlers did not comprehend the complexity—or the necessity—of Indigenous land management regimes. Incoming settlers, reflected through miners' diaries, held three related assumptions about California: "First, they assumed that its diverse natural resources lay idle, untapped, and uncultivated by lazy Indians and Californios. Second, they thought nature's abundance and diversity were going to waste, and they had a God-given right to use them for profit. Third, they viewed the resources of California as inexhaustible" (M. Anderson 2005, 91). Perhaps better than any other moment in American settler history, the California gold rush demonstrates the intersections between resource extraction, violence against Indigenous lands and bodies, and the creation of the settler state: "The settlers' idea of California, mythologized as 'the California Dream,' excluded California Indians" (Akins and Bauer 2021, 10). This systematic attempt to exterminate Indigenous peoples throughout the nineteenth century continues today with the erasure of Indigenous histories and knowledge from public education and consciousness. In other words, "people misunderstand the settler invasion of Indigenous California *as* California history rather than an unsustainable and disruptive episode in it" (4, emphasis in original).

While the current focus is on the experiences of Indigenous peoples and their homelands in California, gold rushing also occurred within an international context. Mae Ngai (2021) positions gold mines as "international contact zones on the frontiers of Anglo-American settler societies" that relied on the imposition of private property regimes and Indigenous land dispossession (3). Wealth accumulation derived from goldfields then enabled the continued colonization and occupation of Indigenous territories throughout the world. The lust for gold (and silver) in Latin America, for example, resulted in the slavery and death of millions of Indigenous peoples. The "silver rush" of Potosí (located in what is now called Bolivia) in the 1500s consumed eight million Indigenous lives over the course of three centuries. Eduardo Galeano (1973) argues that "the metals taken from the new colonial dominions not only stimulated Europe's economic development; one may say that they made it possible" (33). The Brazilian gold rush—at Ouro Prêto, the Potosí of gold—exploded in the eighteenth century. Brazilian production exceeded the total volume that Spain had taken from its colonies in the previous two centuries, and, like in California, harmed the population of Brazil. In 1700 Brazil's population was approximately three hundred thousand, but a century later it had multiplied eleven times. This set the global stage for what was to come in California. Between 1848 and 1896, gold miners and mining companies extracted approximately 435 million ounces of gold, "more than the total amount that had been mined in the previous three thousand years, including the most recent Brazilian gold rush" (Ngai 2021, 7). This was made possible by settler-colonial invasion, genocidal violence, slavery, labor exploitation, and the imposition of private property laws.

Settler-colonial ideas about land and natural resources—and this place we now call California—that were established during the gold rush persist and shape the present, specifically regarding natural resource extraction and management. The California gold rush established the rush mentality influenced by settler-colonial logics of wilderness and *terra nullius*. Therefore, it is necessary to understand the impact that the gold rush had on the landscape and Indigenous peoples, how the violence perpetrated against Indigenous lands and bodies are fundamentally interconnected, and the ways by which Indigenous peoples in California continue to experience environmental injustice as the state moved from gold, to timber, to fish, and now cannabis.

The surge in cannabis production in California alludes to the quintessential origin story of California. Like miners of yesteryear, people from across the country—and even the world—have flocked to California to cultivate and profit on cannabis production. Settler pursuits of gold justified genocidal violence against Indigenous peoples carried out by voluntary militias and financially supported by the state of California and the US government. In tandem with state-sanctioned genocide, Native lands were seized by encroaching settlers and the government's refusal to ratify the eighteen treaties negotiated in California (discussed later). As a noun, a rush refers to a sudden and quick movement toward something, typically by many people. As a verb, to rush means to move with urgent haste—a rush to immediate profit without regard for the life of Native people or future generations. This rush mentality of intense and urgent desire for wealth—the "fervor" articulated by Anderson—could not be met by gold alone; settlers continued to extract other resources, such as timber, fish, and oil.

In retrospect, it is clear that the real gold was in fact the land itself. Such overlapping histories of resource extraction demonstrate that "rushing" is a well-established pattern; cycles of capitalistic extraction—and the inevitable destruction of the resource—are predictably repeated with regularity. The rush mentality is what founded this state, and yet "people act like that was so long ago and we have just definitely moved on and we're just this very green friendly place . . . but what founded Humboldt County is this Gold Rush and I think we've been rushing since 1849" (Risling Baldy 2017). But the gold rush did not end with gold; rather, it set into motion a structure of settler-colonial land dispossession and natural resource extraction that continues to frame settler-Indigenous relations and land use decision-making in Northern California today. California's experience is but one manifestation of multiple gold rushes that took place throughout the globe, all made possible through colonial violence, slavery, and natural resource extraction. California Indians have seen this pattern play out numerous times and we already know the ending.

"WHEN OUR WORLDS CRIED"

When the settler state tells stories about Native peoples, which happens infrequently, it relates stories about our disappearance, our destruction, our death. "While these explorations of the brutal, disquieting history of California are important for intervening on the sanitized history often taught in schools, references only to our genocide, our victimization at the hands of egregious laws and depraved settlers, frame our peoples as passive victims who perished at the hands of settlers thereby erasing our continued presence on this land" (Risling Baldy and Begay 2019, 42). Considering California's attempts to eradicate Native populations, it is miraculous that California Indians continue to speak their languages, gather their acorns, weave their baskets, and hold their ceremonies. This resilience is a testament to the resistance of our ancestors and Native survivance. Jack Forbes (1971) argues how remarkable it is that "Indian people, as a living group of human beings, not only managed to survive but also managed to preserve the essence of their Indianness" (240). I write about the genocides that California Indians survived not to focus on our death or our past, but to understand the relationship between violence against Indigenous bodies and natural resource extraction, and what this mean for Indigenous futures in this place. I must write about genocide *because* I am invested in our futures—because I see the same rush mentality playing out today, because it never stopped. To heal from the genocide that took place here, people and land must heal together. Ecological restoration and land return must occur. To do that, we must understand the history of this place, the ways genocide is written on the landscape, and how relations of genocide are reproduced through settler-colonial orientations to land.

California Indians survived three distinct waves of genocide (Tolley 2006).[2] The death toll of California Indians from American colonization during the California gold rush was the most extreme: between 1846 and 1870 the California Indian population plunged from 150,000 to fewer than 30,000 (Cook 1978; Tolley 2006). These figures, however, are now considered outdated by many California Indian scholars; it is now widely held that the California Indians population exceeded 1,000,000 at the time of invasion (Thornton 1987; Miranda 2010). My task, however, is not to *prove* that a genocide occurred—numerous scholars have already done this (Fenelon and Trafzer 2014; Forbes 1971; Norton 1979; Trafzer and Hyer 1999). Rather, I seek to demonstrate how the settler-colonial ideologies toward land, natural resources, and Native peoples that characterized the California gold rush are interconnected and have persisted into contemporary natural resource management of the present.

It is also important to note that while scholarship on the California Indian genocide has gained recent popularity (due to the work of primarily white male historians), California Indian scholars have been talking and writing about this violence for a very long time (and were often the focus of much criticism from their academic contemporaries). Jack Norton is the first scholar to use the UN Genocide Convention definition to frame his evidence of the California Indian genocide and his work has become foundational for other contemporary scholars. Norton (1979) argues that "in two hundred years of brutal occupation [California settlers] have *repeatedly committed genocide in one form or another*. Its patterns, its pervasiveness, its massive conspiracy is so common and well understood that its horror is diffused. It is so embedded in clichés of white manifest destiny, that the magnitude of the crime is transformed into inevitability or high moral principles" (125, emphasis in original). Norton is making two critical arguments. First, that the centrality and pervasiveness of the California Indian genocide—as the foundation of the state's existence—has become so embedded within the fabric of the state that it is now ubiquitous and thus invisible. The erasure of genocidal and settler-colonial violence is central to mythologizing the California Story and the California Dream—but it also works to mask contemporary ongoing violence. Even so, and despite clear evidence to the contrary, some historians outright deny that genocide took place (Fenelon and Trafzer 2014). Sacramento State University professor Maury Wiseman, for example, feels that genocide is just too strong of a word.[3]

Second, genocide, like settler colonialism, is a necessarily incomplete and ongoing process that takes many forms. This part of Norton's argument is significant because it contrasts with contemporary historical scholarship about the California Indian genocide produced within the past decade. For example, Stephanie Lumsden (Hupa) (2018) has critiqued historical methodologies that temporally bound settler violence. For example, popular texts such as Benjamin Madley's *An American Genocide: The United States and the California Indian Catastrophe, 1846–1873* uphold "a settler narrative of disavowal that locates genocide exclusively in the past" (3). Similar to how settler colonialism is often perceived as an event that has concluded, genocide is temporally bounded by historians. Lumsden, however, stresses that "what must be remembered then, is that the genocide enacted by the settler state against California Indian peoples continues to frame the material conditions of our lives and that the disavowal of that relationship is necessarily incomplete. . . . By locating California Indian genocide in a fixed moment in time Madley, intentionally or not, limits how we might understand the logics of elimination as they are deployed by the state in the contemporary moment"

(11–12). Furthermore, Bauer (2017) points out that texts such as Madley's rely "almost exclusively on non-Native sources to tell the history of genocide in California ... [which creates] a flattened picture of how California Indians responded to and attempted to shape the genocidal policies aimed at them" (140). Scholars like Lumsden, Norton, and Bauer encourage us to consider how contemporary violence employed by the state—from ecological contamination to incarceration—continues the work of eliminating California Indians.

Norton's argument aligns with contemporary scholarship on the relationship between genocide and settler colonialism. Damien Short, in his book *Redefining Genocide: Settler Colonialism, Social Death and Ecocide* (2016), argues that "we should view *cultural genocide* as *central* to our understanding of genocide itself" and the concept of cultural genocide "is an appropriate term to describe *the current experiences* of many Indigenous peoples living under settler colonial rule which has proceeded, as Patrick Wolfe observes, with a 'logic of elimination'" (17). The direct physical killing of California Indians during the gold rush facilitated the land dispossession and the removal of California Indians from their traditional homelands, thereby separating them from their nonhuman relations, sacred sites, and cultural practices. Today, ongoing settler and genocidal violence vis-à-vis natural resource extraction, "pose perhaps the biggest threat to Indigenous peoples' survival, for it is not just the accompanying dispossession which they bring but also the ecocidal 'externalities' of pollution and environmental degradation" (29). We must understand the continued separation of Indigenous peoples from their ancestral homelands and environmental destruction as genocidal outcomes. "Genocidal *outcomes*" result from "complex and only obscurely discerned causes, and in that respect genocide should properly lose its uniqueness of having intentionality as its defining characteristic" (Barta 2000, 238). Writing about the experiences of Indigenous Australians, genocide studies scholar Tony Barta (2000) argues that there needs to be a new conception of genocide, one which "embraces *relations* of destruction and removes from the word the emphasis on policy and intention which brought it into being" (238). Rather than spending our intellectual energy trying to disprove the reality of the California Indian genocide, based on a definitional technicality—which is arguably not a worthwhile academic endeavor, as it does not contribute to the larger project of healing from the settler-colonial violence that took place here—Barta suggests we seek to understand the ways in which genocidal violence, or the lasting repercussions from it, continue to play out in our society. By interrogating the produced relations of genocide we can recognize the ways in which settler-colonial logics of extermination are perpetuated and reproduced.

Settler-colonial orientations to land and land management regimes facilitate what Barta refers to as "relations of genocide." Settler colonialism, driven by the desire for land acquisition, necessarily separates Indigenous peoples from their lands. Because settler colonialism is an ongoing structure, Indigenous land dispossession is continually reproduced and perpetuated. Thus genocidal violence vis-à-vis the breaking down of relationships between Indigenous peoples and their lands—through both dispossession and destruction/contamination—is continually ongoing as well. While it may have started with gold, resource rushing did not end with gold. Subsequent patterns of resource rushing—facilitated by the genocide and removal of Native peoples—has continued to produce colonial ecological violence and environmental injustice for Indigenous communities in California.

Gold was "discovered" in 1848 and California became a state in 1850. The erasure of California Indians—and refusal to acknowledge or respect Indian systems of land tenure and stewardship responsibilities—is pervasive in the economic history of the gold rush. Economic historians Karen Clay and Gavin Wright (2005) posit it this way: "The mining districts of the California gold rush have long been celebrated as remarkable examples of orderly institution-formation in the absence of formal legal authority. This renown is fully deserved. When faced with the need to share access to gold-bearing land, miners gathered, established mining districts, and formalized prevailing customary norms as rules in district codes. The alternative may well have been wasteful and destructive violence. The mining codes thus may be said to have established order, where far worse scenarios may readily be imagined" (177). The erasure resulting from genocidal violence and settler-colonial land dispossession through mining claims is glaring. Miners were not claiming empty lands that lacked legal authority—they were claiming lands that had been tended and cared for by Indigenous peoples for millennia. Throughout the 1850s, the operations of volunteer militia men (many of whom came to California to mine gold) and US Army soldiers were funded by the state of California to kill Native peoples and clear them from the landscape. "Wasteful and destructive" violence did indeed occur and, in fact, was fundamental to the development of mining claims and districts. Furthermore, apart from state-sanctioned genocide, Akins and Bauer (2021) argue that mining exposed California Indians to exploitation and racism. Some traders used what is referred to as the "digger ounce": "a lead slug that weighed more than the weights used for gold and was named after a common and offensive epithet for California Indians" (134).

Moreover, miners heavily relied on the labor (including slavery) of Native peoples. Despite the fact that California was admitted to the Union as a free, nonslavery state, the enslavement of California Indians was widespread by this point (Lindsay 2012; Norton 1979; Reséndez 2016). The demand for labor during the gold rush spurred the slavery of California Indians and a thriving slave trade of Native children between Northern and Southern California (Lindsay 2012; Norton 1979; Risling Baldy 2018). While exact figures are difficult to pinpoint, between 1850 and 1863 Americans had a minimum of ten thousand enslaved California Indians. Some scholars believe that number is closer to twenty thousand (Akins and Bauer 2021). In Humboldt County, kidnapped Native people were valued between $50 and $250 (Lindsay 2012); between 1860 to 1863, of the 110 people enslaved in the county, the vast majority were between the ages of seven and twelve (Risling Baldy 2018). But, of course, the state never called it slavery; in fact, officials called it anything but: indenture, forced labor, custodianship, concubinage, apprenticeship, and so on. Like the state, contemporary historians are also reluctant to use the language of slavery. "The failure of historians to deploy the language of slavery consistently in their analyses of California Indian genocide upholds the narrative of the settler state and erases the violence of captivity" (Lumsden 2018).

A textbook example of settler-colonial strategy, the state of California used law as a weapon to legalize and justify violence against California Indians—whether through the creation of militias or by claiming legal water rights. From an Indigenous perspective, therefore, law must be understood as a tool of colonization that works to justify the plunder of Indigenous territories (Mattei and Nader 2008). For example, legal fictions such as the doctrine of discovery demonstrate how law is used to veil lawless behavior such as genocide and theft.[4] In California specifically, "law works to subjugate Indigenous people to the will of settler society and simultaneously naturalizes their subjugation with punishment. Indigenous criminality becomes the explanation for their low socio-economic position in Euro-American society rather than colonization" (Lumsden 2014, 21).

One of the first laws authorized by the nascent legislature of California, passed in 1850, was the Act for the Government and Protection of Indians (also referred to as Chapter 133). It did neither. Instead, the law had three key intended results, outcomes that were often intertwined and occurred simultaneously. First, the law legalized the corporeal punishment of Indians. Section 9 of the law states that justices of the peace are authorized to "punish guilty chiefs or principal men by reprimand or fine, or otherwise reasonably chastise them"; Section 17 states that "when an Indian is sentenced to be whipped . . . [that] unnecessary cruelty in the execution" not be permitted. Police brutality is not new—rather, it has always been a critical tactic for enforcing white supremacist settler-colonial policies. Moreover, there is a long legacy of colonizers passing off torture as "discipline" (Miranda 2013). Second, the law made Indians criminals until proven innocent. Section 1 states that "Justices of the Peace shall have jurisdiction in all cases of complaints by, for or against Indians," while Section 6 states "but in no case shall a white man be convicted on any offense upon the testimony of an Indian."[5] These in effect create legal immunity for white settlers to kidnap, rape, and murder California Indians. Third, the law established a system of Indian slavery. Sections 3, 14, and 20 outline the provisions. To take a minor Indian, a settler needed to appear before a justice of the peace in their township to be authorized for "the care, custody, control, and earnings of such minor" (Section 3).

Legal immunity enjoyed by white settlers (as a creation of their own law) often was combined with provisions that legalized Indian slavery. As evidence of this practice, Norton (1979) reproduced an 1861 letter written by attorney G. M. Hanson in which Hanson recalls the testimony of a man apprehended for the kidnapping of nine Indian children:

> In the month of October last I apprehended three kidnappers, about 14 miles from the city of Marysville, who had nine Indian children, from three to ten years of age, which they had taken from Eel River in Humboldt County. . . . [The man] who testified [said] that "it was an act of charity on the part of the two to hunt up the children and then provide homes for them, because their parents had been killed, and the

children would have perished with hunger." My counsel inquired how he knew their parents had been killed? "Because," he said, "I killed some of them myself." (*When Our Worlds Cried*, 49)

This man had, presumably, killed the parents of these children so as to legally acquire the children as slaves. To admit to an attorney that you killed two people is a particularly bold move. That this unidentified man felt confident doing so speaks to the legal immunity enjoyed by white settlers at this moment in California history.

Alternatively, settlers could purchase an Indian who had been convicted of a crime. And, considering an Indian could not testify against a white man in court, this also applied to Indians who hadn't been convicted *yet*. Section 14 states that if an Indian were convicted of an offense punishable by fine "*any white man*, by consent of the justice, [could] give bond for said Indian . . . and in such case the Indian shall be compelled to work for the person so bailing" (emphasis added). Section 20 states that Indians found "loitering and strolling about . . . or leading an immoral or profligate course of life" shall be arrested upon the "complaint of *any* reasonable citizen" (emphasis added), and, within twenty-four hours, be auctioned to the highest bidder for a term not exceeding four months. In this way the act defined a relationship between Native labor and Native punishment. "By repeatedly convicting Native Americans under vagrancy and drunkenness laws, magistrates provided cheap Native labor for the benefit of the local economy" (Lindsay 2012, 249). Recall Lumsden's (2018) argument: that the free/slave binary both flattens analyses of labor regimes and is ineffective in describing Native experiences within "the context of a genocide where the meaning of freedom for Indian people was constantly in flux." This binary also must be examined in relation to land dispossession and the desire of the settler state to codify and control land and water rights.

While this law certainly constituted slavery, it also paved the way to state-sponsored genocide. Brendan Lindsay (2012) argues this law served as the "cornerstone of legal genocide" (245). California's first governor, Peter Burnett, stated the following in his State of the State Address on January 6, 1851: "That a war of extermination will continue to be waged between the races, until the Indian race becomes extinct, must be expected. While we cannot anticipate this result but with painful regret, the inevitable destiny of the race is beyond the power or wisdom of man to avert. . . . [California Indians] have no ideas and no recollections of a separate national existence—no alliance with great names or families—no page of history upon which are recorded the deeds of the past—no present privileges—and no hope for the future" (Burnett 1851). Public debates, often occurring through local newspapers, framed the "Indian Problem" as one of domestication versus extermination. Extermination, as illustrated in Burnett's address, saw the genocide of California Indians as the most humane and only sensible option; conversely, advocates of Indian domestication argued that genocide was inhumane and that Native peoples could still be of use to white settlers, just like domesticated livestock. These viewpoints fueled the efforts of the boarding school system that unfolded a couple decades later. Of course, neither advocates of extermination or of domestication envisioned a future in which California Indians could continue their lifeways.[6]

What is important to underscore here is that the genocide in California was not a tragic aberration. Rather, "violence was integral to the success of colonization, it was the policy of the government to 'blink at genocide,' and extermination was considered the most 'practical' approach. These stories of depraved violence are thought of as the isolated experiences of a few and not endemic to a settler colonialism intent on eradicating Indigenous peoples" (Risling Baldy 2018, 57). The California genocide was thoroughly debated and planned, and ultimately carried out by ordinary citizens; the extermination of California Indians was expressed through popular will and facilitated by grassroots democracy (Lindsay 2012). Shortly after the passage of the Act for the Government and Protection of Indians in 1850, the California Legislature passed two laws to create militias specifically to kill California Indian peoples: An Act Concerning Volunteer or Independent Companies and An Act Concerning the Organization of the Militia (Johnston-Dodds 2002; Risling Baldy 2018). Volunteer militias, as opposed to the disorganized and underfunded compulsory militias, were composed of average citizens. Between 1850 and 1859 at least 303 different volunteer militia units were registered, composed of 35,000 individual men (Risling Baldy 2018). Between 1846 and 1873, vigilante and militia campaigns killed between 9,492 and 16,094 Indigenous people (Akins and Bauer 2021). At the time, however, California was strapped for cash, so it employed numerous cost-cutting measures to enforce the law (Lindsay 2012). Because the search for the actual culprits of stock-raidings or other minor offenses was considered too time consuming, the militias were instructed to kill whatever Indians they could find and as efficiently as possible. The militias were directed to keep their company numbers to a minimum, which encouraged shoot-first tactics and surprise ambush attacks (Lindsay 2012). A few years later, in 1854, the California Legislature passed the Act to Prevent the Sale of Fire-Arms and Ammunition to Indians—effectively denying "rights, voting, legal recourse, and gun ownership to California Indians" (Akins and Bauer 2021, 139).

Volunteer militiamen "demanded high compensation because of the gold they expected to miss out on while campaigning against Native Americans" (Lindsay 2012, 240). Low-level privates could earn up to eight dollars per day, and top-ranking majors could earn up to sixteen dollars per day (Lindsay 2012). In 1852 the average earnings of a gold miner was less than six hundred dollars per year, or approximately two dollars per day; by the late 1850s miners were earning, on average, about three dollars per day (Lindsay 2012; Clay and Wright 2005). These wages created a financial incentive to abandon the mines in pursuit of joining Indian-killing militias. And, considering the sparse and uneven deposits of gold, many prospective miners did not strike it rich and sought out other forms of employment.

In addition to direct compensation, numerous economic incentives were put in place by the state of California to encourage Indian killing. Prices for severed heads and scalps of Indian people fluctuated by municipality, but newspapers in Shasta City advertised five dollars for a head and twenty-five cents for a scalp (Johnston-Dodds 2002). In both 1851 and 1852, the state paid out one million dollars to militias that hunted down and slaughtered Indians. In 1857 the state issued a payment of four hundred thousand dollars for anti-Indian militias (Johnston-Dodds 2002). The sharp decline between 1852 and 1857 illustrates the mass reduction of the California Indian population at the hands of American settlers. It also demonstrates the predictability of the resource pattern: capitalize on it until it has been destroyed. "Perhaps the most shocking bounty opportunity was one suggested by the editors of the *Lassen Sage Brush* in 1868, a $500 bounty for 'every Indian killed.' This would be such an incentive as to make killing Native Americans tantamount to California's new Gold Rush" (Lindsay 2012, 212). In this way the rush mentality even applied to the direct killing of Native peoples, who were deemed yet another resource to profit on. "Because California law stipulated that reimbursement was due to citizens who supplied volunteer companies, it was potentially profitable and desirable for Euro-Americans to promote conflict with Indian people. . . . Rewards that necessitated the killing of Indian people, guilty or not, were obviously genocidal in their intent, as they encouraged wanton slaughter for profit rather than allowing for self-defense, as Euro-Americans falsely claimed to be their real intent" (Lindsay 2012, 212). The state of California's first major democratic action was to wage genocide, with the expressed purpose of exterminating California Indians. The murders of Native people, therefore, were not committed by the most violent or dangerous criminals in town, but by average, everyday folks. Killing Indians was one path to achieving the California Dream.

LAND: NEW GOLD, REAL GOLD

Whether they realized it or not, genocide was a method employed by individual settlers and the settler state to acquire land and natural resources. Indeed, "land would prove to be far more profitable for settlers than gold, and would be at the heart of continued struggles as settlers attempted to wrest the land from the rightful Indian owners" (Risling Baldy and Begay 2019, 49). In an editorial published in the *Humboldt Times* dated December 14, 1861, the author attempts to rationalize and justify settler-colonial land dispossession:

> It is a hardship that the natives of the country should be forced to sell their lands. It is hard that California Indians are forced from their homes without even the form of a sale to which they are a party. But the settlers upon public lands are not responsible for the wrong. Government has put the land into market and offered inducements to her citizens to purchase and settle thereon. . . . The settlers must retain possession of the lands they have bought off the Government; but they cannot always submit to being preyed upon by the bands of hostile Indians which roam through the mountains. (quoted in Norton 1979, 91–92)

The lack of responsibility and the faux sympathy for those "forced from their homes" is discombobulating. However, the last line of this excerpt fills the reader in on the author's gap in logic: California Indians are not people, but animals that roam and prey on defenseless settlers. This story is a continuation of missionization, the "stories about savages, heathens, pagans, barbarians, and other lesser, inferior beings" (Miranda 2013, xvi). We continue to see the justification and rationalization of settler-colonial violence in California today. It is found in its absence: absence from school curricula, absence from tourist leaflets, absence from thought. The state-sanctioned and federally funded genocide of California Indians was critical to the development of California and the success of the gold rush. However, after the gold rush—destined, like all capitalistic extractions of resources, to be unsustainable—most miners were not rich beyond their wildest dreams. In fact, gold proved far less profitable than invaders anticipated and the state quickly realized that the real gold was the land (Risling Baldy 2018; Lindsay 2012).

While the gold rush was certainly focused on resource extraction, it also was the process of creating a settler home that was already home to Indigenous peoples. Settlers dispossessed Native people of their lands through a variety of means; as demonstrated earlier, genocide and slavery were quite effective. But also, the conceptualization of land within a settler-colonial framework provided justification and rationale for legally sanctioned land theft. By employing the rhetoric of wasteful California Indians, the California Legislature was determined that valuable lands did not end up in Indian hands.

In response to the genocidal violence perpetrated by individual miners and vigilantes against California Indians, the US Congress sent treaty commissioners to negotiate with California Indian nations.[7] Eighteen different treaties were negotiated with California Indian nations, reserving 11,700 square miles (7.5 million acres) of land, or approximately 7.5 percent of the state (Johnston-Dodds 2002, 23). Treatymaking and the creation of reservations in California was intended to "pacify American and Californio ranchers, who still depended on Indigenous People to work" (Akins and Bauer 2021, 144). However, senators from California called for nonratification of the treaties. Senator Coates, the chairman of the California Assembly Special Committee on Indian Reservations, declared: "Rich and unexhaustible veins of gold-bearing quartz . . . have in the wisdom of the Indian agents, been considered eligible locations for the untutored tribes of the wilderness, and have accordingly been set apart for that purpose, and the energetic and zealous miner has been rudely ordered by those agents to abandon their claims and go beyond the limits of the reservations" (quoted in Norton 1979, 71). Coates characterizes Indians as "untutored" and "of the wilderness," whereas the miners are "energetic and zealous." The language of racism and savagery here is used to justify the denial of property rights and sovereignty of Native Americans; this is, perhaps, one of the oldest and most well-established legal traditions in American history (Williams 2005). Governor Burnett also urged the Senate to reject the treaties because the land, in his estimation, was worth at least $100 million, "a far cry from the $5 million California Indians won through their lawsuit one hundred years later" (Whiteley 2020, 5).

Not only were the eighteen negotiated treaties never ratified, the "federal government had further insisted that an 'injunction of secrecy' be placed upon their very existence. They literally wrapped the eighteen treaties in red tape" (Whiteley 2020, 6). "The President submitted the treaties to the U.S. Senate on June 1, 1852. On June 7, the Senate read the President's message, and referred the treaties to the Committee on Indian Affairs. The treaties were then considered and rejected by the U.S. Senate in secret session. The treaties did not reappear in the public record until January 18, 1905, after an injunction of secrecy was removed" (Johnston-Dodds 2002, 24). Many California Indian tribes were never informed that the treaties had not been ratified and were forced to renegotiate, leaving them with much smaller land bases (Secrest 2003). Some tribes had already left their ancestral homelands and moved to their negotiated treaty areas (Norton 2019), and others were subjected to removal and relocation (Risling Baldy and Begay 2019). Furthermore, many tribes never received land bases or federal recognition (Tolley 2006). "The lack of treaties left Indigenous People vulnerable to the capricious nature of state and federal Indian policy. California settlers consistently called for a policy of ethnic cleansing petitioning the state and federal government to forcibly relocate Indigenous People from their homelands to reservations" (Akins and Bauer 2021, 148).

Simultaneously occurring during the treatymaking process, California passed the Land Claims Act of 1851, which required every person claiming lands in California derived by the Mexican government to file a claim with the Public Land Commission within two years of the act's passage. As Beth

Rose Middleton Manning (2018) argues, because "Indian people were not able to participate . . . [the land claims process] left the vast Native homelands of the state open to non-Indians, who were able to draw on indentured Native labor to settle the ostensibly 'free' new state of California" (25). The Land Claims Act effectively extinguished all aboriginal land titles in the state because no tribes filed claims under the act (McAuliffe 2018).[8]

In 1905 white reformer Charles E. Kelsey and the Northern California Indian Association revealed that the treaties existed and that they had been kept secret for more than fifty years. "Indeed, the secret nickname of the 'lost treaties' and its implication of guilt launched the NCIA's biggest reform. The rhetoric of California's 'lost treaties' offered traction for social reformers and community organizers with which to pressure the federal government to begin to make significant change in its policy toward the state's many indigenous groups. The eighteen unratified treaties were broken not 'lost.' The existence of the treaties was not really a secret as Tribal groups whose ancestors signed the treaties did not forget about them" (Whiteley 2020, 7). As Kathleen Whiteley (Wiyot descent) (2020) astutely notes, the rhetoric of "lost" treaties masks the actions of the settler-colonial state that were aimed at divesting Indigenous peoples of their territories and natural resources. Akin to actions taken against our cultures, our languages, and our belief systems—our treaties were never "lost." They were violently wrested from us.

In 1928 the California Indians Jurisdictional Act authorized California's attorney general to sue the US government on behalf of California tribes whose lands were stolen through broken treaties. In 1942 California tribes "won a symbolic but nearly empty victory in the courts" (Akins and Bauer 2021, 252). This is referred to as the California Indian Claims Case. "To ostensibly compensate Indigenous people for lost lands, the ICC relied on a process that determined the potential value of aboriginal land 'at the date of taking,' paid retroactively, without interest" (Whiteley 2020, 2). Tribes were to be compensated $17,053,942, but the government deducted "offsets" of $12,029,100 for the expense of Indian Affairs administration—leaving behind $5,024,842 for more than 7.5 million acres of land to be distributed among approximately thirty-six thousand "Indians of California." This legal definition included "all Indians who were residing in the State of California on June 1, 1852, and their descendants now living in said state." Like the term "Native American," "Indians of California" is a misnomer that masks the diversity of over one hundred distinct cultural and political entities. Additionally, the creation of this legal term and the consolidation of the many sovereigns in California boundaries within one term affected the impact of federal policies on tribal peoples in California and limited the United States' constitutional obligation of treatymaking with other nations, which according to the US Constitution is the "supreme law of the land." "Thus, the term 'Indians of California' is as unacceptable as referring collectively to the "white men of Europe" if the sovereign nations of France, Spain, and Germany litigated a suit against the United States" (Norton 2019, 118).

A second land claims case involving the land taken from California Indians that was not covered by the treaties was authorized in 1946. This case was appealed and eventually settled in 1963. During this time, nearly forty reservations and rancherias in California were terminated under the Rancheria Act of 1958 (Norton 2019). This settlement awarded $29 million for 64.4 million acres of land to approximately sixty-nine thousand Indians. "In a series of BIA machinations, the 'Indians of California' received only forty-seven cents an acre as 'just compensation' for lands fraudulently taken. Payment of $1.25 an acre for any land in America had been established in 1820. However, the California Indian people were coerced to accept judgment of forty-seven cents an acre and received a federal check for $668.51 on December 22, 1972, three days before Christmas" (Norton 2019, 124). Some recipients did not understand "what the money was for or what it meant to receive payment for stolen lands and 'settle' their aboriginal title claims" (Risling Baldy and Begay 2019, 53). Similar to many Lakota/Dakota refusals to accept money for Paha Sapa (Black Hills), others have refused to cash their checks.

Simultaneously, as the nascent state of California was acquiring lands, so too was it claiming rights over water; indeed, the codification of water rights was integral to the settler-colonial project (Matsui 2009). Andrew Curley (Diné) (2019) argues, "In western states and provinces, water laws became expressions of nineteenth-century utilitarian logics of resource exploitation and commodification. These laws 'produced' or constructed nature according to the ontology of the settler colonialist and exerted claims over Indigenous jurisdictions" (63). Mark Kanazawa's text *Golden Rules: The Origins of California Water Law in the Gold Rush* (2015) documents the emergence of water rights in gold rush–era California. Kanazawa argues that because gold mining was water intensive, the demand for and value of water increased rapidly as more goldseekers flooded into the region. Value, in this context, aligns with the settler ontologies articulated by Curley; within this ontology, value refers to exchange value or profit value, as opposed to the value of water to sustain all life. Gold miners then developed legal rules to govern water development via mining district codes that, prior to the creation of the settler court system, served as a "legal monopoly in any particular locality" (165). The perspective that goldseekers—whom Kanazawa describes as a "horde of humanity" (19)—brought law, order, and civilization to an empty or lawless place relies on a settler-colonial logic that Native peoples did not have their own civilization or maintain legal orders.[9] It explicitly ignores Indigenous stewardship and intimate relationships with water. And, perhaps most significantly, like Clay and Wright, Kanazawa gives the reader no indication that a state-funded genocide of California Indians occurred simultaneously with the development of water law, first in mining camps and then through the court system. This process of dispossession set a precedent for the continuation of water theft from Native peoples that occurs today.

While the origins of settler water rights may have started in the mining camps due to increased disputes over water, by the mid-1850s water disputes had made their way into the courts. Mining had undergone major changes as well. Rather than the initial small labor-intensive activity, mining operations had become large capital-intensive enterprises with large water demands. New incoming miners were dissatisfied with the concentration of water claims; early newspapers articulate how "newly arrived gold seekers have long complained of the injustice of the present system" (quoted in Kanazawa 2015, 173). However, injustice experienced by Indigenous peoples—at the hands of encroaching settlers—did not seem to be of concern:

> Toward the middle of the 1850s, the period of unofficial mining camp law ascendance gave way to emphasis on official judge-made law in the newly operational court system. It was here that the courts stepped in to craft legal principles to create mining and water rights and to resolve disputes over these rights. . . . Water became the subject of much litigation for the remainder of the decade, and the result was the creation of the basic doctrine of prior appropriation, which became the fundamental basis for water law not only in California but also in much of the rest of the western United States. (183)

Kanazawa provides extensive history and analysis of the key case law that built the body of water law as we know it today. However, it is critical to point out that Native Americans were systematically excluded from this nascent court system because the 1850 Act for the Government and Protection of Indians stipulated that Native Americans could not testify against white settlers. Native people were unable to bring water disputes to the court system if it involved a mining district's claim. Moreover, the fact that the state placed bounties on Native bodies likely served as a major deterrent to doing so. (The topic of water rights and the ideological underpinnings of appropriative rights are addressed in chapter 7.)

While scholarly critiques of settler-colonial structures have emphasized how legal mechanisms are designed to acquire Indigenous lands and waters, scholars like Kari Norgaard, Jessica Hernandez, and Kyle Whyte have articulated the necessity of ecological transformation and destruction as integral to the settler-colonial elimination project. The alteration of land and changes to species composition and ecological structures has led to disastrous consequences for Native peoples. The American colonization of California, and the gold rush specifically, was an unimaginable ecological disaster whose legacy impacts are still deeply felt today by California Indians. The subsequent industrial transformation of California resulted in a violent transformation of the landscape, uprooted the lives of many nonhuman relatives, and disrupted every element of Indigenous life. "Habitat loss, lack of foods and plant-based medicines, deforestation, diversion of waters without concern for downstream ecosystems, over fishing, fish-contamination, over-hunting, animal migration for food and habitat, and relocation, and an ongoing genocide of traditional forest stewards all drastically changed the landscape and ecosystems of northern California in a matter of a few years" (Oros 2016, 13). The development of an industrial economy in California—via the fur trade, mining, timber harvesting, grazing, irrigation, and building of dams—led to rampant ecological destruction. Forests were clear-cut, Rivers were diverted and torn up until they turned to mud, and waterways were polluted; these ecological transformations led to a great decrease in Salmon and other populations of more-than-human relatives (Huntsinger et al. 1994; Lichatowich 1999). Because settlers did not understand the complex ecological knowledge of Indigenous peoples, some unknowingly destroyed entire subsistence economies. Others "directly and purposefully attacked the local ecology" as a means of targeting Native communities (Lindsay 2012, 265). "The miners overran native homelands, altering stream courses, destroying salmon runs, scaring away game with pistols and rifles, chopping down oaks and sugar pines, and grazing cattle, hogs, and horses on the grasslands" (M. Anderson 2005, 85). In a letter to Superintendent of Indian Affairs Thomas J. Henley dated 1853, Special Indian Agent E. A. Stevenson (1998) reports that California Indians were starving; because of mining operations there were no fish and few acorns:

> The miners have turned the streams from their beds and conveyed the water to the dry diggings and after being used until it is so thick with mud that it will scarcely run it returns to its natural channel and with it the soil from a thousand hills, which has driven almost every kind of fish to seek new places of resort where they can enjoy a purer and more natural element. And to prove the old adage that misfortunes never come singly, the oaks have for the last three years refused to furnish the acorn, which formed one of the chief articles of Indian food. (110)

Many culturally significant species—including beavers, otters, fishers, foxes, bears, deer, elk, and several bird species—were also impacted by settler activities (Oros 2016, 12). The massive invasion associated with the gold rush caused a rapid decline in traditional food supplies and impacted California Indians' ability to feed themselves (M. Anderson 2005; Norton 1979; Lowry et al. 1999).

Changes to water quantity and quality also contributed to growing food insecurity for California Indians. "Moving the courses of whole rivers and streams to get at the gold in the stream bottoms destroyed not only many of the fish runs but also the freshwater mussels, other aquatic life, and the streamside vegetation from which animal and plant food had been gathered. Hydraulic mining released millions of tons of debris, silt, and gravel into streams, choking salmon-spawning beds" (M. Anderson 2005, 86). Fishing on the Klamath River was unsuccessful after gold mining: "The trout turned on their sides and died; the salmon from the sea came in but rarely. . . . What few did come were pretty safe from the spears of the Indians, because of the colored water" (M. Anderson 2005, 86). The adoption of hydraulic mining dramatically reduced water quality throughout California. Starting in the Sierras in 1853, hydraulic mining "utilized the force of water to wash large quantities of gold-bearing terrace materials into sluice boxes" (Sierra Fund 2008, 15). Hydraulic mining infrastructure consumed timber and other materials for "dams, reservoirs, distributing flumes and aqueducts, pipes and nozzles, tunnels, and sluices" and polluted River systems with debris—causing increased sedimentation in riverbeds—while pressure nozzles destroyed entire mountainsides (Isenburg 2005, 24).

Gold mining in California also would not have been possible without mercury mining (Johnston 2013). Mercury was required for gold mining, and by 1860 gold miners were using more than a million pounds of mercury every year (Isenburg 2005). Mercury contamination remains a concern in California. Until the 1890s mercury mining was the second-largest industry behind gold mining (Isenburg 2005). Scott Johnston (in Sierra Fund 2008) argues that mercury mining—although overshadowed by gold in California histories—was just as important and influential in the development of the state as gold mining. Approximately 26 million pounds of mercury were used during the gold rush. In fact, approximately ten times the amount of mercury was put into the ecosystem compared the amount of gold extracted from it (Solnit 2006). The health impacts of mercury are severe; mercury poisoning affects the brain, kidneys, and the nervous system. Unsurprisingly, those most at risk are Indigenous children from fishing communities (Oros 2016). "In many places, mercury contamination of water forced native North Americans, who have traditionally relied on marine animals and fish as primary food sources, to choose between tradition and health" (Solnit 2006, sec. 3, para. 7). This is a direct impediment to cultural sovereignty and ecological responsibility, and demonstrates the profound connection between violence committed against Indigenous lands and bodies.

According to the Sierra Fund, as of 2008 at least forty-seven thousand abandoned mining sites dating back to the gold rush still exist. Approximately 87 percent of these mines present physical safety hazards and 11 percent present environmental hazards. "Contaminated runoff from abandoned mines impacts land, groundwater, streams, rivers, and lakes. Principal environmental pollutants from abandoned mines are mercury from contaminated sediments, arsenic, lead, and other heavy metals associated with acid rock drainage" (2008, 19). Legacy impacts from the gold rush continue to impact Indigenous subsistence and cultural practices throughout California: "The toxic chemicals that remain from the Gold Rush era also threaten salmon for ceremonies, medicinal plants, and ceremonial plants. The fish that have been the staple of the native diet have become a poison" (25).[10] The settler-colonial violence enacted against Indigenous lands, waters, and bodies during the California gold rush persists through the contamination of our environments. As the state continues to engage in resource rushing—from timber, to fish, and now cannabis—we must understand and evaluate the ecological impacts of contemporary extraction within the context of historic and legacy impacts.

Indigenous political struggles always come back to the issue of land. Contemporary problems that Native American communities face, such as higher rates of disease, poverty, violence, suicide, drug abuse, and language loss, among others, "are all political problems when viewed within the context of settler colonialism. . . . The root causes of these problems are all found in the political economy of settler colonialism, which is inextricably linked to the exploitation of Indigenous lands" (Carroll 2015, 12). To heal from the genocidal violence that occurred in California, we must understand the ways in which genocidal violence is reproduced through the legacies of historic land dispossession and contemporary natural resource extraction. As we move into the timber rush, fish rush, and ultimately the contemporary green rush, we must reflect on the question posed by artist and writer Chag Lowry (Maidu/Yurok/Achumawi): "What price was paid for the Gold Rush?" (Lowry et al. 1999, 12). And who is still paying that price while others reap the profits of the latest resource rush?

2

FORESTS ON FIRE

Constructing Natural Resources and Imposing Ecological Regimes

Our land was taken from us long ago and our Indigenous stewardship responsibility was taken from us too. The land is still sacred and it will forever be part of us. We hold the knowledge of fire, forests, water, plants and animals that is needed to revitalize our human connection and responsibility to this land. —Bill Tripp, "Our Land Was Taken"

Throughout the world, the colonization of diverse peoples was, at its root, a forced subjugation of ecological concepts of nature, and of the earth as the repository of all forms, latencies and powers of creation, the ground and cause of the world.
—Vandana Shiva, "Resources"

Following the gold rush, the timber rush continued settler-colonial processes of Indigenous land dispossession. Like the unratified treaties of 1851 and 1852, vast tracts of land were claimed for timber production during the 1870s, and today the ancestral territories of many tribal nations in Northern California are currently occupied by private timber corporations or labeled state and federal forest reserves. In addition to claiming territory (and producing ecological harm), the settler state facilitated Indigenous land dispossession through the imposition of land management practices and authority. The criminalization of Indigenous land management practices (e.g., fire management) and the imposition of colonialist land management practices (e.g., fire suppression) fundamentally altered the species composition of forestlands—transforming a forest for people (and other more-than-human relatives) to a forest for timber production. From the settler-colonial perspective, California was a wild Eden awaiting taming vis-à-vis industrial development and resource extraction (M. Anderson 2005; Merchant 1998).

Following settler-colonial invasion, Trees were transformed into timber. As James Scott (1998) notes, "Trees that are valued become 'timber' while species that compete with them become 'trash' trees or 'underbrush'" (13). Forests that were understood and managed by Indigenous peoples as dynamic and interconnected systems—not just for the sustenance of human beings but for all of creation—were inventoried and sold for parts. Settler-colonial relationships to land and land management regimes were institutionalized through state and federal land management entities that are largely guided by Western natural resources sciences. Viewing the Earth as composed of "natural resources" is not an objective, neutral, or default position; rather, compartmentalizing entire ecosystems into natural resources is a culturally specific way of thinking about the environment.

Vandana Shiva (1992) argues that the social or ideological creation of "natural resources" is fundamentally tied to colonialism. Whereas the word "resource" originally implied life and reciprocal relationships between humans and nature, natural resources "became those parts of nature which were required as inputs for industrial production and colonial trade" (206). "In this view, nature has been clearly stripped of her creative power; she has turned into a container for raw materials waiting to be transformed into inputs for commodity production . . . it is now simply human inventiveness and industry which impart value to nature. For natural resources require to be 'developed.' . . . This created a new dualism between nature and humans. Since nature needed to be 'developed' by humans, people had also to be developed from their primitive, backward states of embeddedness in nature" (206–7). In what Shiva describes as a conceptual break, relations are transformed into resources. The epistemological, ontological, or cosmological relationships with land that fall outside the realm of property are demarcated as savage, backward, and primitive (Tuck and Yang 2012).

After ecosystems are compartmentalized, plant and animal relatives are transformed into commodities and assigned value. Following the settler-colonial invasion of California, resource extraction traced a clear pattern. Shiva (1992) identifies the phases—or the resource rushing, in the context of settler colonialism—of natural resource extraction: "In the first phase, when nature's wealth was considered abundant and freely available, 'resources' were exploited rapaciously. . . . In the second phase, once exploitation had created degradation and scarcity, the 'management' of 'natural resources' became important in order to maintain continued supplies of raw material for commerce and industry" (207). Within the context of timber production, then, we see the mass destruction of old-growth forests throughout the state within a relatively short time frame following the gold rush. The

Fig 1 An Indian-killing militia poses on top of and next to a fallen Redwood. Courtesy Palmquist Collection, Cal Poly Humboldt Library.

timber rush picked up speed after the 1850s, and by 1900, 40 percent of California's 31 million acres of old-growth forest had already been logged (M. Anderson 2005). Today, more than 95 percent of old-growth redwoods have vanished (Noss 2000).

The deforestation of California's forests under the misconception that these spaces were vast tracts of uninhabited wilderness, and more significantly the corresponding ecological management regimes that accompanied settler-colonial forestry (e.g., fire suppression), has produced colonial ecological violence for California's Indigenous peoples. Akins and Bauer (2021) argue that "by the 1880s, settler violence shifted from overt assaults on Indigenous bodies—by this we mean statements of genocidal intent, state-sponsored body-part bounties, and militia and United States Army massacres—to assaults on Indigenous People's relationships with land, water, and culture" (179–80). In figure 1, originally published in Norton's *When Our Worlds Cried* (1979), a connection is drawn between violence against the landscape and violence against Native people: "They have already murdered the forest. Now they are shown ready to murder the Indians" (69). Moreover, genocidal violence against Native peoples and landscapes formed the basis of contemporary land ownership and management regimes in the region. In addition to the state of California, wealthy settlers also funded Indian-killing militias to clear and secure lands in Northern California, and then shaped federal forest management—often with an emphasis on fire suppression (Lake 2007; Vinyeta 2021).

Land dispossession, deforestation, and fire suppression have greatly impacted Indigenous peoples' abilities to provide for themselves and maintain cultural practices, but it has also changed the very ecosystems that Indigenous peoples steward. While the legal plunder of gold throughout the state demonstrates how violence against the landscape is paralleled in violence against Indigenous bodies, it is important to examine the ideological construction of natural resources and the subsequent imposition of Western ecological management regimes, specifically fire suppression, as a form of settler-colonial ecological violence.

SETTLER CONSTRUCTIONS OF WILDERNESS AND ERASURE OF TEK

Far from the myth of dense virgin wilderness, California's forests were well-tended by Indigenous peoples for millennia. As M. Kat Anderson (2005) cheekily argues, "The new world is in fact a very old world" (1). The notion that this place was "discovered," or that history began when Europeans showed up, is pervasive in all education systems in the United States. Prime examples in California include how schoolchildren are taught about missionization and gold rush history. These myths work to erase the thousands of years of Native history, presence, and knowledge accumulation. In reality, California Indians developed effective stewardship techniques that maintained high levels of biodiversity, and their relationships to their environments provided much in the way of instruction and continues to provide inspiration for contemporary and future populations. As Anderson's *Tending the Wild* so clearly demonstrates, California Indians were active managers of their environments and took advantage of the abundance of wild resources the landscape had to offer. Evidence of traditional ecological knowledge in California is vast, ranging from the plethora of uses of plant and animal species to myriad management techniques and in-depth understanding of plant and animal behavior, to extensive knowledge of food preparation and storage (M. Anderson 2005).

However, by constructing Native American people as primitive savages, wild hunter-gatherers, or even "prehistoric," the settler state erases complex bodies of traditional ecological knowledge, Indigenous governance structures and education systems, and our very humanity. "For settlers, the presence of Indigenous ecologies—from the human activities themselves to their physical manifestations as particular ecosystems and ecological flows—delegitimizes settlers' claims to have honorable and credible religious 'mission,' universal property rights, and exclusive political and cultural sovereignty. To remove all markers or physical manifestations that challenge their moral legitimacy, power, and self-determination, settlers systematically seek to erase the ecologies required for Indigenous governance systems" (Whyte, Caldwell, and Schaefer 2018, 159). The stereotypes of Indigenous land management practices—that they were minimal to nonexistent—were utilized by settlers to demonstrate the lack of use and ownership of the land. For example, Chief Justice Marshall argued in the Supreme Court in 1823 that Native peoples solely "used" the land and were not "owners" of the land because they did not engage in agriculture (Barker 2005). Of course, this is factually incorrect, or the pilgrims would have starved to death on the eastern seaboard. In California, because Indians did not exploit the Earth's resources for wealth accumulation but instead practiced economies of subsistence and reciprocity, they were demarcated as primitive, backward, uncivilized, and wasteful of the abundant resources at their disposal.[1] The impulse to eliminate Native peoples is not solely a process of genocide or assimilation, but rather is a deeply ecological one as well.

Constructions of land, though rife with contradiction, are also key to this process of erasure. Ideological conceptions of *terra nullius* ("nobody's land") marked the landscape of North America as open for business. Notions of manifest destiny engendered a moral justification to colonize and develop territories. "Remaking Native land as settler home involves the exploitation of environmental resources, to be sure, but it also involves a deeply complex construction of that land as either always already belonging to the settler—his manifest destiny—or as undesirable, unproductive, or unappealing: in short, as wasteland" (Voyles 2015, 7). Ideologically at odds with the wasteland is another fictional settler-colonial construction of land: as wilderness. The concept of wilderness is a key element of the settler imaginary that aligns with *terra nullius* and erases Native presence and ecological management practices. That, and the simple fact that it never existed; wilderness had to be *created* (Blackburn and Anderson 1993; Cronon 1996; Spence 1999). As Anderson (2005) argues, California was far from an idealized wilderness when invaders first arrived—what the Spanish and the miners stumbled upon was actually a well-tended landscape. What environmentalists like John Muir championed as pristine virgin forest was the result of careful Indigenous stewardship. "Staring in awe at the lengthy vistas of his beloved Yosemite Valley, or the extensive beds of gold and purple flowers in the Central Valley, Muir was eyeing what were really the fertile seed, bulb, and greens gathering grounds of the Miwok and Yokuts Indians, kept open and productive by centuries of carefully planned indigenous burning, harvesting, and seed scattering" (3). Despite this historically inaccurate framing, the notion of untouched pristine virgin wilderness remains pervasive throughout the environmental movement and environmental sciences that seek to combat the rapid ecological destruction that has unfolded over the past century and a half. Language such as "New World" and "pre-Columbian" are ubiquitous across the United States—from conservative rhetoric, to classrooms, to environmental movements. Expressions like "turn back the ecological clock" emerge. Turn it back to what, exactly? An untouched unmanaged landscape? Native peoples have *always* cared for their landscapes, and the Western notion of wilderness is a socially constructed invention that erases Native presence and knowledge systems.

These diverse bodies of knowledge are rooted in cultures and belief systems that value land not as a commodity, but as a relation with agency. The term "traditional ecological knowledge" (TEK) emerged from academia and became widespread in the 1980s, but the knowledge bodies that inform TEK were developed by diverse Indigenous peoples over millennia. Unlike Western science, TEK does not describe a singular body of knowledge—rather, it encompasses thousands of knowledge bodies that are geographically and culturally distinct. Seafha Ramos (Yurok) (2019), a wildlife biologist who integrates Yurok TEK within her research, writes, "Yurok TEK can be thought of as a branch of Indigenous Science and conceptualized as *hlkelonah ue meygeytohl* ('to take care of the Earth'), a system where Yurok people and wildlife collaboratively strive to create and maintain balance of the Earth via physical and spiritual management in tandem" (86). Native peoples exist within expansive kinship networks that are not limited to other human beings; rather, these kinship networks include more-than-human relatives, like plants, trees, and fish. While Indigenous ecological teachings are traditional—in the sense that they were derived from oral traditions—they are also adaptable and modern.

One critical example of traditional ecological knowledge in California is the widespread fire management regimes employed by Indigenous people throughout the state. Indigenous fire management played a central role in maintaining the biological diversity of plants and animals and facilitated several important ecological tasks (M. Anderson 2005; Kimmerer and Lake 2001; Lightfoot and Parrish 2009). Contemporary research affirms what Indigenous peoples in California have known for millennia: the land needs fire. First and foremost, burning at regular intervals prevents underbrush from building up so when wildfire does strike, it does not burn as hot and goes out quicker. At the California Indian Conference in 2019, cultural fire practitioner Anna Colegrove-Powell (Hupa/Yurok) told a story about burning on her ancestral territory, resisting fire suppression policies; when a wildfire broke out, it hopped over the burned area (Colegrove Powell 2019). Fire management also is necessary for the production of many Native foods and cultural materials. Burning created meadows and prairies for animals to graze and increased the quality and density of acorns, a staple food for many California Indians.[2] Anderson (2005) argues that "for many native shrubs and trees, repeated pruning or burning was not only harmless but beneficial as well. Their repeated resurrection, while appearing to take tremendous energy, may have paradoxically kept them young and vigorous" (236). Fire also increases the production of basketry materials. Tony Marks-Block et al. (2021) found a thirteen-fold increase in California hazelnut basketry stems one growing season postburn, as compared with shrubs growing at least three seasons postburn. This is important because it increased the availability of usable basketry materials and lessened the travel time for weavers to get to their gathering sites—an important consideration as tribal nations are revitalizing cultural practices. In addition, there are important correlations between fire management and water quality. Historically when the first Salmon runs would come up the Klamath, the Karuks, as part of ceremony, would light a log on fire and roll it down the hill. The valley would fill with smoke and block out the sun, keeping the water cold for Salmon during the hot months. One 2018 study found that wildfire smoke cools River and stream water temperatures by reducing solar radiation and cooling air temperatures (David, Asarian, and Lake 2018). While that study was focused on wildfire and not on prescribed burning, it still sheds light on the significance of Indigenous burning practices in relation to water quality and quantity. Indigenous peoples have long observed that when you burn the landscape, the springs hold more water. Elder Ron Goode (North Fork Mono) explains:

> Fire is always about water. Why are these still green? These are beautiful [gestures to surrounding plants]. We haven't seen water for a month. Because they're holding water in their root system. And why is the water still in the river, creek down here? Because all of these plants are still holding water and letting the water go gently down into the trees. When you open this up snow, rain is about to get to the root system and then the root system retains water. What we have done here by opening up this forest in this little ecosystem is we've returned the water. (quoted in Yuan 2016, 17:32–18:17)

"TIMBER!": RUSH MENTALITY AND SETTLER-COLONIAL FORESTRY

Like the goldminers of yesteryear, loggers are also glorified as courageous heroes, and especially in Northern California they occupy a leading role in the United States' national imaginary:

> Today loggers work in an environment permeated with images and narratives memorializing the lives and times of these pioneers—cultural material that saturates schools, parades, museums, and tourist attractions. . . . The celebration of this history is always on display, for example, in the free logging museum at Fort Humboldt State Historic Park in Eureka, where, among a pictorial narrative lining the walls

of the museum, one photograph showing white men working at the base of a redwood tree has a caption with this simple message: "Cut 'er Down, Boys—There's Plenty More Over the Next Hill! Felling the mighty redwoods was a difficult task. But using his strength, his sweat and his Yankee ingenuity, the American Logger chopped and sawed and hammered and hewed and the big trees came down." (Widick 2009, xx–xxi)

Like the gold rush before it, "people came [to California] from everywhere: Arkansas, Oklahoma, Tennessee, Washington, Wisconsin, who knows. . . . Just like in the mining days, a boom town type of thing. The call of the wild, so to speak" (quoted in Raphael 1985, 19). The depiction of settlers "conquering" dense virgin forests and "taming" unclaimed natural resources is critical to the settler-colonial project because it reinforces several parts of the ideological narrative. Loggers are depicted as courageous heroes (Merchant 1998). Bravely entering where no man had gone before—except, of course, for the hundreds of autonomous Indigenous republics that had thrived in California up to and including that time—loggers faced the potential dangers of an uninhabited wilderness and savage Indians. Such narratives reinforce the dualism that Shiva articulates in the construction of natural resources. Understanding human and nature as adversaries—nature as something that needs to be conquered, subdued, or tamed—is at the core of the settler-colonial relationship to land. This is evident from Adam and Eve's betrayal and eviction to contemporary people dependent on industrialized and disassociated food production for their survival. If you only buy your food from grocery stores, nature represents starvation and is thus inherently hostile. Disembodying nature through the "technical domination of the forest" is understood as inventive, thereby marking lifeways that aim to live in relationship with nature as primitive and backward (Whited 1998, 155). "Brute strength was always required—first, that of men and animals, later, that of machines. But brute strength alone would have been helpless without the ingenuity, perseverance and inventiveness of the men who logged the tallest trees on earth" (156). This narrative works to reinforce human superiority to—rather than relationship with—the trees that populate the forest. Moreover, settlers' singular focus on individual species and products (e.g., timber) does not consider other subsistence or cultural uses of the forest or the other beings who also depend on that forest.

Che-Na-Wah Weitch-Ah-Wah (also known as Lucy Thompson, Yurok) authored *To the American Indian: Reminiscences of a Yurok Woman* in 1916 to refute inaccurate representations of Native peoples by media and academics. In it, she shares this story:

> In the early days when a white man arrived among the Indians, he took an Indian woman, and in the fall of the year she would want to gather some pine nuts. The white man would go with her, taking his axe, and cut down the tree, as he could not climb it; and told the woman there they are, what are you going to do about it? At first the women complained, and finally said that the white man would spoil everything. Then the Indians began to cut the trees. In the last few years these trees have become very valuable in the eyes of the white man, and it has become the complaint of the white man that the Indians ought to be arrested and punished. Some of them have gone so far as to say that the Indians ought to be shot for cutting down this fine timber for the nuts. I leave the reader to decide which one ought to be punished for the cutting of the great number of these fine sugarpine trees. (27, 31)

In this short vignette Thompson articulates a central tension between Indigenous and settler-colonial worldviews as they relate to land management: whereas Native forest management is largely predicated on relationships and reciprocity, settler-colonial timber extraction is characterized by domination and control. The male settler in Thompson's story lays claim and exerts entitlement both when "he took an Indian woman" and when he "cut down the tree." Within a settler-colonial imaginary, Native women have long been symbolic stand-ins for the land itself—thus the reason Pocahontas gives male settlers her body, and symbolically the land, in the widely popular Disney film *Pocahontas*.[3] Additionally, the male settler lacks the knowledge and ability to climb the tree to get to the pine nuts. To him, cutting down the tree with the axe is an innovative and labor-saving technology. Indeed, "the mythology of American settlement has celebrated the ax, the saga of forest felling" (Pyne 2001, 62). But what about the Tree? What about the animals that also need to bring pine nuts home to their families? What about the plants that depend on the shade made by the tree? The only beneficiary of that action is the human man (and only for this season at that). This action prioritizes the needs of a singular human above nonhuman relatives and the land itself. While this vignette is but one example, the worldview illustrated here has consistently guided settler-colonial approaches to natural resource extraction and management.

As sugarpine trees increased in value from a settler perspective—meaning, monetarily or for profit value—settlers became concerned about Native American use of sugarpine trees. Within settler perspectives, timber, rather than pine nuts, were the valued product[4]—and thus the reason the tree now has value. Blame was placed on Native peoples for harvesting sugarpine trees, when the loss of sugarpine trees in the first place was rooted in settler-colonial invasion. Native peoples understood how to interact with sugarpine trees in ways that did not destroy the resource. Settler-colonial inclinations to control and dominate the landscape through technological advancement and blatant racism toward Indigenous peoples blinded settlers to traditional ecological knowledge about sugarpine trees. Settler calls for Indians to be punished by being arrested and shot for cutting sugarpine trees are rooted in settler-colonial logics of limiting open access to lands and resources for settler populations only.

Attributing blame to Native peoples for declines in natural resources has become a pattern. Settlers have denounced Indigenous fire management as destructive and irrational (Robbins 1997); have faulted Native peoples for overhunting and overgrazing (Langston 1995); and in the 1970s blamed Native peoples for the great decline in Salmon fisheries in Northern California—even though, of course, the region hosted huge fisheries prior to settler-colonial invasion. This is similar rhetoric to the "Indian Problem" used by the US federal government: the Indian is the problem, and settlers—as the more civilized, modern, advanced, developed—must protect valuable resources from the backward, primitive, savage Indians. Alternatively, the settler-colonial rhetoric also frames Native peoples' lack of exploitation of natural resources as waste: allowing Trees to remain in a forest or letting water stay in a River—neither of which generate profit—is deemed wasteful.

Timber extraction began during the California gold rush. Gold miners needed timber for their sluice boxes. Wood was also necessary for flumes, a basic water channel made out of lumber, to transport cut logs to mills during the hydraulic mining days. As hydraulic mining was replaced by underground hardrock mining, the demand for timber grew when temporary canvas tent shelters were replaced with wooden buildings. A mining technique called square-set timbering also increased demand for wood (Strong 1998, 163). In the Lake Tahoe region—the ancestral territory of the Washoe peoples—as the 1850s came to a close, small-scale lumber and fluming operations composed of a few individuals with small timber claims aimed to supply local timber needs. By 1873 clear-cutting operations were in full force. Large lumber companies established "elaborate networks[s] of logging, barges, railroads, wagon roads, V-shaped flumes, water storage reservoirs, and associated wood cams and mills" (Lindström 2000, 55). In the Sierras, "loggers cut all trees of marketable size, leaving the area nearly denuded. In the process, mostly because of the carelessness in felling and skidding trees, they destroyed a large part of the young growth" (Strong 1998, 164).

The destruction of oak trees specifically presented a significant loss for Washoe peoples because, like many tribes throughout California, acorns were—and continue to be—an important staple food. The benefits of the logging industry, in comparison to the destruction of Indigenous food sources, was minimal. Douglas Strong, in his book *Tahoe: From Timber Barons to Ecologists* (1998), articulates how logging fits within a larger pattern of resource rushing:

> The passing of the logging era marked the end of a period in which a relatively few men—farmers, sheepherders, miners, fishermen, and loggers—attempted to profit from Tahoe's natural resources. Prospectors never found the mineral wealth they sought. Fishermen gradually depleted the resources on which they depended. Loggers quickly decimated the forest and in the process eliminated the employment base it had briefly provided. By the turn of the century, Tahoe no longer offered attractive opportunities for the exploitation of natural resources. Future development, including the urbanization of parts of the basin, rested instead upon the slowly growing tourist trade. (165)

While from a settler-colonial perspective, logging is often perceived as a feat of technological innovation and ingenuity, from an Indigenous perspective, settlers destroyed ecosystems that had sustained Indigenous peoples for millennia. Rhetoric of Indigenous peoples as uncivilized, savage, and backward obfuscate the ecological destruction wrought by settlers in such a short period of time.

As settlers stampeded into northwestern California, they were greeted by towering redwood trees. As early as May 20, 1850, only eleven days after the founding of Eureka, the *Alta California* reported from Humboldt Bay that the *J. R. Whiting* was "inside loading with timber" (Raphael and House 2007, 192). By the fall of 1850, less than a year after the *Laura Virginia* first negotiated the entrance to Humboldt Bay, steam-powered sawmills in Eureka and Bucksport were cutting boards for local use, and come winter the mills were shipping lumber to San Francisco. Within a few short years business was booming. By 1854 Humboldt Bay was sending lumber as far as Hawaii, China, and Australia. At the height of the timber boom, Humboldt mills were exporting three million feet of lumber per month (Raphael and House 2007). When Humboldt County was officially incorporated in 1853, 80 percent of the region was forested with redwood; today, of the approximately 2 million acres of intact redwood forest that thrived prior to settler-colonial invasion, only 4 percent remains uncut (Widick 2009).

Richard Widick, author of *Trouble in the Forest: California's Redwood Timber Wars* (2009), argues that conflict over redwood timber is "about much more than trees. It is a battle for the future, over how this place has been and will be known" (ix). Who owns the forest? How should the forest be used? Whose knowledge systems and worldviews should be centered within forest management? Understanding the transformation that has occurred to forest ecosystems in Northern California during the past century and a half requires grappling with settler-colonial land dispossession and the attempted elimination/erasure of Indigenous peoples. Kyle Whyte (2016) argues: "Settlers can only make a homeland by creating social institutions that physically carve their origin, religious and cultural narratives, social ways of life and political and economic systems (e.g., property) into the waters, soils, air and other environmental dimensions of the territory or landscape. That is, settler ecologies have to be inscribed into Indigenous ecologies" (171). Settler-colonial elimination, therefore, is fundamentally an ecological phenomenon that requires both the claiming of territory but also the elimination of Indigenous lifeways through ecologies. The inscription of settler ecologies is accomplished by transforming kin and relatives into natural resources and property, by imposing management regimes that strive to maximize production of singular species deemed profitable, and by criminalizing Indigenous land management practices that interfere with settler-colonial desires (e.g., fire management).

Settler-colonial paradigms also worked to transform relationships to landscape from one of sustenance and kin to one of extraction and labor. Work and labor figured centrally in Indigenous survival in both nineteenth- and twentieth-century California. William Bauer Jr., in his book *We Were All Like Migrant Workers Here* (2009), examines how Native peoples of the Round Valley Indian Reservation in Northern California engaged in wage labor as an "adaptation to economic change in northern California and their re-creation of community through wage work . . . [thereby] document[ing] efforts of California Indians to survive in the state" (9). Native peoples did not sit idly by during settler-colonial invasion; they tried to resist to survive in every way they could—and one of those ways was through wage labor. Due to a deep understanding of local landscapes, Native peoples were often the best fishermen and loggers. This shift to wage labor, however, coincided with Indigenous land dispossession.

In the decades following the gold rush, both the state of California and the US government created "legal" pathways for settlers to claim forestlands, speeding up the process of Indigenous land dispossession. Congress passed the Homestead Act in 1862, but this law was primarily focused on agricultural land. The Timber and Stone Act and the Free Timber Act, both passed in 1878, applied to lands whose trees and rocks made it unsuitable for agriculture. The Free Timber Act allowed settlers the right to cut timber for domestic and mining purposes; the Timber and Stone Act (applicable only to California, Nevada, Oregon, and Washington) allowed homesteaders to claim 160 acres of timberland in addition to their homesteads (Huntsinger et al. 1994). Prior to the Timber and Stone Act, individual settlers "lacked legal means to buy timberland from the government for the express purpose of logging rather than farming. After 1878, nonarable, nonmineral public land could be purchased at the cut-rate price of $2.50 per acre" (Farmer 2017, 35). Less than a decade later, in 1887, the Dawes General Allotment Act further decreased Indian land ownership; all parcels that were not allotted to tribal citizens were opened for sale to settlers. More than 90 million acres of land were stolen through the Dawes Act.

The rush to claim timberlands led to Indigenous land dispossession, to be sure, but the legislation to facilitate settler accumulation of timberlands also led to the corporatization of the industry and widespread fraud. "By paying 'dummies' to file claims, or simply by buying out titleholders, monopolists and speculators soon controlled the best of California's farmland, range land, and forestland." In short, government "incentives became fodder for land sharks" and "consolidation led to widespread fraud" (Farmer 2017, 35–36). In the Sierra Nevada,

> agents scoured the nearby valley towns, looking for men who had not yet used their timber claim rights and who were willing to bargain for a few easy dollars. . . . Each picked himself out a claim and they were taken back to Visalia where a U.S. Land Office was then located. A stop there, and with a scratch of a pen, they were in possession of a filing on a timber claim where some mighty big trees had flourished for some thousands of years. . . . In course of time the acreage price to the Government was paid off, his deed was delivered and the trees were his. But not for long. There was a wholesale transfer of deeds to the Company, for which each owner received a modest sum, in exchange for his timber right inheritance. All perfectly legal as far as the law was concerned, that is, if he didn't advertise his pre-arrangement concerning the deal. (Merchant 1998, 148–49)

Through this process large companies were able to acquire vast amounts of Indigenous lands. A similar process occurred within the redwood forests of northwestern California as well (Farmer 2017; Middleton Manning and Reed 2019; Widick 2009).

In 1860 local mills in Humboldt County were producing approximately 9.6 million board feet of lumber per year, but by 1875 quantities had increased to 75 million feet (Raphael and House 2007, 196). By the 1870s the redwood timber industry, characterized by overconsumption, was dominated by large firms (Whited 1998). Between 1863 and 1882, redwood production and consumption grew by more than 100 percent (Bowcutt 1998). By 1890 lumber accounted for 80 percent of all Humboldt County's exports (Raphael and House 2007, 207). Clear-cutting redwood forests began in the 1890s and continued until World War II (Bowcutt 1998, 171). By 1900 timber firms had acquired all of the redwood forests (Farmer 2017). This historical context is crucial for understanding the contemporary configuration of timberland ownership in Northern California. Today, most coastal redwood forests in Northern California are privately owned—and most of what hasn't been taken by private firms is within state or federal jurisdiction vis-à-vis national and state parks or forest reserves.

The acquisition of Indian lands and placement under US jurisdiction continues into the present—demonstrating the ways that settler colonialism is an ongoing structure rather than a singular event. The "creation of the Forest Service in 1905 and the BIA's [Bureau of Indian Affairs] Division of Forestry in 1910 provided the administrative vehicles through which scientifically trained foresters were placed in charge of public timberlands and Indian reservation forests" (Huntsinger and McCaffrey 1995, 172). For example, in 1905—the same year the US Forest Service was established—97 percent of Karuk ancestral territory (approximately 1.38 million acres) were confiscated by the US government without compensation and placed under US jurisdiction—first as federal forest reserves and later as the USFS's Klamath and Six Rivers National Forest (Norgaard 2019; Vinyeta 2021). Additionally, the majority of Yurok ancestral territory is now owned by timber corporations or set apart as national parks and national forests (Huntsinger and McCaffrey 1995). Currently, within ancestral territory there are Bureau of Land Management lands, US Forest Service lands (Six Rivers National Forest), Redwood National Park, and other designated wilderness areas. The Yurok Indian Reservation (approximately 55,980 acres) is a small fraction of Yurok ancestral territory (originally approximately 490,000 acres). However, even within the reservation boundaries, significant portions of land are owned by settlers. As of 2014, 44 percent of the reservation is owned by timber corporations—or approximately 26,160 acres (Yurok Tribe GIS Program 2015). The Wiyot Tribe—whose ancestral territory is located in the heart of the redwood and North Coast forest belts—does not presently own any forestlands. They are surrounded by primarily private timberlands (Risling Baldy and Tully 2019).

Characteristic of resource rushing, eventually the booming timber industry came to a bust. Ray Raphael, author of *Cash Crop* (1985), writes: "In retrospect, it appeared as if the logging boom might have been the last gasp of the proverbial Wild West, the final expression of frontier values" (23). Raphael, like loggers and goldminers of the past, relies on settler-colonial logics of wilderness. Reflecting on the aftermath of the logging industry, Raphael reflects: "Although this was technically a part of the most populous state in the nation, the land, now abandoned, appeared as a virtual wilderness" (24). From a settler perspective, the land was no longer valuable and land prices plummeted. The collapse of the timber rush, therefore, paved the way for another wave of settler-colonial dispossession during the back-to-the-land movement, and ultimately birthed the green rush.

In addition to land dispossession, Indigenous peoples must also deal with ecological transformation and destruction of timber extraction within their ancestral territories. The most obvious consequence of timber harvest is the loss of forest habitat as a result of tree removal. Numerous species rely on forest habitat and the ecosystem services provided by forests. Here, the isolation of a singular species deemed profitable by human beings takes precedence within a settler-colonial management context—at the expense of other beings or relatives who also depend on the forest for their livelihood. The Northern spotted owl has garnered public attention and support, but many more species are impacted by the loss of forest ecosystems. Mammals such as the Pacific fisher; birds such as the bald eagle, marbled murrelet, osprey, and snowy plover; fish species such as Chinook salmon, coho salmon, coastal cutthroat trout, and steelhead trout; and many species of amphibians and reptiles are all impacted by forest loss (Carvill 2015; Noss 2000). The use of herbicides and pesticides present additional concerns for wildlife. Atrazine was sprayed aerially on privately owned forests within the Yurok Indian Reservation until 2006 (Fluharty and Sloan 2014).

The removal of trees creates environmental impacts, to be sure, but even worse than removing trees is disturbing the entire habitat. The construction of thousands of miles of roads has disturbed forest soils and caused erosion. Before modern logging equipment—which, arguably "did little to soften the industry's footprint; by most accounts, it worsened it" (Carvill 2015, 25)—skid roads were constructed directly in streams, blocking fish passage. Today, tractors compact the soil and operate on steep slopes and in streams. This is harmful for aquatic habitats specifically. Tree removal eliminates shade, leading to increases in water temperature, which is harmful for coldwater fish species like Salmon and steelhead. Additionally, "dirt laden runoff turns creeks cloudy, impairs water supplies for coastal communities downstream from working forests, and, over time, has changed the very shape of the area's streams and rivers, raising their beds and clogging their channels with fine sediment" (Carvill 2015, 27). In the early days of logging, lumber mills dumped sawdust directly into Rivers and streams by the ton, clogging the gills and suffocating incubating Salmon eggs and juvenile Salmon (Lichatowich 1999). Numerous studies have demonstrated that the loss of Salmon spawning grounds and sediment pollution directly correlate to population declines in Chinook, coho, and steelhead (Carvill 2015). To use Rivers as highways for lumber transportation, settlers cleared Rivers of potential obstructions: trees, rocks, beaver dams, and so forth. As a result, "people came to regard cleared rivers with no large woody debris, beaver dams, or side channels as the standard for how economically healthy rivers should look" (Lichatowich 1999, 64–65). In reality, some large wood is necessary to create pools, riffles, and other elements of functional aquatic habitat. However, throughout the 1980s the state of California paid millions of dollars to remove large woody debris "based on the belief that fallen trees in the channel were barriers to fish passage" (Carvill 2015, 28). The impacts of resource rushing, therefore, do not remain confined to a particular ecosystem; they hold the potential to have vast and far-reaching impacts. Timber extraction does not solely harm forest ecosystems, but also other ecosystems that interact with that forest.

At the turn of the twentieth century, the settler state shifted its focus from acquiring Indigenous territory to imposing ecological management regimes rooted in Western science on those territories. The US Forest Service (USFS) was established by Congress in 1905 to "provide quality water and timber for the Nation's benefit." Native Americans were not recognized as US citizens until 1924, so it is unlikely that the founders of the Forest Service were seriously considering the needs of Indigenous peoples when writing its rules. As a federal agency, the USFS manages public lands in national forests and grasslands. The USFS is the largest forestry research organization in the world. The first chief of the Forest Service, Gifford Pinchot, identified the purpose of the USFS as "to provide the greatest amount of good for the greatest amount of people in the long run" (USFS, n.d.). In reality the government was largely taking Indigenous territory and natural resources—at Native peoples' expense—to meet the needs of settler populations and thus "the institution and expansion of USFS jurisdiction and Indigenous land dispossession are intertwined processes" (Vinyeta 2021, 4).

Scientific forestry—the epistemological basis for USFS and BIA management practices—was originally developed between 1765 and 1800 in Prussia and Saxony. It then spread to the rest of Europe and the United States and was ultimately imposed across the developing world (Fortmann and Fairfax 1989; Scott 1998). Throughout the twentieth century, the Forest Service, along with the Bureau of Indian Affairs, practiced sustained yield forestry: the cutting and harvesting of timber on an annual basis to provide a steady flow of cash income (Huntsinger and McCaffrey 1995). Stemming from a worldview that positions human beings as separate from, and superior to, plant and animal relations, within this approach certain species are deemed profitable and ecosystems are managed to foster the maximum production of whatever species is commercially profitable. Prioritizing fiscal revenue, state-run scientific (fiscal) forestry transformed "the actual tree with its vast number of possible uses [and] replaced [it with] an abstract tree representing volume of lumber or firewood" (Scott 1998, 12). Through its narrow focus on production and profit and its blindness to the interconnectedness of life and the forest, scientific forestry failed to recognize that forests are a complex web of relationships—a central feature of bodies of traditional ecological knowledge. Western science often "reduces a being to its working parts; it is a language of objects"—it cannot recognize or name the agency or kinship within a forest (Kimmerer 2015, 49). This ideological imposition of a settler-colonial relationship to land is reflected in—and perpetuated by—the Euro-American settler vocabulary: useful plants become crops and the species that compete with them are transformed into weeds; insects become pests; tall, straight trees become timber; animals become game or livestock or are relegated to predators or varmints that should be eliminated (Scott 1998).

Not only were the results of a monocropped forest a disaster for those who stewarded the forest for subsistence, but scientific forestry did not achieve its own objectives, since scientific standardization of the forest fundamentally upsets a natural ecological balance that allows the forest to flourish.[5] The significance of the example of scientific forestry is that it powerfully "illustrates the dangers of dismembering an exceptionally complex and poorly understood set of relations and processes in order to isolate a single element of instrumental value" (Scott 1998, 21). This mirrored the historical visions of the Euro-American settler approach to how the forest ought to be and what it ought to produce. Whereas Indigenous peoples throughout California used the forest for a multitude of purposes, such as for food, shelter, clothing, and infrastructure, settlers isolated particular species of trees—which were then transformed into timber—and assessed the value of a forest solely on the monetary value of those resources. Settler-colonial capitalism facilitated "the shift from a forest for people to a forest for trees" (Huntsinger and McCaffrey 1995, 157). Indigenous forest management—largely centered on prescribed cultural burning—was not conducive to maximum timber production.

FIRE SUPPRESSION AND SETTLER-COLONIAL ECOLOGICAL VIOLENCE

The fall of 2020 saw the most devastating wildfires in California to date. On Wednesday, September 9, 2020, the sky turned an apocalyptic shade of orange. I struggled to focus and continue my normal routine because of the physical evidence surrounding me, that what is happening is not normal and that the world is so severely out of balance. As animals, homes, and entire settlements were engulfed in flames, a national debate raged over the cause of wildfires. Though climate change certainly exacerbates the damage from wildfire and impedes the ability to douse fires quickly, it is not the whole picture (Fried, Tom, and Mills 2004; Westerling and Bryant 2008). To understand forest health in California requires an understanding of traditional ecological knowledge and the ecological transformations wrought by settler colonialism—specifically, colonial orientations to land and the relationship between fire suppression and the social, political, economic, and ecological oppression of Native peoples (Norgaard 2019). As Kirsten Vinyeta (2012) explains, "in California, as in many other places across the country, the absence and presence of fire is steeped in Indigenous/settler conflict. The Forest Service's erasure of Indigenous knowledges has led to incalculable ecological and cultural consequences for Indigenous peoples especially, but also for settlers living under constant wildfire threat. Addressing the history and mechanisms of this erasure is a matter of environmental justice" (2). Fire suppression policies are illustrative of a settler-colonial relationship to land and are symptomatic of the rush mentality that isolates a single species deemed profitable. The legacies of inept settler-colonial land management practices are burning the world down.

Tied to invasion and settler colonialism, fire suppression policies in California ignore and erase Indigenous knowledge of how to manage California's forests. Spanish soldiers and missionaries were able to identify human populations because they could see fire on the landscape, and some of the first recorded writings of Spanish soldiers illustrated how baffled they were by the intentional fires set by these "primitive" people (Jones 2019; Lightfoot and Parrish 2009). Early settlers did not recognize or understand the necessity and complexity of Indigenous land management practices. Fire is a holistic and integrated management approach that does not seek to only maximize the quantity of trees; it also considers habitat, food, and material production. Bill Tripp (Karuk), the deputy director of Eco-Cultural Revitalization, a unit housed within the Karuk Tribe's Department of Natural Resources, explains:

> Prescribed fire and cultural burns are fires that are intentionally set during favorable conditions, sometimes at regular intervals to achieve a variety of socio-ecological benefits. They reduce the density of small trees, brush, grass and leaves that otherwise fuel severe wildfires. Clearing undergrowth allows for a greater variety of trees and a healthier forest that is more fire-resistant, and it provides more room for wildlife to roam with beneficial effects such as enhancing the success of our hunting. Fire suppression, meanwhile, involves extinguishing fires using teams of people, bulldozers, fire engines, helicopters and airplanes by land management agencies assigned that duty by federal, state and local governments. (2020, para. 3)

But Indigenous fire management was not conducive to settler views on how the landscape ought to be. Within a settler-colonial orientation, the ecosystem is organized into working parts and specific species are assigned value based on their ability to accrue monetary profit.

Dismayed by California Indians' reluctance to "learn proper usage of land or gold," Spanish missionaries were the first to impose fire suppression policies in southern and central California (Miranda 2013, 97). The following century, the nascent state of California instituted fire suppression policies during the gold rush genocide. Section 10 of the Act for the Government and Protection of the Indians (passed in 1850) states: "If any person or persons shall set the prairie on fire, or refuse to use proper exertions to extinguish the fire when the prairies are burning, such persons shall be subject to fine or punishment, as Court may adjudge proper." Preventing California Indians from carrying out their ecological management regimes—built upon generations of knowledge and experimentation spanning millennia—was, in the perspective of the state, an act of protection and imposition of governance. The settler state started to "enact large-scale land management practices through the development of forestry agencies beginning in 1876 with successive iterations in 1881, 1891, and 1901 until reaching its present form and title as the U.S. Forest Service in 1905" (Norgaard 2019, 59).

Since the inception of the US Forest Service in 1905, a primary objective has been to protect forests from fire. Under the direction of Gifford Pinchot, "a national forest fire policy was initiated and the agency began systemic fire suppression including the development of an infrastructure of fire control facilities, equipment, fire stations, lookouts, and trails. The forest reserves were created partly because Congress believed the nations' forests were being destroyed by fire and reckless cutting" (Stephens and Sugihara 2006, 433). The result of this approach was exacerbated by the Great Idaho Fire, which killed seventy-eight firefighters and burned 2.5 million acres of forestland. The Weeks Act of 1911 was passed by the US government the following year.[6] This law called for fire protection efforts and authorized the federal government to purchase private (read: Indigenous) lands to protect the headwaters of Rivers and watersheds.

Vinyeta (2021) argues that the USFS has—both historically and in the present—racialized Indian fire management and erased and delegitimized Indigenous knowledge systems through fire suppression policy and rhetoric. Historically, Indigenous fire management was referred to as "light burning" or "Piute burning" (now spelled Paiute). Aldo Leopold—considered the father of wildlife conservation—believed Forest Service policies of fire suppression were "directly threatened by the light-burning propaganda" (quoted in Vinyeta 2021, 7). Light burning became "racialized code for forestry that is 'savage' [and] lacking expertise." Situating USFS rhetoric on fire management through a framework of settler colonialism, Vinyeta identifies three commonly used tropes: *terra nullius*, Indian savagery, and the vanishing Indian narrative. These tropes are deployed in USFS rhetoric to discredit Indigenous land management practices as unscientific, to downplay the scale, quantity, and impact of Indigenous burning, and/or exclude

Native peoples from fire discourse altogether. Thus, the existence of the US Forest Service has always been tied to fire suppression. The Bureau of Indian Affairs mimicked this model and also criminalized Indigenous fire management practices (Norgaard 2019).

In Northern California, specifically in the Klamath watershed, fire suppression efforts increased exponentially during World War II, when timber prices were at an all-time high (Norgaard 2019). The USFS began using military force and command structures to fight fire.[7] Kari Norgaard argues that even the word "firefighter" illustrates a settler-colonial orientation or relationship to fire. Within this framework, fire is something to be fought and protected from; humans and fire are at war. In 1942 the Smokey Bear campaign and his catchphrase—"Only you can prevent forest fires"—was born.

The USFS did not recognize the value of prescribed burning until the 1960s—and has failed to recognize its role in generating the current wildfire crisis. Vinyeta (2021) argues "it is now acknowledged among Western scientists that absolute fire suppression was a misguided management approach—that in fact, 'light burners' had been right all along. Yet contemporary USFS discourse diffuses blame for a century of forest mismanagement and continues to erase Indigenous peoples and knowledges, even as the agency seeks Indigenous expertise and collaborates with Tribal governments to remedy the damage. . . . [Instead, USFS rhetoric suggests] it was 'science' that discovered the benefits of fire, when in fact the USFS refused to scientifically assess the value of low-intensity burns while actively discrediting Indigenous burning practices" (11).

The rhetoric of discovery—like civilization—is a widespread trope within a settler-colonial logic system. From the Doctrine of Discovery to Columbus Day—the notion that Indigenous territory was an empty wilderness, *terra nullius*, and thus free for the taking, is foundational. As of 2020 the Klamath National Forest rhetoric was still utilizing civilization/savagery terminology. Vinyeta (2012) notes that its website included the following statement: "As civilization moved deeper into the forest, fire came to be seen as an enemy that destroyed lives, property and natural resources" (11). The implication—that civilization arose in California *after* European arrival—is deeply rooted in settler-colonial logics designed to justify invasion and conquest. Of course, Indigenous peoples in California had sophisticated knowledge systems and land management regimes—the refusal to recognize them as such is rooted in white supremacy.

The imposition of Western ecological management regimes is a continuation of settler-colonial structures that dispossess Indigenous peoples of lands and livelihoods—and a continuation of settler-colonial elimination. Scholars such as Norgaard, Kirsten Vinyeta, and J. M. Bacon suggest that fire suppression policies facilitate colonial ecological violence. Indeed, policies of fire suppression led to severe negative consequences for California Indians. In *Salmon and Acorns Feed Our People* (2019), Norgaard provides a history of fire suppression policies in California and argues that fire suppression continues to enact settler-colonial violence against Indigenous peoples. "The new fire regime in turn supported the installment of white settlers by enabling the establishment of an economic system based in capitalistic commodity production. . . . Today, the narratives of loggers, pioneers, and gold miners as 'first peoples' enact settler replacement on the land as the real 'first peoples.' Fire suppression became a central mechanism to the performance of this erasure by disrupting human-fire relationships that were central to sustenance as well as spiritual and social practice. Fire regime alteration matters because it shifts economic, cultural, and political power relations" (101). First, "fire suppression has profoundly disrupted the existing relationships across species that underlie Karuk economic, ecological, and food systems" (59). Fire suppression policies effectively created food deserts (in combination with water quality contamination and depletion of Indigenous fisheries; see next chapter). Fire management is necessary for healthy acorn production and also for creating spaces to hunt game. Fire suppression has eliminated many usable basket materials; weavers reported a limited supply of weaving materials by the 1950s (Norgaard 2019). Furthermore, as a result of fire suppression policies and the buildup of fuels, fires have drastically increased in size and severity (Steel, Safford, and Viers 2015). For one example, the average number of fires per thousand acres in California has doubled since the 1970s (Norgaard 2019).

The 130-year legacy of fire suppression, Norgaard argues, continues the process of land dispossession into the present. As Tripp also notes, California forestry management continues to prioritize timber production while erasing and excluding Indigenous knowledge and ties to land.

> We know the solution is to burn like our Indigenous ancestors have done for millennia. But too often we are told we can't burn. Simply put, it's either because we don't have the proper environmental clearance for burning under the National Environmental Policy Act, because of liability[,] or because there aren't enough personnel available to supervise the burn. This year it is because smoke will be bad for Covid-19 patients. These are excuses, not solutions. We carry the same qualifications as the federal and state agencies when it comes to prescribed burning or otherwise managing fire, and we hold the Indigenous knowledge that is needed to get the job done right. We have the knowledge to conduct cultural burning that is perfectly safe, and in many cases, we do not even need fire lines. Yet the federal agencies still do not allow us to lead prescribed burns on lands administered by the National Forest System. (2020, para. 12)

3

SALMON IS EVERYTHING

Controlling Rivers and Commodifying Kin

Most believe that the salmon's precarious state is due to events of the last twenty or thirty years—perhaps not surprisingly, since during those few decades we have witnessed the rapid disappearance of forests, construction of the last big dams, rapid urbanization of large areas of the landscape, and a host of other assaults on the salmon and their rivers. But the salmon's dilemma goes back much further—back to the arrival of the first Euro-Americans in the Northwest. The whites brought cattle, plows, seeds, axes, and other essentials they needed to survive; unfortunately for the salmon, the settlers also brought their worldview and their industrial economy. —Jim Lichatowich, *Salmon Without Rivers*

Salmon navigate sometimes hundreds of miles to return home to spawn; they live by their relationship to their homelands. They know intrinsically and biologically where they come from and where they have been. Salmon cross borders fluidly; they build relationships across Indigenous cultures and also across nations, counties, and states. The Hupa people believe that it was the K'ixinay (First People) who taught humans how they were supposed to live so that the earth would remain balanced and good. The salmon became a part of that, and the Hupa were told that salmon "will be good wherever it grows." The Hupa also say that when the K'ixinay left the world, they went into "everything," like the rocks, rivers, trees, plants, and salmon. Salmon are our First People; they are much older, much wiser, and here for us, embodying our spirituality and our culture. We pray for them to return when we do our ceremonies. We are grateful for what they give to us, and we build ceremony to remind ourselves not to take them for granted. "Let the salmon return" goes one of our prayers. We have always been told salmon must return so that we can live. And we live so that we can make sure they return. —Cutcha Risling Baldy, "Why We Fish"

On June 1, 2021, the Karuk Tribe declared a state of emergency in response to drought conditions and a potentially looming fish kill. Over 95 percent of juvenile Salmon sampled by the Karuk Tribe tested positive for *Ceratonova shasta* (C. Shasta), a parasite that for decades has been linked to Klamath Salmon decline. The combination of water-heating dams and the Bureau of Reclamation's irrigation diversions for agriculture creates the ideal habitat for disease to flourish. As of June 2021, "a massive fish kill is currently underway in the Klamath River that could result in losing an entire generation of salmon" (Karuk Tribe 2021). Two weeks later, the Wiyot Tribe similarly declared a state of emergency on its ancestral Rivers, including the Baduwa't (Mad River) and the Wiya't (Eel River), due to extreme low flows and drought conditions. Low rainfall and above-average temperatures caused by anthropogenic climate change, coupled with water diversions associated with agriculture and excessive nutrient runoff, have impeded water quantity and quality, especially for small tributaries that provide Salmon-rearing habitat and cold-water refuges during dry summer months (Wiyot Tribe 2021). Unfortunately, these are not new phenomena for tribal nations in this region. Patterns of settler-colonial resource extraction, specifically dam construction and agricultural irrigation, have inflicted violence on Salmon and other fish relatives for decades.

Twenty years ago the Klamath River experienced the largest fish kill in American history. The 2002 fish kill—wherein over thirty-four thousand Salmon died prematurely and rotted on the Klamath River bank—was ecocide, an indirect genocide via livelihood destruction.[1] We typically use the word "genocide" for people only, but within Indigenous epistemology Salmon are understood as relatives or ancestors. To us, the fish kill was genocide. Fisheries biologist Barry McCovey (Yurok) (2002) reflects on the events of that summer:

> In my lifetime, I have never seen the Klamath so shallow. Over the past month, the lack of water has actually stopped the tribal fisheries program from completing tasks that were routine last year. There is so little water that people are unable to safely travel the river by jet boat or by raft. I've seen rocks that I didn't know existed protruding from dangerous rapids, making the attempt to count dead and dying fish a risky endeavor. Yet even in its shrunken state the river humbles me and demands my respect. I am fortunate enough to spend time within its grasp and to be able to know and understand the power of the Klamath. For me, nothing is greater. Civilizations will come and go, but the river will remain. This I know. (para. 2–4)

Violence perpetrated against Indigenous lands and waters directly affect Native cultural practices, worldviews, and cosmologies. In an important documentary about memory and the Klamath River, Cutcha Risling Baldy (quoted in Orona 2013) reflects on the larger cultural and ecological ramifications of the 2002 fish kill:

> I remember [my grandfather] talking about how it's very—not damning, but scary to see all of these dead fish because—it's not just because it's a sad thing because all of these dead fish and you feel bad, but because for him and for I think a lot of people in that area, those are like relatives. They're close to you. You don't go out and fish because you want to get the biggest fish so you can hang it on your wall and tell everybody you caught a big fish. You go out and fish because it's your responsibility to sort of maintain that balance because you're interconnected with that fish because it becomes a part of you and takes care of you from the inside. So to see all of that I think it felt like what does that really mean for where we are at in terms of the balance of our people and our system. (13:34–14:18)

It wasn't always this way. Our elders say that before settler invasion, when the Salmon came in, the River turned silver. There were so many you could walk across the River on the backs of the Salmon. Salmon, like Native Californians, populated vast tracts of area throughout the state—from the Smith River in the north to the Carmel River in the south. More than thirty river systems and hundreds of creeks supported millions of Salmon in six thousand miles of spawning habitat. Native peoples throughout the state ate more than five million pounds of Salmon each year (M. Anderson 2005).

Many tribes in Northern California understand themselves as Salmon people and engage in reciprocal relationships with the more-than-humans.[2] Salmon are central to both subsistence and the spiritual life of many Indigenous peoples in this region. For example, Yuroks' relationship with Salmon is established in the Yurok creation story, as told by Elder Geneva Mattz (Yurok): "In the beginning of time, the Creator came to the mouth of the Klamath. He stood on the beach and thought: 'This is a great river. I want to leave my children here. But there's nothing for them to eat.' So the Creator called to the spirit of the river, Pulekukwerek. . . . Pulekukwerek answered, 'I can feed them. I can send fish.' . . . Greatest of all, Nepewo entered the river each fall, leading the salmon people. Then the river spirit made human people" (quoted in Most 2006, 69). Yurok relationships to Salmon are reflected within ceremony and religious practice, ecological management regimes, community organization, and principles of laws and governance. Writing about human-fish relations in First Nations territory of Paulatuuq, Zoe Todd (Métis) (2014) argues that for Indigenous peoples, "human-fish relationships represent a whole host of social, cultural, and legal-governance principles.... Humans and fish, together, share complex and nuanced political and social landscapes that shape life in the community ... fish exist in a plurality of ways" (218).

As a keystone species, Salmon deliver ocean nutrients throughout the River basin and nourish not only human beings, but all wildlife. We—people, plants, and wildlife—all depend upon Salmon and the often-unacknowledged ecological labor they perform. In addition to being ecologically significant, Salmon are also a cultural keystone species.[3] In the same way some species are integral to the structure and function of an ecosystem, some species are integral to human culture. In other words, the decline or elimination of fish represents a profound violence for Indigenous peoples that have moral and cultural obligations to fish; but, simultaneously, the attempted elimination or criminalization of Indigenous stewardship practices that facilitate reciprocal relations with our more-than-human relatives enacts violence against fish, resulting in devastating fish kills. Salmon are part of our creation stories, our ceremonies, and our laws and governance systems—they are a part of everything, because Salmon are everything.[4] Salmon demonstrate the importance of ties to place and connection to ancestral territory and the strength and perseverance necessary to return to and remain in those places.

In her seminal text *All Our Relations: Native Struggles for Land and Life*, Winona LaDuke (Anishinaabe) (1999) argues that "the stories of the fish and [Native] people are not so different. Environmental destruction threatens the existence of both" (1). Patterns of Indigenous land dispossession and fish habitat destruction coincide; Indian relocation policies of the twentieth century were forced onto Salmon, too, with the construction of dams that blocked their spawning grounds. This violence enacted against fish relatives is paralleled in violence against Indigenous bodies. Before going on, however, the starkest comparison that must be drawn is to note the way the settler state has documented the decline of Native peoples and fish, that it is normal and natural. Akin to Benjamin Madley's lauded tome that meticulously documents the details of Native deaths, histories of fish populations and habitats document Salmon's seemingly inevitable demise and decline. Such histories are void of emotion, tragedy, and heartbreak. For Native peoples existing in a settler state, to read histories of fish and California Indians is a process of grief. And too often this colonial ecological violence is boiled down to statistics: for example, during settler-colonial invasion, 90 percent of California Indians died (Cook 1978). Today, 45 percent of California's Salmon, steelhead, and trout are likely to be extinct in the next fifty years if present trends continue; and 74 percent will be extinct within the next one hundred years (Moyle, Lusardi, and Samuel 2017). Transforming the elimination of Native peoples and our fish relatives into a statistic removes the violence and settler culpability, and reduces our genocide to a natural disappearance and an inevitable consequence of modernity. I aim to extend Risling Baldy's (2021) call for Indigenous peoples to "continue to take responsibility for our relationships with our more-than-human relatives by demonstrating and utilizing our salmon rhetorics to dismantle settler colonial rhetorical logics that value salmon only as a 'resource'" (174). As Indigenous people struggle to defend their lands and waters from development, deforestation, and now cannabis cultivation, Salmon struggle—and sacrifice their lives—to travel up a River choked off by dams. The water is too hot and it is hard to breathe, but Salmon cannot stop swimming. Neither can we.

INDIGENOUS FOOD SOVEREIGNTY AND LEGAL ORDERS

Indigenous relationships to Salmon in this region depart from colonial understandings of fish as an economic resource, commodity, or product. In Yurok language, the word for Salmon, *nepuy*, literally means food, or that which is eaten. Within Yurok epistemology, the River is a living being. The River and Salmon are considered relatives. Geneva Mattz's telling of the Yurok creation story situates Yurok people in relation to the Klamath River and the Salmon people. The Klamath River is central to the "sacred geography" of Yurok people (V. Deloria 1994, 199) and is often referred to as "vein" or "umbilical cord to the Earth" (Orona 2013).[5] Risling Baldy (2021) writes that the Hupa people understand more-than-human beings as relatives while also recognizing their "dependence on them and so regard them in a way that understands this relationship as complex, dynamic, and informed by our practices of reciprocity and respect" (167). The significance of the River and the more-than-human relatives are difficult to situate within the so-called objective Western frameworks of science, and it may be impossible to understand for those who measure Mother Earth's bounty in numeric values. Salmon are intricately connected to every facet of Indigenous life in this region. For Yurok people, "catching the first salmon of the season had significance beyond the return of a major food source. Traditional Yuroks understood that salmon are somehow responsible for the renewal of life on land as well as in the River. This is a biological fact. Salmon bring nitrogen from the ocean to the forest floor via the intestines of mammals that eat them. But for Yuroks, it was and remains a spiritual reality that their ceremonies are part of the annual cycle of life within their world" (Most 2006, 73). Zoe Todd, in her writings on the relationships between fish and First Nations peoples in Canada (2014), articulates the concept of fish pluralities: multiple ways of knowing and defining fish. For many Indigenous people, fish are more-than-human: "Rather than treat fish as separate from humans or humans as separate from fish, fish are intimately woven into every aspect of community life" (225). Traditional Native food systems, ecological practices, and Indigenous scientific knowledges have long included sophisticated, well-thought-out, and complex food systems that require ongoing ecological management. "Indigenous people also managed and monitored fish, much as scientists do today. Native people monitored numbers of fish, the impact of fishing practices on spawning and migration, and the impact of water quality during various fish seasons" (Risling Baldy 2021, 171). Native peoples sustainably managed fish populations through governance structures and ceremony (Norgaard 2019).

Because the settler-colonial logic of elimination—aimed at justifying conquest of preexisting civilizations—depicts Native peoples as uncivilized, savage, and lawless, there is a widespread and incorrect assumption that Native peoples did not have legal orders. This thinking works to justify the imposition of settler law and sovereignty within occupied Indigenous territories. Indigenous peoples had sophisticated legal orders embedded within their own social, political, economic, and spiritual institutions. "Indigenous peoples applied law to harvesting fish and game, the access and distribution of berries, the management of rivers, and the management of all other aspects of political, economic, and social life" (Napoleon 2007, 3). As more-than-human relatives, Salmon are integral to Indigenous legal orders in this region. Traditionally, within Indigenous worldviews and knowledge systems there is a concept of natural law. Settler-colonial societies mistakenly believe that human beings alone decide the laws of the land. Indigenous scholars challenge this notion. C. F. Black (Kombumerri/Munaljahlai) (2011) argues that in fact the land itself is the source of the law. Specifically, she argues that "the central focus of the law is thus not humans and their rights, but the maintenance of a sustained place in the pattern of the web" (107). The ecosystem decides which activities can and cannot happen; when human beings ignore these laws, tragedy ensues (e.g., the 2002 fish kill). "In other words, fish are an integral part of Indigenous legal orders and we can and should think through our obligations to one another by also considering the duties and obligations we have to fish" (Todd 2016a).

Indigenous food sovereignty is a continuation of the anticolonial struggle that reconnects land-based food systems with political structures and spiritual teachings. Our traditional foods hold significance beyond caloric intake. "The concept of Indigenous food sovereignty is not focused only on *rights to* land, food, and the ability to control a production system, but also *responsibilities to* and culturally, ecologically, and spiritually appropriate *relationships with* elements of those systems" (Mihesuah and Hoover 2019, 11, emphasis in original). For many tribes, Salmon is everything: "Karuk and other Indigenous people speak of the foods they eat as relations. They speak of a longstanding and sacred responsibility to tend to their relations in the forest and in the rivers through ceremonies, prayers, songs, formulas, and specific stewardship practices they call 'management'" (Norgaard 2019, 161). In addition to the relational and spiritual nourishment that traditional foods provide, they are also important because "the activities of managing, gathering, preparing, and consuming traditional foods serve the functions of passing on traditional ecological knowledge, stories within the community and from one generation to the next. Food-related activities serve as social glue that binds the community together; they outline social roles that provide a sense of identity and serve as the vehicle for the transmission of values" (Norgaard 2019, 151).

Because of the significance of traditional foods to Indigenous communities, settler-colonial violence strategically focused on Indigenous food sources. In California, settlers attempted to not only kill and remove Native peoples, they also supplanted Indigenous peoples' ecological management, which dramatically reduced food production they were dependent upon.[6] In Southern California, during the Spanish Mission takeover, Catholic padres outlawed Native people from eating their traditional foods, such as acorns, as a way of civilizing and controlling them (Costo and Costo 1987). "With colonization, there was a big attack on acorns on top of everything else. And what you saw was that with the restrictions that came from colonial mentalities about who native people were supposed to be they really went after our acorns because they knew that that was our staple food. That's what held us together as people. That's what made us *k'iwinya'n-ya: n* [acorn eaters]" (Risling Baldy 2020). Dramatic dietary changes among tribal communities primarily occur from the lack of access to traditional foods, either because environmental contaminants such as mercury and persistent organic pollutants make the food too risky or because of the lack of food availability entirely due to environmental destruction and state land management regimes.

For many Northern California Indian peoples, "diet change—rather than being inevitable—was tied to ecosystem decline that was in turn a function of the improper management of the rivers and forests by federal and state agencies" (Norgaard 2019, 141). For example, the links between dam construction, Salmon population decline, and changing diets along the Klamath River demonstrate how colonial ecological management regimes have altered both the ecology of the region and the diets of California Indians (Norgaard 2019). The Bureau of Reclamation Klamath Project was completed in the 1960s to bring irrigation and hydroelectric power to farmers. The project initially included four large dams on the Klamath River that diverted 1.3 million acre-feet of water to irrigate approximately 240,000 acres in both Oregon and California (Doremus and Tarlock 2003, 2008). Today the Klamath River is impeded by seven dams, forty-five pumping stations, more than 185 miles of canals, and 516 miles of irrigation ditches—all of which have damaged Salmon habitats and populations (LaDuke 2005). Dams raise water temperatures, decrease River flows, and block off Salmon spawning grounds, and agricultural runoff from upriver creates algae blooms and other nutrient overloads. This deadly combination has caused Salmon populations to plummet. Salmon runs on the Klamath River have declined by as much as 95 percent (May et al. 2014). Data from the Karuk Health and Fish Consumption Survey, completed in 2005, revealed that over twenty-five species of plants, animals, and fungi that once formed part of the traditional diet are no longer available due to habitat destruction and lack of access (Norgaard 2005). Approximately 80 percent of surveyed Karuk households were unable to gather adequate amounts of Eel, Salmon, or Sturgeon to meet family needs, and 40 percent reported that some fish species their family historically harvested are no longer present (Norgaard 2005).

This lack of access to traditional foods is rooted in structural changes wrought by settler colonialism: "Largely due to denied access to traditional food as salmon populations have plummeted, mushrooms have been overharvested by competing commercial interests, and acorn yields have been reduced in the absence of proper fire management" (Norgaard 2019, 146). But perhaps the most illustrative example of the toll taken by settler colonialism on Indigenous food sources is the decline in fish consumption. The Karuks, for example, ate approximately 450 pounds of fish per person per year prior to invasion. "Now, given that per person salmon consumption has recently averaged less than 5 pounds per person per year, Karuk people appear to have experienced one of the most dramatic and recent diet shifts of any tribe in North America" (Norgaard 2019, 13). Throughout California, the construction of dams has led to Indigenous displacement and cultural genocide: "The social impacts, cultural disruption, and destruction of communities represent incalculable and irredeemable costs, and yet they are dismissed as externalities in a narrative of national progress" (Middleton Manning 2018, 9).

Food security continues to threaten Indigenous peoples throughout the region. The Klamath Basin Tribal Food Security Project found that 92 percent of Native American households in the Humboldt/Del Norte region are food insecure and 70 percent never or rarely have access to Native foods.[7] Sixty-four percent of Native households rely on food assistance, and a further 84 percent worry about their next meal (Sowerwine et al. 2019). The work we do for the ongoing food sovereignty of our tribal peoples is necessary because our communities have been targeted for exploitation, both historically and through contemporary practices. Rural and poor communities, like tribal groups, have less access to healthy foods and often face some of the nation's highest rates of diabetes and other health problems. Food sovereignty is not only about reconnecting to our knowledges and practices; it is also an issue of environmental and social justice. Our traditional food knowledge can help us to build stronger communities and brighter futures.

The loss of traditional foods has led to numerous health problems within Indian Country; therefore, systemic health disparities must be understood as colonial ecological violence. The Indian Health Service estimates that American Indian/Native American rates of death from diabetes is three times the national average. This is attributed to poverty, cultural differences, discriminatory health services, and a lack of education. But, as Dina Gilio-Whitaker (2019) rightfully points out, "nowhere is the United States' history of violence and land dispossession implicated as a source of these health problems" (74). Kari Norgaard and Ron Reed's study (2005) found that diabetes first appeared among Karuk families (over 60 percent) in the 1970s—the same decade when spring Chinook salmon was largely eliminated from Karuk diets; this "was the first study to link increasing tribal diabetes rates to the loss of a traditional food in the context of generalized environmental degradation, species declines, and the loss of traditional food sources" (157). The Karuk Tribe's natural resources director, Leaf Hillman (Karuk), explains that "while many non-Indians are aware of the U.S. government's destruction of the North American bison as a tool to subjugate the Indian, to Native people, it all looks the same. It's understood to be the same phenomenon—destruction of the Salmon, destruction of the acorns—they all lead to the same thing. Genocide" (quoted in Norgaard 2019, 150). Gilio-Whitaker (2019) further argues that "if we understand settler colonialism as a genocidal structure, the health disparities (and virtually all the negative sociopolitical indicators that characterize the American Indian demographic) can clearly be linked as elements of environmental injustice" (75).

FISH DECLINE AND SETTLER COLONIALISM

Exploitation of California's fisheries—like many contemporary issues in California—began with the gold rush.

> Along with the attempts to destroy the environment in the name of seizing as much gold as possible, miners also began clear-cutting the old-growth forests, which often resulted in soil collapse that led to disastrous results for the local ecosystem. Oros notes, "The bioaccumulation of mercury in fish and other water species in local rivers such as the Klamath, Trinity, Salmon, Mad, Eel, Van Duzen, Eel, Elk, Mattole,

and Smith occurred in tandem with the massive impacts of debris and sediment, called slickens, run-off from mountain and hillside destruction and also the soil erosion from clear cuts."[8] These methods of destruction also led to habitat loss, contamination of waters, and contamination of fish and other wildlife. Settlers were not concerned with sustainable practices, often overfishing, overharvesting, and overhunting various regions. (Risling Baldy 2021, 178)

Environmental impacts that occurred during the gold rush, specifically the destruction of riverbeds and water quality, had disastrous consequences for Native fisheries. Gold miners diverted entire streams without concern for downriver ecologies and tore up rivers until they turned to mud. By 1872 the California Board of Fish Commissioners suggested that "the most important cause for the decrease of salmon in our rivers is from mining" (McEvoy 1986, 84).

[A settler] describes the failed attempts of Indians to fish on the Klamath River after gold mining: "The trout turned on their sides and died; the salmon from the sea came in but rarely. . . . What few did come were pretty safe from the spears of the Indians, because of the coloured water; so that supply, which was more than all others their bread and their meat, was entirely cut off." The situation was the same on the American, the Yuba, the Feather, and the other salmon streams along which gold mining was practiced. (M. Anderson 2005, 86)

On top of that, much of the twenty-six million pounds of mercury used during the gold rush found its way into waterways and the bodies of fish. Mercury contamination continues to be a major concern for tribal subsistence fishing communities to this day. The destruction of fisheries—and the continued exploitation of fish species and habitat destruction—contributed to a massive decline in available traditional foods that is still felt by Native Californians today.

Overharvesting was a common practice during the gold rush. The Sacramento and San Joaquin watersheds—located in the ancestral territory of numerous Indigenous nations, including the Wintus, Nisenans, Miwoks, Yokuts, and others—was ground zero of settler economic activity for much of the nineteenth century. In the late 1840s, miners "could pitchfork fifty-pound salmon out of the Yuba and Bear Rivers in unlimited quantities" (McEvoy 1986, 67). In 1852 one settler reportedly harvested thirty-five hundred pounds of river perch near Sacramento City in a single day. The fishing industry in the Sacramento–San Joaquin Watershed didn't take off until the 1860s—after floods and drought had brought an end to the gold rush. In the 1860s the settler Salmon trade took off. Steamship services to Hawai'i began in 1861, to China and Japan in 1867, and to Australia in the late 1860s and 1870s.

The timber rush killed fish and destroyed fish habitat in numerous ways. Lumber mills dumped tons of sawdust into Rivers and streams, which suffocated fish—either by clogging their gills or suffocating the incubating and juvenile Salmon (Lichatowich 1999). Moreover, as fisheries biologist Jim Lichatowich (1999) argues, the timber rush "helped shape an erroneous vision of healthy rivers" (64). Prior to invasion, many Rivers would contain logs, beaver dams, side channels, and other objects that provided habitat for fish. Desiring to use Rivers as highways, logging industries cleared out all obstructions by blowing up rocks and blocking side channels. Lichatowich argues this has resulted in people regarding cleared Rivers as the picture of economic and ecological health.[9] Moreover, this thinking has pervaded fisheries biology "to the detriment of salmon" (65). In 1953 the director of Washington State's Department of Fisheries wrote that "fish need clean, unobstructed rivers and streams" (65).

In the Humboldt region, canneries started popping up as early as the 1850s, primarily on the Eel River. Commercial fishing was slower to develop on the Klamath River, both because Requa, at the mouth of the River, was recognized as Indian reservation land and because the Klamath and Trinity Rivers were being heavily mined.[10] "From the Gold Rush on, miners had increased the turbidity of the water when they dug up the riverbed, and this interfered with salmon spawning grounds" (Raphael and House 2007, 1:211). These problems were exacerbated by the advent of industrial hydraulic mining in the 1860s and 1870s. Commercial fishing and canneries on the Klamath materialized in the late 1870s and 1880s, as white settlers began encroaching and dispossessing Yurok peoples of their land through allotment policies. Martin Van Buren Jones established the first commercial fishery at the mouth of the Klamath in 1876.[11] Largely because of the proliferation of internal combustion engines, ocean fisheries began to flourish by the turn of the century. Simultaneously, recreation and sport fishing increased as well. "In the mid-1920s, several small canneries opened to cater to the hundreds of sportsmen lining the banks and trolling the waters of the estuary. . . . In the mid-1950s recreational fishing in the Klamath had only increased in popularity; anglers in 1956 landed 15,000 fish in the estuary alone. In 1955–56 from 1,200 up to 3,200 salmon per day were landed by sportsmen in the estuary" (Pierce 1998, 9). This would eventually culminate in conflict between settlers and Indigenous fishermen along the banks of the Klamath River in the 1970s, a conflict that came to be known as the Fish Wars.

On Sunday, August 27, 1978—five years after Yurok fishing rights were secured through the Supreme Court case *Mattz vs. Arnett*—the US Department of the Interior issued a fishing moratorium on all sport and Indian fishing in the Klamath River estuary. Adding to restrictions that had been established by the Bureau of Indian Affairs a year prior, the moratorium further limited Yurok fishing to specific time slots without regard to tides or seasons (Most 2006). Consequently, the moratorium went into effect at the height of the fall run. That Monday morning a squad of heavily armed federal agents, backed by sheriff's deputies and the coast guard raided and patrolled Yurok gill nets from the estuary to the bridge over Highway 101, three miles upriver. Boats were rammed, fish were confiscated, and Yuroks were jailed. The next day "about twenty agents with billy clubs grabbed five Indians" and confiscated their nets and Salmon (Most 2006, 111). By Wednesday night there was "a miniature naval battle . . . on the estuary of the Klamath River" (quoted in Most 2006, 112). Five boatloads of heavily armed federal agents, all wearing bulletproof vests, raced down the Klamath to the cheers of sport fishermen along the bank. Twenty boatloads of Yurok Indians were waiting for them and a violent clash ensued. Fisherman Richard McCovey (Yurok) was repeatedly held under water by an agent who then placed a gun to his head before hauling him off to jail. McCovey recalls: "None of us were armed . . . [and they] never told us what we were charged with" (Most 2006, 113). Shortly thereafter, the "secretary of the Interior came to the Klamath Basin . . . [and] unleashed SWAT teams on jet boats to arrest people who were denying the federal moratorium on fishing" (242). From an Indigenous perspective, settlers depleted a culturally significant traditional food source by prioritizing economic growth while simultaneously policing the Indigenous fishermen who had not created the problem in the first place.[12]

Other tribes have experienced similar declines in their fish populations. The Winnemem Wintus have stewarded a fishery in the McCloud Watershed. Their traditional fishery was depleted over approximately fifty years of settler management. Between 1880 and 1883, ten million pounds of fish were harvested from the McCloud River. Because the sole motivation underlying the settler fishing industry is profit—a fundamental difference from Indigenous subsistence fishing economies—exploitation was rushed and waste was extreme. In September 1880 settlers "simply threw 9,000 dead salmon back into the river because no one would buy them. Only one-half of the 10.8 million pounds of fish harvested that year ended up in cans; the rest were dumped on the San Francisco retail market, with huge quantities going to waste. Such bountiful harvests lasted only four years, or precisely one normal salmon generation, and were no more" (McEvoy 1986, 80). By 1884 there were twenty-one canneries and over fifteen hundred boats to service them; not uncoincidentally, the fish commissioner reported that the fall run of 1884 on the McCloud River was "the lightest that was ever known in the memory of the oldest fisherman" (McEvoy 1986, 80). Fish populations continued to decline until the McCloud River cannery closed in 1919.

The decline of fish populations throughout the state continued for the duration of the twentieth century. Studies conducted over the past fifty years have all pointed to a similar conclusion: fish species are declining and it is largely due to habitat destruction. In 1974 a survey of native fish populations in the streams of the Sierra Nevada foothills found that the ranges of native freshwater fish—including California roach, hardhead, Sacramento squawfish, and Sacramento sucker—had declined due to "habitat and water quality deterioration coupled with the introduction of exotic fishes" (Moyle and Nichols 1974, 72). In 1998 another study found that Central Valley Salmon had declined for several reasons, including overfishing, blockage and degradation of streams by mining activities, and reduced Salmon habitat and streamflows due to dams and water diversions. "Although substantial investment has been made by the state of California in managing the chinook salmon resource since the early years of the commercial fishery, chinook salmon have declined over the decades to small fractions of their previous numbers" (Yoshiyama, Fisher, and Moyle 1998, 487). In 2011 a quantitative study on native freshwater fish in California revealed that out of 129 freshwater species, 5 percent were extinct and more than 75 percent were on an extinction spectrum (Moyle, Katz, and Quiñones 2011). Specifically, 26 percent were in danger of extinction in the near future (endangered), 26 percent were on a future trajectory of extinction (vulnerable), and 26 percent were declining but not in immediate danger of extinction. The root of these declines was attributed to the "19th and early 20th centuries when unrestricted mining, logging, and wetland conversion, combined with wide-scale dam building, severely altered most rivers, lakes, and estuaries" (2420). In 2017 a study done through a collaboration between the University of California, Davis, and the nonprofit California Trout reported that if present trends continue, 45 percent of California's Salmon, steelhead, and trout are likely to be extinct in the next fifty years and 74 percent will likely be extinct in the next one hundred years. Regarding Salmon specifically, the report suggests that California could lose 52 percent of its native anadromous salmonids and 27 percent of inland salmonids within the next fifty years if present trends continue (Moyle, Lusardi, and Samuel 2017). Reader, have you detected a pattern here?

Put simply, settler-colonial management regimes are eliminating fish—and the elimination of Salmon is, simultaneously, an elimination of Salmon people. Arthur McEvoy, in his 1986 text *The Fisherman's Problem: Ecology and Law in the California Fisheries, 1850–1980*, describes the "fisherman's problem" this way: "Every harvester knows that if he or she leaves a fish in the water someone else will get it, and the profit, instead" (10). In the case of California, McEvoy argues:

> the commercial development of California's lush and varied fisheries has followed a repetitive pattern of boom and bust, one typical of fisheries the world over. Usually, after a few pioneers demonstrate a fishery's profitability, capital and labor rush into it, and the harvest increases exponentially for a time. At some point, unable to bear the strain of exploitation indefinitely without sacrificing its ability to replenish itself, the resource begins to yield less and less to economic effort. As depletion erodes its productivity, a fishing industry may even improve its technical ability to find and catch more fish, thereby sustaining profits for a time but drawing ever more effort into the harvest

and ever more life out of the stock of fish. Ultimately, harvesting so depletes the resource as to cripple it. (6)

While the "pattern of boom and bust" articulated by McEvoy is emblematic of the rush mentality, this "pattern" began relatively recently and erases the history and knowledge of Indigenous fisheries prior to "pioneers." How did the numerous Indigenous nations within California deal with the fisherman's problem? The fisherman's problem, as explored by McEvoy, is actually rooted in settler-colonial orientations to land, water, and nonhuman species; fish—rather than being viewed as kin or relatives—are reduced to commodities or products. Within the settler state, for example, Salmon are understood as "economic resources" or "natural resources." What is lacking in the scenario McEvoy describes is relationship to Salmon predicated on something other than the market. There is no engagement in reciprocal relationship: "Enshrined in the rhetorics of salmon governance in the State of California is not only a reliance on Western scientific conclusions, but also a classification of salmon as 'economic resources' or 'natural resources.' Salmon are also constantly treated as impediments to economic development and though they have recently been added to the endangered species list in several regions, this does not mean that government agencies make decisions that incorporate salmon protection" (Risling Baldy 2021, 170). The settler state doesn't sing for the Salmon, nor dance them home. It doesn't treat Salmon as the gift that they are. Salmon have been transformed from a relative to a commodity. To settlers, Salmon is *a* thing, but to Indigenous peoples in this region Salmon is *every*thing.

The conceptual foundation that guides settler management of Salmon populations prioritizes the industrial production of commoditized fish (Lichatowich et al. 2018): "To achieve this, it is acceptable to replace wild salmon with fish produced in an industrial process (hatcheries). . . . The current conceptual foundation describes a salmon management paradigm that simplifies the production system by replacing ecological processes and relationships with industrial processes" (4–5). Much like the way complex forest ecosystems have been dismembered, inventoried, and sold for parts within a settler-colonial management paradigm, so too have Salmon habitats been altered: "This dominant worldview defines ecosystems as warehouses for the storage and production of commodities, insists that humans stand apart from those ecosystems, and demands that they control, manipulate, and 'improve' them" (Lichatowich 1999, 6). While this settler worldview is dominant in Salmon management today, it is a recent phenomenon. For millennia Native peoples have been able to facilitate relationships with Salmon based on reciprocity, care, and respect. The attitude that Lichatowich speaks to—in this part of the world, specifically—cannot be disentangled from settler colonialism and the settler-colonial orientation to land that is based on domination and commodification. For Native peoples the destruction of fisheries is a prime example of the ecological mechanics of settler-colonial domination. If Native people were able to thrive within fish-based economies for thousands of years, then settlers and settler management practices drastically altered (if not destroyed) every fishery in California within 170 years, what happened? Put simply, the habitats of fish have been destroyed to make way for the desires of settlers. As Lichatowich points out, "There is not just one threat to their existence but a continuous series of threats at nearly every point in their range, through their entire life cycle" (46), from logging and mining in the headwaters to agriculture in the Rivers' lower elevations and the accompanying infrastructure (e.g., dams), to cities and industry in the estuaries and pollution and large-scale fishing in the oceans.

While the commodification of kin and domination of River systems remains at the root of fish decline, the settler state has tried a variety of ineffective solutions to maintain domination and control over the natural world. One such solution, sustained yield forestry—the cutting and harvesting of timber on an annual basis to provide a steady flow of cash income—is also being applied to the fishing industry. The quantity of fish that any given level of harvesting will yield over the long term is a function of both the intensity of fishing and the capacity of the stock to reproduce. The maximum sustainable yield, then, is the maximum amount of fish that can be harvested without impairing the resource's long-term productivity (McEvoy 1986). This worldview reduces and dismembers complex ecosystems into their working parts. It necessarily excludes the ecological and cultural necessity of fish as an active member of Indigenous worlds, and clearly, given the documented decline in fish populations, is an ineffective approach to sustainability.

West Coast fisheries were not a significant concern to the settler state until after the Civil War, when East Coast fisheries began to collapse due to industrial pollution and overharvesting (McEvoy 1986). The California

State Board of Fish Commissioners was established in 1870, and by 1900 the state had developed a "nationally acclaimed body of fishery management law" (95). California's fisheries program was considered a success for two primary reasons: first, it successfully introduced non-Native fish species into California's waters. For example, shad and striped bass were stocked into the Sacramento River after settlers had depleted the native fish. Second, California artificially propagated fish species—both of which set "important precedents for resource management nationwide" (101).

Between 1875 and 1900, fish hatchery programs (primarily for Salmon) constituted half of all funds appropriated for state and federal fishery agencies (McEvoy 1986). Instrumental to the proliferation of hatcheries in the United States, Spencer Baird was appointed to lead the U.S. Commission of Fish and Fisheries in 1871. In a letter to the Oregon Legislature that is now considered "one of the most significant documents in the history of salmon management," Baird identified three major threats to the survival of Salmon in the Pacific Northwest. They included: "Excessive fishing, especially when salmon were in nursery streams and in the act of spawning; dams that blocked the migration of salmon to their spawning grounds; and changes in the physical habitat of the streams. These three problems identified by Baird over 120 years ago are the same threats still facing the salmon in the late twentieth century" (Lichatowich 1999, 112). To solve these three problems, Baird proposed fish culture as the solution—based on one incomplete experiment in a hatchery located on the Sacramento River. Lichatowich argues that "Baird's letter gave birth to the myth that artificial propagation could maintain or enhance salmon abundance, no matter how many fish were caught. Salmon managers with no better evidence of hatchery success, extended Baird's promise further: hatcheries not only could make up for excessive harvest but would compensate for habitat destruction as well. This myth has continued to guide salmon management for the past 120 years, and its effect on salmon cannot be overestimated" (112–13). In July of 1872 Baird sent Livingston Stone to California with five thousand dollars to acquire Pacific Salmon eggs. Stone did not even know where to find spawning Salmon, so he asked the members of the California Fish Commission, but they didn't know either. Eventually Stone met a railroad engineer who had seen Winnemem Wintu fishermen at the junction of the McCloud and Pit Rivers. Stone found the fishing Indians in late August of 1872 and he began the first Pacific Salmon hatchery the following day (Lichatowich 1999).

Winnemem Wintus initially protested the construction of the hatchery. War Dancers assembled on the opposite bank of the McCloud River and held demonstrations that Stone interpreted as an attempt to "drive us off" (Yoshiyama and Fisher 2001, 9). If such was the case, Stone disregarded the message. Stone's writings about the development of the hatchery indicate several sites of tension between Winnemem Wintus and incoming settlers. Ranchers neighboring the hatchery let their sheep graze on Wintu pastureland, "destroying every blade of grass, and leaving a desolate waste for their horses, the Indians resented it, as well they might. It certainly seemed cruel in the extreme, but, agreeably to the maxim that there is not great loss without some small gain, our camp was kept in capital mutton" (9). Additionally, Wintus expressed concern that hatchery employees would desecrate Wintu burial sites, "caused without doubt by the casual remarks of our party on the subject" (10).

The Winnemem Wintus eventually struck a deal with Baird: "Stone could capture the salmon for breeding, but we promised our sacred fish that they would always be able to return home" (Winnemem Wintu Band, n.d.). Of course, the Winnemem Wintus were indispensable to Stone's effort because their intimate knowledge of and ability in the McCloud River were essential to hatchery operations. Stone records: "The water was very cold and very swift, and it would have been extremely difficult for white men . . . I do not know how we should get along without them. . . . They are the best men we could have when work is to be done in the water or fish are to be handled" (Yoshiyama and Fisher 2001, 13). Winnemem Wintu women, most assuredly due to their practice and skill in basketry, were lauded by Stone for their skill in sorting eggs, specifically their "dexterity and delicacy of touch," so much so that he "could hardly get through the picking season without them" (13).

Apart from the first batch of eggs that were spoiled due to water supply problems, the first decade of Baird Hatchery's existence was relatively successful. During the first eleven years of the Baird Hatchery's operation, thirty million Salmon eggs were stripped from the McCloud River and shipped to the eastern United States, Hawai'i, Holland, Denmark, Germany, France, Russia, Australia, and New Zealand (Lichatowich 1999). However, by the 1880s the evidence of Salmon decline was apparent. In 1885 Stone wrote: "Instead of catching five hundred or a thousand salmon, we caught but one, and that a small one. . . . Instead of seeing from 6,000 to 8,000 jumping in an hour. . . . I did not see one jump for several minutes. In the meantime all the Indians we met had the same story to tell—that there were no more salmon in the river" (16). The decline in Salmon correlated with the demographic decline of Winnemem Wintus. In 1879 Stone writes: "Settlers are beginning to come to the McCloud River. They take up a claim, burn the Indian rancherias, shoot their horses, plow up their graveyards, and drive the Indians back into the hills, the ultimate result of which must be approximate starvation" (16). By 1897 Wintus were no longer a part of the Baird Hatchery workforce and by 1935, due to diminished Salmon runs, the hatchery closed. In 1943 the construction of the Shasta Dam was completed, blocking all Salmon runs from their spawning grounds in the upper Sacramento, McCloud, and Pit Rivers. The Winnemem Wintus were never compensated for lands taken under the Central Valley Project Indian Lands Acquisition Act of 1941.

Baird Hatchery was largely a failure, which has been ascribed to "haphazard allocation of salmon eggs and fry to destinations determined more by the enthusiastic imagination of sportsmen and fish culturists, as well as political demands, than by their ecological suitability for the fish" (Yoshiyama and Fisher 2001, 19). However, there was one exception: the Rakaia River in Aotearoa (New Zealand), the ancestral territory of the Māori people. In the spring of 2010, Winnemem Wintus traveled to New Zealand to conduct a four-day ceremony, called Nur Chonas Winyupus, to atone for the Winnemem Wintus' failure to stop the Shasta Dam. The Winnemem have appealed to the US Bureau of Reclamation and the National Oceanic and Atmospheric Administration to bring home the descendants of the McCloud River Salmon (Houck 2019). However, "despite records and genetic testing proving that eggs were shipped from the McCloud River to New Zealand, biologists working with the U.S. government are reluctant to allow 'foreign' species of fish into the waters of California" (Red Road Project, n.d.). Fortunately, on July 11, 2022, the Winnemem Wintus celebrated the return of winter-run Chinook salmon eggs to the McCloud River for the first time since the construction of the Shasta Dam.[13]

With the exception of the transplanted eggs to the Rakaia River—which was likely possible due more to luck than science—early Salmon hatcheries were an abysmal failure. McEvoy (1986) argues "the failure was due primarily to the early scientists' ignorance of the life history of salmon, especially of the importance of the young fishes' environment during the months they spend in freshwater" (107). So, essentially, by the turn of the twentieth century, settler fisheries scientists still did not know the basics about Salmon (McEvoy 1986). Scientists were still "discovering" that young Salmon spend the first part of their life in freshwater, that they must spend several years in the ocean, that Salmon spawn in their natal streams, that Salmon breed in cycles of four to six years, or that Salmon die after they spawn. Yet it is Native people who have been deemed primitive, backward, and uncivilized by settlers throughout the nineteenth and twentieth centuries. This is a prime example of how the refusal of settler science to acknowledge or consider traditional ecological knowledge—developed by Indigenous peoples who have been fishing the waters of California for millennia—has harmed settlers as well.

Initially, hatcheries were considered comparable to agriculture. "At the time, agriculture represented both the triumph of civilized societies. . . . Comparing a fish hatchery to a farm fixed the ideas of progress associated with agriculture onto artificial propagation" (Lichatowich 1999, 117). The correlation between agriculture and civilization, notably, was used as rationale for the legal justification of the colonization of what became the United States. Chief Justice John Marshall's infamous Supreme Court ruling in *Johnson vs. McIntosh* (1823) claimed that Native peoples were merely users—not owners—of the land because they did not practice agriculture (Barker 2005). This is not true. Marshall concocted what Pawnee legal scholar Walter Echo-Hawk (Pawnee) (2010) has referred to as a legal fiction. In actuality, Indigenous peoples of the Americas domesticated many of the foods considered to be central to European cuisines, including corn, beans, squash, tomatoes, peppers, avocados, quinoa, cacao, sweet potatoes, peanuts—and the list goes on (Dunbar-Ortiz 2014). Likening fish hatcheries, then, to civilization perpetuates settler-colonial logics and demarcates Indigenous relationships to fish and their fish knowledge as uncivilized, backward, and savage. Moreover, Lichatowich argues that linking hatcheries to agriculture had two long-lasting impacts: agricultural success was prematurely applied to hatcheries without evidence of their success and the science of fisheries management prioritized an agricultural paradigm and departed from the science of ecology. Just like Livingston Stone needed Native peoples' knowledge so he could locate Salmon, the settler state needs Native peoples' knowledge of Salmon habitat and life cycles that have been developed over millennia for continued Salmon survival.

One example of settler ignorance can be seen in the transfer of eggs between hatcheries. Despite the fact that this practice has created numerous problems, it is still common and widespread. As soon as multiple hatcheries were established in the Northwest, settlers relied on egg transfers to keep ponds filled to capacity (Lichatowich 1999). However, "for millions of years, the salmon and their habitats had evolved into a complex tapestry of individual populations adapted to the habitats of their home streams. Now the relocation of non-native fish species into western rivers, together with the transfers of the salmon among rivers within the region, was unintentionally ripping that tapestry to shreds. The early transfers of the salmon between rivers could be blamed on a lack of knowledge" (127). In addition to settler ignorance and disregard for Salmon lifeways, we can see here how the colonial logics of elimination, such as removal, have been wielded against our more-than-human relatives as well.

The conceptual framework of hatcheries prioritizes artificial propagation over habitat restoration. Essentially, "underlying this approach to management was the assumption that hatcheries could maintain salmon production without healthy rivers" via technological fixes (Lichatowich 1999, 131). Hatcheries, then, "provided the perfect vehicle for ordering and controlling the aquatic realm" (Lichatowich 1999, 128). Technological fixes absolve settlers from changing their behavior or giving up unsustainable practices. The same worldview pervades other strategies as well—such as trucking young Salmon to the oceans or around barriers such as dams, rather than limiting diversions or habitat restoration. Ultimately, however, hatcheries rely on a "flawed conceptual foundation with its reliance on technology [that] actually enabled irreversible decisions when habitat and wild salmon were traded for hatcheries. Over time, the irreversible decisions gradually accumulate causing habitat to degrade and wild salmon to decline in abundance" (Lichatowich et al. 2018, 24). In other words, early hatcheries provided a way for settlers to have their cake and eat it too—for a little while, at least.

The decline of fish species throughout the state of California was caused by a multitude of factors—all rooted in a view of the world that transforms relations into commodities and prioritizes the wants of human beings over the needs of other species. The result of this has been dammed Rivers and water diversions, habitat destruction, and fish kills.

Like the Salmon, Indigenous peoples who have stewarded their ancestral territories since time immemorial also experienced colonial patterns of removal and dispossession. Historian Donna Akers (Choctaw Nation of Oklahoma) (2011), writing about the removal of Choctaw peoples in the southeastern United States during the infamous Trail of Tears, argues that Choctaw peoples saw themselves as *part of* their homelands and "could no more be separated from these lands and survive than could the pine forests of the Southeast be uprooted and transplanted hundreds of miles to the west" (111, emphasis added). Deep within their ancestral memory, Salmon know what they are supposed to do: "Salmon navigate sometimes hundreds of miles to return home to spawn; they live by their relationship to their homelands. They know intrinsically and biologically where they come from and where they have been" (Risling Baldy 2021, 188). Winona LaDuke's words ring true: the stories of the fish and people are not so different. We heal together.

4 BACK TO WHOSE LAND?

Hippies, Environmentalism, and Cannabis

In American Indians, they, like Thoreau and Muir before them, saw a relationship to nature that should be emulated, inspiring a back-to-the-land movement and an aesthetic that unequivocally evoked the Indian—long hair, headbands, moccasins, beads and feathers, leather and fringe, turquoise and silver. . . . The problem was not so much that hippies looked to Indian country for answers. It was that as settlers they unconsciously brought with them worldviews and behavior patterns that were inconsistent with Indigenous paradigms and tried to fit Indigenous worldviews and practices into their own cognitive frameworks. —Dina Gilio-Whitaker, *As Long as Grass Grows*

There are many layers of colonization in this place [the Klamath River Basin]. This is evident through the various settler groups still present, including descendants of original gold miners, missionaries, loggers, farmers, different waves of "back to the landers," and now marijuana growers. Unfortunately, to Indigenous peoples the newest batch of settlers might look different than past invaders, but the implications of our presence is one in the same. Back-to-the-landers, who are a large portion of the current settlers, left mainstream society to live a better, more sustainable life and yet our/their return to the land is in direct relationship to Indigenous Peoples' displacement from it. In this area, as in other settler colonial situations around the world, non-Indigenous residents indisputably benefit from this system of land dispossession. —Laura Sarah Hurwitz, "Settler Colonialism and White Settler Responsibility in the Karuk, Konomihu, Shasta, and New River Shasta Homelands"

The origin story of the green rush in Northern California begins with the back-to-the-land movement. Often associated with peace and harmony, the movement constructs a particular ideological relationship to land of "free land for free people"—the unofficial motto of the Black Bear Ranch commune in Northern California (see Monkerud, Terence, and Keese 2000). Notions of "free land" erase Indigenous presence and continue the long legacy of colonial dispossession. The mass movement of young people into Northern California in the late 1960s and into the 1970s was a continuation of the settler-colonial occupation lived by their ancestors before them.

Dina Gilio-Whitaker (2019) offers a more critical perspective on the back-to-the-land movement, as "counterculture settlers who migrated to the area and built a cannabis industry that has led to skyrocketing land values and profound ecological impacts that further alienated Indigenous peoples from their homelands in the last half century" (158). The back-to-the-land movement, and the early cannabis farming that went with it, continues to replicate and perpetuate settler-colonial land dispossession. In the aftermath of termination, urbanization, and relocation policies imposed on Native Americans—which are forcing Native communities to leave their rural homelands and take up positions in the service industry within urban centers—the "back-to-the-land" movement facilitated another process of settling. This led Laura Hurwitz (2017) to pose a critical question in her master's thesis: Back to whose land?

Organized into three sections, this chapter examines the relationship between the back-to-the-land movement, settler colonialism, environmentalism, and the birth of cannabis production in northwestern California. First, a brief history of the back-to-the-land movement, specifically within the context of California, is juxtaposed to other relevant laws and events affecting Native American communities at the time, including policies on termination, relocation, and urbanization and the patterns of "white flight" that were occurring throughout the United States. Second is an examination of the appropriation of Native cultures and spiritualities within the context of American environmentalism and the role of the American environmental movement within the project of settler-colonial land dispossession. Third is an investigation of the significance of cannabis production to the back-to-the-land movement in northwestern California and how this region came to be known as the "Emerald Triangle."

THE BIRTH OF THE BACK-TO-THE-LAND MOVEMENT

Emerging in the 1960s and 1970s, the back-to-the-land movement is associated with counterculture and the New Age. To escape the capitalist culture of urban centers, primarily white young people began to flock to rural areas they considered "empty"—which in truth was a reenactment of settler-colonial land dispossession predicated on the false idea of *terra nullius* and wilderness. Many back-to-the-landers were able to acquire cheap land that had been logged following World War II; "Cutover land that was deemed worthless was sold by ranchers and realtors, especially in California, to 'back-to-the-landers' of various types at $10,000 to $12,000 for 40 acres in the late 60s and early 70s" (Gienger 2018, 17). Discussions of race and class have not been central to histories of this movement because rural communes created through the movement were overwhelmingly white, middle class, and well educated (Boal et al. 2012; Corva 2013). Although typically not considered in this way, the back-to-the-land movement nevertheless constitutes another example of white flight.[1] It was made possible by the timber rush, accompanying deforestation, and federal Indian policies of the mid-twentieth century focused on terminating Native American reservations and facilitating mass transfers of Native peoples from their reservation homelands to urban centers.

The history of the back-to-the-land movement and communal living in Northern California is often romanticized and viewed with a heavy dose of nostalgia. The edited collection by Boal et al. (2012), *West of Eden: Communes and Utopia in Northern California,* provides an overview of the history, challenges, and motivations of back-to-the-landers in the region. Historian of communal living in California Timothy Miller (2002) argues that the back-to-the-land movement was not the first of its kind, but rather built upon a historical tradition of communal living in California. Settlers established religious-based communes in the late nineteenth century. In the 1880s two different communes derived from fictional novels were established: Icaria Speranza and Altruria. They were both short-lived. Several other back-to-the-land–style communes arose in the early twentieth century as well, including Little Landers (1909), Los Angeles Fellowship Farms (1912), and Llano del Rio (1914). "Communal living has been an ongoing, if little-noticed, theme in California for over a century and a half. One could push the story back farther: the record could begin with American Indian communities, or perhaps the Spanish missions, both of which had elements of intentional community about them" (Miller 2002, 3).

Conceptualizing Native American communities as communes erases tribal specificity and the unique social, political, economic, and governance structures of the hundreds of autonomous republics within California pre-invasion. California Indian peoples had complex interactions, relationships, and trade networks with Indigenous peoples across the state, Turtle Island,

and the Pacific. Moreover, "commune" does not translate in an Indigenous worldview because the settler state prioritization of individualism, property, and human superiority represents a radical divergence from Indigenous ideological foundations. Within Indigenous knowledge systems, however, we understand ourselves as part of—not above—our environments. Rather than utilizing "resources" collectively, those "resources" are relatives or kin to whom we have obligations and for whom we have responsibilities. Additionally, for California Indians, the mission system, like the California gold rush, was an apocalypse.[2] California Indians were subjected to physical, emotional, spiritual, and sexual violence. Rather than creating a safe space to practice Catholicism, the Spanish mission system is fundamentally about colonialism and acquiring Indigenous territory.

Hurwitz's master's thesis, "Settler Colonialism and White Settler Responsibility in the Karuk, Konomihu, Shasta, and New River Shasta Homelands: A White Unsettling Manifesto" (2017), interrogates the back-to-the-land movement and asks the question: Back to whose land? As a white settler that moved to the Black Bear Commune located in Karuk ancestral territory, Hurwitz reflects on her own lack of understanding of settler colonialism upon her arrival to California:

> When I came to the Rivers for the first time I had never heard of Karuk, Konomihu, New River Shasta or Shasta people. I [was] unaware that Indigenous Peoples remained strong here in their ancestral territories. Nor did I realize that I was coming to one of the last places colonized, in what is now called the United States. I merely knew that I was leaving suburbia to come back-to-the-land and live a better life. I had known about Black Bear Ranch for many years before making the cross-country journey. . . . However, prior to coming here, I never had heard anything about the Indigenous people whose homelands this commune sits upon and neighbors with. (4)

Hurwitz situates the back-to-the-land movement within the longer historical trajectory of settler-colonial land dispossession. Back-to-the-landers, like goldseekers and loggers before them, benefit from Indigenous displacement from the land. Depictions of back-to-the-landers occupying "empty" wilderness upholds settler-colonial logics of *terra nullius*—thus the necessity of Hurwitz's critical question: Back to whose land? Through qualitative research with settlers living along the Klamath and Salmon Rivers, many with ties to the Black Bear Commune, Hurwitz identifies a lack of engagement or understanding of settler colonialism as an ongoing structure and pattern, which Eve Tuck and K. Wayne Yang refer to as "settler moves to innocence." Tuck and Yang (2012) describe settlers' moves to innocence as a set of strategies or evasions that attempt to alleviate or reconcile settlers' guilt in order to preserve settlers' futures in settler states, including settler nativism (claiming Indigenous ancestry) and colonial equivocation (homogenizing all experiences of oppression as colonization). In the Klamath River Basin, Hurwitz identifies several settler moves to innocence, including People Have Always Migrated Around, The Land Welcomes Us, and One Love/One People, among others.[3] Perhaps the most salient settler move to innocence for the American environmental movement that Hurwitz (2017) identifies is the position taken by the name The Land Welcomes Us: "The land 'speaks,' showing acceptance and welcoming the settler to be here" (75). This provides settler entitlement to continue to disrupt Indigenous relationships to lands that have been safeguarded over millennia and is particularly pronounced within preservation/conservation discourse. The notion of One Love/One People evokes elements of settler nativism through the argument that because Native and settler families have intermarried, we've all become "one people," which thus absolves the settler state of retribution for genocidal violence land theft.

To contextualize the historical moment of the back-to-the-land movement from an Indigenous perspective necessitates an understanding of twentieth-century federal Indian policy. As Hurwitz points out, "Fifty years ago, when back-to-the-land settlers began to arrive in force . . . [Indigenous] experiences of suffering abuse at boarding schools [were] fresh and raw" (5). The boarding school system began in the late nineteenth century with the infamous mission to "kill the Indian, save the man."[4] In both the United States and Canada, young Indigenous children were abducted from their homes and sent to live at residential schools far away from their homelands and apart from their parents, siblings, and cousins. Upon arrival, a student would be given a new name, new clothing, and, it was hoped, a new identity. Students were punished for speaking their own languages and many endured physical, emotional, spiritual, and sexual abuse (Child 1998; M. Jacobs 2009; Lomawaima 2002; Trafzer, Keller, and Sisquoc 2006). Native American studies scholars widely understand the boarding school system as cultural genocide. Moreover, the forcible transfer of children from one group to another group constitutes genocide as defined by the United Nations in 1948. While conditions of the schools improved during the 1930s, boarding schools persisted well into the mid-twentieth century. Today, former boarding schools are revealing the presence of the human remains of students, and tribal nations are struggling to repatriate them (E. Jacobs 2021; Yellowhorse Kesler 2021).

In the early twentieth century, the survivors of the boarding schools returned to their reservations only to find they were under threat of termination. Vine Deloria Jr. (Standing Rock Sioux), in his canonical 1969 text *Custer Died for Your Sins*, argues that termination was the single most important problem for Native Americans at the time. Passed by Congress in August 1953, House Concurrent Resolution 108 aimed to "make the Indians within the territorial limits of the United States subject to the same laws and entitled to the same privileges and responsibilities as are applicable to other citizens of the United States, *to end their status as wards of the United States*, and to grant them all the rights and prerogatives pertaining to American citizenship" (quoted in Akins and Bauer 2021, 256, emphasis mine). Disguised as a plan to offer Native peoples full citizenship rights,[5] Deloria (1969) argues that "in general, the public does not understand the issue of termination, and public statements of termination-minded Senators make it appear to be the proper course of action" (75). Termination was all about absolving the United States of its treaty obligations to Indian nations. A treaty, by definition, is an agreement between sovereigns and one party cannot terminate the agreement alone. Thus, if anything, the United States' violation of every treaty ratified with Indian nations should necessitate a return to pre-treaty terms, delegitimizing US occupancy.

Between 1945 and 1960, more than 109 tribal nations were terminated by the US government, affecting over 1.3 million acres of land and more than eleven thousand individual Native people. California Indians were specifically targeted in 1958, when Congress passed the California Rancheria Act to abolish the trust status of rancherias in California and formally terminate the relationship between rancherias and the federal government. "In return, the federal government pledged to complete surveys of rancheria land to ensure clear boundaries, to improve roads and bring them to comparable standards for state roads, to install or repair irrigation systems, to assist

Indians in protecting their water rights in the court, to cancel reimbursable debts for existing projects, and to resolve any lingering disputes that might affect property distribution" (Akins and Bauer 2021, 272–73). Additionally, the federal government promised to create education and training programs to help Indian people "assume responsibilities as citizens without special services because of their status as Indians" (273). This kind of rhetoric is prevalent in US-Indigenous relationships, wherein the United States' legal treaty obligations are reenvisioned as special help or special rights. In 1964 the act was amended to include all rancherias in California. Ultimately, forty-six rancherias in California were terminated. This meant that Native peoples from those rancherias lost land holdings and became subject to taxation, and existing programs and services created in 1934 under the Indian Reorganization Act were liquidated and their trust status was dissolved (Fixico 1986). "In practice, termination is used as a weapon against the Indian people in a modern war of conquest" (Deloria 1969, 76).

The federal government's next strategy to solve "the Indian problem" was the twentieth-century version of removal: relocation and urbanization. The idea was that rural reservations kept Indian people uncivilized and impoverished. The intention behind relocation and urbanization policies was to get Native people to leave their reservations and move to urban areas; reservation poverty was the problem and urban prosperity was the solution. It was assumed Native people would forget their Native heritage and assimilate to American culture, and the Indian problem would finally be solved. Throughout the 1950s, 1960s, and 1970s, Indian people were relocated to Chicago, Seattle, Denver, Los Angeles, Detroit, San Francisco, and Minneapolis, among other cities. In 1956 the US government spent over $1 million relocating Indians to urban areas. "Between 1955 and 1962, the Indian population of the San Francisco Bay Area quadrupled, from twenty-five hundred to ten thousand. By 1970 it ranked as the third-largest urban Indian population in the United States, at twenty thousand. Los Angeles grew in a similar manner. Eventually, proponents of relocation believed, American Indians would melt into the urban populace" (Akins and Bauer 2021, 272). By the 1990s more than two-thirds of the total Indian population in the United States lived in urban areas. Today, close to 80 percent of Native people are "off-reservation." However, despite separation from their ancestral homelands, "many urban Native Americans maintain connections to tribal communities or assert their tribal identities while living away from a land base" (Ramirez 2007, 3).

While the federal government intended for relocation and urbanization programs to complete the assimilation policies of the boarding school days, that plan backfired. Native peoples from across the country suddenly found themselves as neighbors and coworkers with each other. This enabled Native peoples to share their experiences on their reservations and form pan-Indian movements to demand the government fulfill its empty promises. The Red Power movement emerged in the late 1960s with the founding of the American Indian Movement in Minneapolis in 1968 and the occupation of Alcatraz Island in 1969, led by Indians of All Tribes (IAT).[6] From November 20, 1969, to June 11, 1971, Native Americans claimed and occupied Alcatraz Island, the site of an abandoned federal prison in the San Francisco Bay. IAT's authority to act relied on the 1968 Treaty of Fort Laramie negotiated between the Oceti Sakowin Nation (along with several other tribal nations) and the US government, specifically the clause that states "retired, abandoned and out-of-use federal lands" would be returned to Native people. After the federal penitentiary closed in 1963, the United States declared the island as surplus territory. The now-infamous Alcatraz document, titled "Proclamation to the Great White Father and All His People," articulated Native peoples' frustrations and demands:

> We, the native Americans, reclaim the land known as Alcatraz Island in the name of all American Indians by right of discovery.
>
> We wish to be fair and honorable in our dealings with the Caucasian inhabitants of this land, and hereby offer the following treaty:
>
> *We will purchase said Alcatraz Island for twenty-four dollars ($24) in glass beads and red cloth, a precedent set by the white man's purchase of a similar island about 300 years ago. We know that $24 in trade goods for these 16 acres is more than was paid when Manhattan Island was sold, but we know that land values have risen over the years. Our offer of $1.24 per acre is greater than the 47¢ per acre that the white men are now paying the California Indians for their land. We will give to the inhabitants of this island a portion of that land for their own, to be held in trust by the American Indian Affairs and by the bureau of Caucasian Affairs to hold*

> *in perpetuity—for as long as the sun shall rise and the rivers go down to the sea. We will further guide the inhabitants in the proper way of living. We will offer them our religion, our education, our life-ways, in order to help them achieve our level of civilization and thus raise them and all their white brothers up from their savage and unhappy state. We offer this treaty in good faith and wish to be fair and honorable in our dealings with all white men.* (quoted in Smith and Warrior 1996, 28–29)

The proclamation plays on several enduring settler-colonial tropes and inverts language repeatedly deployed by the settler state—such as the "discovery" of the New World, inequitable land transactions, a bureau of Caucasian Affairs, and the offer to relieve settlers from their "savage and unhappy state." The proclamation also makes a powerful statement about Indian lands: it identifies Alcatraz as a suitable spot for a reservation because it lacks fresh running water and productive soils, among several other reasons. Here, IAT points to the discrepancy in the quality of lands that Indigenous peoples were able to hold onto, as reservations were often of lower quality and the best areas of ancestral territory were often appropriated by settlers.

Janferie Stone, in her essay "Occupied Alcatraz: Native American Community and Activism," attempts to put Alcatraz and the back-to-the-land movement in conversation. Stone (2012) argues that "the visibility and symbolic power of Alcatraz coalesced in the imaginary of California that led young back-to-the-landers to settle in the northern state and to support the Alcatraz action" by sending aid (food, clothing, money, etc.) (88–89). From Stone's perspective, what connected the two movements was the centrality of land: "Both groups saw land/space as essential to their endeavors. The Rock was a symbol of the reservation system, of the loss and endurance of all native peoples.... The land that was the magnet for communalists was logged over forests, amenable to slow regeneration as back-to-the-landers established their homesteads, singularly or in experimental groups" (89–90). However, missing from Stone's analysis is engagement with how settler colonialism, specifically land dispossession, contributes to the "loss" experienced by Native people and how settler-colonial structures are ongoing and continue to frame Indigenous-settler relations.[7] Stone illustrates reconciliation "which motivate[s] settler moves to innocence," rather than what Tuck and Yang (2012) refer to as "an ethic of incommensurability, which guides moves that unsettle innocence" (35). Incommensurability "recognizes what is distinct, what is sovereign for project(s) of decolonization in relation to human civil rights based on social justice projects. There are portions of these projects that simply cannot speak to one another, cannot be aligned or allied" (28). Whereas the IAT proclamation is claiming territory that does not and cannot support cultural lifeways (fishing, hunting, agriculture, production of cultural materials, etc.), back-to-the-landers are claiming ancestral territory that has been stewarded by Indigenous peoples for millennia. In other words, you cannot purport to stand in solidarity with Indigenous peoples at Alcatraz while simultaneously colonizing Indigenous lands elsewhere.

The critical perspectives of the back-to-the-land movement explored in the works of Hurwitz and Gilio-Whitaker are important because they "succeeded in metaphorically unsettling the settler population by blowing the lid off myriad unspoken assumptions about what it means to 'go back' to a land that was stolen to begin with, and it exposed the ways in which even the most progressive and antiestablishment of countercultures are rooted in white supremacy and settler privilege" (Gilio-Whitaker 2019, 159). To illustrate some of the arguments put forth about the back-to-the-land movement, and its segue into the New Age movement, we turn to a long-standing commune nestled in the ancestral territory of the Karuk people. Located in a former mining town and surrounded by US Forest Service land, Black Bear Ranch is an 80-acre commune in Siskiyou County originally purchased in 1968 for $22,500 (T. Miller 2002). The numerous writings about the commune highlight its "remoteness," "the wilderness of Black Bear Ranch," and its "virgin timberlands," making it "an ideal hideaway, a Badlands for dissidents and political activists on the run" (Drew 2012). This language replicates settler-colonial logics of *terra nullius*: the land was empty and free for the taking. But, like the Badlands, this is an important place to Native peoples that has been renamed and taken by settlers. Black Bear Ranch has brought to the region more than a thousand settlers, and counting.

Black Bear Ranch is the ancestral territory of the Karuks, but the Karuk Tribe does not have a reservation to serve as its land base. Approximately 97 percent of Karuk land was incorporated into the US National Forest reserves in 1908, and only thirty-five of the ninety original Karuk allotments remain in the ownership of Karuk families (Norgaard 2019). Very little land is in private ownership within Karuk ancestral territory and it is often too expensive for Native families to purchase. Additionally, due to the emergence of cannabis cultivation in the region as part of the back-to-the-land movement, "the new 'gold rush' (aka marijuana cultivation) has artificially inflated real estate prices astronomically" (Norgaard 2019, 60).

While not diminishing the efforts at social justice organizing that occurred at various communes, the notion of "counterculture" that pushes back against economic and social injustice also relies on the erasure of Indigenous peoples, cultures, and relationships to *their* land. Jesse Drew (2012) writes that the remoteness of the commune "created the perfect laboratory environment to explore and develop alternatives to an oppressive and shallow status quo, from social governance to technology to food production" (48). While Black Bear Ranch residents toil away at reinventing the wheel, Karuk peoples who have been living in this region for millennia have developed sophisticated land management and food production regimes. While many writings produced at Black Bear Ranch do refer to "Indian neighbors," there seems to be a pervasive lack of understanding of the history of the region. For a century prior to the settler acquisition of Black Bear Ranch, Karuk people were experiencing genocide. The state of California was compensating individual vigilantes to murder Native people and bring back their severed heads or scalps (see chapter 1). Sixty years prior to the settler acquisition of Black Bear Ranch, 97 percent of Karuk land was taken by the US Forest Service, and widespread fire suppression policies were enforced. Fifty years prior to the settler acquisition of Black Bear Ranch, Karuk children were being abducted from their homes, separated from their families, and forced into boarding schools, an attempt to eradicate Indigeneity by waging a cultural genocide.

The motto of Black Bear Ranch is "free land for free people." As Gilio-Whitaker (2016) points out, the irony of this statement lies in it being "oblivious to the fact that the land was stolen in the first place." For the communes themselves, the notion of "free land" was an "attempted critique of capitalist property relations of exclusion and enclosure. But it has deep historical connection to Jacksonian dispossession and the Westering Anglo empire. To the expropriated grandchildren and great-grandchildren of the Miwok and Modoc, it would be hard for 'free land' to not trigger the memory of recent genocide. It is all the more bitter to some that the rusticating hippies spent a lot of time playing Indian, in all sincerity romancing 'the red man' and intending to honor the ancestral inhabitants of Alta California" (Boal

Fig 2 "Indian Land for Sale." This poster, dated 1911, is advertising the sale of Indigenous territory in the aftermath of the 1887 Dawes General Allotment Act. Source: Library of Congress, Rare Book and Special Collections Division.

et al. 2012, xxiii). Indeed, the notion of "free land," like the rhetoric of pristine virgin wilderness, relies on the erasure of Indigenous presence and the assumption that the land was always meant to be settler land (regardless of the property relations constructed). Back-to-the-landers maintained "settler entitlement to land based on that very system of capitalist greed they were trying to overcome. Most of them hadn't thought twice that the lands they were buying were stolen from the very people they were trying to emulate . . . repeat[ing] the patterns of settler colonialism they were simultaneously condemning" (Gilio-Whitaker 2016, para. 5).

In 2016 Unsettling Klamath River—an organization of settlers living on the Klamath and Salmon Rivers—wrote an open letter to the Black Bear Ranch Commune. Calling for the repatriation of land, the letter asks: "Can it be 'free land' if it is stolen land?" (Unsettling Klamath River 2016, para. 3). Linking Black Bear to historical patterns of settler-colonial land dispossession, Unsettling Klamath River argues that "ultimately, beckoning people 'back to the land' is part of the same system that created westward expansion, advertised famously with the promise of 'Indian Land for Sale'" (para. 8). This is a reference to the Dawes Allotment Act, by which the US government authorized the sale of Indian "surplus" lands and advertised it to settlers (see figure 2). Between 1887 and 1934, over 90 million acres of land were stripped from Native nations by the settler state.

APPROPRIATION, SPIRITUALITY, AND ENVIRONMENTALISM

Back-to-the-landers, sometimes referred to as "new settlers," sought to "emulate native ways" (Robinson Bosk 2000, x)—a markedly different approach to the state-sponsored genocide of a century prior. "From the birth of the Back-to-the-Land movement, settler people have turned to Indigenous ways as an inspiration and a guide for the spirituality that is sought. Until the more recent illumination and naming of cultural appropriation, 'hippie' society has felt completely free to take what it desires from Native culture and try to claim it for its own" (Hurwitz 2017, 65). The appropriation of Native cultures, belief systems, and spiritualities relies on assumptions that Native peoples are absent or have been erased from the landscape and are unable to carry on their cultures for themselves. Gilio-Whitaker (2017) argues that appropriation (especially within the context of environmental ethos) is fundamentally rooted in settler-colonial dispossession: "Native American appropriation is enmeshed with—really, a product of—the American imperative to claim ownership of that which is not one's own, beginning with land, and inevitably identity." In other words, settler-colonial entitlement extends beyond land (manifest destiny) to include Native cultures and spiritualities, Native images (e.g., mascots), and Native bodies (e.g., human remains housed in museums and college campuses).

Phillip Deloria (Standing Rock Sioux) (1998) situates Native appropriation by the counterculture/New Age movement within a historical trajectory of "playing Indian." From the Boston Tea Party to the Rainbow Tribe growing cannabis in the Pacific Northwest, "playing Indian" is a widely documented American practice. Whereas Indianness has been used to represent identities that are, as Deloria notes, "unquestionably American," countercultural communes sought to oppose capitalism and United States military interventions of the time (183). In a departure from earlier enactments of Indian identity, "now, countercultural rebels became Indian to move their identities away from Americanness altogether, to leap outside national boundaries, gesture at repudiating the nation, and offer what seemed a clear-eyed political critique. The wearing of the symbols of the Indian . . . signified that one's sympathies lay with both the past and the present targets of American foreign policy. To play Indian was to become vicariously a victim of United States imperialism" (161). By emulating Native Americans—and marking themselves as victims of American imperialism—back-to-the-landers have obfuscated their ongoing role in settler colonialism and continued land dispossession. They are doing the same thing they are critiquing the United States for doing: taking land from Indigenous peoples.

As Deloria explains, "many communes toyed with symbolic Indianness; [but] they were in reality largely disconnected from Indian people" (159). Rather than authentic traditional ecological knowledge or actual political allyship to return lands or halt genocidal federal Indian policies, back-to-the-landers largely imagined Indianness on their own terms in ways that were beneficial and useful for them. Much of their rhetoric is also based on erasure, a tried and true logic of settler colonialism. The book *The New Settler Interviews: Boogie at the Brink,* for example, considers itself "a continuation of the ancient Deer Dance among Yurok and Hupa peoples" (Robinson Bosk 2000, x). Presumably new settlers must continue this Ceremony because Native peoples are no longer able—either they've "vanished" or "lost" their cultures. In this way, new settlers become Indigenous and complete the replacement of the Native populations. In reality, Native peoples are still practicing their religions and conducting these ceremonies—even the White Deerskin Dance—despite more than a century of religious suppression by the United States. Many cultural thieves have come under fire by Native nations for spiritual appropriation; settlers often cite the First Amendment, arguing they have a "right" to Native American religions (Dunbar-Ortiz and Gilio-Whitaker 2016b).

Despite the constitution's First Amendment, Native Americans have had religious freedom for only a little over forty years. To put it into perspective, Black Bear Ranch has existed longer than Native American religious freedoms in the United States. In 1883 Secretary of the Interior Henry Teller developed the Indian Religious Crimes Code as a means to prohibit Native American ceremonial activity; general guidelines were disseminated to all Indian agents to ensure all dances and feasts were discontinued and to compel medicine people to abandon their practices. Religious offenses on the reservation were later codified by Commissioner of Indian Affairs Thomas J. Morgan in 1892. Morgan established a series of criminal offenses aimed at Native American religious practices. What is key to point out here is that throughout much of the 1960s and 1970s—when back-to-the-landers were widely appropriating Native American religions and spiritualities—it was still *illegal* for Native Americans to practice their own religions. Native Americans could not legally practice their own religions—which predate the invasion of Turtle Island—until 1978, following the passage of the American Indian Freedom of Religion Act.

Nevertheless, and despite the passage of the American Indian Freedom of Religion Act, many tribal nations struggle to access and/or protect their sacred sites from desecration and appropriation. Because the majority of sacred sites are not within the jurisdiction of the tribal nations that maintain relationships to those places, many sacred sites are on what are now called "public lands." This is especially so for federally unrecognized tribes. Another fallout from the back-to-the-land movement, New Agers flocked to conduct appropriative, inappropriate, and spiritually dangerous ceremonial activity within Indigenous sacred sites. For example, Bulyum Puyuik (Mount Shasta) and Panther Meadows are sacred sites for the Winnemem Wintu peoples. In 1987 the Harmonic Convergence "turned Mount Shasta into a Mecca for the New Age" wherein incoming settlers vastly outnumbered Winnemem Wintus much like a century prior during the gold rush (McLeod 2001). As Chief Caleen Sisk (Winnemem Wintu) explains, because place-based Indigenous religions do not share material conventions with Christianity, Indigenous sacred spaces are not granted the same respect or level of protection:

That area right there is our church and this is how you behave in our church. But they believe that it's as much theirs as anybody's because it's out here. If we built a building around it and said this is our building and inside this building is our sacred spring and this is how you behave in it, then maybe they would because then they can see the boundaries of what is ours, you know. Just like we couldn't walk into the Catholic Church and say "hey, I think we should have a little fire right here because that's our way." (quoted in McLeod 2001)

The erasure of Indigenous peoples and their relationships to land through colonial logics of wilderness and *terra nullius* creates the ability to "play Indian."

In tandem with the appropriation of Native spiritual practices, back-to-the-landers have also looked to Native peoples for environmental ethos. This often operates under the assumption that "Natives are one with the land" or "Natives are the original environmentalists." This is known as the "ecological Indian" stereotype, defined by Gilio-Whitaker (2019) as "a revamped version of the noble savage who became the stand-in for an environmental ethic the US should aspire to" (103). While it is certainly true that Native peoples have fundamentally different ways of relating to and tending landscape than the settler state, the ecological Indian trope is actually rooted in early European portrayals meant to dehumanize Native peoples by equating Native peoples to animals or to the land itself. This, of course, necessitates human-centric hierarchies that view the land or other species as less than, but, furthermore, the generalization of the "ecological Indian" stereotype "overlook[s] the meaning of the concept of environmentalism on the one hand, and on the other . . . mischaracterize[s] Native peoples' actual relationship to land" (Gilio-Whitaker 2017, para. 2).

American environmental movements—informed by conservation and preservation ethics—are rooted in manifest destiny and white supremacy, both of which rely on a historical fiction that Native lands were once empty and assume Native peoples are "incapable of managing their own lands in intelligent and innovative ways" (Gilio-Whitaker 2019, 97). Celebrated early environmentalists, such as John Muir, Henry David Thoreau, and Ralph Waldo Emerson, advocated for the conservation/preservation and enclosure of "wilderness" for the benefit of the American public. From an Indigenous perspective, however, wilderness does not exist. Wilderness is a socially constructed notion that necessarily erases Indigenous histories, cultures, ecological management practices, and relationship with the landscape (M. Anderson 2005). "While naturalists worked to protect lands acquired through centuries of aggressively imposed treaties and a variety of other legally sanctioned land grabs, tribes struggled to hold on to what remained of their land bases and culture" (Gilio-Whitaker 2019, 101). In fact, Native peoples had to be forcibly removed to "create" the wilderness that naturalists worked to protect (Spence 1999).

Acclaimed as "America's greatest idea," the national park system was yet another wave of Indian removal. Mark David Spence (Métis), in his book *Dispossessing the Wilderness: Indian Removal and the Making of the National Parks* (1999), argues:

> The American wilderness ideal, as it has developed over the last century, necessarily includes a number of strange notions about native peoples and national parks. In the rare instances that park literature even mentions Indians, they tend to assume the unthreatening guise of "first visitors." Just like tourists today, it seems these ancient nature lovers did not really use or occupy future park areas. Apparently, they possessed an innate appreciation for wilderness as a place where, to paraphrase the 1964 Wilderness Act, humans are visitors who do not remain. Amazingly, if we follow this reasoning to its logical extreme, the park service has managed to protect the only areas on the North American continent that Indians did not use on a regular basis.
>
> Of course, this all sounds absurd, but scholars and park officials alike have long asserted that native people avoided national parks because these places were not conducive to use or occupation. Yet nothing could be further from the truth. The foothills, mountains, and canyons of most western parks provided shelter from winter storms and summer heat, sustained seasonal herds of important game animals, and served as the locale for tribal gatherings and important religious celebrations. In short, native people made extensive use of these areas—often well into the twentieth century. To the degree that such practices ceased, the lack of use was the result of policies to keep Indians away

from these areas. Unfortunately, subsequent denials of native claims on parks have served only to perpetuate the legacy of native dispossession. (16–17)

In reality, the national park system and creation of forest service lands separated Native peoples from their ancestral territories, sacred sites, and critical hunting and gathering grounds.

The ideological underpinnings of both historical and contemporary Western environmental movements are fundamentally at odds with Indigenous understandings of and relationship to place. Western notions of conservation/preservation and exploitation are two sides of the same Eurocentric coin; they "assume that humans are autonomous from, and in control of, the natural world" (Pierotti and Wildcat 2000, 1333). The paradigms of both conservation and exploitation rely on worldviews that separate one's environment from one's self and maintain a humancentric hierarchy wherein land is an object to be utilized for human purposes—whether material or aesthetic. Furthermore, as Jessica Hernandez (2022) argues, the very notion of conservation does not align with Indigenous philosophies, because "conservation is a Western construct that was created as a result of settlers overexploiting Indigenous lands, natural resources, and depleting entire ecosystems" (72). Just as many tribal nations do not have a word for wilderness in their languages (M. Anderson 2005), many Indigenous languages also do not have a term equivalent to conservation, as reciprocal relationships with landscape are woven into one's very being (Hernandez 2022). Indeed, many "conservationists often fail to recognize that many Indigenous environments are endangered or in constant threat because of the practices and beliefs of settler colonialism introduced to the Americas and not because of the Indigenous communities themselves" (82).

Despite the role of environmental movements within the larger project of settler-colonial land dispossession, they simultaneously appropriate Indigenous identity and culture. "In the settler-colonial context, these usages of Native stories, symbols, and images serve to obscure both the historic events related to colonization and the ongoing occupation of Native lands" (Bacon 2019, 62). Perhaps the most prominent example of this is the character of Iron Eyes Cody. In 1971 "Indians unwittingly became the symbol" of the modern environmental movement (Gilio-Whitaker 2019, 103). Popularly known as the "Crying Indian," Iron Eyes Cody starred in an anti-littering commercial released by the Keep America Beautiful campaign. "The image of a buckskin-clad Indian, with a single tear rolling down his face as a factory spews toxic smoke in the background and trash thrown from a car lands on his beaded moccasins, seared itself into America's collective consciousness. Never mind that the Indian, Iron Eyes Cody, was no Indian at all, but a 100 percent Sicilian American actor named Espera Oscar de Corti who had built an entire career—and personal life—on Indian impersonation" (Gilio-Whitaker 2019, 103). The fact that one of the most recognizable Native faces to the settler population is not a Native person is quite fitting. Both playing Indian and the reduction of actual Native people to settler stereotypes has been pervasive throughout American history. As scholars have articulated, the symbolic repurposing of Native identity for the environmental movement furthers the settler-colonial project of elimination in multiple ways. First, by creating an Indian symbol—and then reflecting settler values onto that image—actual Native peoples and our contemporary struggles are discursively erased. Iron Eyes Cody is not demanding the deconstruction of dams, land return, or the end of capitalism. Second, it facilitates a settler move to innocence wherein settlers, through emulation/appropriation of Native ways, become the caretakers of the land and thus discursively replace Indigenous peoples on the landscape.

The erasure of Native peoples perpetuated through the historical and contemporary environmental movements was also pervasive within the back-to-the-land movement. Often back-to-the-landers are hostile when asked to confront settler privilege. While many have lauded the activism efforts of back-to-the-landers (see S. Smith 2012), others have pointed out the ways in which back-to-the-landers participate in the settler move to innocence and reproduce the white savior narrative (Hurwitz 2017). "Some claimed to have 'saved' the area due to their land stewardship and environment activism, asserting their presence prevented logging, pesticide spraying and other environmental ills" (Gilio-Whitaker 2019, 158). Because cannabis cultivation in Northern California has emerged with the back-to-the-land movement, much of this rhetoric bleeds into cannabis culture as well.

HIPPIES GROWING WEED

The origin of cannabis production in Northern California is rooted in the back-to-the-land movement—helping foster an ideological connection between hippies, environmentalism, and weed. Part of the countercultural rebellion of the 1960s, cannabis became an important symbol. "By championing the plant as part of an alternative lifestyle that emphasized peace, love, personal expression, and a oneness with nature, the counterculture shattered the popular consensus of the marijuana menace . . . pot smoking was transformed from a petty individual vice into a powerful collective symbol for hippies, back-to-the-landers, and other cultural rebels" (Johnson 2017, 84–85). Because cannabis production developed in tandem with environmental activism among many communities, it has been difficult for some to disentangle cannabis from an environmental ethos or face the reality that cannabis production has developed into an environmentally harmful site of exploitation. However, both the back-to-the-land movement and the emergence of cannabis agriculture in this region must be understood as reproductions of settler-colonial structures of Indigenous land dispossession that have produced colonial ecological violence for the region's Indigenous peoples.

Many of the stories of back-to-the-land hippies cannot be separated from stories about cannabis cultivation and the history of the plant in this region. The language used to describe the "new settlers"—like the language used to describe the individualistic miners or courageous loggers of yesteryear—is important to examine. One of the first, and perhaps most influential, texts on early cannabis cultivation is Ray Raphael's *Cash Crop*. Published in 1985, this text emerged as the War on Drugs was in full swing and many cannabis cultivators in the region were at risk of militarized violence due to cannabis prohibition. Raphael—in opposition to drug war violence—argues that the sensationalized violence of the green rush perpetuated by the media is "fake news." In interviewing cannabis farmers, law enforcement, and other community members, Raphael seeks to find out: "What happens to the indigenous backcountry culture of a once-neglected region which is thrust, willy-nilly, into the limelight?" (4). It is important to note here that Raphael's use of the term "indigenous" is not referring to Wiyot, Karuk, Yurok, or Hupa peoples (or actually *any* Indigenous peoples). He is actually referring to the back-to-the-landers who began cultivating cannabis prior to the 1980s, as a means for differentiating the first wave of cannabis cultivators and the back-to-the-land movement from the more recent cannabis cultivators of the green rush.

As demonstrated by Raphael, the "good grower"—who appeared during the back-to-the-land movement—is distinguished from the newer generation of growers. Journalist Emily Brady, in her book *Humboldt: Life on America's Frontier* (2013), describes the "Green Rush grower" as "the kind of men who migrated to Humboldt County every year. They came from around the country and sometimes from abroad, like miners of old, hoping to strike it rich. . . . These newcomers often lived in isolation out in the hills, where they clear-cut hillsides and grew pot. Or they filled buildings with impossibly bright lights and grew their plants indoors, with diesel-powered generators" (17). In the writings of Raphael and Brady, the profile of the green rush grower is in direct contrast to the back-to-the-lander's, which, according to Brady, represents "one of America's last great pioneer movements" (61). The division among the so-called good growers and more recent newcomers continues today. Again, the disconnection between pioneering and Indigenous land dispossession is palatable: "This first wave of new settlers—the ones who came to Humboldt before it became synonymous with its clandestine crop—would, in later times, promptly remind people that they hadn't moved there to grow pot. They'd come to be righteous and free. *What happened next was Manifest Destiny*" (66, emphasis added). Manifest destiny—an imagined concept—serves as a bedrock of settler-colonial logics: God ordained white settlers to claim and settle the United States. Brady's use of manifest destiny to describe the surge in cannabis production speaks to both its inevitability and its justification, at least from a settler-colonial perspective.

Raphael's text is concerned with how the "old-time inhabitants" navigated and have responded to the social, political, and economic transformations associated with the green rush. One of these concerns is drug war violence. Raphael (1985) asks: "What happens to a once peaceful countryside when it is besieged by one of the largest domestic military operations in our nation's history?" (5). Militarized state violence exerted on citizenry is inexcusable in every context, and cannabis cultivators in Northern California are not an exception. However, to describe Northern California as a "once peaceful countryside" is to severely misunderstand the history of this place. Raphael concedes that "from 1860 to 1865, the Indians were systematically and ruthlessly massacred," but in this version of history it seems as though settler violence came to an end in 1865 (169). Raphael's distortion of settler-Indigenous relations in this place is not due to ignorance of these events but is used to illustrate the imagined peacefulness of the physical and ideological origins of cannabis cultivation in Northern California.[8] Writers like Raphael and Brady romanticize the cannabis farmers of yesteryear and fail to see the ways in which cannabis farming rooted in the back-to-the-land movement perpetuate the same patterns of Indigenous land dispossession of the previous century. This is necessary, albeit difficult, to reckon with, because the ideological connection between cannabis, social and environmental justice, and resistance persists.

Hippies took to growing weed for several reasons, but, put simply, they needed cash. Even if settlers had been able to purchase lands outright, communities still had to come up with funds for land taxes, building materials, vehicle parts, stoves, storage tanks, and other equipment (Johnson 2017). The realization that back-to-the-landers needed money—and that due to the collapse of the timber industry, there weren't any employment options—led folks to turn to cannabis cultivation. "Communes had to deal with the politics of working on the commune for no obvious monetary gain, versus working off the land in professions or trades with salaries and status. But the economics of backcountry living meant that many individuals turned to marijuana cultivation, an enterprise linked with a secrecy that challenged the group ethos. Land itself, acquired at low prices in the early days, gained in value in the market economy" (Stone 2012, 90). Cannabis cultivation—like gold mining, logging, and fishing—was a way to generate cash from the landscape. But as cultivation continued throughout the 1960s and 1970s, and exploded in the 1980s, land prices continued to increase. During the gold rush the real gold was never actually gold; it was land. The same holds true today. The real gold is not cannabis, but the land itself.

Geographer Joseph Leeper argues cannabis production flourished in the region now known as the Emerald Triangle because of its geographical isolation, established economic dependence on natural resource extraction, and the social politics of prohibition.[9] Due to recent logging activity, much of the land is not economically advantageous or accessible. Inaccessible lands are conducive to illegal activity—and in the past the illegality of cannabis artificially raised its value. In addition, the crop was conducive to California's mild climate (Raphael 1985). However, the reasons the geography of the North Coast made it the perfect spot to keep an illegal activity hidden—with forests that are still intact and infrastructure almost nonexistent—are now the same reasons that make large-scale cultivation economically nonsensical. For example, of Humboldt County's 2.3 million acres, 75 percent is heavily forested (Humboldt County 2017). Much of the county is mountainous and the terrain is steep. According to Humboldt County (2017), "Most marijuana cultivation operations are in areas that were previously suited only for forest or grazing lands, too steep and without sufficient water or adequate soils to support commercially viable cultivation of other legal field or orchard crops" (3.2–8). This has engendered ecological impacts that environmental scientists have now begun to study.

The impact of early cannabis cultivation, in comparison to trespass cultivation today, is considered to be negligible (Silvaggio 2018). However, the inclination to romanticize the environmental ethos of the back-to-the-landers works to erase the ways in which cannabis cultivation since its inception has contributed to settler-colonial land dispossession. Some back-to-the-landers take it a step further and view the start of cannabis cultivation in the region as fundamentally tied to environmental restoration in the region. "Cannabis production enabled restoration because it funded the livelihoods of restorationists and helped to fund restoration projects. In the words of one back-to-the-lander, 'In my mind, the restoration economy grew out of the weed economy. Weed allowed people to settle in the hills'" (Kelly and Formosa 2020, 4). To say that cannabis cultivation enabled ecological restoration in Northern California obfuscates the relationship between settler colonialism and the necessity for ecological restoration in the first place. Cannabis cultivation is as embedded in the pattern of resource extraction that necessitates ecological restoration as it is within the restoration movement itself. While many small-scale cannabis farmers openly criticize the environmental harms of the green rush and understand it as in tension with restoration movements, neither position engages with ongoing structures of settler colonialism or the centrality of land. "In the Klamath River region, the principal way that [settlers] have profited is through access to land. Here, land directly equates to more wealth through gold mining, logging, farming and marijuana cultivation" (Hurwitz 2017, 44). In other words, settler possession exists in relation to Indigenous displacement.

While cannabis may have been a powerful cultural symbol for back-to-the-landers, the emergence of cannabis farming in Northern California has only continued a pattern of settler-colonial resource rushing. "From the moment of colonization 'boom and bust' economies have largely profited the settler. The marijuana industry on the Klamath and Salmon Rivers today is a prime example of this. Settlers, controlling almost all of the private land, profit from the growing of marijuana while this economy remains less accessible to Indigenous peoples" (Hurwitz 2017, 34). The shift to cannabis cultivation was part of a historical trajectory of resource rushing and must be understood as a response to the economic decline of natural resource extraction industries in the region. To survive in a capitalist economy, back-to-the-landers continued the pattern of settler-colonial resource extraction that, like other extractive industries, has continued to grow—until, of course, that now-familiar crash.

Given its clandestine nature, it is difficult to ascertain how much cannabis was produced throughout the region during the back-to-the-land era—but law enforcement efforts give us a good indication of the recent rise in production. In Mendocino County from 1936 to 1966 there were six total cannabis-related arrests. By July 1967 there had been twenty-nine arrests in nine months. Within Yurok ancestral territory, growers produced over 230 pounds of cannabis near Weitchpec in October 1970 alone (Johnson 2017). The small family-farmed cannabis era quickly transformed into big business. "Indeed, it happened so fast that the growers themselves didn't even realize it, arguing that the thousands of plants they grew were simply part of their efforts to have 'peace and quiet'" (Johnson 2017, 114). While the first cannabis cultivators who settled in the region during the back-to-the-land movement may not have anticipated the green rush explosion, that bomb has already been detonated and many of the tribal nations in the region are at ground zero.

5 WEED GREED

Explosion of the California Green Rush

As a rags-to-riches story, the marijuana boom goes straight to the heart of American mythology. There is nothing that titillates our fancy more than a get-rich-quick scheme, with its promise of instant fortune for anyone who is willing to take a little risk.
—Ray Raphael, *Cash Crop*

What was started with the intention of supporting an escape from the greater capitalistic society has become another aspect of its resource extraction, impoverishing the disadvantaged to the benefit [of] the privileged. Like the timber and mining industries before it, the marijuana economy has begun to eat its own tail.
—Laura Sarah Hurwitz, "Settler Colonialism and White Settler Responsibility in the Karuk, Konomihu, Shasta, and New River Shasta Homelands"

The summer of 2014, the third year of an extreme drought in Northern California, was especially concerning for tribal nations. Rivers and streams were running dangerously low and water temperatures were high due to the dams and water diversions into the Central Valley Water Project for industrial agriculture farther south. In the summer of 2014, and in most summers since, tribal nations had to petition the Bureau of Reclamation for water releases. That summer I was an intern at the Yurok Tribe Environmental Program and, because instream flows were so low and water temperatures were so high, concern arose that another fish kill could occur. I still vividly remember prepping fish kill kits so that Yurok Tribe staff would quickly be able to count the bodies of deceased fish along the River banks. On top of these existing "on the book" diversions, however, there was another source of water diversion that was causing great concern to tribal nations: trespass cannabis cultivation.

In Yurok ancestral territory, cultivators were tapping into creeks that feed the tribal and private water systems, so much so that tribe members reported to the Yurok Tribal Council that entire streams—and even creeks with year-round flows—had been entirely dewatered. The *Yurok Today* newspaper reported that cannabis cultivators who had moved onto and near

Yurok lands—largely from out of state—had increased significantly in the previous five years. As the paper noted, "Klamath River tributaries that are being pilfered for marijuana production normally provide cold water refuges for the migrating salmon on the way to spawn. Instead, the important Klamath tributaries are barely making it to the main stem" (Yurok Tribe 2014, 5). In response, the Yurok Tribe collaborated with local, state, and federal law enforcement to protect water and fish from illegal water diversions for cannabis production. This collaboration came to be known as Operation Yurok. From illegal diversion of water to chemical pollution to clear-cutting to the dumping of hazardous waste, unregulated trespass cultivation in the biologically sensitive watersheds of Yurok ancestral territory is widely deemed an ecological nightmare.

Aptly named the green rush, this surge in cannabis production evokes gold rush–era ideology of manifest destiny, resource extraction, and wealth accumulation. References to the green rush, and reflections on the similarities between the gold rush and the green rush, date back to as early as the 1980s: "The story has been told many times, and the story is always the same: There's a modern gold rush underway in the hills of California . . . the new gold is green and it's called *sinsemilla*, a high-potency marijuana which commands astronomical prices" (Raphael 1985, 1). The rags-to-riches story of the twenty-first century, the green rush, predicted to potentially be a $40 billion industry (Silver 2016), holds a dream of wealth and profit similar to its predecessor. Indeed, despite decades of cannabis eradication efforts, cannabis is—hands down—the largest cash crop in California (Brady 2013; Carah et al. 2015; Lee 2012).[1] By 2006 cannabis produced in the United States was worth $35.8 billion (by comparison, corn totaled $23.3 billion that same year and wheat fetched $7.45 billion). In California alone it topped $14 billion, more than a third of the entire US yield (Lee 2012). In 2011 the medical marijuana market (including illicit marijuana sales) in California was estimated at $1.4 billion and possibly as high as $4.5 billion (Hecht 2014). Since the 1970s California has supplied the bulk (60 to 70 percent) of the nation's cannabis supply. In 2020 cannabis sales in California hit $4.4 billion and were $5.6 billion in 2021 (Bartlett 2021; Lange 2022).

An ideological descendant of the gold rush, the green rush serves as yet another get-rich-quick fantasy founded on the erasure of Native people. Like celebrated and memorialized gold rush narratives that exclude the volunteer militias and bounties placed on Native peoples' bodies, the narratives of the green rush often leave Native people out of the discussion. This is specifically problematic because cannabis cultivation in California occurs on occupied Indigenous territory and Native people experience environmental injustice as a result of both licit and illicit cannabis cultivation in their ancestral territories. Like precedent resource rushes, the cannabis industry maintains and relies on settler-colonial land dispossession through extractive violence and imposed land-use decisions. Governed by settler-colonial relations to land that seek to control and commodify the landscape, the pattern of resource rushing, even the rush mentality itself, suggests that eventually the growth will come to an end. This chapter examines the buildup to the contemporary California green rush and the marked shift in cannabis production within California in response to different policy regimes over the past few decades.

Militarized eradication campaigns in the 1980s created a profitable market and incentivized people to flock to the area. Medicinal legalization in the 1990s created a quasi-legal gray market, facilitating ecologically devastating trespass grows on public and tribal lands. As of this writing, recreational cannabis has been legal in California for over five years, warranting an in-depth examination of the impacts of cannabis cultivation on Indigenous peoples in Northern California, both because it is a present and urgent issue and historically Native perspectives have largely been absent from public discourse on cannabis cultivation and policy. However, it is important to stress here that the problem at hand is not the unique impacts of cannabis cultivation itself, but rather the continuation of extractive environmental relationships that disproportionately benefit settler populations at the expense of Native American stewardship, health, and culture. While the relevant environmental research remains in its early stages, it is becoming quite clear that the rapidly growing cannabis industry—like the gold rush, timber rush, and fish rush before it—is depleting and damaging critical ecosystems and cultural resources of Indigenous peoples in Northern California (see Wartenberg et al. [2021] for a review of the existing literature). Like the preceding rushes, the green rush isolates a single species deemed profitable by human beings and sacrifices healthy ecologies for its maximized production while perpetuating both settler-colonial land dispossession and colonial ecological violence in the process. Like what occurred with gold, timber, and fish, the extractive relationship eventually reaches a breaking point.

EMERGENCE OF THE GREEN RUSH

Though cannabis has been present on the continent since invasion—settlers in Jamestown, Virginia, were mandated to grow it on their property for hemp production—it did not emerge in large quantities in California until the mid-twentieth century. Anthony Silvaggio (2018) has identified four distinct eras of cannabis cultivation and related policy regimes: industry emergence (1970–83); militarization of eradication (1983–96); the gray market (1996–2012); and legalization (2012–16). Cannabis emerged in Northern California during the back-to-the-land movement. After decades of mining, logging, and fishing, the monetary value of land had declined and enabled young white people to flock to the region. Then, after the collapse of the timber industry, back-to-the-landers turned to cannabis cultivation for a source of cash (Silvaggio 2018; Johnson 2017). During this period, cannabis cultivation was not considered a large ecological burden, but this began to change by the early 1980s.

The scale of cannabis cultivation in Northern California increased in the 1970s and 1980s because the US government eliminated the region's primary competition.

> Around the same time that marijuana growers in Humboldt and the neighboring counties of Trinity and Mendocino began producing sinsemilla, the U.S. government inadvertently helped create a market for their new industry. In the mid- to late 1970s, the American government supported the Mexican government's spraying of the toxic herbicide paraquat on the Mexican marijuana crop.[2] At the time, more than 90 percent of the marijuana smoked in the United States came from abroad. . . . Marijuana continued to flow north from Mexico, but after the Centers for Diseases Control and Prevention (CDC) warned of the serious health risks that paraquat-laced pot posed to consumers, there was a sudden interest in other sources. (Brady 2013, 70)

Despite CDC warnings, the US Drug Enforcement Administration (DEA) continued to use paraquat in the United States well into the 1980s. By order of the Reagan administration in August 1983, the DEA undertook a paraquat campaign in Georgia's Chattahoochee National Forest. But when environmental organizations sought an injunction due to the DEA's failure to complete an environmental impact review, the DEA abandoned paraquat campaigns on federal lands in 1984 (Johnson 2017). However, "In 1985, the DEA quietly revived the practice of spraying cannabis with paraquat. This time the program targeted cannabis grows on nonfederal lands, which included state-owned, private, and Indian land" (Johnson 2017, 134). Paraquat-laced cannabis, primarily from Mexico, led to an increase in demand for homegrown cannabis, leading to "an ambitious crowd of profit-hungry outlaw farmers" flocking to Northern California, triggering the first green rush (Johnson 2017, 120). By 1979, 35 percent of the marijuana smoked in the United States was produced in California, and by 2010, 79 percent of the marijuana smoked in the United States was grown in California (Brady 2013).

A militarized war on drugs formed the backdrop of the early green rush of the 1980s. Inflated prices, attributed to prohibition tactics, drew people to the region—at times during the 1980s an ounce of cannabis was worth more than an ounce of gold (Brady 2013). The Campaign Against Marijuana Planting (CAMP), established in 1983, was a joint task force that coordinated federal, state, and local agencies for two months every summer to locate and eradicate outdoor cannabis grows (Corva 2013). Northern California was a key target of CAMP raids. Heavily militarized, complete with helicopters and camouflaged men with automatic weaponry, CAMP raids were part of the Reagan administration's War on Drugs. CAMP was unique in that state and federal land management departments, like the US Forest Service, the Bureau of Land Management, and the California Department of Fish and Game, were also involved in CAMP (Raphael 1985). From 1983 to 2012, CAMP utilized militarized eradication tactics to suppress cannabis cultivation. "After spotting and photographing marijuana grows from the air, authorities would return on raids. Pot would be chopped down, hauled out, and burned or buried. Whenever possible, the grower was arrested" (Brady 2013, 76).

While initially focused on southern Humboldt County and northern Mendocino County, CAMP created a "balloon effect": law enforcement pressure spurred production to move elsewhere, usually expanding onto public and tribal lands. Additionally, CAMP—through a marginal reduction in supply—dramatically increased the price of cannabis. As a result, "'old settler' families who were suffering through the timber bust found in cannabis agriculture a way to preserve and indeed enrich rural livelihoods. This [increase in cannabis production] was the first 'Green Rush' and it never really stopped" (Corva 2013, 6). Former Yurok Tribe vice chairman David Gensaw (Yurok) recalls seeing reports about cannabis production and the CAMP raids on the news in the early 1980s: "They were cracking down on marijuana and one of the crackdowns is because people started putting booby traps out. One area where this forester was walking out and he tripped over a line or something across and that triggered it and killed him" (David Gensaw, author interview, July 6, 2018). CAMP was discontinued in 2012 and overall did very little to decrease cannabis production in the region. On the contrary, CAMP raids served as a "protective subsidy" that resulted in increased cannabis prices and thereby incentivized more cannabis producers to flock to the region (Corva 2013).

For Indigenous people of the region, CAMP also posed a continuation of colonial violence via military presence in our homelands. Elder Richard Myers (Yurok) recalls: "Many years ago, when we did our World Renewal [Ceremony], in 1986 or 1987, we were hiking out to High Country in the Blue Creek range and helicopters came overhead and they thought we were marijuana growers, they thought we had machetes. They chased us around a little bit. . . . [The growers] make it a little scary, but we have to have faith and march forward" (Richard Myers, author interview, June 22, 2018). Myers's comments demonstrate one of the many ways Indians experience violence simply for being Indian. Getting chased around by CAMP helicopters is reminiscent of Yurok fishermen getting chased around by US Fish and Wildlife officers a decade prior during the Fish Wars, or California Indians running for their lives away from voluntarily formed militias during the gold rush. And while the theoretical and geographical focus of this text is the construction and perpetuation of settler-colonial ecologies in Northern California, the War on Drugs has far-reaching global implications. Dawn Paley (2014) argues in her book *Drug War Capitalism* that drug war violence must be understood within the context of territory, land, and resources. Indeed, "rather than stopping the flow of drugs, funding the drug war has bolstered a war strategy that ensures transnational corporations access to resources through dispossession and terror" (15). The War on Drugs is not about prohibition or drug policy but about "the expansion of the capitalist system into new or previously inaccessible territories and social spaces" (Paley 2014, 15).

In 1996 California legalized medicinal cannabis under the California

Compassionate Use Act (Proposition 215), garnering 56 percent of the vote and marking the beginning of what Silvaggio refers to as the gray market era (1996–2012). This likely resulted from drug war fatigue and growing compassion for patients, but Nick Johnson (2017) offers another explanation—one that requires "delving deeper into the history" of the American West:

> For centuries before 1853, when the United States lay claim to the last piece of land that makes up today's American West, the region had been shaped by the ideas and interactions of people from many cultures and backgrounds from indigenous to Spanish, French, Mexican, and even Russian. . . . [this] continued during the American period, as industrial and agricultural opportunities in the West drew thousands of newcomers during the nineteenth and twentieth centuries. However else one wishes to define it, the West has always been a destination. Whether it was gold, glory, land, labor, health, climate, or even the current draw of legal grass, thousands of people have acted on the belief that something better waits in the West. (150)

Perhaps unsurprisingly, Johnson reproduces the same California Story critiqued by William Bauer and other California Indian scholars. Bauer (2009) argues that these manifest destiny narratives rationalize settler colonialism, exculpate settlers for nineteenth- and twentieth-century violence, and erase Native people from the past, present, and future. While Johnson (2017) concedes that "frontier justice" ("the lynchings and other forms of vigilante justice carried out across the West before the arrival of the courts") was "particularly bloody" (150), the erasure of state-sponsored slavery and genocidal violence toward Native peoples throughout the nineteenth century has been and continues to be pervasive. This is not an indictment of Johnson's work specifically, but rather an attempt to demonstrate the widespread historical amnesia of the settler population of the genocide Indigenous peoples experienced in this place. The founding of California, the infamous gold rush, and the subsequent patterns of resource extraction cannot be disentangled from the land theft and genocide of California Indians—all of which are predicated on dispossession. Dispossession, like settler colonialism, is not a one-time occurrence; it is a continually perpetuated structure, as evidenced by the green rush.

While the initial boom in cannabis cultivation emerged in the 1980s, medicinal legalization of cannabis in California triggered another wave. "Proposition 215 began an era in which industrial cannabis cultivation became normalized in the region, leading to a surge in the number of grows and migration of people to [Humboldt] county for the sole purpose of growing cannabis. . . . Shielded by the protections of Proposition 215 and SB 420, people from all over the United States moved to the region to engage in cannabis agriculture in a second Green Rush, and by 2009 California was producing more outdoor cannabis than all of Mexico" (Silvaggio 2018, 20). During this era, "mega-grows" of several thousand plants became commonplace. As a result, the price for cannabis plummeted. By 2009 "the price of outdoor cannabis dropped almost by half, to around $1,500 per pound" (Silvaggio 2018, 22). The following year, another legalization initiative was proposed. Proposition 19, the Regulate, Control and Tax Cannabis Act, was defeated on the statewide ballot in 2010. The Proposition 19 campaign failed for several reasons, including a lack of funding after achieving ballot status, the timing of the vote during a nonpresidential election year, and because a few months prior Governor Arnold Schwarzenegger had reduced charges for possession of less than an ounce of cannabis to an infraction punishable by a traffic ticket (Reiman 2018). Humboldt, Mendocino, and Trinity Counties, all located in the Emerald Triangle, rejected the measure and bumper stickers that read "Save Humboldt County—Keep Pot Illegal" were displayed on vehicles throughout the region. Within the next two years the number of outdoor mega-grows had ballooned into the thousands near most watersheds in the region (Silvaggio 2018). The large and thriving cannabis industry in the region continues to pose significant challenges to cannabis legalization in the state, as many cannabis farmers opt to stay outside of the legalized market due to financial, administrative, and psychological barriers (Bodwitch et al. 2021).

In 2015 California established a comprehensive state regulatory framework for medical cannabis. Three separate bills—Assembly Bill 243, Assembly Bill 266, and Senate Bill 643—formed what is known as the Medical Cannabis Regulation and Safety Act (MCRSA). MCRSA outlined the licensing and enforcement of cultivation, manufacturing, retail sale, transportation, storage, delivery, and testing of medicinal cannabis throughout California. Senate Bill 837 built on this framework by requiring comprehensive environmental safeguards; SB 837 requires the California State Water Resources Control

Board (SWRCB), in collaboration with the Department of Fish and Wildlife, to create guidelines governing the use of water for cannabis cultivation.[3]

Proposition 64, the Adult Use of Marijuana Act (AUMA), passed in November 2016 with 57.1 percent of the vote. This law stipulates that adults twenty-one years of age or older can legally grow, possess, and use cannabis for nonmedicinal purposes. Cultivation of cannabis for personal use is limited to six plants; those opting for personal use cultivation do not have to apply for a license, nor are they subject to environmental regulations outlined in places such as the SWRCB's cannabis policy. Starting on January 1, 2018, it became legal to sell and distribute cannabis through a regulated business, as stipulated in AUMA. However, the California state regulatory framework that arose following the passage of Proposition 64, and as outlined in MCRSA, applied specifically to medicinal cannabis only. In June 2017, Senate Bill 94 integrated MCRSA with AUMA, creating the Medicinal and Adult-Use Cannabis Regulation and Safety Act (MAUCRSA). Under MAUCRSA the newly formed Bureau of Cannabis Control (BCC) is the lead regulatory agency.[4] The other two primary licensing authorities include the California Department of Public Health (specifically the Manufactured Cannabis Safety Branch) and the California Department of Food and Agriculture (specifically the CalCannabis Cultivation Licensing Division).[5] Numerous other state agencies are involved as well, including the California Department of Fish and Wildlife (CDFW), the State Water Board, and the California Department of Pesticide Regulation, among others.

With legalization—and a set of stringent environmental regulations—the hope was that the ecological toll of cannabis cultivation would be lessened considerably, as many scholars have linked the environmental damage of cannabis cultivation not to the plant itself but to federal cannabis prohibition policies (C. Miller 2018; Corva and Meisel 2022). Silvaggio (2018) argues that "prohibition exacerbates environmental harms and incentivizes cannabis cultivators to set up environmentally damaging grow sites on public and private lands with little regard for the natural environment" (25). Johnson (2017) also argues that environmental destruction is a direct consequence of federal prohibition, and thus "why California can't get its salmon-killing pot industry under control" (177). Wildlife biologist for the Hoopa Valley Tribe Mark Higley et al. (2018) echo these concerns: "Many proponents of the new legislation have stated that this will make the trespass-growing problem simply go away. We are skeptical at best about that result, primarily because a large black market still exists throughout the United States and around the world. Most of the marijuana grown on California's public and tribal lands has been destined for places outside of California, and this continues to be the case" (67).

Clearly a more accurate understanding of the current ecological toll of the cannabis industry must take into account the impacts of large trespass grows *in addition to* regulated cannabis in California. While prohibition certainly plays a role in the contemporary ecological impacts of the cannabis industry, it is not the whole problem. Rather, we can understand prohibition as an extension of settler-colonial state power. To focus on prohibition as the only or even the primary cause of environmental harms, in fact, masks a problematic relationship with the natural world that organizes space in terms of property and transforms plants into commodities. This is why it is useful to frame the green rush within a historical pattern of settler-colonial resource rushing; the similarities in extraction between the gold rush, the timber rush, the fish rush, and the contemporary green rush help illustrate other factors at play, apart from prohibition, that contribute to the ecological toll of cannabis cultivation.

Some tribes have expressed frustration at the lack of protections afforded to ecological and cultural resources within the legal regulated industry. For example, since 2016 the Yocha Dehe Wintun Nation has consistently provided feedback and recommendations to the Yolo County Board of Supervisors regarding its Cannabis Land Use Ordinance and accompanying Environmental Impact Report, but the nation's input has largely been ignored. Capay Valley, the ancestral territory of the Yocha Dehe Wintun Nation, is currently overconcentrated with cannabis cultivation sites. The tribe has expressed concern that Capay Valley "has become flooded with cannabis grows since the County first unleashed its interim program four years ago" (Roberts 2021). As of 2019, nearly half (twenty-six of fifty-nine) of Yolo County's cannabis operations are located in Capay Valley (Roberts 2019). "In sum, a disproportionate concentration of cannabis cultivation in the Capay Valley is neither sustainable nor equitable, and it threatens to overwhelm our small valley's sensitive natural resources and undermine the Valley's fledgling agri-tourism industry" (Roberts 2019). The tribe has recommended caps be placed on cultivation; the county has acknowledged that overconcentration is, indeed, a problem in Capay Valley, but the Cannabis Land Use Ordinance does not address this problem. The Yocha Dehe Wintun Nation has gone so far as to offer to purchase all parcels in Capay Valley that are actively engaged in cultivation, at the price each grower paid for the parcels, with an additional premium paid to each grower for relocation costs (Roberts 2021). Yolo County has not taken the tribe up on this offer. Moreover, it is particularly curious considering the county tried to prevent tribal land acquisitions less than a decade ago under the pretense that it would lessen protections for Capay Valley. "The irony of where we find ourselves bears noting. Just over seven years ago, when the Tribe sought to take 853 acres of land into federal trust ownership for Yocha Dehe's sovereign benefit, the County challenged that effort, informing the Bureau of Indian Affairs it had to oppose the trust acquisition to protect the treasured Capay Valley from the possibility that the Tribe might engage in 'some degree of commercial activity'" (Roberts 2021).

Cannabis cultivation and the cannabis industry as a whole amount to natural resource extraction for profit accumulation. They are part of a larger historical pattern of settler-colonial land dispossession and ecological transformation. While environmental regulations are important and necessary, regulations alone do not challenge settler-colonial orientations to land, but rather they maintain the perspective that the natural world exists for the material accumulation of human beings. Just because environmental regulations exist does not mean they are comprehensive or effective, that people will understand and follow them, or that they will be enforced. Questions of environmental justice are also important to consider here. What groups are primarily benefiting from either regulated or trespass cultivation? In many cases white settlers are profiting on production and damaging Indigenous territory in the process, while other people of color remain incarcerated for cannabis-related charges.

TRIBES' EXCLUSION FROM CALIFORNIA'S CANNABIS INDUSTRY

As sovereign nations, tribal governments exercise self-determination to make their own decisions about land stewardship and economic development, although this self-determination is often challenged by local, state, and federal entities. For example, the Pit River Tribe (2015) in northeastern California—a federally recognized tribe composed of eleven autonomous bands—developed a comprehensive medicinal cannabis operation. In April 2015 the tribe adopted a tribal medical cannabis program under tribal law that was also consistent with California's medicinal cannabis laws. The Pit River Tribe provided the US Attorney's office with its Medical Marijuana Program Ordinance, and during consultations with the federal government the tribe "asked the U.S. Attorney's office to identify any concerns and to advise the tribal government before taking any enforcement action against the tribal project" (2). Speaking on behalf of the tribe, former Tribal Council chairman Mickey Gemmill Jr. (Pit River Nation) (2015) declared: "We have been transparent in our conversations with the federal government and made no secret of our intent to exercise our sovereignty in the manner we believe appropriate" (2). Despite this public statement, tribe-owned High Desert Farms was raided by federal agents, who confiscated twelve thousand cannabis plants and one hundred pounds of processed cannabis.

On July 8, 2015, dozens of law enforcement agents from the Bureau of Indian Affairs (BIA) and the DEA invaded a tribal cannabis operation located on Pit River tribal land in Modoc County, California (NoiseCat 2015). According to Gemmill, some tribe members were subjected to excessive police force, severely injured, and arrested during the search (Pit River Tribe 2015). Agents destroyed plants, seized processed cannabis, and confiscated confidential patient information and other documents (Armitage 2015; Eid 2015). The tribe issued a press release on July 9, 2015, titled "Federal Government Fails to Respect Tribal Self Governance":

> We are very disappointed with the decision of the Bureau of Indian Affairs, as the lead federal agency, to descend on sovereign land with an army of nearly fifty law enforcement officers . . . that the BIA would take such a disrespectful approach to an Indian tribe on its own land is a serious assault to the Tribe's right to self-governance. We believe that it is important to remind the BIA of its responsibility to protect Indian tribes, not to undermine legitimate tribal efforts to create jobs and improve the health and welfare of tribal members. (2)

The BIA is the federal agency responsible for upholding the United States' trust relationship with Native nations. Its mission is to "enhance the quality of life, to promote economic opportunity, and to carry out the responsibility to protect and improve the trust assets of American Indians, Indian tribes and Alaska Natives" (Bureau of Indian Affairs, n.d.). Gemmill's critique of the BIA highlights the imposition of colonial rule over California Indians, the ways in which the settler state continually narrows the ability of Native nations to develop politically and economically of their own accord, and the failure of federal authorities to protect their economic well-being.

While some tribal nations are pursuing cannabis operations, other tribal nations in the state speak out against the ecological harms levied against their homelands. Reconciling the differences between tribal groups within the context of cannabis requires engagement with settler colonialism and the way in which settler-colonial structures continue to frame the material realities of Indigenous peoples today. Referring to tribal nations' participation in environmentally extractive industries as a "Faustian bargain," Dina Gilio-Whitaker (2019) argues: "The need to escape poverty and assert sovereignty, weighed against cultural obligations to protect land, forces tribes into what can seem like an impossible double bind. It is a realm of difficult choices that exists beyond binaries of black and white and right and wrong, necessitated by the unforgiving and unrelenting demands of capitalism" (69). Extreme rates of poverty characteristic of many Native American reservations often frame Native nations' engagement in extractive industries. Through long-term processes of settler-colonial land dispossession, many tribal peoples now hold mere fractions of their ancestral territories; untold numbers of tribal peoples were removed from their homelands entirely, and in California many tribes were left without land bases at all. As such, many Indigenous peoples have been separated from their traditional means of subsistence and must participate in systems that commodify relatives. In other words, settler-colonial society has created a system in which Native people are often forced to exploit their own lands to survive.

In *Roots of Our Renewal: Ethnobotany and Cherokee Environmental Governance,* political ecologist Clint Carroll (Cherokee) (2015) situates Indigenous environmental governance on a continuum of resource-based and relationship-based practices. The latter refers to traditional management practices that foster reciprocal relationships between ecosystems and nonhuman relatives, whereas resource-based environmental governance describes settler-colonial approaches of "allocating and administering the resources themselves to achieve mostly economic goals" (8). Prime examples of resource-based environmental governance include monocrop forestry, fire suppression, and damming Rivers. Carroll argues that Indigenous environmental governance is situated on a continuum because both resource-based and relationship-based approaches are currently necessary within a settler-colonial framework: "In speaking the language of 'resources,' Indigenous nations are able to assert some form of sovereignty over them. As flawed as this discourse may be, commensurate within it are Indigenous assertions of territory and resource control" (xiii). In other words, resource-based approaches allow tribal nations to be legible to the settler state, and in this way they work to protect relationships between the land and nonhuman relatives.

Sovereign tribal nations' decisions to participate in the cannabis industry do not negate the colonial ecological violence of the green rush. For example, during the timber rush Indigenous peoples experienced land dispossession through the creation of timber corporations and state and federal forest reserves; clear-cutting destroyed and impaired habitats for many culturally significant species. On top of that, the imposition of fire suppression policies prevented many Native peoples from cultivating the materials and food sources necessary for subsistence. The combination of land dispossession, habitat destruction, and fire suppression facilitated colonial ecological violence for Indigenous peoples. And yet many Native peoples worked in the timber industry (Bauer 2009). The Baird Hatchery would not have had any successes without Winnemem Wintu peoples—but now Winnemem Wintus are separated from their Salmon relatives (Yoshiyama and Fisher 2001). Some Native people worked in the gold mines, but a state-sponsored genocide continued to exist into the mid-nineteenth century. Native peoples have always had complex ways of navigating and surviving settler-colonial structures aimed at the elimination of Indigenous peoples. And while California Indians did not have a seat at the table during the gold rush, many tribal nations are asserting their own self-determination during the green rush. Gilio-Whitaker (2019) reminds us, however, that "modernity's challenge to Native governments is to balance the material needs of the nation with the original instructions of the Creator within a governing structure that forces choices between resource-based and relationship-based management" (72). The newly emergent legal cannabis industry is one space in which Native nations are trying to strike that balance.

Several tribal nations in California have expressed interest in and commitment to engagement in the cannabis industry as a source of economic development. However, Proposition 64—which legalized recreational cannabis in California—does not include, incorporate, or even address Native American tribes. Former executive director of the California Growers Association Hezekiah Allen suggested that "tribal cannabis is probably the last big unsettled question in California cannabis policy" (quoted in Lewis 2016). State policymakers argue that addressing tribes in Proposition 64 would have been too complicated and time consuming. Instead, they claimed they would deal with it later. In short, because tribal nations were not included in state legislations to legalize and regulate recreational cannabis in California, Native American tribes have been shut out of California's regulated cannabis industry. To participate, tribal nations must waive their sovereign immunity.[6]

In response to the exclusion of tribes from the California state market, the California Native American Cannabis Association (C-NACA) formed in 2017. C-NACA currently represents 25 federally recognized tribes in California (of 109 total). Most of C-NACA's membership tribes are located in remote locations that are unsuitable for gaming, have high levels of unemployment, or are targeted by illicit cultivators and manufacturers as well as the criminal justice system. Their mission as stated on their website in 2019 is to "protect tribal sovereignty and promote tribal self-reliance by assisting California tribes in designing and implementing comprehensively regulated, legal cannabis and hemp enterprises that benefit tribal communities." On behalf of the member tribes, C-NACA has voiced to state regulatory agencies tribal concerns and frustrations on being excluded from the state cannabis market. But currently there is no mechanism for tribes to participate in the state cannabis market without waiving sovereign immunity and submitting to state licensing authority and unfettered regulatory jurisdiction on tribal lands (BCC n.d.).

Representing tribal governments, C-NACA aimed to negotiate with California to reach a fair and equitable agreement for tribe participation in the state cannabis market. Using agreements in Oregon, Washington, and Nevada as models, C-NACA helped develop Assembly Bill 924 to provide tribal access to the state's legal cannabis market. Similarly to tribal gaming, AB 924 would allow a tribe's government to enter into a regulatory agreement or compact with the governor to develop a tribal cannabis regulatory commission. Under AB 924 tribes would still agree to comply with state regulations but would remain the regulatory authority. However, the state pushed for complete regulatory jurisdiction on tribal lands and authority to keep any taxes levied by the tribe (Levitan 2019). Moreover, proposed amendments to the bill by the California Legislature would have forced tribes to waive sovereign immunity, receive approval from local governments, and defer jurisdiction to state regulators (Herrington 2019). These terms were unacceptable to C-NACA and its membership tribes. The bill was killed in a Senate committee meeting in November 2018. California Indian tribes continue to be excluded from the state cannabis market.

Despite this exclusion, the Iipay Nation of Santa Ysabel, located in a rural part of eastern San Diego County, opened the Mountain Source Cannabis Dispensary on the reservation in February 2019. The operation is conducted and regulated pursuant to the Santa Ysabel Cannabis Enterprise Code, which created the Santa Ysabel Tribal Cannabis Regulatory Agency (TCRA) and was ratified by membership in August 2015. In a press release dated March 5, 2019, the TCRA stated: "While denying Santa Ysabel's cannabis operators access to the California market, this action by the State also denies the State a share of revenues generated by Santa Ysabel's cannabis sales because Santa Ysabel is not obligated to charge state taxes for the sale of cannabis products from the Nation's lands" (Santa Ysabel Tribal Cannabis Regulatory Agency 2019). As the experiences of the Iipay Nation demonstrate, numerous barriers to access—primarily access to state markets while retaining sovereign immunity—persist for several tribal nations in California. In April 2019 C-NACA sent a letter to Governor Gavin Newsom that outlined tribal concerns with California's cannabis industry. Because AB 924 failed to get through the California Legislature, there are significant access issues for tribal nations. These include: "The inability of tribal enterprises to supply cannabis products to state-licensed distributors and retailers, a lack of coordination between state cannabis regulators and tribal cannabis regulators, impediments to state-licensed laboratory testing of cannabis products generated by tribal cannabis operators, and a lack of state resources to address the on-reservation adverse impacts of the State's legal cannabis commerce" (Braithwaite 2019). In a presentation to the California Bureau of Cannabis Control Advisory Committee in June 2019, C-NACA articulated the crux of the issue: "Unfortunately, the State of California, has created barriers to tribal nation participation in the California cannabis market by enacting regulations which treat tribal nations as business entities rather than sovereign governments, establishing requirements that either don't apply to tribal nations or which tribal nations as sovereign governments cannot meet due to their federal designation as dependent sovereign nations (i.e. CEQA requirements). In spite of repeated overtures, state cannabis regulatory agencies have refused to interact with tribal cannabis regulatory agencies for the benefit and consumer protection of California's cannabis consumers" (C-NACA 2019). C-NACA requested that the BCC advisory committee encourage the governor's office and state cannabis regulatory agencies to interact with tribes on a government-to-government basis. Because the state has failed to engage with tribal nations, the Iipay Nation of Santa Ysabel has implemented a cannabis business exclusively on tribal lands that does not contribute revenue to the state of California.

C-NACA makes an important connection between the support of tribal cannabis operations and the issue of trespass cultivation. "If history can be a guide on matters of marijuana, a failure to recognize responsible tribal governments that regulate cannabis in safe, controlled environments will serve to encourage undesirable non-tribal operators growing marijuana on tribal reservations 'off the radar' and will only exacerbate safety and law enforcement concerns. Cannabis has been and is still grown illegally in many of the State's less accessible and hard-to-police locations, like tribal reservations. A well-regulated and economically successful legal cannabis enterprise on tribal lands provides the resources necessary to discourage and eradicate illegal marijuana operations" (Braithwaite 2019). Similar to tribal lands in Northern California, tribal lands in Southern California are often remote and targeted for trespass cultivation, leading to a variety of ecological concerns and safety hazards.

While some tribal nations in California experience direct environmental impacts on their ancestral lands and waters from cannabis cultivation, other tribal nations are excluded from the emerging legal industry altogether. Both experiences demonstrate the ways the green rush systemically benefits settler populations at the expense of Indigenous peoples. This is a repetition of a familiar pattern: like the gold rush, timber rush, and fish rush before it, the green rush has disproportionately impacted Native territories and lifeways and the settler state reaps the benefits. The potential implications of tribal exclusion from the cannabis industry have important considerations for tribal sovereignty as well. Tribal nations maintain a unique government-to-government relationship with the United States. This is fundamentally different from other racialized minorities in the United States because tribal governments are sovereign nations with a right to self-determination, and the upholding of this nation-to-nation relationship serves as the basis for the US government's legitimacy. If the state refuses to engage in a peer relationship with a tribe, and if tribal sovereignty is not acknowledged and taken seriously within the California commercial cannabis industry, it could set a dangerous precedent for the exercise of tribal sovereignty in other capacities and ultimately put tribal rights in jeopardy. Tribal nations have much at stake; our sovereign right to determine our own laws is critical to our livelihoods and collective continuance as culturally and politically distinct peoples. Though tribal nations are not immune from critique of the ecological impacts of resource-based management approaches, it is critical to make space for tribal sovereignty within cannabis policy.

CANNABIS AND ENVIRONMENTAL RESEARCH

The environmental impacts of cannabis cultivation have only recently become a subject of concern in California and beyond. Prior to 2012 very few scientific studies focused on the environmental impact of cannabis cultivation (Wartenberg et al. 2021). Even as late as 2019 the North American Cannabis Summit featured only three panels—out of hundreds—that pertained to environmental concerns. From an environmental science perspective, most of our knowledge about cannabis has been developed in the past decade, and put simply, we don't know much. Historically, we have gained understanding of the ecological impact of the gold mining, timber harvest, overfishing, and, other resource-extraction processes by documenting the ecological impacts. Typically the approach of Western science and the settler state is to allow ecological harms to occur and then quantify them and use that in future decision-making.[7] While scientifically sound environmental regulations are beneficial, ecological concerns, especially concerning water, are becoming more and more urgent. And who is paying the cost of ecological harms in the meantime, while we wait for scientists to study them?

Economic projections tell us that cannabis production will continue to expand and we can therefore assume that the current ecological impact of cannabis will continue to expand as well. In the context of settler-colonial resource rushing, cannabis is not unique. Many ecological concerns resulting from corporate agriculture in California (e.g., water use and drought and climate change) are also applicable to cannabis production. Theoretical critiques of capitalistic resource extraction levied against the gold rush, the timber rush, and the fish rush remain relevant. Our ecosystems are already overtaxed and now we're adding a new industry into the equation.

To understand the ecological impacts of cannabis cultivation, it is necessary to understand the variety of cultivation techniques employed by cannabis cultivators. While much of the focus in Northern California is on the ecological impacts of outdoor cultivation, indoor cultivation also increased significantly as a result of the War on Drugs–era prohibition tactics of the 1980s, as it provided protection against constant surveillance in the hills. By 1985 one-quarter of all cannabis was produced indoors and between 1986 and 1987 there was a 49 percent increase (Johnson 2017). In addition to evading law enforcement, indoor cultivation was attractive to many because it "removed two key obstacles to high-quality cannabis growth: the once-a-year harvest and the removal of male plants to produce the coveted sinsemilla" (Johnson 2017, 138). Indoor cultivation facilitated controlled environments that allowed growers to manipulate particular characteristics of the plant. *Mother Jones* enticed readership with hopes of profit: "You can grow $30,000 worth of top-grade sinsemilla in a space as small as your master bedroom" (quoted in Johnson 2017, 137). Today, however, many farms do not adhere to one or the other but use a combination of indoor and outdoor techniques, referred to as mixed-light. Indoor and outdoor cultivation present a different set of environmental concerns; whereas outdoor cultivation can disrupt surrounding ecosystems, indoor and mixed-light cultivation often require more energy (e.g., lighting, water, and air circulation) and fertilizers (Wartenberg et al. 2021). "Cannabis factory farming involves energy-intensive lighting, space conditioning, dehumidification, artificial CO_2 fertilization, water reclamation, and other processes to boost yields while maintaining year-round tropical indoor conditions irrespective of the outdoor climate" (Mills 2021, 483). In one 2012 study, the electricity use of legal and illegal indoor cannabis cultivation was estimated to be 1 percent of national electricity use, with a total cost of $6 billion a year (Mills 2012). This is the energy equivalent to 4 percent of all US agriculture (Mills 2021). In Northern California, especially within tribal territories, we are primarily dealing with outdoor and mixed-light cultivation strategies (and while indoor cultivation is a rapidly growing ecological concern in urban areas, it is not the focus of this work). Thus, a more significant and impactful contrast among cannabis cultivation sites in this region is between licit and illicit farming.

California has two cannabis industries: a rapidly expanding and corporatizing legal commercial industry and the ever-present robust black market. The existence of a thriving illicit market makes it more challenging to detect, quantify, and regulate the resulting environmental harms. While mitigating environmental harm has been a critical argument for legalization, trespass cultivation persists. Optimistically, even if legalization is able to eliminate trespass cultivation—which, as long as federal prohibition persists, remains unlikely—it will be a gradual process, and in the interim, environmental impacts occurring from both licit and illicit cultivation will continue to occur simultaneously. We must be cognizant of both when analyzing the environmental impacts of the green rush. Illicit cultivation sites, usually located on public lands or tribal lands, are referred to as "trespass grows." However, it is critical to note here that within a framework of settler colonialism, public lands are tribal lands, and the dispossession of those lands should be understood as an ongoing process, not a settled event. Regardless of whether tribal nations hold jurisdiction over all extents of their ancestral territory, tribal peoples maintain relations and obligations to their homelands.

Trespass cultivation is pervasive throughout the state (see figure 3) and often presents a wide-ranging variety of ecological hazards including, but not limited to, unregulated water diversions, clear-cutting, road construction, waste dumping, and harm to wildlife through pesticide contamination. Because illicit cannabis operations are invested in remaining undetected, the actual ecological impact of cannabis is very difficult to quantify. To avoid detection, illicit cannabis production is often found in remote biologically sensitive watersheds (Carah et al. 2015). In other words, the reasons that Northern California was an attractive place to cultivate cannabis during prohibition—inaccessibility and heavy forest cover—are the reasons why, ecologically speaking, it does not make sense to cultivate large quantities in the region. However, in California, land management agencies reported a 300 percent increase in trespass cannabis grow sites between 2006 to 2010 (Rose, Brownlee, and Bricker 2018).

During Operation Yurok, which began in 2014, the Yurok Tribe Environmental Program (YTEP) documented environmental harms and threats of trespass cultivation sites in Yurok ancestral territory. At the Yurok Tribe annual membership meeting in August 2018, YTEP (2018) reported on the primary environmental concerns of trespass cultivation within Yurok ancestral territory: first, the lack of sanitation facilities at cultivation sites and resulting human waste pollution has potential impacts to water quality and human health; second, solid and hazardous waste, including household garbage, abandoned vehicles, spent irrigation lines, and other equipment are left behind at cultivation sites; third, non–point source pollution, such as pesticides, fertilizers, and spent soils, come into contact with both groundwater and surface water, risking local wildlife exposure; fourth, unpermitted roadbuilding and the clearing of land for cultivation facilitates sedimentation in surface waters, thereby filling in critical Salmon spawning habitat; and lastly, and of grave concern during Operation Yurok, are ruinous water diversions. In some cases entire streams have been diverted for cannabis cultivation, which has detrimental effects to endangered Salmon, steelhead trout, and sensitive amphibian species and simultaneously diminishes water quality and quantity for public and private water systems. This was especially significant for Yurok Tribe members, because not everybody on the reservation has access to a community water system and many folks obtain household water directly from a stream or a spring—making it more likely for residents to suffer negative impacts from chemical fertilizers, solid waste, and sediment due to cannabis cultivation. The documentation of environmental harms is critical for the tribe's efforts to protect ancestral lands and waters. That being said, the environmental research conducted during Operation Yurok required collaboration with local, state, and federal law enforcement (discussed in further detail in chapter 6). While the Yurok Tribe should be lauded for bringing this collaboration together and making environmental research at illicit cultivation sites possible, the experience illustrates the existing barriers of conducting research on illicit cannabis cultivation. In other words, had Operation Yurok not been carried out, the Yurok Tribe Environmental Program likely would not have the data it needs to advocate for land and water protection.

Not only does illicit cultivation make it more difficult to quantify the ecological harms of cannabis production in the region, it also makes the

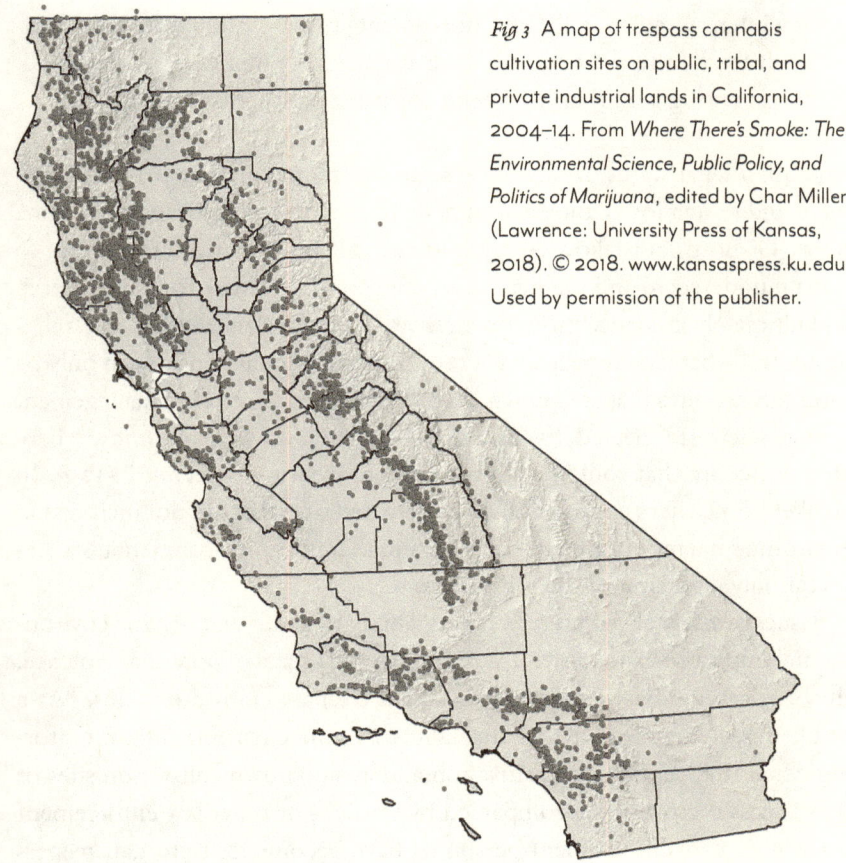

Fig 3 A map of trespass cannabis cultivation sites on public, tribal, and private industrial lands in California, 2004–14. From *Where There's Smoke: The Environmental Science, Public Policy, and Politics of Marijuana*, edited by Char Miller (Lawrence: University Press of Kansas, 2018). © 2018. www.kansaspress.ku.edu. Used by permission of the publisher.

process of conducting research far more difficult and, at times, dangerous. Higley et al. (2018) write:

> This research is far more difficult to conduct than most ecological studies in North America. The sites are hidden, and when they are in use they are typically defended by armed workers. The value of the crops they are protecting is generally in the tens to hundreds of thousands of dollars, and therefore their guards are likely to protect their crops with violence. To conduct our research, then, requires us doing so under the protection of large groups of [law enforcement] officers at the time of eradication; even if we visit in the nongrowing months

of winter, we still need [law enforcement] presence for safety concerns, albeit few of them. In addition, we are generally limited to visiting and documenting sites that have been recently eradicated. (62–63)

The quasi-legal status of cannabis creates substantial barriers to the assessment and mitigation of the environmental impacts of its cultivation. As Anne Short Gianotti and fellow researchers (2017) show, cultivators' desires to remain undetected and physical safety concerns both work to limit research and ultimately influence "who does research, how and where that research is done, and what data is collected" (129). Environmental impacts can only be monitored at sites that are known. As one California-based land management agency scientist reflected, "When we're sampling, do we really know where all the sites are that could be contributing to what we're seeing?" (129). In all likelihood, there continue to be undetected sites that are not included in environmental monitoring or datasets, and therefore, environmental studies reveal only a portion of the full picture.

Issues of safety also limit researchers' ability to gather data on the environmental impact of cannabis cultivation. Due to threats of potential violence, they are often advised to avoid occupied trespass cultivation sites. "As a result, researchers report that they abort routine environmental monitoring when they see signs of cultivation and avoid known cultivation sites or only access them when accompanied by wardens or other law enforcement personnel. Law enforcement personnel have become de facto gatekeepers for field research" (Short Gianotti et al. 2017). Environmental sampling is time sensitive, and if the availability of law enforcement does not align with when areas can be accessed, environmental monitoring can be compromised. For example, "you might have a [cannabis] grow site where they have a lot of herbicides, chemicals, pesticides just sitting there, but they're not in the water. When you have your first big rain event, a lot of that could wash into the water and, unless you're sampling right then, you may have no clue that it was even there. And it has an effect but you have no way of being able to quantifiably or defensibly capture the contribution of that" (129). Requiring the presence of law enforcement and the time sensitivity of environmental sampling both limit the in-the-field research on the impacts of cannabis cultivation.

To avoid contact with sites entirely, much research has relied on aerial imagery to estimate the scope of production and the landscape-level impacts. Aerial imagery can detect greenhouses and visible outdoor cultivation, but it cannot detect cultivation in the understory (Bauer et al. 2015). Additionally, the aerial approach also limits the ability to understand how historic production trends have shifted. "We see this explosion in the open, photographable kind of cultivation because of the rise of the greenhouse in the end of the nineties, beginning of the 2000s. But that doesn't mean there wasn't a lot of weed growing in those watersheds before. So, you know, it's really hard to parse out how the impacts of [cannabis cultivation] have increased over time when you just don't know how much, you know, Mr. A grew on that parcel all through the 80s and 90s" (Short Gianotti et al. 2017, 130). Policy liberalization has contributed to the increase in visible cultivation—and thus why we're now able to detect cultivation via aerial imagery. In Humboldt County there was a nineteen-fold increase in greenhouses from 2004 to 2014 (Butsic and Brenner 2016). However, "while the current patterns of greenhouse production and visible outdoor cultivation make this a defensible technique for assessing *current* cultivation on private lands in the North Coast, it cannot be used to assess historic production or production on public lands because areas in cultivation may not be visible in aerial images" (Short Gianotti et al. 2017, 130, emphasis in original). Additionally, while aerial imagery can detect location, size, and placement of a grow site, there are many significant environmental indicators it cannot detect, such as "roads, trails, latrines, agrochemical storage sites, and waste dumps. Many of these features, along with impacts such as agricultural runoff, loss of water in streams, disturbance to wildlife by humans or domestic animals, and energy consumption, are invisible in satellite imagery and detectable only through fieldwork" (Wang, Brenner, and Butsic 2017, 500). Even fieldwork—in addition to the necessity of law enforcement and the time-sensitivity of environmental sampling—has its own constraints: "While researchers aim to account for cultivation sites in their study region, some sites inevitably go undetected leading to substantial uncertainty regarding the location and scope of cultivation . . . [thereby limiting] researchers' ability to establish baseline conditions" (Short Gianotti et al. 2017, 130).

Despite existing limitations, environmental research on cannabis cultivation has begun to materialize within the past decade. Published in 2018,

Where There's Smoke: The Environmental Science, Public Policy, and Politics of Marijuana is an interdisciplinary anthology that explores the environmental consequences of cannabis production. "The first of its kind," this text bridges the humanities and natural and social sciences to examine the environmental impacts of prohibition and cannabis cultivation on public, private, and tribal lands in a variety of contexts, including California, Colorado, and Oregon (C. Miller 2018). One chapter in particular addresses the impact of cannabis cultivation on Hoopa tribal lands, noting that in addition to the environmental impacts felt throughout the state, cannabis activity also negatively impacts Hoopa cultural and spiritual activities (Higley et al. 2018).

While the impacts of cannabis cultivation on Hoopa lands is explicitly discussed in *Where There's Smoke*, the relationship between cannabis cultivation and settler colonialism is not. In 2019 the University of California, Berkeley launched the Cannabis Research Center (CRC) (n.d.) to engage in "interdisciplinary scholarship on the social and environmental dimensions of cannabis production." This is significant because it indicates an important shift in research priorities and voices concern about the ecological toll of cannabis production. The CRC has compiled briefs on water and land use in cannabis agriculture, produced several peer-reviewed publications, and facilitated webinar series to disseminate information. Ariani Wartenberg et al. (2021) conducted a literature review of documented pathways of environmental impacts related to cannabis. They examined qualitative literature published between 2012 and 2020 and identified six distinct environmental impact pathways from cannabis cultivation and consumption, including land-cover change, water use, pesticide use, energy use, air pollution, and water pollution. However, with few exceptions, studies thus far have "focus[ed] on single environmental pathways, suggesting that systematic or cumulative analyses of cannabis cultivation impacts are currently lacking" (100). Additionally, environmental analyses of cannabis cultivation must also consider legacy impacts of previous waves of resource rushing.

The way the settler state acknowledges cumulative legacy impacts is through the creation of a baseline in an environmental impact report. A baseline refers to the original status of the environment in the area before the development work of the project is started; in California, the baseline is established at the time of the initiation of the California Environmental Quality Act (CEQA) process. Environmental impacts are then considered within the context of the established baseline. Critiques of baselines are not new, by any means—scholars have long pointed out that the year or two establishing baseline conditions prior to conducting an environmental impact report is insufficient (Hilborn and Walters 1981). However, baselines also reinforce the idea that existing environmental harms are part of the "original" status of the environment. So, in the context of cannabis cultivation, "prior illegal activity is not a project for purposes of cumulative impact analysis under CEQA; rather, it is a baseline condition against which the impacts of the project under consideration are assessed" (Humboldt County 2018a, 2–7). Baselines serve to normalize settler-colonial ecological inscriptions by including the past century of environmental destruction as the original status of the environment. From Indigenous perspectives, our baselines do not include dammed Rivers, clear-cut forests, or corporate agriculture. Our baselines include Rivers that turn dark when the Salmon come home to spawn and healthy forests managed with cultural fire and acorns for everybody. Our baselines preceded the gold rush, the timber rush, the fish rush, and the green rush. In Humboldt County, baseline cultivation operations include the legacy impacts of unpermitted cultivation sites, including large-scale sites (Lazar 2016, 12). Notably, Humboldt County did not initially express the need to invest the time or financial resources to conduct an environmental impact report and only did so when faced with the threat of litigation.

Despite the legalization of cannabis, trespass cultivation remains a concern for tribal nations. Prohibition at a federal level ensures a market for unregulated cannabis grown in California—all without the permitting fees and tax obligations. While the goal of a legal regulated cannabis industry is the elimination of trespass cultivation and associated ecological harms, that has yet to happen. And many are skeptical of this outcome due to the continuation of federal prohibition policies (Higley et al. 2018). The ecological impacts of trespass and regulated cultivation may very well differ considerably, but the impacts of trespass cultivation remain relevant for tribal nations; it is an ongoing issue both within and outside of reservation boundaries. Moreover, the legacy impacts resulting from decades of the unconsented taking of natural resources for cultivation and numerous abandoned cultivation sites yet to be cleaned and restored present numerous environmental and human health concerns for tribes. Tribal nations, specifically tribal environmental agencies and departments, face many challenges to environmental monitoring and assessment as well as unique sets of challenges due to land dispossession and the resulting lack of jurisdiction. Because significant cultural resources are often located on ancestral territory—and not within the boundaries of the reservation, therefore not within tribal jurisdiction—in order to take action to monitor and assess trespass cultivation, tribes must collaborate with local, state, and federal law enforcement and various land management agencies that hold jurisdiction over ancestral territory. Additionally, environmental impacts, such as water diversions, that occur off-reservation also impact cultural resources within reservation boundaries.

Trespass cultivation is ongoing and impacts are still accumulating. In 2020 the California Department of Fish and Wildlife issued a special issue of the *California Fish and Wildlife Journal* focused on the impacts of cannabis cultivation on fish and wildlife. In the introduction, Mourad Gabriel and Greta Wengert (2020) reflect on the current historical moment we find ourselves in: "This issue [is] coming on the heels of an unprecedented cannabis cultivation season where both unpermitted private as well as trespass public land cultivation appear to be unbridled in plant production and environmental damage. This is our ninth season of data collection on the vast environmental impacts of this activity, and collectively, we have documented over 650 cannabis cultivation sites. Nevertheless, this season is proving to be on par with our first data collection season in 2012 in terms of impacts to California's natural resources" (10). Since legalization, law enforcement has consistently detected illicit cultivation and illegal water diversions. In July 2021 Humboldt County law enforcement, in collaboration with several land management agencies, served twenty-five search warrants for illegal cannabis cultivation across four watersheds; in total they eradicated thirty-five thousand plants and documented approximately ninety-seven environmental violations. Violations included water diversions, water pollution, and trash deposits in or near waterways (Humboldt County Sheriff's Office 2021). Trespass cultivation also continues to flourish in other areas of the state. In July 2021 the Los Angeles County Sheriff's Department seized sixteen tons of cannabis from over two hundred locations, with an estimated value of $1.19 billion; illegal water diversions were also documented at many of these sites (Powell 2021). Much of the damage to the environment that has already occurred has yet to be addressed. While the ecological impacts of regulated cannabis—which are also varied depending on method, geography, and scale—are just now beginning to be studied, trespass cultivation provides us with important information about the ecological toll of cannabis production in northwestern California over the past decade.

The relationship between legalization and production—and especially trespass cultivation—is complex. On the one hand, legalization has led to increased production. Trends and characteristics associated with cannabis legalization include cultivation expansion, shifts toward urban areas, and increased size of cultivation facilities (Wartenberg et al. 2021). Scott Bauer, a senior environmental scientist at the California Department of Fish and Wildlife (2017), notes: "There's just more. The sites are bigger; there are more of them. So [legalization has] kind of opened the floodgates." Legalization, therefore, has provided an opportunity for newcomers to enter the market and given preexisting growers the confidence to increase production. In this regard cannabis is not unique to other agricultural products. When prices drop, you have to grow more. Moreover, early data suggests that many cultivators in California are not going through the permitting process. A California Growers Association report published in 2018 estimated that California had approximately sixty-eight thousand cultivators prior to the development of the regulated market. For some perspective, there were sixty-eight hundred active temporary cultivation licenses issued statewide at the end of 2018, accounting for only 10 percent of cultivators. However, only twenty-eight hundred entities hold those sixty-eight hundred licenses, meaning only 4 percent of cultivators in the state are entering the regulated market (California Growers Association 2018). An online survey of 1,750 cannabis consumers in California and Colorado in 2018 revealed that 18 percent of California cannabis consumers still purchase from an unlicensed source, and 84 percent of those consumers plan to continue obtaining their supply from an illicit source (Price 2019).

On the other hand, some studies suggest that legalization has reduced trespass cultivation. One study found that legalization policies have decreased the reports of illegal cannabis operations within 111 national forests throughout the country (Prestemon et al. 2019). The reduction of trespass cultivation within national forests is a step in the right direction—especially considering that California has the highest number of cannabis grows on national forests. However, there are many variables that could affect this trend. For example, the imposition of taxes on legal cannabis sales could make trespass cultivation in national forests "somewhat more frequent" (Prestemon et al. 2019, 11). Another study (Klassen and Anthony 2019) examined the impact of legalization on trespass cultivation in national forests in Oregon and Washington and found that recreational cannabis legalization significantly contributes to a reduction in trespass cultivation in national forests in Oregon but not in Washington:

> According to the US Forest Service, while there may have been a decline in discovered grow sites in the Pacific Northwest in recent years, they are of the opinion that this is unlikely to be the result of recreational cannabis legalization. It is posited that decreases in resources and partnerships are more likely to be contributing to a decline in the agency's ability to discover and document grow sites. In fact, the US Forest Service suggests that legalization of recreational cannabis has resulted in many state and local cooperators reducing or eliminating resources that typically assist the Forest Service with counter marijuana cultivation operations. . . . It should also be noted that the US Forest Service reports no observable difference in the size and location of grow sites after the implementation of legalization in the Pacific Northwest, and does not believe that the long-term effects of legalization will reduce illegal marijuana cultivation in national forests. (45)

Additionally, oftentimes the categories of legal and illegal are not so simple to delineate. Though a cultivator may be licensed, they may not be in compliance with all existing environmental regulations. Environmental regulations are difficult to enforce, especially for farms sited in remote or difficult-to-access areas.

What does all of this mean? The hope was that a legal cannabis industry would make the illicit industry economically unfeasible and the rational economic subject would abandon ship. But data tells us that's not happening. Thus, we have a regulated cannabis industry with measured ecological impact—but *on top of that* we also have an illicit cannabis industry whose ecological harms we are unable to quantify, or even survey. We must recognize the limitations of contemporary environmental science of cannabis which, admittedly, remains in its infancy. Considering the clandestine nature and safety concerns of monitoring trespass cultivation, the ecological impacts of cannabis production in California are certainly more than what we are able to quantify. The following three chapters—organized around land dispossession, water, and toxics—provide a more in-depth examination of the available environmental research on cannabis cultivation and situates these impacts within a context of settler colonialism.

6 NO JUSTICE ON STOLEN LAND

Cannabis Cultivation and Land Dispossession

Marijuana farming is the perfect embodiment of a people's capitalism.
—Ray Raphael, *Cash Crop*

[Capitalism] relies on violence to meet its goals, so when you hear this green rush you start to think what's going to happen is maybe a sincere effort at making marijuana a money-making venture, but out of that comes capitalism and violence. You can't get away from it. And I think about what that means to Native people in this area, if people are going to call it a rush . . . you can't get away from what that really means. It has always meant a dispossession of land, land use, land rights of Native peoples at the behest of capitalism. The idea that what is more important is making money than anything else. —Cutcha Risling Baldy, author interview, August 28, 2017

In April 2019 I participated in a panel discussion titled "The Social, Economic, and Ecological Sustainability of Cannabis Production in Northern California." As one might have expected, I was asked the question, What does a socially and/or environmentally just cannabis industry look like to you? While perhaps I should have anticipated this question, I was baffled. The idea that any just industry rooted in capitalist logics of property and commodification could be built on stolen territory requires a strong dose of historical amnesia. The very territory on which the cannabis industry is built was acquired through violent force. Settler-colonial violence is not temporally bound to a bygone past, but rather is "reasserted each day of occupation" (Tuck and Yang 2012, 5). Tribal nations in Northern California have experienced environmental and cultural harm directly attributed to cannabis cultivation—including both illicit and legally regulated cultivation. My central claim is that justice—social, environmental, or otherwise—is impossible to achieve on stolen land; more specifically, a socially and environmentally just cannabis industry is impossible to achieve on stolen Indigenous lands. Lots of folks seem to want to prioritize social and environmental justice as central features of the cannabis industry, yet I encounter very few who are willing to engage with the history of land dispossession and genocide in California and with their positionality as settlers profiting from stolen Indigenous territory.

Cannabis cultivation as a wave of resource extraction continues to maintain and rely on settler-colonial processes that, by definition, work to facilitate Indigenous dispossession. The former natural resources director of the Karuk Tribe, Leaf Hillman (Karuk), illustrates the repetitive nature of settler-colonial resource extraction in Northern California and draws connections between legal cannabis cultivation in Humboldt County with preceding waves of resource extraction: "Humboldt's Tribes have had to struggle through the gold rush, then the timber rush, and now the green rush. Each wave of resource extractors deals another critical hit to the fishery resources that are central to Tribal culture and economies" (quoted in Kemp 2018a). The gold rush facilitated land dispossession through state-sanctioned genocide and unratified treaties. The timber rush continued dispossession through legal processes (e.g., Free Timber Act, Timber and Stone Act) and the creation of federal and state forest reserves. The fish rush and construction of dams have decimated Native food sources, making it difficult, if not impossible in some areas, for Indigenous peoples to harvest, gather, or consume traditional foods. The impacts of cannabis cultivation cannot be examined in isolation; rather, they must be understood within a historical legacy of settler-colonial resource extraction that has perpetrated violence against Indigenous bodies and lands. The political and economic structures that facilitate patterns of extractive industries maintain Indigenous dispossession through settler-colonial processes, including policymaking, consultation, and impact assessments, while providing to the settler state the ethical justification to continue to perpetuate violence against Indigenous lands and bodies (Simpson 2017).

In California schools we're taught that genocide—if that word is uttered at all—is ancient history. In reality we are only 170 years out. For a people who have stewarded and cared for this region for millennia, the gold and green rushes are but a blip on the time scale. Our ancestors survived the volunteer militiamen, composed of average settler citizens, who slaughtered Native people, families, and communities and were then reimbursed by the nearest municipality. Our ancestors fought to retain our homelands, despite the fact that the US government refused to ratify any of the eighteen treaties negotiated in California. Our ancestors maintained and passed down knowledge about the land and how to steward our ecosystems despite fire suppression legislation that targeted the ability to feed ourselves. Our ancestors endured genocidal boarding schools—where they are now unearthing the remains of Indigenous children—as back-to-the-landers settled our clear-cut territories and called it free land. Our ancestors resisted as they watched settlers dam our Rivers and kill our fish. Now we find ourselves located at ground zero of cannabis production.

Like awareness of genocidal violence in California, Native perspectives are largely absent and underrepresented in environmental decision-making and natural resource management throughout the state and beyond (Hernandez 2022). Native peoples' concerns over River health and fish kills are consistently delegitimized. Frequent lip service is given to Native peoples—like the land acknowledgment that was spoken before the 2019 panel presentation—but little to no engagement with how the cannabis industry maintains settler-colonial violence. We're continually told that it's just a plant. Cannabis cultivation is small scale. Growers are *really, really* trying. We all care about the environment. We all have equal claim to these "natural resources." Or, we're told to quit complaining about cannabis, because other extractive industries are much worse. In comparison to other agricultural industries, cannabis doesn't use *that much* water. Native folks should be grateful we're now growing cannabis instead. But what is the reality that tribal peoples in Northern California have experienced? We have seen entire streams dewatered. Our more-than-human relatives have been poisoned. Our forests have been cleared to make way for cultivation and roads. Our basketweavers and cultural practitioners have been held at gunpoint for the mistake of wandering into a grow site on their own ancestral territory.

The next three chapters explore the ecological and cultural impacts of cannabis cultivation on Indigenous peoples in Northern California, organized around land, water, and toxics. Of course, these distinctions are artificial in that impacts to lands and waters are interconnected and cannot be disentangled. Even the concept of land itself is limiting: "The concept of land itself may be a result of colonial capitalism. That is, Native peoples have a spiritual relationship to the entire biosphere, not just the land. However, colonialism separates land from the rest of the creation as a marker of territorial expansion" (Teves, Smith, and Raheja 2015, 66–67). But this kind of rhetorical separation is necessary in order to transform land as kin into land as property, and it facilitates the commodification and dismemberment of ecosystems. Land dispossession, like settler colonialism, is an ongoing structure rather than a singular completed event. The forms of land dispossession discussed here include ecological destruction and land alteration, physical and financial barriers that prevent Indigenous peoples from accessing their homelands, and the threat of physical violence for tribe members and employees who cross paths with a trespass cannabis cultivation site.

CANNABIS CULTIVATION AND LAND DISPOSSESSION

Dispossession is a term used to critique the macrohistorical processes through which Indigenous peoples have been divested of their lands and central to settler-colonial logics of territorial acquisition. However, within the critique of dispossession is a critique of the capitalist logics of possession, property, and ownership—all at odds with Indigenous conceptions of and relations to land built on kin, reciprocity, and mutual care. Robert Nichols (2020) responds to the question often asked by critics of Indigenous resistance and decolonial thinkers: "If Indigenous peoples didn't conceptualize their relationship to land in terms of property, how could it be stolen?" Nichols refers to this as the dilemma of dispossession: either you reinforce colonial property relations through discourse of dispossession *or* you admit to not being the "original possessors" and thus not a victim of theft. Of course, this critique privileges a specific form of land tenure and relationship that emerges from a specific cultural context. There is nothing natural or inherent in organizing geographical space in terms of property. Additionally, even proponents of this critique of dispossession will concede that relations of importance that are not marked in property relations can be forcibly altered. If one's grandmother is kidnapped, the fact that she was not your property does not condone or justify the act of theft. Nichols (2020) argues that Indigenous theorizations of dispossession both presuppose *and* resist the language of possession: "Dispossession of this sort combines two processes typically thought distinct: it transforms nonproprietary relations into proprietary ones while, at the same time, systematically transferring control and title of this (newly formed) property. In this way, dispossession merges commodification (or perhaps more accurately, 'propertization') and theft into one moment" (8). The process of transforming living Earth and kinship networks into property and commodities is itself an act of dispossession, a dispossession that is maintained through the spatial organization of the settler state—which works to facilitate processes of land dispossession long after lands have been claimed or contested. In other words, the settler state "as a structure of domination [is] *predicated* on our ongoing dispossession" (Coulthard 2014, 23).

Dispossession is more than just land loss; the loss of lands also separates Indigenous peoples from the place-based practices and knowledges that shape Indigenous political systems, economies, and nationhood (Simpson 2017). "For just as colonialism is not a single event of the past, we must think beyond the notion that 'land theft' and land dispossession are single events of the past. Instead, colonialism is an ongoing process that takes place through the alteration of land, the alteration of species composition and ecological structures, and the alteration of relationships between people and the more-than-human entities known as nature" (Norgaard 2019, 20). Indigenous land dispossession occurs and is maintained in a multitude of ways, including alternating land and species composition, imposing management regimes, severing Native relationships with place via extraction and removal, and imposing settler-colonial conceptions of land and capitalist economies that transform relatives into commodities. As such, land dispossession is fundamentally an ecological process. Kyle Whyte (2018), among others, argues that settler-colonial dispossession requires the inscription of settler-colonial ecologies on top of existing Indigenous ecologies (see also Whyte, Caldwell, and Schaefer 2018; Whyte 2016). "In other words, settler colonial societies seek to inscribe their own homelands over Indigenous homelands, thereby erasing the history, lived experiences, social reality and possibilities of a future of Indigenous peoples. Settlers seek to inhabit the territories they newly inhabit as if they are—so to speak—the 'Indigenous' populations" (Whyte 2016, 159). This requires transforming Earth and more-than-human relatives into natural resources, which can then become the property of settlers or the settler state. Then those now-created natural resources are used for the benefit of settler populations at the expense of Indigenous populations. The conversion of Indigenous homelands into agricultural lands, the damming of ancestral Rivers, the suppression of fire and other fire management practices, to name just a few examples, all work to erase necessary socioecological contexts for Indigenous peoples and continue the work of settler-colonial elimination. "Colonialism as alteration of the land persists by denying people access to the practices needed to care for the land . . . [and] ecological alteration reworks the way people interact with knowledge and the land" (Norgaard 2019, 109–10). These acts facilitate what J. M. Bacon (2019) refers to as colonial ecological violence; however, Bacon warns that understanding colonial ecological violence cannot be limited to aggressive capitalist expansion, but rather must be viewed as part of the settler-colonial structure. This structure is maintained through settler-colonial processes such as policy-making, consultation, impact assessments, regulations, and contemporary forms of land management perpetuated by the state and private industry (Simpson 2017). These are then reinforced through management practices: "Since their inception, the federal government and the state of California have implemented land management policies on the Klamath that reflect and privilege non-Native values, economic systems, cultural practices, and cosmologies" (Norgaard 2019, 12). This control has been well documented, as California has long engaged in the patterns of resource rushing and continues to do so today in cannabis cultivation: landscape alteration, financial barriers that prevent Indigenous peoples from accessing their homelands, and threats of physical violence that prevent tribe members and employees from accessing territory or otherwise deterring cultural practices.

Environmental research on cannabis cultivation, as explained earlier, is challenging and limited. However, it has become clear that "land-use change from cannabis has the potential to directly and indirectly impact natural ecosystems at multiple scales" (Wartenberg et al. 2021, 100). In Northern California specifically, the emergence of cannabis cultivation took place under federal prohibition and during a domestic fight against drug production and use. Many early cultivators sited their farms in clandestine areas away from roads and infrastructure, so there is a historical precedent for grow sites to be predominantly clustered in remote and biologically sensitive watersheds that are near sensitive habitat and critical Salmon spawning areas. Van Butsic and Jacob C. Brenner (2016) conducted an aerial survey to map greenhouse and outdoor grow sites using imagery taken from the fall of 2012 and 2013. Randomly sampling 60 watersheds of the total 112 in Humboldt County, they located 4,428 grow sites, with an estimated average of 70 sites per watershed. Cannabis production was ongoing in 83 percent of sampled watersheds (as of 2014), suggesting it is already widespread. In Humboldt

County alone there was a nineteen-fold increase in greenhouses from 2004 to 2014. As part of their results, Butsic and Brenner argue that because there are "abundant grow sites clustered in steep locations far from developed roads, potential for significant water consumption, and close proximity to habitat for threatened species" there is a "high risk of negative ecological consequences associated with cannabis agriculture as it is currently practiced in northern California" (6). The impacts that environmental scientists are able to quantify are useful in that they provide a glimpse of what is occurring, although it is possible that we're only seeing the tip of the iceberg.

One source of ecological degradation associated with cannabis cultivation does not have anything to do with the plant itself, but rather is related to the infrastructure required. While some growers take advantage of old logging roads, many construct additional roads to access clandestine sites, which often creates habitat fragmentation, erosion, and sedimentation in surface waters that is harmful to critical Salmon spawning habitat. Within their sample, Butsic and Brenner found that over 68 percent of grows were located more than 500 meters from a developed road and only 15 percent were within 100 meters of a developed road. This means that the majority of grow sites required new road construction for access. They also found that over 23 percent of grows (both greenhouse and outdoor) were located on slopes exceeding a 30 percent grade. Such siting facilitates increased erosion, sedimentation, and landslides, and when it rains, toxicants and nutrient-heavy fertilizers slide down into the creeks and tributaries. Butsic and Brenner found that one-quarter of all grows in their sample were located within 500 meters of Chinook salmon habitat, and 6 percent were located within 100 meters.

The Butsic and Brenner study also found that grow sites tend to be spatially clustered within particular watersheds that can, in some cases, magnify ecological impacts. Thus, even if the footprint under cultivation is relatively small in comparison to the footprint required for timber extraction, the environmental impacts may extend far beyond the grow sites themselves and have disproportionate effects because of how they are clustered together. This finding is also reproduced in a follow-up study by Butsic et al. (2017): "Biophysical drivers are less important to location choice for cannabis farmers than for other farmers . . . areas with steep slopes, poor irrigation access, and location far from roads are just as likely places for cannabis cultivation as areas more suited to conventional agriculture" (78).[1] Historically, grow sites were clustered together because prohibition policies meant no how-to guides for cannabis existed at local gardening shops. Folks relied on knowledgeable neighbors. Indeed, there is an observable network effect within the cannabis industry; proximity to other cultivation sites both positively and significantly increases the likelihood of cultivation. "On one hand, clustering may diminish the spread of cannabis into further remote areas of the County. That is, cannabis impacts may be localized by virtue of clustering. On the other hand, clustering may actually magnify the effects of these grow operations, thereby intensifying local environmental impacts. Clustering thus presents a classic trade-off involving localized but relatively severe impacts versus widespread but relatively modest impacts" (Butsic et al. 2017, 78). This "support effect" is another example of the way in which responses to prohibition (remote siting, clustering, etc.) established patterns and magnified the effects of cultivation that are ecologically harmful to the region. And these magnified localized impacts are of most concern to tribal nations. As will be demonstrated in the next chapter regarding water usage, the cannabis industry often publishes statewide data to argue for the sustainability of cannabis cultivation in comparison to other industries, but statewide data is irrelevant to tribal nations that are experiencing localized impacts, such as the the dewatering of entire streams. These magnified and localized impacts occurring within tribal territories perpetuate the colonial ecological violence that tribal nations have experienced since invasion.

Another study examined the spatial distribution of cannabis agriculture in relation to forest fragmentation. Ian Wang et al. (2017) compare the effects of cannabis agriculture and timber harvest from 2000 to 2013. Building on Butsic and Brenner's 2016 study of the ways in which the clustered placement of cannabis farms creates disproportionate environmental effects, Wang, Brenner, and Butsic (2017) found that 1 square kilometer of land used for cannabis agriculture generates effects on forest fragmentation similar to 1 square kilometer of timber harvest and in some cases cannabis had a greater impact: "Timber harvest, which affects large stands of forest, causes greater patch and landscape division and more forest loss per unit area, whereas cannabis grows, which are typically more isolated and placed away from roads in forest interiors, generate proportionately greater losses of core area and greater increases in forest edge and shape complexity" (499). Diminishing the core of a forest interior disrupts habitat for culturally and ecologically sensitive species, and the increase in forest edge increases the vulnerability of species to predators and invasive species.[2] This study is significant because it upends the argument of many cannabis advocates, who routinely scapegoat the timber industry for ecological damages in the region as a means for inflating the sustainability of their own industry. Others argue that cannabis benefits the landscape because, in comparison to other patterns of resource extraction such as timber harvest, the effects are smaller scale. However, this assumption operates under the baseline assumption that land is meant to be extracted for the pursuit of human wealth accumulation. Cannabis cultivation can be better for the environment than timber extraction yet still produce environmental harm. CDFW biologist Scott Bauer (2017) explains:

> I give a lot of presentations. I talk to thousands of people about this. One of the things I try and point to is, you know, people want to argue that "well, the timber industry is worse." I get this kind of, typically from the cultivation industry, right? "Oh, timber is—what about timber?" Well, I said "timber is regulated." A clear-cut grows back. What you're doing doesn't grow back. So you take an acre, 5 acres, and you clear off a forest and you put up structures, and you put people out there, mainly year round. That's a permanent impact and it's not just that area of land that you've cleared because now you've got generators. How far does that noise impact the forest environment? And you've got lights—everybody is doing mixed lighting now. And sometimes they'll tarp it, it looks like a damn stadium out there, right? How far does that impact extend beyond the actual clear-cut or the cultivation area? (author interview, August 30, 2017)

Pointing fingers at another extractive industry does not lessen the impact of cannabis cultivation. Moreover, every extractive industry in California must be understood as part of a pattern of resource rushing. What we're really talking about here is adding to the list of legacy impacts, rather than stand-alone impacts.

In addition to the ecological transformations associated with resource rushing, the green rush has also drastically increased real estate prices. From an economic development perspective, the spike in land prices is good news. The wealth of landowners increases and tax revenues to the county and state increase. Of course, this beneficial perspective requires the privileging of settler-colonial worldviews that conceptualize land as property and work to benefit individual settlers and the settler state at the expense of Indigenous dispossession. Resource rushing in California has always been less about the specific resource/relative in question, and more about access and control over lands and the ability to assert ecological managerial authority. The real gold is not gold, after all, but the land itself.

Prior to legalization, green rush land-grabbing had to be conducted somewhat secretively. Cultivators "had to read between the lines when hunting for weed growing property. Savvy real estate agents knew to brag about supply and privacy, but outsiders browsing local listings would be none the wiser" (Burns 2017, para. 1). Many tribal peoples brought up this issue during their research interviews. Former interim director of the Yurok Tribe Environmental Program Micah Gibson (Yurok) recalls: "There was a realtor located in the Willow Creek area that had a map of all of the reservations and surrounding areas and was targeting properties that had streams or headwaters running through them for the sole purpose of making that his pitch to whomever is buying land, that it's located on 30 acres of land with this pristine stream running right through it that you can draft water to your garden from" (Micah Gibson, author interview, August 11, 2017). Following legalization, however, media coverage of the green rush land boom increased. In 2017 the *Cannifornian* reported on spikes in land prices in Humboldt County, noting that "local Realtors have likened the recent property demand to California's Gold Rush days" ("Marijuana Market" 2017). One real estate agency based in Eureka reported that prices increased for large acreages and ranch properties by 90 percent—and some increased by as much as 150 percent if they had the right conditions for cannabis cultivation.

Economic studies have correlated increasing property values and cannabis cultivation. Analyzing a dataset of over three thousand property transactions between 2000 and 2015, one study identified a positive and statistically significant relationship between cannabis cultivation density and property values, specifically the median existing cannabis density in a watershed is associated with a 3 to 4 percent increase in property price (Schwab and Butsic 2016). A subsequent study analyzed the impact of cannabis legalization on property values using fifteen hundred property transactions between 1990 and 2016, with particular attention to the effects of two legal changes in

2008 and 2016, respectively. In 2008 the *Kelley* decision eliminated quantitative limits on medicinal cannabis cultivation, which allowed growers to increase the number of plants under cultivation. After 2008 the doubling of cannabis production caused an approximate 8 percent appreciation in land values. In 2016 Humboldt County enacted the Commercial Cannabis Land Use Ordinance to create a legal permitting system for cannabis cultivation. Properties that were ineligible for a permit decreased in value and properties that were eligible for a permit increased markedly—ranging from a 49 to 98 percent increase (Schwab and Butsic 2017).

Many tribal nations are currently working to purchase lands that were, in many cases, unlawfully taken during the late nineteenth and early twentieth centuries.[3] The green rush, however, has complicated these efforts by forcing tribal nations to compete with incoming growers for land:

> I know that in our area there has been land that is part of the aboriginal territory of our tribe in Hoopa that was for sale and [the] Hoopa [Valley Tribe] offered the full price for the land but a weed grower came in and offered more for the full price of the land because it had water access and because it was, you know, it's in a so-called "isolated" space. And of course the landowner is going to take—and it was an all-cash offer, you know—so again you're dispossessing Native peoples and land. (Cutcha Risling Baldy, author interview, August 28, 2017)

Kari Norgaard (2019) articulates similar struggles for Karuk people: "Land that does come onto the market remains too expensive for most Indian families or even often for the Karuk Tribe to purchase. Today the new 'gold rush' (aka marijuana cultivation) has artificially inflated real estate prices astronomically" (60). Laura Hurwitz's (2017) work on settler colonialism and the back-to-the-land movement also identifies similar concerns. One informant said: "There is definitely a competing interest in land/property in the area and it's unfortunate that local Native people have such a hard time acquiring property on their own ancestral territory because they can't afford to keep up with rising costs as outside interest in moving to the area increases" (61).

In addition to landscape alteration and financial barriers, cannabis cultivation also poses threats to tribal cultural resources. The Wiyot Tribe has expressed concern about tribal cultural resources, specifically ethnobotanical resources, such as white oak, tanoak, and hazel stands, that risk further loss as a result of cannabis-related land-clearing (Canter 2017). The Blue Lake Rancheria Tribe has expressed concerns about cultural resource disturbance due to past and ongoing cannabis cultivation (Fuller 2017). Both archaeological sites and sacred sites have been disturbed by cultivation. Areas sought out for cultivation are often the places Native peoples reside. Many cultivators seek out "a flat spot, [a] great spot for greenhouses, and [with] a spring right there. Well, what does that mean? It was an occupied site most likely. Oak woodland, flat, spring—you're going to have an archaeological site, and so cultivation sites are typically found in the same location" (Scott Bauer, author interview, August 30, 2017). While legalization may be one way to prevent archaeological destruction, via the California Environmental Quality Act (CEQA) or county-level regulations, cultivators could be deterred from surveying their property if it could potentially result in ineligibility to participate in the state market. Additionally, non-tribe archaeologists may not be able to adequately recognize or identify sites of significance to tribal nations.

Clandestine trespass grows and the threats of physical violence associated with them can also deter cultural practitioners and thereby limit Indigenous peoples' abilities to access their ancestral territories. At one cultural committee meeting composed of Yurok elders in June 2018, many expressed their concerns about the ways in which large-scale cannabis cultivation has caused environmental destruction and will affect Yurok culture overall. Many elders are concerned about the safety of plant materials for basketry and how the various chemicals used to cultivate cannabis are impacting culturally important plant species and animals. Cultural activities such as gathering are

> a demonstration of the continuing revitalization of Indigenous societies, epistemologies, and world view. It is here that we gather, not just because it is important to carry on this tradition, but also because this continues the interrelationship the people formed with this land at the beginning of time. We gather not only because it is our right but because it is our responsibility, a responsibility that we have built through cultural and spiritual interaction with the land, and a responsibility that we must continue in order to maintain the bio-cultural sovereignty of our Indigenous spaces. (Risling Baldy 2013, 9)

Our ability to interact with and tend the natural world is critical to the survival of our cultures. Elder Janet Morehead (Karuk) makes a really important historical connection between settler surveillance on her ancestral territory and contemporary green rush violence:

> I know we're supposed to be able to gather berries and harvest mushrooms, but me and my sister have been harassed so many times that sometimes we wonder how long we're going to be able to keep this up. We both wear our tribal IDs around our neck—and heck, we're two old ladies that are obviously Indian—but I don't think people know that we are supposed to be able to do it on public lands. And then there are the marijuana growers. I'm afraid to get shot and I'm sick of being treated like I'm doing something wrong. (quoted in Norgaard 2019, 115)

Morehead makes an important connection between contemporary cannabis cultivators and imposed ecological management authorities, such as fish and game wardens. Although quite different and frequently in opposition, both trespass cultivators and fish and game wardens surveil, ultimately to prevent, Indigenous activity within ancestral territory.

Director of the Yurok Tribe Environmental Program Louisa McCovey (Yurok) is deeply concerned about the ecological and cultural impact of illicit cannabis production within the context of her professional duties but also "as a weaver, a gatherer, as a tribal citizen": "One of the biggest things that you see from grows is, like, the community, the social, sort of, fabric changes in communities where there are big grows. . . . They're militant in a lot of ways, so they're taking over areas where normally you'd go get mushrooms or gather basket materials . . . [Illegal cannabis grow sites are] hindering our ability to do that and just changing the face of, the feel of the community is a big impact" (author interview, August 10, 2017). Like the wave of 49ers who preceded them, the flood of cannabis cultivators to the area have shifted the demographics of the region. Familiar faces are few and far between and strangers line the sidewalks, hoping for a ride. McCovey speaks to the deterrent many traditional gathers and weavers feel: a looming threat of violence. McCovey also speaks to the wide-reaching impacts of this deterrent: the violence, or threat of violence, is pervasive and prevents community relations and cultural activities from flourishing. "There's generally a sense that [gathering is] not an okay thing to do anymore. Because you might just get a gun pulled on you." Tribe members may be reluctant to take their children out and teach them how to gather.

This fear is shared by many members of the community. Micah Gibson explains this fear: "The biggest concerns, from what I've heard from the community, is just the ability to be able to walk around in your ancestral territory, to be gathering [what] you need: the resources for basket making, for praying, or gathering for subsistence foods, hunting, anything like that. There are people who are actually scared to go down certain roads, even in broad daylight. It doesn't have to be at night" (author interview, August 11, 2017). Richard Myers reiterates this point: "It's about our livelihood; we need to gather mushrooms or deer or different things like that." But unfortunately, he jokes, "they usually have bigger guns than we do" (Richard Myers, author interview, June 22, 2018). Growers are often heavily armed and, as Myers points out, a hunting rifle provides little protection. The threat of violence functioning as a deterrent to the practice of cultural activities is reminiscent of gold rush–era genocide and miners' violent attacks on Indian communities. Assaults on our cultures are part of a larger settler-colonial pattern predicated on the consumption of Indigenous lands, bodies, and cultures.

Another concern about cannabis cultivation that frequently comes up among community members is sexual violence and sex trafficking. Shoshana Walter (2016) has reported on sex trafficking in the cannabis industry in Northern California. Survivors of sexual violence that occurred during their employment share their stories. Rape crisis centers and service providers have also received an increasing amount of calls over the past few years, which they attribute to the rise in cannabis cultivation in the region. In April 2018 Humboldt State University students organized a panel discussion about sex trafficking in the cannabis industry. Students in the room shared experiences and tips about how to protect yourself when working in the industry. Humboldt County has the highest per capita rate of missing people in California, and the region also has the largest Native population per capita. Research on murdered and missing Indigenous women and girls also shows high rates of violence against Native women in the region (Abinanti, George, and Lucchesi 2020). More research needs to be conducted to draw a direct correlation to the green rush. Research also would add to other scholarly discourse within critical Indigenous studies that examine the relationship between rape, sexual violence, and settler colonialism (see Deer 2015; Risling Baldy 2018) and the relationship between sexual violence and natural resource extraction (K. Anderson 2011; Nagle and Steinem 2016; A. Smith 2005; Warren and Erkal 1997).

In addition to the threat of physical violence, physical barriers erected by cultivators also prevent Indigenous peoples from accessing their ancestral territory. One of the most visible physical barriers associated with trespass cannabis cultivation is the construction of gates. Cultivators often place gates on roads to prevent access to sites in order to remain either undetected or undisturbed. These gates prevent cultural practitioners from accessing hunting, gathering, and ceremonial sites and present an added obstacle to tribal employees who need to access different places throughout tribal homelands (e.g., environmental monitoring stations). Director of the pollution prevention division of the Yurok Tribe Environmental Program Koiya Tuttle (Yurok) explains: "Gates come up. . . . It just pisses me off when gates come up on tribal roads, I flag them with a GPS, come back, double check, triple check, and if that gate and fence is on tribal lands, it's out. I'm going back up there and pulling it out because tribal people, tribal employees, and tribal staff shouldn't have to ask permission to travel on tribal roads" (Koiya Tuttle, author interview, June 4, 2018). Here Tuttle evokes tribal peoples' right to access roads on their own homelands. The imposition of gates associated with cannabis cultivation, viewed through this lens, can be seen as an infringement of tribal sovereignty and tribal peoples' abilities to be in relationship with their homelands. In a critical analysis of the installation art piece created by Bob Haozous (Chiricahua Nde'/Apache/Diné/Spanish/English) called *Gate/Negate*, Natchee Blu Barnd (Ojibwe/Portuguese/Scots-Irish) (2017) theorizes the gate as an important symbol for settler-colonial control: "Gates can be and are used simultaneously as points of denial and as points of invitation and welcoming. . . . The gate presents the passage or site of entry for immigrants and settlers who have come to occupy the US American territories and other Indigenous lands . . . [but the gate also symbolizes] the act of negation. As a historical mechanism for controlling access to land and nationhood . . . entry is not guaranteed" (140). The gate, then, by preventing Indigenous peoples from accessing their territories, serves as a powerful symbol of the ongoing nature of land dispossession. And in this particular instance there is another layer of impact: tribe employees are tasked with gathering the data to document the ecological impact of cannabis cultivation, but physical barriers such as gates can prevent tribal nations' abilities to monitor their environments and prove that cannabis cultivation is causing negative ecological impacts to tribal homelands.

Tribal environmental programs must also worry about the safety of employees as they complete their fieldwork, and during the time of my research, all Yurok tribal employees within the Natural Resource Division were encouraged to wear identifiable clothing and bring a partner into the field (McCovey 2017). Employees of the Hoopa Valley Tribe have also experienced similar threats of violence and intimidation in the field. This is important to note because it suggests the far-reaching impact cannabis cultivation is having on Indigenous peoples throughout northwestern California. Dawn Blake (Hupa)—a former biologist at the Hoopa Tribe Forestry Department—shared a story of growers preventing her from her employment duties. Blake and a high school intern set out to conduct fieldwork, specifically to track pileated woodpeckers. She recalls:

> We got out of the car and got our backpacks on. I specifically had left my phone in the office that morning, so I had realized that at some point, but just decided to leave it. We got out, got our backpacks on, and got ready to hike in the woods and started our hike. When we took a few steps in and I heard a phone power down, you know the Verizon power down? And so I turned around and asked her, "Was that your phone?" She said, "No, I left my phone in the truck." I realized that there was someone else out there with us. I didn't want to scare her, but I said, "We're going to go back." She didn't argue. We packed up and got into the vehicle, came back down and reported what happened. We did something else that day, but later that year, they busted a grow right there. (Dawn Blake, author interview, July 3, 2018)

Blake's colleague at the Forestry Department, Aaron Pole (Hupa), has had similar experiences. He recalls:

I found myself right in the middle of this patch and I was like "Oh crap," and it was July, so they were all budded out and big so I tiptoed out. . . . [I was] getting a little paranoid because when I was trying to exit the area, I went the wrong way because I just kept on running into more plants, more plants, more plants and usually that time of year—they have this old expression when there's buds on the plants, that's when the patch dogs are out. Patch dogs are just people who stay out there and make sure their plants aren't getting ripped off. (Aaron Pole, author interview, July 3, 2018)

Patch dogs are frequently armed. Whether real or perceived, this violence is unacceptable.

During Operation Yurok in 2017, YTEP employee Koiya Tuttle was tasked with collecting a water sample from an active grow site:

We thought to access below the grow site we would hike in from a grow that was below it and kind of traverse the side of the mountain to get under it. As we were doing that, we didn't find any water, didn't find any running water. We eventually get right below that grow and there was a little bit of water and it's trickling out. "Tink tink tink." The National Guard guy gets on his [communication device] and was going to call and he said, "We're finishing up here with the water guys. We're going to be coming up out of the bushes to the grow. Just to let you know that is us because the grow we decided to sample is also where they detained suspects." We thought they were up there because we had heard voices, a lot of people talking, we heard an ATV running, chainsaws running . . . [Then] he gets a message that they had left and released the suspects, returned their firearms, and that law enforcement was no longer present at that grow. So we're there, right underneath the suspects that had their firearms returned, listening to them talk, waiting for our water sample, and it was going "Tink, tink, tink," waiting for our one hundred milliliter. . . . So, we are just waiting and waiting for our sample. It's crazy. So we get the water sample and it was really surreal. We put the lid back on, put it back in the cooler, and [we're] trying to sneak off back the way we came, which wasn't very quiet and was quite a hike. We had hiked for a good amount of time, maybe a half an hour or more . . . halfway back we heard these monkey sounds coming from right below us that we couldn't see, from down the hill. We were looking down there and it's kind of freaky because there were monkey sounds and obviously there were no monkeys around . . . we didn't know what was going on and we thought maybe it was other people in the raiding party trying to mess with us. But it was still pretty freaky. So I stood up and I started meowing really loudly because I didn't have any other animal sounds to give. So, I just started to go "Meow, meow, meow," and the monkey sounds stopped. We just hauled ass all the way back to where we started, and Frankie Jo and Yurok Public Safety were there waiting for us. They were like "We were just about ready to come look for you, we just got back from looking at that fourth grow area up the hill." . . . So, it was totally someone else. (Tuttle interview)

Unfortunately, "these types of experiences and some much worse have become commonplace" (Higley et al. 2018, 59). Tribe members and employees literally put their lives at risk to carry out their non-law-enforcement job duties or cultural obligations.

Lastly, cannabis cultivation has negatively impacted sacred sites. For example, cannabis activity on and around the Hoopa Valley Indian Reservation has deterred Hupa peoples from accessing their sacred sites. This is not a new phenomenon. The inability to practice Native religions is rooted in settler-colonial policies aimed at eliminating Native peoples and cultures and has been weaponized against Indigenous peoples since invasion. Native peoples have been able to legally practice their religions in the United States only for the past fifty years as a result of religious suppression policies enacted in the early nineteenth century. During the gold rush, genocidal violence from militias deterred Native peoples from gathering or practicing ceremony; for the Hupas specifically, the desire to protect their young women from violence meant that they stopped conducting their Flower Dances because it was not safe to do so (Risling Baldy 2018). Today, tribe members need not fear state-funded militias, but another form of violence awaits in the hills: "We have actually detected and eradicated grow sites from spiritual sites and sacred sites on Hoopa lands. In several instances Hupa tribal members could not go near these sites. There is one occurrence where Hupa tribal members who have gone out to go gather have been shot at by drug trafficking organizations" (Gabriel 2017). This serves as a deterrent from practicing culture and ceremony and is a widespread concern among tribe members. As Dawn Blake explains, when speaking

> with a tribal elder about the changes that result from the trespass marijuana grows, she was informed that the elder used to enjoy gathering materials alone but now is encouraged to only go out with others as a matter of security. Because the Hupa's gathering practices involve prayers and one-on-one connection with Ninis'a: n (interpreted as both Creator and Mountain), these new security concerns compromise the ceremony and its sacred purposes. . . . Cultural, spiritual, and recreational activities of the Hupa are compromised twofold. First, the presence of potentially violent defenders of marijuana patches creates a risk of going into the forest in the first place, which has become a deterrent. Second, the chemicals used are a concern for protected resources, such as fish-bearing streams, as well as trophic level effects that can reach human consumers. (Higley et al. 2018, 67)

The potential threat of violence represents a continuation of settler-colonial violence that Indigenous peoples continue to experience in their own territories. Moreover, the ecological violence described earlier is also significant to consider within the context of sacred site protections. Making a distinction between cultural and ecological impacts originates from a settler-colonial worldview that aims to separate human culture from nature. From an Indigenous perspective, ecological impacts *are* cultural impacts.

In 2014 the Karuk Tribe discovered a trespass cultivation site at Tishawnik, the dance grounds where Pikyavish (World Renewal Ceremonies) have been held since the beginning of time. The Karuk Tribe does not possess a reservation, nor does it have jurisdiction over Tishawnik. Tishawnik is located on private property, but the owner has allowed the tribe to conduct ceremonies at the dance grounds for the past few decades. On April 28, 2014, while checking eel traps, Karuk Tribe members noticed strangers at the dance grounds and decided to investigate. River access roads had been blocked with cables and two men—both of whom claimed to be members of the Native American Church—were in the process of planting six hundred cannabis plants.[4] By the next morning, more tribe members had arrived to protect the site and wait for law enforcement. Deputies seized 615 plants (Bacher

2014). In this particular instance, tribal religion is used as justification for cannabis cultivation that, in actuality, threatens the integrity of sacred sites of the very people who are Indigenous to the region. Karuk ceremonial leader Leaf Hillman explains: "While we acknowledge that peyote is considered a sacrament by the Native American Church, Marijuana has never been sacred to the Karuk People" (quoted in Bacher 2014). While this particular situation was able to be rectified without causing permanent or long-standing damage to tribal cultural resources, the case demonstrates the vulnerability of traditional ceremonial sites.

Until this point in the discussion we have been primarily focusing on illegal trespass cultivation. However, legal cultivation also poses potential threats to tribal cultural resources. Specifically, sacred sites and sites of cultural significance that lie outside of reservation boundaries remain vulnerable. Because reservations are small portions of many tribes' ancestral territories, it is common for sites of spiritual and cultural significance to be located outside of reservation boundaries and thus beyond tribal jurisdiction. Some 75 percent of Indigenous sacred sites in the United States fall outside of tribal jurisdiction (LaDuke 2005). While compliant cultivators need to abide by the CEQA, and some counties have developed protections for tribal cultural resources, if the county or state does not recognize a place as a sacred site, the site remains vulnerable. However, some tribal nations have developed creative strategies to protect sacred sites from cultivation. For example, the Yurok Tribal Council defined a ceremonial district so that it was compatible with Humboldt County language and the definition of the tribal cultural resources used within the county's cannabis land use ordinances. In 2018 the Yurok Tribe Tribal Council passed Resolution 18–87 to formally define the Ke'wet Ceremonial District as a tribal cultural resource included within the Yurok Tribal historical register and the state historical register "because of the features, places, cultural landscapes, sacred places, and objects with cultural value to the Yurok Tribe" (Yurok Tribe 2018a). The Yurok Tribe is able to deny permit requests for cultivation sites within the Ke'wet Ceremonial District; however, provided a proposed site is not within tribal jurisdictional boundaries, Humboldt County still has the final say.

The Bluff Creek Company—located on fourteen acres in the Weitchpec area, within both the Yurok and the Karuk Areas of Traditional Tribal Cultural Affiliation—applied for a cultivation permit at a location within the Ke'wet

Ceremonial District. Humboldt County relayed the Yurok Tribe's objection to cultivation within the Ke'wet Ceremonial District and the company then requested a hearing with the Humboldt County Planning Commission to receive a special use permit. The hearing occurred on February 7, 2019, in Eureka. Representatives from the Yurok and Karuk Tribes spoke about the cultural importance of this site and the inability to mitigate harms from cannabis cultivation. The Humboldt County Planning Commission ultimately denied the Bluff Creek Company's special permit request and protected tribal cultural resources in this particular instance. Following the decision, Yurok Tribal vice chairman Frankie Jo Myers (Yurok) stated in a press release that "the planning commission deserves a lot of credit for protecting this sacred area" (Yurok Tribe 2019). While this example illustrates a positive working relationship between Humboldt County and the Yurok Tribe, legal cannabis cultivation within ancestral territory remains a concern. Had the Yurok Tribe not been prepared by legally defining a ceremonial district that aligned with Humboldt County's definition of the term "tribal cultural resource" used in the commercial cannabis land-use ordinance, this hearing may have turned out differently. This illustrates the inherent vulnerability embedded in sacred site protection when tribal nations must rely on the settler constructions of law and property to protect them. Moreover, if a cultivation permit is approved, despite a tribe's objections, there is much less legal recourse for tribal nations to protect their ancestral lands and waters from permitted legal cultivation, in comparison to illegal cultivation.

Indigenous peoples in northwestern California face a plethora of problems as a result of cannabis cultivation. Ultimately, from an Indigenous perspective, the green rush represents a continuation of settler-colonial erasure and elimination and demonstrates "disrespect for and no acknowledgment of the tribal government and our authority and our jurisdiction to manage our own lands and disrespect for tribal culture. . . . It's blatant disregard for our way of life in my opinion. Because we're so intimately connected to our land and our river that we need, we need to help the environment to be healthy Yurok people and that's not even a thought or recognized at all by these growers. They're just trying to make money; it's all just about making money" (McCovey interview). I am reminded of the Oceti Sakowin prophecy of the Black Snake. It is foretold that the Black Snake will bring great destruction to the landscape, but the story does not end there. It also foretells resistance and resurgence of tribal nations, in the face of colonial violence and capitalism, to protect our lands, waters, and relatives. While tribal nations did not have a seat at the table during the gold rush, tribal nations are taking a stand against the ecological and cultural toll of cannabis cultivation.

RESISTING GREEN RUSH DISPOSSESSION: OPERATION YUROK

Operation Yurok demonstrates how the Yurok Tribe rose up to fight against the repetitive patterns of resource rushing in California and protect its lands, waters, and more-than-human relatives from the urgent environmental concerns of illicit trespass cannabis cultivation. Begun in 2014, Operation Yurok was a collaborative effort between numerous tribal, county, state, and federal entities that targeted cannabis cultivation sites within Yurok ancestral territory and documented environmental damages. The intended goals of Operation Yurok were to protect the environment from cannabis-related damages and protect tribe members from cannabis-related violence. From 2014 to 2018 Operation Yurok considerably decreased the amount of cultivation sites within the Yurok Indian Reservation.

Operation Yurok was my entry point to the magnitude and scale of the damage caused by cannabis cultivation, from denuded hillsides to dewatered streams. When the effort entered full swing in 2014, I was an inexperienced intern at the Yurok Tribe Environmental Program. I recall sitting at my desk, sipping my coffee and pretending to look busy, when a colleague emailed to me a *Los Angeles Times* article titled "Massive Raid to Help Yurok Tribe Combat Illegal Pot Grows" (Romney 2014). Tribe members and employees, accompanied by dozens of law enforcement officers clad in camouflage and carrying assault rifles, made their way upriver. They were gathered together that morning to eradicate cannabis cultivation and document the environmental damages both within and beyond the exterior boundary of the Yurok Indian Reservation. It would be another two years before I would see Operation Yurok up close and personal, but that summer I had the privilege to talk with other tribe members and employees about their experiences with and concerns about trespass cultivation within ancestral territory. Almost everybody I talked to knew of at least one person who had had a close call with a cultivation site—from on-duty environmental scientists heading to a water monitoring station to cultural practitioners out gathering plant medicines, foods, or other materials. Folks unanimously expressed deep concern for the River and the fish—and the harmful effects of continued water diversions to agriculture operations in southern Oregon and Northern California and what large-scale cannabis production meant for them and the continuation of Yurok ways of life. Operation Yurok was necessary.

Well before Operation Yurok began, the Yurok Tribe had passed two key pieces of legislation to protect the reservation from cultivation. On August 25, 2006, the Yurok Tribal Council unanimously adopted Resolution 06–65, entitled Zero Tolerance Policy and 215 ID Card Non-Recognition. The resolution (Yurok Tribe 2006) states: "No person shall cultivate marijuana within the exterior boundaries of the Yurok Indian Reservation." Jurisdiction is delegated to the Tribal Court, the Tribal Police, "and any other law enforcement agency having jurisdiction on the Yurok Reservation." Penalties include fines up to $500 and additional costs associated with litigation and the investigation, seizure, forfeiture, or destruction of plants. It is important to note that the language of this resolution is specific to cultivation, not individual consumption. Despite the law, trespass cultivation flourished on Yurok tribal lands. While some tribes in California struggle to enter the cannabis industry (see chapter 5), other tribes—like the Yurok Tribe and other tribes in northwestern California—are struggling to fend off the encroaching industry.

Seven years later, on August 29, 2013, the US Department of Justice issued a memorandum concerning medical marijuana, referred to as the "Cole Memorandum." This document did not change the legal status of cannabis at the federal level, but rather it outlined eight cannabis-related law enforcement priorities. Nor did the document explicitly mention tribes.[5] It did, however, create a sense of ambiguity regarding what would be enforced and what would not. Concerned that this could potentially lead to an increase in cannabis cultivation on and near tribal lands, the Yurok Tribal Council put forth its own Controlled Substances Ordinance to be considered for emergency adoption within one week after the Cole Memorandum was released. The ordinance was selected for emergency adoption because "the Reservation community is under siege from unlawful cultivation of marijuana and drug manufacture" (Yurok Tribe 2013a, 18). Other concerns that were highlighted in the ordinance included physical violence toward and intimidation of tribe members as well as violence toward our water, our resources, our wildlife, and our ecosystem. The legislation highlights the negative effects that cannabis cultivation has had on tribal lands and waters and on the social fabric of the community. Because "marijuana cultivation and harvesting is at a peak during the fall season, presenting additional risk of physical violence against and intimidation of Tribal members and the Reservation community" (18), the ordinance was an urgent matter. The ordinance was officially adopted on February 6, 2014. While the zero-tolerance resolution, passed in 2006, had already made cannabis illegal within the Yurok Indian Reservation, the Controlled Substances Ordinance established penalties for use, possession, distribution, and production within the reservation.

During this time period, the Yurok Tribe had "observed a large number of non-tribe members purchasing land on the Reservation for the sole purpose of starting clandestine cannabis operations" (Yurok Tribe 2013a). Despite the tribal laws forbidding cannabis cultivation on the reservation, non-Indian landowners have continued to disrespect Yurok sovereignty and culture. In response, "there was a group of community members from the Weitchpec area that came to the Tribal Council and said [cannabis cultivation] is starting to get out of hand. We don't feel comfortable, people are driving around, shooting around at all hours of the night. . . . They informed Tribal Council of the problem [and] the Tribe took rapid steps to try to solve it" (Matt Mais, author interview, September 6, 2017). Thus, it became both urgent and necessary to reclaim tribal lands from trespass cultivators.

These events led to the Yurok Tribe–spearheaded cannabis eradication campaign known as Operation Yurok. As former vice chairman David Gensaw has reflected, "We had to get out there and we had to make calls, write letters, and meet with people. And know our concerns. We had to have proof that these things were happening. . . . [Humboldt] County wasn't going to step in and help us because it was already going that route [of legalization] and so we had to go the environmental route" (David Gensaw, author interview, July 6, 2018). In January 2014 the state of California declared a drought emergency. In response to the drought emergency, various California state government entities formed the unified command structure referred to as the Drought Task Force. This task force included representatives from the governor's office, the Office of Emergency Services, the Department of Water Resources, and the State Water Resources Control Board. Tribal policy advisor for the Department of Water Resources Anecita Agustinez (Diné Nation) has noted an important gap in drought services for Native American tribes in California (Anecita Agustinez, author interview, August 14, 2017). Tribes are often forgotten within state policies and many had made the assumption that federally recognized tribes would be protected under federal acts and federal emergency protocols; this was, however, not the case. Agustinez and former tribal advisor to the governor Cynthia Gomez (Tule River Yokut) created the Statewide Monthly Drought Consultation report and a webinar for tribal governments in California (Agustinez interview). Through this process the Yurok Tribe informed the state of the disastrous impacts of illegal cannabis cultivation on state and tribal water resources—namely, impacts to tributaries and streams affected by illegal diversions for the illegal grow operations, impacts to ceremonial plants, and access to traditional ceremonial sites. "Through the governor's outreach of tribal drought consultation we were informed that there were illegal diversions of streams, so you're dealing [with] drought issues and you're dealing with curtailment of water" (Agustinez interview). Following outreach by Agustinez and Gomez, the Yurok Tribe (2014) declared a state of emergency on January 29, "proclaiming that the record-setting drought conditions pose a threat to Yurok people, natural and cultural resources." The Yurok Tribe was the second tribe in California to do so, the first being the Hoopa Valley Tribe. The Yurok Tribe was then able to request assistance from the governor's office, which then sent members of the California National Guard Counterdrug Task Force to help rein in the rampant water thefts and environmental damage caused by cannabis cultivation on tribal lands (Yurok Tribe 2016). The funding for Operation Yurok was deemed critical under the governor's Emergency Declaration and directed funding allocations from several agencies, including CalFire, CalOES, the national guard, and local law enforcement. In subsequent years the Yurok Tribe created a broader coalition to include funding from the US Department of Justice and local law enforcement (Anecita Agustinez, letter to author, May 28, 2019).

Operation Yurok is unique and serves as an important model for other tribal nations because it illustrates successful strategies for protecting the entirety of ancestral territory. Through processes of historic land dispossession, many Native American reservations are small fractions of their ancestral territory. And yet, tribal peoples maintain relationships and responsibility for their entire homelands. Neither Indigenous relationships to land nor ecological impacts are confined to artificial borders drawn on a map. The Yurok Tribe mobilized to form multi-agency partnerships and collaborations to respond to urgent environmental concerns beyond the boundary of tribal jurisdiction. "The approach is to look at it as aboriginal territory, not current reservation boundaries, which aboriginal territory extends well beyond current reservation boundaries and that's what we're always looking to protect. . . . never think of where you're currently confined to as far as your reservation is, but think of it as how we were since time immemorial. That is what we're here to protect and maintain or enhance. And I think that's a great way to look at things" (Gibson interview).

The primary limitation of Operation Yurok—albeit one negated by the Yurok Tribe's strategic collaboration with county, state, and federal law enforcement—is the limitation of tribal jurisdiction within ancestral territory. Currently, tribal lands outside of the reservation boundaries but within ancestral territory are under the jurisdiction of Humboldt County, the state, or federal land management agencies. The Yurok Tribe does not have the jurisdiction to prosecute cannabis cultivators outside the reservation boundary, even if they are creating environmental hazards that impact tribal members within the reservation. This led the Yurok Tribe Public Safety Department (tribal law enforcement) to collaborate with a variety of county, state, and federal entities to aerially survey trespass cultivation sites and issue search warrants outside of tribal jurisdiction.[6] This multilevel collaboration served as a strategic mechanism for the Yurok Tribe to protect the entirety of ancestral territory, rather than being forced to limit their scope to solely reservation lands.

The first large-scale cannabis bust—coordinated by the Yurok Tribe—occurred in summer of 2013. The eradication effort was initiated "after residents living on the upper reservation nearly ran out of drinking water as a result of illegal water diversions from creeks that feed the Tribe's and individual water systems" (Yurok Tribe 2016). This eradication campaign targeted eight privately owned non-Indian properties on the Yurok Reservation. More than two thousand cannabis plants were destroyed—a small percentage of the parcels used by non-Indians to cultivate cannabis (Yurok Tribe 2013b). All eight of these properties were located upriver on the eastern end of the reservation, specifically near the community of Tulley Creek. The Hoopa Tribal Police, the Bureau of Indian Affairs Division of the DEA, and the US Forest Service assisted the Public Safety Department (Yurok Tribe 2013b).

The following summer—July 21–29, 2014—was the inaugural year of Operation Yurok. During the nine-day operation, forty-three search warrants were issued and over fifteen thousand cannabis plants were destroyed. The grow sites spanned the area on the eastern side of the reservation, from Bald Hills Road to Weitchpec. In 2014 Operation Yurok was composed of tribal, state, and federal law enforcement officers, the Yurok Tribe Public Safety Department, the California National Guard Counterdrug Task Force, the Humboldt County Drug Task Force, and the California Department of Fish and Wildlife. "The Humboldt County Sheriff's Office served 20 of the warrants to property owners living off the Reservation and the Yurok Public Safety served the remaining 23 on the Yurok Reservation. Officers from the California Department of Fish and Wildlife were on hand to assess environmental damage on off-Reservation properties" (Yurok Tribe 2014). Numerous environmental violations were recorded by the Yurok Tribe Environmental Program, including several water diversions and impoundments, unpermitted clear-cutting, human waste, and herbicides, pesticides, insecticides, and petroleum products (Yurok Tribe 2012).

In addition to the collaboration among law enforcement, the Yurok Tribe Environmental Program plays a central role in Operation Yurok. As Gensaw explains, it was important for the Yurok Tribe to have documented evidence of environmental destruction directly resulting from cannabis cultivation in order to acquire support from Humboldt County and California for Operation Yurok (Gensaw interview). Prior to Operation Yurok, YTEP had seen evidence of the environmental impacts of cannabis production, namely lower water quantity and diminished water quality. Environmental monitoring conducted by YTEP provided the necessary evidence to convince collaborators to participate in Operation Yurok. During Operation Yurok enforcement actions the primary role of YTEP is to document environmental damages, including "anything and everything from sediment inputs to soil and nutrients concentrations, pesticides, brownfields, and fuels" (Matthew Hanington, author interview, June 20, 2018). YTEP employees are already tasked with the environmental monitoring of reservation lands and, given the legacy impacts of the gold rush and subsequent resource extraction, this is a large task. In terms of personnel, participation in Operation Yurok "depends on who's available and willing to go out because it is outside of the scope of peoples' job descriptions" (Louisa McCovey, author interview, August 10, 2017). Additionally, "because of the enforcement nature and the danger factor . . . it is asking a lot of staff to do that." The increase in cannabis cultivation, and the necessity to document associated environmental impacts, adds additional strain to YTEP, a department that primarily relies on grant funding to meet the needs of the Yurok Tribe.

Operation Yurok's first year was successful and it continued to grow. By 2015 a team of over seventy-five law enforcement officers from multiple agencies, headed by the Yurok Tribe Public Safety Department, eradicated more than forty grow sites. "The summer long operation has so far resulted in the removal of approximately 55,000 marijuana plants, nearly 1 ton of marketable buds and one butane-based hash lab. The marijuana alone was valued at more than $110 million" (Yurok Tribe 2015). The number of cannabis plants destroyed in 2015 was significantly higher than that of the previous year. While "there were fewer grows on the Yurok Reservation, the pot plantations just beyond the Tribe's border were much larger, a possible result of looming legalization in the state of California" (Yurok Tribe 2015). The Yurok Tribe estimates approximately 95 percent of the illegal operations were conducted by non-Indians.

In July 2016 over fifty law enforcement officers served forty-one search warrants and destroyed over twelve thousand plants. In 2017 Operation Yurok destroyed approximately four thousand plants. The amount of plants eradicated in 2016 and 2017 is significantly smaller than the fifty-five thousand plants destroyed in 2015, but the Yurok Tribe argues this is a "clear indicator of the progress that is being made toward putting an end to this kind of rampant ecological destruction" (Ferrara 2017). However, in 2017 there was significantly less participation from collaborating entities, including the Humboldt County Sheriff's Office, the national guard, and the Bureau of Indian Affairs. According to the Yurok Tribal Justice Center, there were eighteen infractions issued for cannabis cultivation in 2014, sixteen in 2015, thirty in 2016, and forty-three in 2017. None were issued in 2018 (Abby Abinanti letter to author, August 14, 2018). The reason for the marked decline in citations during 2018 can be attributed to both a reduction in trespass cultivation and a lack of Operation Yurok activity during the summer of 2018.

In 2018 Operation Yurok eradication was conditionally postponed because of the tribe's success in decreasing cultivation within reservation boundaries. The Yurok Tribe issued a press release, stating: "This year, the Tribe is going to push pause on the operation, but we will continue to closely monitor tribal lands for the foreseeable future to prevent any further damage to the environment. We are also working closely with Humboldt County officials to investigate potentially illegal gardens just outside of the reservation's borders" (Kemp 2018c). The Yurok Tribe strategically and successfully mobilized to take action against urgent threats to the Yurok environment and culture. While trespass cultivation has decreased within ancestral territory boundaries, legalized cultivation remains concerning. Nevertheless, Operation Yurok provides an important example of Indigenous resistance to ongoing settler-colonial resource extraction. Following the first Operation Yurok, in 2014, former Yurok tribal chairman Thomas O'Rourke (Yurok) declared: "The operation was a huge success. Creeks that were dry on the first day were flowing by the second. It is almost beyond belief how much water was being stolen from the watershed" (Yurok Tribe 2014).

7

CANNABIS AND WATER

Use, Rights, and Infrastructure

The waters that run through Indigenous lands are the arteries that feed us—humans and more-than-humans. Water runs through our human veins and connects us to everything. The water that we drink is the water the salmon breathes, is the water the trees need, is the water where Bear bathes, is the water where the rocks settle. Many of our stories foreground relationships to water. These stories show us that water is theory; theory that is built from relationality to the land, the earth, everything.
—Melanie K. Yazzie and Cutcha Risling Baldy, "Introduction: Indigenous Peoples and the Politics of Water"

The historical amnesia that characterizes contemporary natural resource decision-making is, in part, a factor of institutionalized racism. The lack of attention to the histories of Indigenous peoples and their land [and water] rights is the direct result of manifest destiny— or doctrine of discovery-based approaches to European appropriation of Indian land [and water]. —Beth Rose Middleton Manning, *Upstream*

Two weeks after the Karuk Tribe declared a state of emergency on the Klamath River in response to drought conditions and a looming fish kill, on June 16, 2021, the Wiyot Tribe issued a press release that declared a state of emergency on its ancestral Rivers—the Wiya't (Eel River), Hikshari' (Elk River), Baduwa't (Mad River), and Gidughurralilh (Van Duzen River)—due to extremely low flows and drought conditions.[1] Low rainfall and above-average temperatures caused by anthropogenic climate change, coupled with water diversions associated with large-scale agriculture and excessive nutrient runoff, have impeded water quantity and quality, especially for small tributaries that provide rearing habitat and cold-water flows during dry summer months. For reference, in 2014, a drought year, flows at Scotia were measured at 300 cubic feet per second (cfs). That summer, "the lower Wiya't ran dry near Fortuna, immediately above the reach where the tides affect the river's height, impeding the rriqhawu'rruwalh (Chinook salmon) run and causing fish death from disease associated with high water temperatures" (Wiyot Tribe 2021). On June 10, 2021, in the Wiya't, flows at Scotia were measured at 210 cfs. The Gidughurralilh was reporting flows only 20 percent of average in the mainstem and some tributaries. One tributary, Hely Creek, no longer provides a viable connection to Gidughurralilh or supports an active Salmon run. The Hikshari' is plagued by sediment and effluent from a local sewage plant. Testing by the Blue Lake Rancheria in the lower Baduwa't has identified hazardous toxins in the water that are particularly dangerous for pets and small children. Temperatures in Baduwa't are also running high. On June 11, Baduwa't was 18 degrees Celsius, a "level where fish begin experiencing acute levels of stress if exposed for extended periods of time" (Wiyot Tribe 2021).

While the Wiyot Tribe does not explicitly name cannabis cultivation in its press release—although it does refer to water diversions for agriculture, of which cannabis would be included—the Wiya't sources water to a substantial amount of cannabis production in southern Humboldt County. A 2015 study by Jennifer Carah et al. compared the water demand for cannabis irrigation in the Wiya't watershed to water yield: "For comparison, the areally averaged water yield from the Eel River during the marijuana-growing season is approximately 50,000,000 L per km^2 [liters per square kilometer] per season . . . ten times lower than the estimated marijuana water requirement of 430,000,000 L per km^2 per season. Marijuana plantations, even if relatively small in area, can have a disproportionately large impact on water resources and flow" (Carah et al. 2015, 824). The estimated water demand for cannabis irrigation exceeds the water yield of the Wiya't by almost ten times. As the cannabis industry continues to expand, Wiyot ancestral Rivers remain threatened. "These rivers are sacred cultural resources to the Tribe and are considered the bloodlines of Wiyot culture, providing nourishment, medicine, spirituality, sustenance, and cultural knowledge to the Wiyot people" (Wiyot Tribe 2021).

In the press release issued by the Wiyot Tribe (2021), contemporary water issues are contextualized within a legacy of settler-colonial ecological violence:

> Before Euro-colonial settlement, Wiya't produced the largest salmon runs in California and provided salmon for the rest of the United States. Beginning in the early 1900s Wiya't has suffered numerous deleterious impacts, including water diversions, invasive predators,

logging, sedimentation, dams, overfishing, extreme summer conditions, and low flows, which have led to significant loss of habitat and ecological degradation, contributing to diminished native fish populations that are critical to the survival of the Wiyot culture and people. . . . Presently, Wiyot people risk their health and safety when choosing to consume fish or eels out of Wiya't because of hazardous algal blooms and diseased animals. The health of the Wiya't is intrinsically tied to the health of the people. The survival of the people relies on the health of Wiya't. Threats to the Wiyot's subsistence practices through irresponsible water diversion on the Wiya't represent a continuation of settler-colonialism and environmental injustice. (para. 2)

Violence inflicted against the Wiya't is violence inflicted against the Wiyot peoples. Contemporary water concerns cannot be divorced from the legacy of settler-colonial violence that has erased Indigenous peoples from natural resource decision-making and disproportionately harmed Indigenous lands, waters, and peoples, which are framed by Indigenous studies scholars as "sacrifice zones" for the benefit of settler populations (see Voyles 2015).

Native peoples throughout California, and throughout Turtle Island, have always been in relationship to their water relatives. Like the veins and arteries that transport blood throughout our bodies, the River systems of California and beyond nourish and sustain us. What links Indigenous relationships to water across time and space is the emphasis on interconnectedness and relationality. To employ the metaphor of the human body: one cannot block an artery without causing catastrophic impacts to the entire vascular system; the resulting heart attack or stroke leaves permanent damage and lowered capacity to deliver blood. Likewise, one cannot dam a part of a River without causing damage to the entire River system. The River systems throughout California (as well as on Turtle Island) are linked and interconnected, so to sacrifice a River system for irrigation or hydropower does not solely impact that River. It impacts all of the Rivers—and the humans and more-than-humans who depend on them. Native peoples of California have long deeply understood this interconnection, as well as the interconnections between humans, more-than-humans, and water. These relationships are reflected in the traditional ecological management of our water resources and Indigenous water governance. Anderson (2005) argues that California Indians throughout the region effectively stewarded their lands and water in ways that successfully increased biodiversity and promoted habitat heterogeneity. Far from the pristine untouched wilderness that John Muir and his disciples fantasized about, the entirety of California was actively managed by Indigenous peoples. Furthermore, Kari Norgaard (2019) reminds us that capitalist wealth accumulation from natural resource extraction has been and continues to be possible only because of the success of Native land and water management practices.

Contrary to settler-colonial natural resource management ideologies, Native stewardship does not seek to categorize, codify, or control natural resources. Rather, Native management, rooted in sound ecological principles, is attuned to the biology of specific species and has sought to work with or enhance the natural function of the ecosystem (M. Anderson 2005). Rather than create an agency responsible for each element of the ecosystem (air, water, forest, and so forth), Indigenous land management practices are fundamentally interconnected and holistic (Hernandez 2022). Forest management *is* water management. Fisheries management *is* water management. Prescribed burning is an excellent example of integrated and holistic ecological management. In the past, by regularly burning the landscape, Native peoples maximized food production and cleared prairies for wildlife. Low-intensity fire also cleared out brush in the understory, which can build up as fuel for catastrophic fires. That brush also sucks up a lot of water, so burning (removing) it increases the flow of the River. Burning, therefore, influenced local hydraulic cycles and increased seasonal runoff into creeks (Norgaard 2019). But even more significant than technique is the relationship that Native people hold with their waters. We understand ourselves as caretakers of the River, rather than owners of a River. Melanie Yazzie and Cutcha Risling Baldy (2018) articulate a concept called "radical relationality": radical relationality "brings together the multiple strands of materiality, kinship, corporeality, affect, land/body connection, and multidimensional connectivity . . . [that] provides a vision of relationality and collective political organization that is deeply intersectional and premised on values of interdependency, reciprocity, equality and responsibility" (2). Drawing from the work of several Indigenous feminists, Risling-Baldy and Yazzie describe radical relationality as the ability to see water as self and self as water. Water is ancestor, relative, teacher, narrator, theory, and agent deserving of the same respect and care given to other members of the community. Water runs throughout human veins and connects to everything.

This book opens with a description of the Lakota prophecy of Zuzeca Sapa, the Black Snake: "Extending itself across the land and imperiling all life, beginning with the water" (Estes 2019, 14). It is particularly fitting that Zuzeca Sapa begins by infecting the water. First, not only is water necessary to sustain all life, but Native nations hold an intimate relationship with water that informs their purpose and place. The second reason it is fitting for Zuzeca Sapa to begin with water is because the settler state relies on the control and codification of water resources. Eve Tuck and K. Wayne Yang (2012) argue that land, water, and air are the most paramount concerns to settler colonialism because these natural resources become the source of capital for settler societies and because they disrupt Indigenous relationships to land, water, and air. In other words, all settler-colonial relationships to land and water must be reconfigured to the one that exists between owner and property: relationships to water are rooted in notions of private property that take on a mechanistic view of Nature wherein its parts can be extracted and manipulated for profit. Guided by a manifest destiny ideology, the claiming of water rights in the settler state's perspective demonstrates legitimacy but simultaneously works to eliminate Native peoples' existence and claims. From water rights claimed in miners' camps during the genocidal gold rush to sacrificing Native lands and waters during the creation of the State Water Project, settler-colonial relationships with water have been marked by exploitation and disrespect. And thus the legal codification of water rights and the creation of state water infrastructure were (and continue to be) an integral part of the settler-colonial project (Matsui 2009).

Settler-colonial commodification and control of water has, in large part, led to its destruction and contamination—from mercury contamination during the gold rush to mass deforestation during the timber rush to the decimation of fish populations during the fish rush, and now to the additional diversion and contamination associated with the green rush. California Indians recognize this pattern. The history of water development and extraction in California has disproportionately impacted Indigenous peoples, water, plants, and wildlife. For this reason, when scholars refer to Indian lands as "sacrifice zones" they mean that the environmental destruction necessary for the consumption of settler society is conveniently sited on Native lands

(Voyles 2015). As Beth Rose Middleton Manning (2018) argues, "Native lands and communities have been treated as sacrifice zones for national priorities of irrigation, flood control, and hydroelectric development . . . leaving a painful legacy of displacement and cultural and community disruption" (4). The subjugation and control of water relatives is reflected in the state's attempts to control and eliminate Native peoples. And, because all life is dependent on water, this has disastrous impacts for our nonhuman relatives as well.

This is the proper context and frame for any contemporary discussion of water use and water rights within the cannabis industry. As a result of the legacy of the settler state's toxic relationship with lands and waters, coupled with the impacts of climate change, our River systems are reaching their breaking points. Our Rivers are choked and contaminated, yet more is demanded from them every day. Our River systems need time to heal, to recover. Demanding water allocations for yet another industry is like asking your relative, still in the intensive care unit recovering from a heart attack, to help you move your furniture. This is not to say that the cannabis industry, specifically, is the cause of this problem. Rather, it is a worldview that considers our water systems as resources to be plundered for export-based agriculture and other industries. The next discussion is organized into two main sections. The first examines the relationship between settler colonialism, water rights, and water infrastructure in California. The second covers cannabis cultivation and water use and examines public discourse over water use in the cannabis industry with an explicit focus on tribal concerns, the difficulty of quantifying water use for cannabis cultivation (considering the many cultivators that remain outside the regulated market), and the recent studies on water usage for cannabis cultivation in California. The arguments put forth here are twofold: First, cannabis is a significant cause of water diversion in Northern California. In this region, cultivation is geographically clustered within sensitive watersheds, and while water use for permitted cannabis cultivation throughout the state may be significantly less than other industrial agricultural products, within this region, cannabis exacerbates the stress on already beleaguered River systems. Cannabis-related water diversions are not the sole culprit by any means, but the expansion of the cannabis industry—in addition to all the other extractive industries currently threatening our River systems—has the potential to substantially reduce instream flows (which, in turn, poses significant water quality issues such as higher temperatures), to dewater entire streams, and to destroy critical Salmon spawning habitats. Second, the cannabis industry's reliance on the creation of water rights and water infrastructure—both of which have systematically erased Native peoples from the landscape and from natural resource decision-making—cannot be disentangled from the settler-colonial violence that made them possible. In these two ways, cannabis cultivation facilitates colonial ecological violence.

WATER AND SETTLER COLONIALISM: INVENTING RIGHTS AND IMPOSING INFRASTRUCTURE

As discussed in chapter 1, settler-colonial water rights in California emerged and began to take shape during the gold rush. Contemporary water rights in California are notoriously complicated and the task at hand is not to articulate the minutiae of California water law, but rather to demonstrate that the way settler water rights were constructed in California specifically, and in the United States broadly, worked to continue the settler-colonial dispossession of Indigenous peoples. The codification of water rights (and land rights) is an integral part of the settler-colonial project (Matsui 2009). "Water colonization was part of a larger project of settler colonialism in the United States and Canada. Like land and territory, settlers intruded onto Indigenous water systems. In western states and provinces, where the climate is drier, settlers displaced Indigenous communities and diverted limited waterways into expanding agricultural fields and livestock watering holes. They built towns and dams while denying the flow of water downstream to Indigenous peoples, who were forced onto reservations" (Curley 2019, 62). Dependent on Lockean theories of private property, settler-colonial water rights created during the California gold rush formed the basis of the "prior appropriation" doctrine (Kanazawa 2015). This doctrine of prior appropriation was designed to meet the needs of settler water users and encouraged westward expansion (Colby, Thorson, and Britton 2005; McCool 2002; Thorson, Britton, and Colby 2006). The central principle of prior appropriation is "first possession," or "first-in-time is first-in-right." Similar to the doctrine of discovery—a legal fiction that justifies American colonization—water rights are based on a glorified "finders keepers, losers weepers" arrangement:

"the first water user to file a water claim with the state has priority over all subsequent water users" (McCool 2002, 11). Contemporary senior water rights stem from this assumption. The problem, however, is that California Indians were not eligible to file for water rights during the gold rush. Native American tribes did not have a means to file for federally recognized water rights until 1908, following the US Supreme Court case *Winters vs. United States*. Tribal water rights in California, specifically, retroactively trace back to the date that tribal land in question was set aside as federally reserved land (Parr and Parr 2009). Even if Native peoples could have reserved water rights between 1850 and 1870, the state-sanctioned bounties placed on Native bodies likely served as an effective deterrent from their doing so.

The second broad principle on which western water rights are founded is beneficial use; this refers to both the type of use (e.g., mining, agriculture) and the amount of water needed for said use (Kanazawa 2015). The assumption here, of course, is that Indigenous peoples had not been putting water to beneficial uses, but rather that waters were lying in wait for settlers to put them to beneficial uses. Kenichi Matsui (2009) argues that categories of beneficial use for water stem from the Lockean notion of private property, which are established by investing labor for beneficial uses of land (i.e., agriculture). Political scientist Barbara Arneil argues that "Locke's purpose was to justify the practice of dispossessing Indigenous peoples of their ancestral lands in order to facilitate European settlement and plantation agriculture" (quoted in Matsui 2009, 18). Deciding which uses of water are recognized as "beneficial" directly "reflects social values and scientific understandings" of the settler state (Halvorsen 2018, 941). Settler states and individual settlers have historically been the primary beneficiaries of use at the expense of Indigenous peoples' uses for and relationships with their water relatives (Robison et al. 2018). Beneficial uses, put simply, are uses that generate profit. California currently has twenty-three beneficial uses that may be applied to water bodies statewide. These include activities such as mining, irrigation, and hydroelectric power, as well as habitat preservation, endangered species protection, and groundwater recharge. While some environmentally focused beneficial uses (e.g., providing cold freshwater habitat) have been added to this list, initial state-recognized beneficial uses were those that produced income and reduced waste. Keeping water in the River for fish to thrive and for the River's health does not generate profit and historically these were not considered beneficial uses. California Indian nations have developed additional beneficial uses, such as preservation of tribal tradition and culture, tribal subsistence fishing, and broad subsistence fishing. However, laws governing these uses are not enforced statewide, nor does the state designate water bodies for them. Instead, these "additional" beneficial uses must be voluntarily adopted by individual regional water boards and applied to specific waterways (Reed, Middleton Manning, and Martinez 2021; SWRCB, n.d.).

Last is the "use-it-or-lose-it" principle. A water rights holder who does not put that water to a designated beneficial use may lose their rights over it—hence the water law mantra to use it or lose it. Scholars suggest this thinking emerged from the principle of abandonment at mining claims: if a mining claim was not being worked and was considered abandoned, another miner could start working that claim (Kanazawa 2015). Put simply, if one does not use a water claim, one runs the risk of losing it. This principle incentivizes the exploitation and overconsumption of water resources. Together, these principles form the doctrine of prior appropriation, the ideological basis of water law in California.

Perhaps unsurprisingly, water rights in California are already overallocated. The first comprehensive evaluation of appropriative water rights, aiming to identify where and how much water has been allocated in California, took place less than a decade ago. As of 2014, water rights allocations totaled 400 billion cubic meters, approximately five times the state's mean annual runoff. In many of the state's major River basins, water rights allocations add up to 1,000 percent of existing surface waters and "most of California's major river basins have water rights allocations that exceed their natural, unimpaired annual supply" (Grantham and Viers 2014, 5). And, because of numerous large dams, very few of California's Rivers are unimpaired. Though the state keeps tabs on how much water has been allocated, water use is a different story. "To date, the state simply does not have accurate knowledge of how much water is being used by most water rights holders. As such, it is nearly impossible to curtail or re-allocate water in an equitable manner among water users and to effectively manage for environmental water needs" (Grantham and Viers 2014, 9). The authors of the study project difficulty in the state's ability to meet current water demands long into the future—let alone increased demands from additional industries. The addition of widespread unregulated water diversions makes this puzzle even more complex. Put simply, settler-colonial "ontological constructions that convert rivers into notions of 'acre-feet,' divorcing water from the land, species, and kinship networks," are fundamentally unsustainable (Curley 2019, 61).

State control and management of water resources in California are rooted in the same processes of Indigenous dispossession as water rights. In *Upstream: Trust Lands and Power on the Feather River*, Middleton Manning (2018) demonstrates how the dams and reservoirs constructed as part of the State Water Project (SWP)—often framed as "unquestionable public goods"—displaced Indigenous peoples and destroyed cultural landscapes. She argues that "placing the histories of Indian land and water rights alongside the development of California water resources reveals the ways in which the dispossession of Indian people enabled the development of the economy of the new state of California" (25): "The seizure and transformation of the state's water resources that began during the gold rush continues in contemporary water infrastructure. The dams, power plants, aqueducts, and reservoirs that compose this infrastructure have become embedded in the socioeconomic, political geography of the state, where it underlies industries from tourism to agriculture to construction" (62). Middleton Manning demonstrates how the SWP, framed as a "public works" project for the public good, in actuality only benefited a narrow few, such as large landowners and hydroelectric providers, at the expense of Native peoples:

> Throughout the development of the SWP and the Central Valley Project (CVP), the articulated purpose was to capture the "surplus" waters of the north state's rivers (i.e., the Feather, Sacramento, San Joaquin, Eel) from the Delta and export them to the farms and cities located to the south. Native California nations on both ends of these systems were impacted. The northern tribes lost water and land rights to private and public projects, as well as the associated fisheries and cultural practices tied to the land area, while the southern tribes were displaced from their homelands for development and, if compensated, received far less than non-Native landowners. Tribes on both ends of the system struggled to access any "benefits" of the supposed progress built on their displacement. (40)

As others have shown, "all along the foothills and mountains across the entire state, surveyors and engineers identified sites on Indian land to build dams for water storage for agricultural and increasingly urban use" (Akins and Bauer 2021, 178). By 1870 Tulare Lake—a lake that sustained Yokut peoples for more than ten thousand years—was putrid and salty due to hydrologic modifications for irrigation; by 1930 it was gone (Akins and Bauer 2021; EPA 2007).

The California Legislature passed the first State Water Resources Act in 1945, which included a detailed State Water Policy. Under the directives of this legislation, the State Water Resources Control Board began developing what would become the SWP. The project occurred over three phases: inventorying California's water resources (1951), examining current and future water needs (1955), and creating a planning document for the management and conveyance of California's water resources (1957). These studies cost more than $8 million in total and found that 7 million irrigated acres used 90 percent of California's water, while up to 13 million more acres were irrigable. Additionally, the study found that in 1953, hydropower potential in the state could have been as high as 10.7 kW but the state was generating only 2.8 kW (Middleton Manning 2018). The way this study is framed and the questions that were asked perfectly embodies a settler-colonial relationship to land: it is all about conquering, controlling, and maximizing production. "This view, that all water available could be put to a 'productive' use of development and agriculture, controlled by storage to ensure availability throughout the year and to reduce flood risk, completely ignored diverse cultural perspectives and needs of upstream tribes, tribal water rights, and ecological needs such as in-stream flows that support the life cycles of anadromous fish" (Middleton Manning 2018, 48). By January 1960 Governor Edmond Brown argued that Northern California was "wasting huge quantities of water" by letting rivers flow back into the ocean, while central and southern California faced "'critical' water shortages" (quoted in Middleton Manning 2018, 48). The SWP was approved that same year.

The goal of the State Water Project was "to make water available throughout the State in a manner which will most adequately and equitably meet the economic and social needs of all of the people of California" (quoted in Middleton Manning 2018, 61). Functionally, this serves as a greater good argument, wherein Native lands and waters had to be sacrificed for settler populations to pursue their economic development:

> This pattern of flooding Indian lands for the "greater good" of non-Indian peoples repeated itself across California time and time again. Between 1923 and 1961, major dams built on the Colorado, Feather, Merced, Sacramento, San Joaquin, Stanislaus, Trinity, and Tuolumne Rivers flooded lands of the Chemehuevi, Hupa, Maidu, Miwok, Paiute, Wintu, Yokuts, and Yuroks, among others. The state has left few rivers untouched. Forty of the fifty largest lakes in the state are man-made reservoirs, and every one of them flooded Indigenous land. A hydrological map of the state is a map of Indian dispossession. . . . A map of California highlighting reservoirs *is* a map outlining theft and erasure of Indian land. (Akins and Bauer 2021, 245–46, emphasis in the original)

Though Indian water rights were recognized by the Supreme Court in 1908, Native peoples in California "have not had formal roles (aside from the work facilitated by tribal liaisons or tribal working groups) on state water policy and management bodies" (Middleton Manning 2018, 44). Settlers benefit and reap billions of dollars through agribusiness, but Native peoples have paid the price for the State Water Project—and continue to do so with each rush of resources.

WATER AND WEED

There is much contention and public debate over how much water cannabis production actually uses. On the one hand are narratives that cannabis does not use much water. Articles with headlines like "Cannabis Farms Not as Thirsty as Previously Thought" (Vanderheiden 2021) and "Legal Marijuana Farms Are Not a Drain on Water Resources" (NORML 2021) challenge the notion that cannabis production, and legal cannabis specifically, is a significant strain on water resources. As these authors argue, growers are falsely blamed for drought, when they are actually the victims of a suppressive state that makes it difficult for them to get water. Examining 416 articles published in and about Northern California between June 2015 and December 2019, Betsy Morgan et al. (2021) examine how public discourse frames perceptions of water use/availability for cannabis cultivation. They write:

Media portrayed illicit cannabis as culpable for "literally sucking rivers dry" as dry-season diversions coincided with drought to diminish flow. Concerns over developing effective regulations for cannabis water use were largely discussed from 2016 onward, as recreational cannabis was legalized. Some articles reflected that, despite legalization, illicit cannabis was still a large concern, potentially causing streams to "dwindle down to near trickles." Yet, even newly legal cannabis was still a cause of concern. One media source offered that under the current law, "a vegetable garden is an acceptable use but a cannabis garden of the same size is now environmental degradation." (11)

In this view, cultivators are unfairly scapegoated for water diversions that are equivalent, if not less than, other industries.

On the other hand, some narratives emphasize concerns over unregulated water diversions, causing streams to run dry, depriving tribe members of drinking water, and decreasing much-needed River flows for Salmon populations. In this view, cannabis cultivation is associated with environmental harms, such as decreasing instream flows and increasing water temperatures, which facilitate the destruction of salmonid habitats and increase the disease susceptibility of aquatic organisms (Bauer et al. 2015; Carah et al. 2015; Miller 2018; Wartenberg et al. 2021). In other words, "the combination of limited water resources, a water-hungry crop, and illegal cultivation in sensitive ecosystems means that marijuana cultivation can have environmental impacts that are disproportionately large given the area under production" (Carah et al. 2015, 1).

Tribal perspectives are rarely included in popular media, which Betsy Morgan et al. (2021) describe as "an unfortunately common occurrence in water management" (13). However, long before recreational legalization in 2016, tribal nations were expressing their concerns over illicit cannabis cultivation, situating water-related issues within a longer legacy of colonial ecological violence. The *Two Rivers Tribune*, a local newspaper based in Hoopa, California, drew this connection in a 2013 article with the headline "Drought and Expanding Marijuana Grows Paving Way for Repeat Fish Kill." The article reads: "Severe drought, desperate farmers, and migrating fish struggling to survive in the shallow, over-heated and fertilizer-laden waters of the Klamath and Trinity Rivers: almost all of the pieces are in place for a repeat of the 2002 fish kill" (Korns 2013). The possibility of another genocidal fish kill has been a concern for tribal nations since 2002, and the Karuk Tribe even declared a state of emergency on the Klamath River in 2021. Trespass cultivation on and around the Hoopa Valley Indian Reservation has resulted in loss of water. "On the trespass grows, they'll completely dewater headwater streams, divert it, pond it up into makeshift tanks that they make out of tarps, and either dig a pit and line it with a tarp or build a frame out of wood and then line it with a tarp and divert the water over to the tank or grow, and then all the water that was flowing downstream no longer flows downstream" (Mark Higley, author interview, September 7, 2017). As river flows and river health decrease every year and are magnified by the effects of climate change, the continuation of extractive industry (and even more threatening, the growth of that industry) threatens the livelihood of Salmon and Salmon people.

Operation Yurok began because streams in Yurok ancestral territory were being dewatered and tribe members lacked access to drinking water. The Yurok Tribe's newspaper, *Yurok Today*, frequently reported on concerns over trespass cannabis production within Yurok ancestral territory. In August 2014 the paper reported on the Operation Yurok raids that had occurred a month prior:

> In addition to diminishing people's access to clean water, the ballooning number of grows is also causing large-scale environmental destruction. The marijuana growing season coincides with the spring and fall runs of Klamath River salmon. The river is already flowing at a historically low level and the amount of *ceratomyxa Shasta* and *parvicapsula minibicorniss*, both potent fish pathogens, is off the charts in the alarmingly warm water body. The Klamath River tributaries that are being pilfered for marijuana production normally provide cold water refuges for the migrating salmon on the way to spawn. Instead, the important Klamath tributaries are barely making it to the main stem. (4–5)

In 2014 and 2015 tribal leaders and their collaborators investigated seventy-five sites, averaging 861 plants per site;[2] more than 55,000 plants in total were eradicated. During my participation in the Operation Yurok raids in the summer of 2016, I personally witnessed extensive evidence of illegal cannabis-related water diversions. Large tanks and fifty-five-gallon drums were filled to the brim. Black plastic irrigation tubing—Northern California's version of the black snake—ran up and down entire mountainsides. Pipes, some as large as five inches in diameter, were placed directly into streams. Yurok Tribe members were experiencing a direct impact on their own water sources. "Streams that had, since time immemorial—as well as within a generation of direct memory of tribal members—those springs and creeks had always had water, [but] they were drying up. . . . So . . . anecdotally, when they started growing above me, tribal members would say, 'My water went away. What can I do? I don't have any water to drink.' So did the drought do it? Did the growers do it? . . . or not? And so then we said what we need to actually do is figure out how much [water cannabis agriculture is taking]" (Suzanne Fluharty, author interview, August 10, 2017). In addition to diminished water quantities, many involved in Operation Yurok have seen evidence of "leaky plumbing, whether it's bears chewing on pipes, which we see all the time, or they're just incompetent plumbers. So you have water leaking twenty-four-seven" (Matt Mais, author interview, September 6, 2017).

One of the primary arguments in favor of cannabis legalization in California, then, was that it would provide a mechanism for addressing illegal water diversions through state regulation. The creation of water rights for cannabis cultivation cannot be disentangled from settler colonialism and Indigenous dispossession, as the very creation of settler water rights in this state are rooted in violence against Indigenous peoples. Ryan Stoa, in a 2016 article titled "Weed and Water Law: Regulating Legal Marijuana," reflects on the incapacity of traditional doctrines of water law in the West to cope with water scarcity in the face of a new legal industry that overuses water. Stoa suggests that for many states, cannabis legalization could place additional strain on existing water regulations and rights and argues that "if the legal marijuana industry were to enter this traditional conception of prior appropriation, it is very likely that many marijuana farmers would remain on the black market by virtue of the priority afforded to senior rights holders" (582). While many cultivators in California have chosen to stay unregulated, the state has created water rights and regulations specifically for the cannabis industry.

In 2016 the California Legislature, under Senate Bill 837, authorized the SWRCB to develop policies and guidelines for water use and diversion for legal cannabis cultivation. In collaboration with the California Department of Fish and Wildlife (CDFW) and the California Department of Food and Agriculture, the board issued the Cannabis Cultivation Policy in 2017 to "ensure that the diversion of water and discharge of waste associated with cannabis cultivation does not have a negative impact on water quality, aquatic habitat, riparian habitat, wetlands, and springs" (SWRCB 2017). As Joanna Hossack (2019) writes, "On an individual scale, many of the cultivators are not diverting a large amount of water. However, the SWRCB found that the cumulative impact of cannabis cultivation significantly affects waterways and habitats in California (cultivators often divert flows in remote and sensitive watershed areas, exacerbating these effects). It is death by a thousand cuts: if everyone takes more from the river, eventually the river stops flowing" (288). In response, the SWRCB developed several requirements for cannabis cultivators, and ownership of a water right requires compliance with the Cannabis Cultivation Policy.

First and foremost, any cultivator who plans to divert surface waters for cannabis production is required to obtain a Cannabis Small Irrigation Use Registration (SIUR) Water Right: a "streamlined option to obtain a small appropriative water right (less than 6.6 acre-feet per year) to divert and store surface water for commercial cannabis" (SWRCB 2021). The first appropriative water right of its kind, Hossack argues, the SIUR is a "novel approach to bridge the gap between surplus water in the wet season and widespread water scarcity in the dry season" (290). Cannabis SIURs cannot be obtained on designated Wild and Scenic Rivers and streams, on fully appropriated streams, or within CDFW instream flow study areas.

To combat the cumulative impacts of water diversion for cannabis cultivation, the Cannabis Cultivation Policy established minimum instream flow requirements and a forbearance period. Cultivators must first check their local compliance gauge to ensure that the daily average flow is greater than the monthly instream flow requirements for a period of seven consecutive days prior to diversion. In response to potential impacts of surface water diversions during the dry season—which are stated as "likely to significantly decrease instream flow and, in some instances, reduce hydrologic connectivity or completely dewater the stream"—water use regulations for cannabis cultivation in California stipulate a forbearance period during the growing season. This prohibits cannabis cultivators from diverting surface water during the dry season (April 1 to October 31) and requires cultivators to divert surface water during the wet season and store it. While both of these protective measures are steps in the right direction, concerns about water availability and River health remain.

Despite implementation of the Cannabis Cultivation Policy, quantifying the water usage of cannabis cultivation in Northern California is notoriously difficult for multiple reasons. First, due to the long-term illegality of cultivation, there are no studies that have quantified historic cannabis water use. Studies aiming to identify water sources and quantify water usage have only begun within the past decade. Even these contemporary studies are limited to analyzing permitted cultivation sites and estimations of water use leave out unpermitted and trespass cultivation, which make up a large portion, likely the majority, of cultivation in the region. Second, widespread variability makes it impossible to determine how much water cannabis production requires, as it depends on a plethora of factors including the soil quality, elevation, agricultural practices being utilized, length of growing season, size, quantity, and density of plants, and so on (Thiesen and Plocher 2016).

Current scientific literature describes cannabis as a water-intensive plant (Carah et al. 2015), but debate over how much water cannabis requires continues. The water demand estimate of 22.7 liters (approximately 6 gallons) per plant per day during the growing season (approximately 150 days) is based on calculations from the 2010 Humboldt County Outdoor Medical Cannabis Ordinance draft; this number translates to approximately 900 to 1,200 gallons of water per plant per season (Gabriel 2016). Mourad Gabriel (2016) estimates that in 2012 there were approximately 870,000 plants on public lands in California utilizing 1.04 billion gallons of water. In 2013 and 2014 there were approximately 500,000 plants on public lands in California utilizing 600 million gallons—the amount of water San Francisco uses in a month. Jennifer Carah et al. (2015) put it into perspective: "For comparison, wine grapes on the California north coast are estimated to use a mean of 271 million L of water per km^2 of vines per growing season. Marijuana is therefore estimated to be almost two times more 'thirsty' than wine grapes, the other major irrigated crop in the region" (2). Studies in Northern California, such as Scott Bauer et al.'s (2015) "Impacts of Surface Water Diversion for Marijuana Cultivation on Aquatic Habitat in Four Northwestern California Watersheds," are based on the 22.7-liter calculation.

Outdoor cannabis cultivation in Northern California largely depends on irrigation, as precipitation during the growing season is negligible. As Bauer et al. argue, "Given the lack of precipitation during the growing season, marijuana cultivation generally requires a substantial amount of irrigation water. . . . Diverting springs and headwater streams are some of the most common means for [cannabis cultivation sites] to acquire irrigation water, though the authors have also documented the use of groundwater wells and importing water by truck" (2).

Through high-resolution aerial photographs, Bauer's team (2015) estimated the number of cannabis plants being cultivated in four different watersheds: Upper Redwood Creek, Redwood Creek South, and Salmon Creek (all located in Humboldt County), and Outlet Creek (in Mendocino County). Plant estimates were then validated through search warrants served by law enforcement. The researchers then calculated water demand and documented stream flows in each watershed. When comparing these numbers they found that cannabis cultivation has the potential to divert substantial amounts of water, decreasing instream flows by up to 23 percent. Perhaps most alarming, the research team found that "water demand for marijuana cultivation exceeds streamflow during the low-flow period . . . diminished streamflow is likely to have lethal or sub-lethal effects on state-and federal-listed salmon and steelhead trout and to cause further decline of sensitive amphibian species" (1). In Redwood Creek South, located in Yurok ancestral territory, the data indicated the estimated water demand for cannabis cultivation was up to 165 percent of the annual seven-day flow.

However, the figures used in Bauer et al.'s (2015) study have recently come under fire from legal cannabis lobbyists. The California chapter of the National Organization for the Reform of Marijuana Laws (Cal NORML)—one of the leading lobbyists for the cannabis industry in the state—argues that the figure of 22.7 liters per plant per day during the growing season presented in Bauer et al.'s study "has been extrapolated to cause law enforcement to overestimate the water consumption of gardens they raid, much as they have always overestimated plant yields and prices" (Cal NORML 2015, sec. 1, para. 2). After canvassing growers from eleven farms in El Dorado, Placer, Humboldt, and Mendocino Counties, the California and Sacramento chapters of NORML found that water usage ranged from 1 gallon per plant to 3.5 gallons per plant: "Six gallons a day is possible for July and August, but not for 150 days. . . . The average number of gallons used on plants daily was 2.30 in Cal NORML's study" (sec. 2, para. 1). In fact, Cal NORML argues that using a metric of gallon per plant is not the most appropriate; rather, they encourage gallons of water per day per gram of cannabis bud produced. Based on this suggested metric, they argue that only "an average of 0.72 gallons of water is needed to produce a gram of marijuana, no matter how many plants are grown or how big they are" (sec. 2, para. 3).

While this figure may be technically accurate, it misses the point because it does not address the fact that cannabis grow sites in Northern California are often densely concentrated in sensitive, remote ecosystems (Bauer et al. 2015; Butsic et al. 2017; Butsic and Brenner 2016; Carah et al. 2015). The issue is not about how many gallons are required per plant or per gram of product (though those are important), but rather the geographic clustering in overtaxed River systems and the timing of diversions, as the height of the growing season is the dry season and overlaps with a crucial time for Salmon populations. Butsic and Brenner (2016) articulate this point as well: "Total stocks of land and water resources consumed by cannabis agriculture are not in themselves troubling. Rather, it is the spatial distribution of cannabis agriculture that determines environmental harm" (9). The creation of a universal number that applies across the state aims to simplify diverse cultivation practices and localized ecological impacts. James Scott's *Seeing Like a State* is useful here. In a discussion of land tenure, Scott (1998) articulates the goals of the colonially imposed state to measure, codify, and simplify land tenure to make it mappable and easily legible to the state. Akin to scientific forestry (discussed in chapter 2), "these state simplifications, like all state simplifications, are always far more static and schematic than the actual social phenomena they presume to typify" (46). While it may be more legible to the state to have a measured and fixed quantity of water for cannabis production, the reality is that there is great variation across the state, and water diversions in one region may have significantly more devastating impacts on water systems than a diversion in another region. Cannabis industry lobbyists also often highlight a comparison to other crops in the state to demonstrate the insignificance of cannabis's water use. However, it is not as if water for all cannabis cultivation in the state is taken from one water system, or that those water systems have equal amounts of water available. The fact that other crops use more water than cannabis does not negate the harms of cannabis-related water diversions. In Northern California, farms are geographically concentrated in sensitive ecosystems that are already experiencing stress due to climate change, causing low flows and high temperatures and threatening Salmon habitats.

In 2016 the Yurok Tribe Environmental Program released a (rarely cited or considered) study on water demand from cannabis cultivation within the watersheds that discharge to the Klamath River located within the Yurok Indian Reservation boundaries. YTEP also based its study on the water use estimates provided in the Bauer team's (2015) study. A water demand estimate study prepared for YTEP in 2016 elaborated on this debate:

> Furthermore, in an attempt to be impartial, Hezekiah Allen, Chair and Executive Director of California Growers Association (CGA) was contacted about the numbers that were used for plant densities and the water demands per plant (personal communication via phone and email, January 15, 2015). . . . Mr. Allen's answer to the question "how much water" was that it depends on the agricultural practices being utilized and that there exists a wide range in water usage based on the length of the growing season and the size of the plant. He explained that the growers his organization represents refer to the size of a plant by the amount of marketable product. Based on surveys and research they have completed, the best formula they've developed is, "1 gallon per pound of product per growing day" and that generally means, the larger the plant, then the longer the growing season, and the more water required. . . . However, Mr. Allen commented that he's known of some outdoor grows with plants that require up to 15 gallons a day due to their larger size and more exposed growing conditions. The final comment is that grow operations are diverse in their practices. (Thiesen and Plocher 2016, 1)

The study estimates the daily cannabis-related water demand within the reservation to be approximately 75,453 gallons per day (Thiesen and Plocher 2016, 14).

Water use studies based on permitted cultivation offer only a partial and preliminary understanding of water use, as the majority of cultivation in this region remains unpermitted. Unpermitted sites, obviously, do not need to comply with local or state regulations such as the forbearance period, and thus, "unpermitted sites may be more likely to use surface water opportunistically throughout the summer" (Dillis et al. 2020, 9). Assessments of trespass cultivation sites during Operation Yurok, for example, found leaky storage tanks, pipes placed directly into streams, and some streams that had been entirely dewatered. Additionally, "field observations from warrant inspections on unpermitted cannabis farms have found stream and spring diversions that feed directly into storage tanks without overflow protections, dispersing excess water to upland areas" (Dillis et al. 2020, 9). Tribal nations have made numerous documentations of illicit water diversions within ancestral territory and Humboldt County has uncovered illicit water diversions made as recently as 2021 (see Humboldt County Sheriff's Office 2021). Contrary to NORML's position, it is the safest and most reasonable course of action for Indigenous people to operate under the assumption that water use estimates developed through these studies are conservative underestimations and total water use is likely much more than reported.

Moreover, while the development and implementation of regulations for water use in cannabis cultivation is certainly a step in the right direction, it certainly will not make water magically appear. The availability, source, and timing of water diversions are all critical to understanding water allocation and its potential impacts. Morgan et al. (2021) examine how current water policy instituted by the SWRCB influence water availability for cannabis cultivators in Northern California. To assess how well current policy is providing water to growers, Morgan's team compared current water use regulations against historic streamflow data from 1980 to 2019. (This study only considered surface water and excludes groundwater extractions and illegal water diversions for cannabis.) Applying the forbearance period to streamflows in 2014–17 showed that the number of diversion days varied between 24 (2014) and 128 (2017), with an average of 71 diversion days. Water availability varied depending on water right permit volume and hours per day of irrigation. Small water rights holders (for grow sites less than 600 m^3) would have secured their water right in full for more than 90 percent of the years between 1980 and 2019. Approximately 65 percent of registered cannabis water rights holders have a small water right. For water right permits greater than 900 m^3, there was often insufficient water to secure the full water right. Approximately 20 percent of registered cannabis water rights holders in this region hold a water right greater than 900 m^3. Water access is particularly unreliable for water rights exceeding 1,200 m³ (under 50 percent) and for growers unable to divert water for twenty-four hours a day. Put simply, the larger your water right, the less likely there is available water to meet it. When faced with the decision to comply with state water regulations or let one's crop fail, growers may be incentivized to either divert surface waters despite low instream flows or acquire water from additional sources.

Water-related concerns over cannabis production have primarily focused on surface water diversions, but cannabis cultivation relies on a variety of different water sources. Chris Dillis et al. (2019) was the first study to analyze where cannabis sites source their water in Northern California. Analyzing data from annual reports submitted by cannabis cultivators enrolled in the Cannabis Waste Discharge Regulatory Program administered by the North Coast Regional Water Quality Control Board, Dillis's team compared monthly patterns for each water source and the differences between compliant and noncompliant sites.[3] In the annual reports, growers must report the water source(s) and the amount of water they use each month of the year. Water sources include surface, spring, well, rain, and off-site; off-site water sources include water deliveries and municipal water sources. The amount of water usage is self-reported and "farms were not required to use water meters, and those without meters often estimated usage based on how frequently they filled and emptied small, temporary storage tanks (250–500 gallons)" (147). This study does not include trespass cultivation or unpermitted cultivation—which undoubtedly describes a great share of the cultivation occurring in the region.

There is variation in water sources across counties throughout the Emerald Triangle (Humboldt, Trinity, Mendocino, and Sonoma). Humboldt County relied on surface water (33.1 percent) and spring diversions (23.9 percent) more than the other three counties did, and fewer relied on wells (40.9 percent).[4] Additionally, cultivators in Humboldt County who relied on surface water were 33.8 percent more likely to use an additional source of water. One explanation offered in this study for the difference in water sources across counties is the availability of various water sources that exist: because Humboldt County receives more rain annually than Trinity, Sonoma, or Mendocino Counties, surface waters are more available and cultivators are likely to use them. "Conversely, the potential necessity of groundwater use in counties that receive less rainfall holds particular importance in consideration of emerging areas of industry growth throughout California" (151–52).

Groundwater, rather than surface water, is the predominant source of water available for legal cultivation in Northern California (Dillis et al. 2019). Groundwater describes the portion of water under the Earth's surface that forms aquifers. The state has been monitoring groundwater withdrawals only since 2014. Groundwater pumping has increased at an alarming rate and is now 64 percent of all water used in California; Southern California, specifically the San Joaquin Valley, is already dealing with substantial land subsidence due to groundwater overdraft (Kaufmann 2019). Cultivation sites access groundwater by drilling a well on-site. In the Dillis 2019 study, 58 percent of sites relied on groundwater—compared to surface water diversions (22 percent) and spring water diversions (16 percent). Rain catchment (12 percent) and off-site water sources (5.4 percent) were the least commonly used water sources. Notably, while only one-third (33 percent) of noncompliant sites had wells, 68 percent of compliant sites had wells, suggesting a possible increase in groundwater use as the regulated cannabis industry expands. Additionally, noncompliant sites were more likely to rely on surface and spring waters (39.4 percent and 36.1 percent, respectively) than compliant sites (14.9 percent and 8.6 percent, respectively) (151). The use of groundwater—provided there is sufficient recharge during wet months—may affect streamflow less than surface water diversions; however, "in the upper reaches of small watersheds, streams are dependent throughout the summer months on subsurface water flows from the landscape into the stream. Well water extraction may reduce cold water inputs—limiting streamflow or, in extreme conditions, dewatering stream channels" (151). Streamflow impacts from groundwater depletion depend on the degree to which water sources are hydrologically connected, which is unknown in many watersheds in California.

Building on the findings from Dillis et al. (2019) that groundwater is the predominant water source for legal cannabis in Northern California, Sam Zipper et al. (2019) aimed to quantify the impact of groundwater pumping for cannabis cultivation. Zipper et al.'s study compares cannabis irrigation to residential groundwater use in the Navarro River Watershed in Mendocino County. Using high-resolution aerial imagery, the team examined 411 parcels; 302 (73 percent) were estimated to use groundwater. Again, unpermitted and trespass cultivation are excluded from data analysis. The Zipper study found that residential groundwater use greatly exceeds groundwater use for cannabis cultivation. Simply put, this is because there are far more residences within the watershed than cannabis operations. However, "if the number of cannabis parcels increased to match the number of residential structures, groundwater abstraction for cannabis would exceed residential use for June–September" (6). Additionally, water demand for cannabis cultivation fluctuates during the year to a much greater extent than residential water use. This supports the findings from Dillis et al., specifically that cultivation sites dependent on groundwater do not divert all year long to store water but rather extract as needed during the growing season. Additionally, Zipper et al. found that a small number of wells (thirty-two) caused a disproportionate amount of streamflow depletion (more than 50 percent) and that "pumping close to stream segments with high habitat potential has the largest potential negative environmental impacts. All else being equal, streamflow depletion would have larger negative impacts in smaller stream segments with lower flow" (9). Groundwater pumping for cannabis cultivation, therefore, is both a current and a future concern that will exacerbate preexisting depletion due to residential, industrial, and other agricultural uses.

The timing of extraction also varies by water source—which is important to consider because the environmental impacts of stream diversions are likely to be greatest during the dry summer months, which coincides with the peak of the cannabis growing season. To address this, the state has created a forbearance period for legal cultivation. Cultivators are prohibited from diverting surface waters during the dry season (April 1–October 31), requiring cultivators to divert surface water during the wet season and store it. To protect aquatic species in drier years with lower flows, the diversion season begins once there are seven consecutive days with flows greater than the instream flow criteria recorded or after December 15. Once the wet season has begun, diversions can only occur on days when the daily average flow is greater than the instream flow criteria. Whereas most groundwater extraction occurs during the growing season (April–October), surface/spring water diversions are more evenly distributed across the year—suggesting that surface/spring water diversions are being stored. But studies also show that many cannabis farms lack the storage capacity to meet their own water demands during the growing season; in Northern California, roughly 80 percent of farms do not have the necessary storage capacity to meet the forbearance period (Dillis et al. 2020): "This suggests that many farms may need to expand water storage capacity or find other sources of water in order to forbear from surface water extractions during the growing season, as currently required by the State Water Resources Control Board" (7). The larger the area of a cultivation site, the less likely that farm is able to store enough water to meet its forbearance requirements. Only cultivation sites with ponds—approximately 10 percent of the total number of sites reviewed—had sufficient water storage to comply with forbearance.

There are logistical and regulatory constraints that will likely limit the forbearance option for many sites. "Aside from the engineering required to build ponds on rugged terrain, there may be difficulty in siting ponds to avoid seasonal watercourses, as required by state and county regulations. Depending on their location, ponds may also serve as habitat for invasive species" (Dillis et al. 2020, 7–8). Alternative storage methods, such as covered tanks, also pose challenges of site grading on rugged terrain. Barriers to water storage may incentivize growers to drill wells, further depleting groundwater rather than developing storage infrastructure. If cannabis cultivators are unable to acquire the water storage necessary to comply with the forbearance period, "these farmers may choose to scale back operations to reduce their water demand, cease operations entirely, or leave the regulated market" (8). And, of course, forbearance and water storage policies operate under the assumption that there is water available; however, "an extremely dry year or multi-year drought may make it difficult to fill reservoirs, superseding concerns about storage capacity altogether" (8).

Interestingly, on July 8, 2021, Cal NORML reported on the Dillis study, with the headline: "Study: Legal Marijuana Farms Are Not a Drain on Resources." The organization writes: "Licensed outdoor marijuana farms in northern California do not put undue strain on limited water resources." The only reason provided is that other crops—like tomatoes and almonds—use more water. They certainly do, but Cal NORML misses the point of the Dillis study. The key finding is that over 80 percent of the legal cannabis farms in Northern California lack the storage capacity to meet the forbearance period.

As we look to the future, research on the geographic trends of legal cannabis production indicate that it is moving southward (Dillis et al. 2021). Optimistically, one might suggest that the problem is moving out of Northern California. Unfortunately, however, this is unlikely to be the case, most obviously because unpermitted cultivation persists in the region but also because water use for agriculture in central and southern California are dependent on water infrastructure that diverts water from Rivers in Northern California. The water infrastructure required for agribusiness in California cannot be disentangled from the dispossession of Indigenous peoples. In February 2021, New Frontier Data, in collaboration with the University of California, Berkeley, Cannabis Research Center and the Resource Innovation Institute, released a report on water usage in the cannabis industry. The researchers argue that cannabis is not a major contributor to water use in United States agriculture:

> The volume of water used to grow cannabis is poised to increase significantly as demand for cannabis (especially in the legal market) surges. However, compared to typical major crops in the U.S. agricultural economy, the cannabis industry has a nominal impact on water used for farming. The impact of the industry's water use may be more pronounced in the drought-prone areas in the Western states. However, even in California and Oregon—two of the country's largest cannabis production markets—the volume of water use is dwarfed by other crops (e.g., fruit trees, grapes, corn, cotton, and rice). (60)

One of the arguments made by the cannabis industry to justify its water usage is that, relative to other agribusiness in California, cannabis is a water-economical crop. According to a study by the Resource Innovation Institute, cannabis uses .0003 million acre-feet, whereas orchards use 6.95 million acre-feet. Of course, the .0003 only describes the legal industry, a small portion of cultivation in the state. From this perspective, statistically cannabis—compared to other agribusiness—is not a major contributor to California's water challenge. The other part of this line of argumentation is that cannabis has a higher market value than other crops (e.g., whereas rice may fetch roughly seventy cents per pound, a pound of smokable cannabis runs from $1,500 to $3,000) (New Frontier Data, Berkeley Cannabis Research Center, and Resource Innovation Institute 2021). In this telling, the value of water lies in its economic value and the best way to use water is putting it toward the product that will produce the most income. Attempts to justify cannabis-related water diversions by comparing diversions by larger industries that consume more water, such as almonds, wine, rice, and other crops, fundamentally mischaracterizes the problem of settler-colonial appropriation of waters for profit, at the expense of Indigenous peoples and our more-than-human relatives.

Statewide data on water usage does not show how individual streams and River basins are impacted, nor does it reveal the genocidal violence and displacement of Indigenous peoples that made contemporary water infrastructure possible. If our fish are dying, it's irrelevant whether that water is being used for wine, tomatoes, or cannabis. All resource rushing in California has been steeped in extractive relationships with water. The green rush is continuing an unsustainable and ecologically violent pattern of water appropriation that benefits settler populations at the expense of Indigenous peoples, our cultures, and our more-than-human relatives.

Discussions of water use among the regulated water industry exclude unregulated cultivation, so water use data only provides a glimpse of the total water use actually happening. And while bringing cannabis cultivation under regulation is a primary goal for its legalization, unregulated cultivation continues to thrive in this region. Therefore, tribal nations have concerns about both illegal *and* legal cultivation. Several tribal nations within Humboldt County articulated their concerns by submitting statements in the county's commercial cannabis environmental impact report. As former natural resources and environmental policy director for the Karuk Tribe Leaf Hillman (2017) writes: "Within Karuk's Aboriginal Territory, legal and illegal cannabis growing operations are dewatering many of the streams our fisheries depend on and associated herbicides, insecticides, and rodenticides are negatively affecting our water quality and killing wildlife" (Humboldt County Planning Dept. Public Comments, 38). On June 1, 2021, the Karuk Tribe also declared a state of emergency, "acknowledge[ing] the reality that climate change is upon us, and the dangers that it poses to rivers, forests, wildlife and communities" (Karuk Tribe, para. 1). Due to low flows and warmer-than-normal water temperatures, 97 percent of sampled juvenile Salmon have tested positive for a deadly pathogen called *Ceratonova shasta* (or C. shasta) (Karuk Tribe 2021). In June 2021 the Wiyot Tribe declared a state of emergency for low instream flows, high temperatures, and toxins present in the water: "The Blue Lake Rancheria Tribe has concerns about cannabis cultivation activities in the ancestral Wiyot territory, and specifically in the Mad River watershed. . . . The Mad River is our source for drinking water, and is home to many culturally-important (and threatened or endangered) species. . . . Impacts from cannabis cultivation have been felt in the lack of cool tributary water as water is siphoned off for grows, in sediment delivery to the river from grading and other ground-disturbing activities, and in the change of aesthetics of the watershed as we see it become over-run with cannabis cultivation" (Humboldt County Planning Dept. Public Comments, 2). A month later the Yurok Tribe announced to tribe members that, due to drought, drinking water in the upper half of the Yurok Reservation was at a historic low and pallets of drinking water were being distributed to elders on an as-needed basis.

Tribal nations have and continue to experience the impacts of the green rush. And while legal cultivation is regulated, it still requires the extraction of resources that are already in peril. The 2016 YTEP study conducted by Stan Theisen and Orrin Plocher (2016) articulates the crux of the issue: "Ecosystem wide impacts are being felt and the water availability throughout a watershed is often diminished. . . . [Yurok Tribal member] concerns range not only for their own uses but for all life, including the plants and animals of the area that are also dependent on the watershed. It is often expressed that the marijuana growers have brought 'un-balance' to the natural world, a deep felt-cultural and ceremonial concept, central to the Yurok" (2). Balance is a central idea to many Indigenous peoples' traditional ecological knowledge and management practices. Yurok scientist Seafha Ramos (2019) describes Yurok TEK (*hlkelonah ue meygeythol*) as "a system where Yurok people and wildlife collaboratively strive to create and maintain balance of the Earth via physical and spiritual management in tandem" (86). Settler colonialism has disrupted this balance. The green rush—like previous rushes—relies on an extractive relationship to landscape that dismembers vast kinship networks and violently transforms them into commodities driven by a singular goal: profit. The reality of the current situation is that Indigenous peoples are experiencing colonial ecological violence due to the lack of water in our ancestral Rivers. Put simply, tribal peoples are already experiencing crisis-level water shortages while much of the state enthusiastically predicts and celebrates the leading cause—increased growth in the cannabis industry.

8 TOXIC ENVIRONMENTS

Cannabis, Chemicals, and Legacy Impacts

Toxicity is violence. More specifically, it is settler colonial violence. Toxicity and the invasive infrastructures it spills from separate us from the land by damaging our relations to it. If our lands are toxic, the more we engage in our cultural practices, the more we risk harming our bodies. Toxicity turns our relations against us. It kills us through connection. It eliminates us as Indigenous peoples by making Indigenous practices dangerous. Don't eat the fish, don't drink the water, don't gather the berries. It does the work of settler colonialism by destroying to replace.
—Anne Spice, "Processing Settler Toxicities: Part 2"

On May 10, 2014, the *Los Angeles Times* reported on the poisoning of environmental scientist Mourad Gabriel's dog with the headline: "Was the Poisoning of Scientist's Dog a Warning from Humboldt Pot Growers?" (Cart 2014). Two years prior, Gabriel and his collaborators had published their findings on exposure and poisoning of the Pacific fisher populations on Hoopa tribal lands and the northern Sierra Nevada. The fisher, a culturally significant species for many tribal peoples in California, is a candidate species for listing under the federal Endangered Species Act. Almost 80 percent of the fishers tested in the study by Gabriel et al. (2012) had been exposed to an anticoagulant rodenticide, an acutely toxic and restricted-use rat poison. Usually found in urban and industrial agricultural settings, it was a surprise to the researchers involved to find large quantities of rat poison in fisher populations whose habitats are found in remote places.

> A likely source of AR exposure to fishers is the emerging spread of illegal marijuana cultivation within California public and private lands. . . . In 2011, a three week eradication operation of marijuana cultivation removed over 630,000 plants and 23,316 kg of trash including 68 kg of pesticides within the Mendocino National Forest in the northern California fisher populations range. Anticoagulant rodenticides and pesticides are typically dispersed around young marijuana plants to deter herbivory, but significant amounts of AR compounds are also

placed along plastic irrigation lines used to draw water from in order to deter rodent chewing. . . . Placement of ARs at the grow sites and along irrigation lines which jut out great distances from the grow site itself may explain why there are no defined clusters of AR exposure. (sec. 4, para. 11)

This research represented an important milestone for turning mainstream attention to the potential ecological ramifications of cannabis cultivation in Northern California. But unfortunately, this attention hasn't been received without violent pushback. Gabriel's labrador retriever, Nyxo, was poisoned with anticoagulant rodenticides.

Cannabis cultivation presents its own toxic challenges, but they must be understood within a larger context of settler-colonial toxicity. In Northern California a pattern of resource rushing has left a toxic legacy that shapes the historic context of emerging industries in the state. From the widespread use of mercury during the gold rush and its disproportionate impact on Indigenous fishing communities to the aerial spraying of atrazine over Yurok forests as late as 2013, the use of toxics within settler resource rushing has negatively impacted tribal peoples since invasion. Trespass cultivation sites on Yurok ancestral territory have left behind numerous toxic substances, and other tribal nations have reported similar findings as well. "Because we do not know the long-term ecological ramifications of these toxicants left on site long after marijuana grows are dismantled, heightened efforts should be focused on the removal of these toxicants at these and adjacent areas at the time of dismantling" (Gabriel et al. 2012, sec. 4, para. 14). Environmental regulations imposed on legal cultivators in the state of California prohibit the use of the chemicals, but trespass cultivation remains an ongoing concern. Additionally, many people within the legal framework are out of compliance and the state lacks sufficient environmental enforcement resources to enforce the regulations.

This chapter examines the pollution impacts of the cannabis industry and the ways in which the green rush maintains and perpetuates settler-colonial toxicity. Cannabis cultivation, specifically trespass cultivation, presents urgent and acute contamination concerns that need to be resolved, but these concerns are exacerbated by past legacy impacts and future impacts of climate change and must be understood within a historical context of settler colonialism and environmental injustice. This chapter concludes with some remarks on the relationship between toxicity, environmental justice, and settler colonialism.

TOXICITY AND CANNABIS

In July of 2016, as Operation Yurok began its third consecutive season of busting trespass cultivation sites in Yurok ancestral territory, I witnessed for the first time the magnitude of pollution associated with trespass cultivation sites. I remember navigating my way through abandoned greenhouses lined with dozens of bags of spent soils and fertilizers. I had to step high to clear the scores of plastic bottles and containers—some empty, some filled with brightly colored chemicals, almost all of them unlabeled and no longer in their original containers. I was shocked by the sheer quantity of chemicals on-site and my head swirled with questions: What did the bottles contain? How harmful were they to the soil and water? To surrounding wildlife? To the unprotected tribe members and Yurok Tribe Environmental Program employees who were engaging with and taking inventory of the site? How much money would it cost to test all of these unlabeled chemicals? Were they legal to purchase in the United States? How much soil and water contamination had already occurred here? How long would these contaminants remain in the ecosystem?

Many of these questions remain unanswered, as the research on toxicants and cannabis production (like most cannabis-related environmental research) remains in its infancy. Outside of the structures that served as pop-up greenhouses, there is often even more pollution: abandoned structures, vehicles, and equipment are commonplace at many trespass cultivation sites. At many sites human waste also poses pollution concerns as there is often a lack of infrastructure such as latrines, which has caused increased levels of coliform and E. coli in the River system. Finally, the amount of garbage left behind is staggering and poses financial and logistical challenges for cleanup. Combined, these sources of pollution present serious harms to tribal homelands. "The Yurok Tribe has determined that there is a significant impact to soil and surface water from illegal marijuana cultivation to the land and water on the Yurok Reservation. Possible impacts identified in a 2014 contracted study with Freshwater Environmental Services include the presence of petroleum compounds used for generators, construction equipment, pumps, and other uses; the use of insecticides for insect control; the use of herbicides for vegetation control; the use of anticoagulant rodenticides for rodent control; and the use of fertilizers and nutrients to enhance growth" (Middleton et al. 2019, 4).

I encourage everyone to think of the impacts of the green rush not as a unique or isolated instance of contamination, but rather as a continuation of historic contamination that has not stopped since settler-colonial invasion in Northern California began with the gold rush. For example, on the Yurok Indian Reservation, there are "over 200 potential environmental pollutant sites, including illegal dumpsites, abandoned autos, herbicide spraying, burned homes, faulty septic systems, old mill sites, old mining sites, previously cleaned dumpsites, old home sites, and historic logging activity where machinery fluids were often improperly disposed into soil and waterways" (Middleton et al. 2019, 4). This is all before cannabis cultivation is added into the mix. Toxins *already* present in species that are culturally significant to the Yurok people include carbamates, dioxins/furans, mercury, microcystins, and organophosphate pesticides. Five legacy organochlorine pesticides that were banned between the 1960s and 1980s were detected across several tested species. (These include Chinook and fall coho salmon, winter steelhead, green sturgeon, and Pacific lamprey, among others. Residues and derivatives of DDT were also detected [Fluharty and Sloan 2014].) While exposure does not necessarily imply health impacts, Yurok Tribe members report disproportionate health impacts compared to the general US population, including higher rates of cancer and reproductive complications (Fluharty and Sloan 2014; Middleton et al. 2019). The Yurok Tribe is not alone in this. The Copper Bluff Mine in Hoopa, for example, is a hazardous waste site and may qualify as an EPA Superfund site. Used to collect copper, zinc, silver, and gold from 1928 to 1964, the mine continues to impact the Klamath River Basin (Estrada 2018). Featured in the *North Coast Journal*, director of Hoopa Valley Tribal EPA Ken Norton (Hupa) explains that chemicals are still seeping out of the mine and into the water, impacting the soil, salmon, lamprey, sturgeon, and human health (Estrada 2018).

As tribal nations speak out against the environmental harms perpetuated by the gold rush and take action to protect ancestral territory (e.g., Operation Yurok), the onus of cleaning up the aftermath of trespass cultivation falls to tribal peoples, who disproportionately experience the harms of trespass cultivation when growers set up shop on tribal and public lands. If we understand the history of settler-colonial dispossession, we know that public lands are just tribal lands that have been taken by the government. Trespass cultivation sites profit on the unconsented taking of natural resources and leave a legacy of ecological degradation and violence. The fact that tribal nations have to clean up these sites highlights the ways in which settler-colonial relationships to land and natural resources work to benefit settlers and simultaneously harm Indigenous peoples through the creation of toxic environments.

Toxicants are chemicals put into the environment by human activity that can kill or harm humans, animals, or plants. Toxicants are used at cannabis cultivation sites for a variety of reasons: "to mitigate herbivory of cannabis plants by wildlife, curtail pilfering of food stores at trespass cultivation site camps, and reduce damage to cultivation infrastructure by wildlife" (Gabriel and Wengert 2020, 10). Additionally, concentrated toxicants are sometimes intentionally placed in cans of tuna, sardines, and cat food and distributed around a site (Levy 2014; Thompson et al. 2018). Many sources of pollution associated with cannabis cultivation are referred to as nonpoint source pollution. Nonpoint source pollution results from many diffuse sources, as opposed to a confined, discernible source—the latter defined as point source pollution. According to the EPA (2021), nonpoint source pollution generally results from land runoff, precipitation, drainage, or hydrologic modification. This pollution includes excess fertilizers, herbicides, insecticides, petroleum products, sediment, bacteria, and nutrients. "As the runoff moves, it picks up and carries away natural and human-made pollutants, finally depositing them into lakes, rivers, wetlands, coastal waters and ground waters" (sec. 1, para. 1). Fertilizers, for example, are added to the soil and then eventually seep into the groundwater, where they are transported to surface waters, creeks, and Rivers. For the Klamath River, already plagued by low flows and toxic algae blooms due to the impact of installed dams, the added elements present a grave concern for water quality.

Various herbicides and pesticides—ranging from the readily available over-the-counter Roundup varieties to banned and restricted-use pesticides—are used by cannabis cultivators and are then indiscriminately eaten by numerous wildlife species. In a research interview conducted in 2017, Gabriel shared with me that he has recovered a plethora of toxicants, including—but not limited to—organophosphates, carbamates, pyrethrins, molluscicides, and phosphides. These chemicals pose ecological risks to the environment and also threaten human health:

> [There is a] misconception that because it's just a plant . . . what's the worst thing that could be out there? Maybe some fertilizer, but what people don't realize is that cultivators use chemicals and pesticides that are systemic—that means that they can go on clear, the plant can absorb them, and they're sequestered in the phloem or xylem—which is the sap material of that plant—and you may see a normal marijuana plant, but that plant is pumping through its sap pesticides. And you pick it up, you sample it, or you touch the soil, or you touch the shovel, you touch other material that the cultivators use . . . that is just a fraction of the health impacts that can occur from people just interacting at the site. (Mourad Gabriel, author interview, August 29, 2017)

If touching contaminated plants is a human health concern, the impacts from ingestion are even greater. Moreover, many of the recovered pollutants are restricted use, meaning only licensed applicators should be able to purchase them. "Unfortunately, there is no traceability for that; so when we find a lot of restricted use pesticides out there, we can't trace it back to whoever purchased it" (Gabriel interview). For example, the Mill Creek Watershed—the large tributary of the Trinity River on the eastern side of the Hoopa Valley Reservation—has repeatedly been polluted with toxicants over the past decade. In 2012 the Hoopa Valley Tribe, in collaboration with law enforcement, visited and documented recently eradicated sites. At the first grow site they visited, located in the Mill Creek Watershed, researchers

> documented well over a ton of empty chemical fertilizer bags and 11 pounds of poisoned rat bait on that first visit, among other pesticides, and several gallons of liquid fertilizers. Human waste was common within feet of the main channel of Mill Creek; this creek is a key domestic water source for the tribe as well as one of the most important anadromous fish-bearing streams on the reservation. Our in-depth investigation into this first site was an eye-opener: it was hard to believe

what we were seeing. Intricate trail systems connecting the patches, camps, dumps, drying areas and water sources were extensive throughout this grow-site complex. At least three major water sources were used, and we noted several miles of ¾- and 1-inch black plastic source lines in addition to miles of ½-inch irrigation lines within patches, fitted with drip lines and emitters. (Higley et al. 2018, 63)

Six years later, on October 2, 2018, the Trinity County Department of Environmental Health issued a quarantine of a private parcel in the Mill Creek Watershed being used for cannabis cultivation. Following a search warrant executed by the California Department of Fish and Wildlife, several pesticides currently banned in the United States that were used for cannabis cultivation were recovered from the site: "Due to these findings, [Trinity County Environmental Health] is warning the public that there has been a potential spill into an unnamed tributary of Mill Creek, a tributary to the Trinity River, of suspected Carbofuran, Methamidophos, and Avermectin B1 pesticides. The private parcel is located off of Underwood Mountain Road in the Burnt Ranch area, and the site is being quarantined at this time" (Kemp 2018b). Carbofuran, primarily used to control insects on crops such as corn, potatoes, and soybeans, is a Class 1 pesticide, meaning it is extremely hazardous. Carbofuran is very toxic to birds and has been illegally used to intentionally kill wildlife. For humans, Carbofuran has one of the highest acute toxicities of any insecticide; Carbofuran poisoning can lead to death. Banned in both Canada and the European Union, Carbofuran was supposed to be banned by the EPA in 2006, but "FMC, carbofuran's U.S. manufacturer, has fought the Agency's decision" (Pesticide Action Network 2010). Also a Class 1 pesticide, Methamidophos is used on crops such as potatoes and rice. Methamidophos is rapidly absorbed through the stomach, lungs, and skin of humans. Methamidophos is very toxic to both birds and aquatic organisms (EXTOXNET 1995). While Avermectin B1 and other Avermectin pesticides are relatively not harmful to mammals, they are highly toxic to fish and aquatic invertebrates. Avermectin B is also highly toxic to bees (EXTOXNET 1994). Gabriel (2017) predicts that, regarding cannabis cultivation, "we may be dealing with legacy impacts. And therefore, we may have water and soil contamination for months to years to possibly decades, especially if we do not do cleanups" (Gabriel interview).

Perhaps the primary toxicant of concern at trespass cultivation sites—and the subject of Gabriel's research—is rat poison, technically referred to as anticoagulant rodenticide (AR). The intended purpose of ARs is to kill relatives deemed "pests" (primarily rat populations) in agricultural and urban settings. On cannabis farms, ARs are typically placed near young cannabis plants to prevent animals from eating them; they are also placed by plastic irrigation lines to prevent animals from chewing on them (Gabriel et al. 2012). Inhibiting the recycling of Vitamin K, the ingestion of a rodenticide prohibits blood clotting and causes massive internal bleeding. Additionally, it also makes a poisoned animal more susceptible to predation and, through the process of bioaccumulation, toxicants make their way up the food chain. However, the problem is not only accidental consumption of poison; wildlife species are purposefully poisoned as a preventative measure against crop disruption. Examples include hot dogs stuffed with carbamate insecticide, wherein a dead fisher was found less than 20 meters away (Gabriel 2016). In recent years there have been rodenticide replacements, such as Bromethalin, which can be flavored—bacon-scented and bacon-flavored poisons have been detected at abandoned grow sites. One grow site uncovered in 2014 had over twenty-four pounds of Bromethalin on its premises (Gabriel 2016). Other animals—such as coyotes and even a black bear—have been found dead near grow sites heavily laced with poisonous chemicals (Hamann 2013; Shogren 2014).

Described as the "canary in the coal mine" of trespass cultivation, the fisher (Hupa 'ista:ngq'eh-k'itiqowh; Yurok le'go'; Latin *Pekania pennanti*) has been subject to pesticide poisoning and the focus of recent research (Thompson et al. 2018). Once abundant throughout western North America, the fisher has experienced significant population decline. While it was proposed for listing under the federal Endangered Species Act, the fisher was denied protection (Gabriel et al. 2012; Higley et al. 2018). Since 2005 the Hoopa Valley Tribe has collaborated with researchers, including Gabriel, to conduct the "longest-running fisher demographic study in western North America" (Higley et al. 2018, 61). Gabriel et al. (2012) conducted a study on the spatial distribution and exposure of anticoagulant rodenticides among the fisher population in California. Gabriel's team tested fifty-eight carcasses from two isolated fisher populations—one located on Hupa ancestral territory in Northern California (including tribal, private, and public lands) and the other on the northern Sierra Nevada/southern Cascade Mountain borderlands in northcentral California—and found forty-six (79 percent) had been exposed to anticoagulant rodenticides and 96 percent had been exposed to one or more second-generation anticoagulant rodenticide compounds.[2] An additional study by a Gabriel team from 2015 found that exposure rates statewide had increased to 85 percent and toxicant-related mortality had increased from 5.6 to 18.7 percent between 2007 and 2014. Also important to note is that this significant environmental impact of trespass cannabis cultivation was discovered by accident; researchers were studying fisher populations for reasons unrelated to cannabis (Thompson et al. 2018). Had this research not been taking place, the toxic threats of trespass cultivation may not have been made public. Additionally, because trespass sites are difficult to access and researchers are often only able to access them *after* they have ceased cultivation, concerns remain high that there are other sources of contamination that environmental scientists have thus far not been able to identify.

On par with wildlife pesticide poisoning, impacts to water quality remains an important ecological concern of trespass cultivation as well. Because of the cultural importance of water and multiple exposure pathways experienced by Indigenous peoples, water contamination is an affront to Indigenous peoples' relationships and responsibilities to their homelands. Water quality impacts are then magnified by a reduction in water quantity. Cannabis-related water diversions have impaired instream flows and in some cases have entirely dewatered streams in crucial Salmon spawning creeks and tributaries (Bauer et al. 2015). When stream flows are reduced, the impacts on water quality by, for example, chemical pollution, are magnified. Less water in the River also means that water temperatures rise and water quality is compromised—and the dams intensify this as well. Forest manager for the Hoopa Tribal Forestry Department Jeff Lindsay explains: "If you take all the water out, that kills off the wildlife and it has a ripple effect all down the watershed. Amphibians and bugs that are a food source for fish lower down aren't there anymore" (quoted in Korns 2013). "Hotspots for human waste, sewage, illegal dumping," these trespass cultivation sites contaminate tribal water supplies through the application of pesticides, insecticides, and herbicides (toxicants), as well as by illegally dumping (toxins) (Suzanne Fluharty, author interview, August 10, 2017).

> Basically, because of this, and then low flows [which have] their own water quality issues . . . It can make contaminants more concentrated because they're not being diluted; on the other hand, they could also be so dry they're not being transported into the water, but what we've seen is spikes of the E. coli and septic coming down, so people can't drink. So we have tribal members, because of different issues with their water, not enough water or water that's contaminated, have to leave the reservation. And so the tribal members can't even live on their homeland . . . this is a big deal. Water is a basic human right and it's not being protected. (Fluharty interview)

The lack of safe water has led to hardship for many tribal families, with some going so far as leaving the reservation to live in towns on the coast. This is especially significant considering the legacy of removal in this country. From the aftermath of the Indian Removal Act of 1830 to the abduction of Native American children into boarding schools, Native peoples have experienced geographic, social, and psychocultural removals (Wildcat 2009). Daniel Wildcat (2009) draws connections between historic removals of Native people in the nineteenth century and the removal we see today via environmental destruction and climate change: "This removal is not simply a governmental social policy imperative of the non-indigenous majority population. This relocation is mandated by a much deeper, more fundamental crisis: the way we live" (4). Like previous waves of removal, it is Indigenous folks who pay the price for settler desires.

Widespread use of nutrients and fertilizers also pose a threat to water quality. In Humboldt County, for example, 90 percent of the county has poor-quality agricultural soil, so many growers import soil and amendments for both outdoor and greenhouse grows (Schwab and Butsic 2016). During Operation Yurok, one of the most common features of trespass cultivation sites were three-hundred-gallon containers of highly soluble nitrate fertilizers (Yurok Tribe 2014). When it rains, these kinds of fertilizers can contaminate drinking water and cause eutrophication, or toxic algae blooms, in the waterways. The combination of warm water and high nutrient loading provides ideal habitat for the rise of toxic blue-green algae. Increased water temperatures, stagnation and low water movement, and high nutrient concentrations lead to algae blooms. These blooms provide a class of toxin called microcystins. The presence of microcystins in surface waters is a growing concern for the Yurok Tribe due to tribe members' multiple sources of exposure to the toxin. Toxic algae blooms already appear periodically in this region and tribe members are already experiencing chronic exposure. Symptoms of microcystin exposure in humans include rashes, hepatotoxicity, muscle fasciculations, abdominal breathing, and convulsions (Fluharty and Sloan 2014; Middleton et al. 2019). Additionally, when those algae blooms die, the oxygen that decomposes the algae is pulled out of the water and the Salmon suffocate. This is referred to as hypoxia. To make matters worse, Salmon then transport these toxins into the ocean and the mouth of the Klamath River delivers fresh water "quite a ways out into the ocean and so it would be carrying any toxins, chemicals, nutrients out into the ocean environment as well" (Fluharty 2017). These toxins can be absorbed by ocean plankton that both rockfish and mussels feed on—both of which are a major subsistence food for the Yurok Tribe. Finally, not everyone living on the Yurok Indian Reservation has access to a community water system; some tribe members obtain household water directly from streams or springs—increasing the likelihood that they will be exposed to and suffer the negative impacts from the chemical fertilizers, solid waste, and sediment resulting from cannabis cultivation.

Another potential source of water quality impacts is human waste. Many trespass cultivation sites on tribal and public lands are transient; growers have no intention of staying in our hills after the harvest. Therefore, they are not accountable to these places nor do they invest in these places. Often growers do not construct latrines or outhouses. Illicit cannabis cultivation sites, therefore, are hotspots for human waste and sewage. Some sites documented during Operation Yurok had built outhouses over a creek so that the water would flush away waste. Another site utilized five-gallon plastic buckets as toilets. After the site has been abandoned, "What do you do with one hundred five-gallon buckets filled with human sewage?" (Fluharty interview). YTEP has also detected increased levels of coliform and E. coli in the River system (Micah Gibson, author interview, August 11, 2017).

In addition to water quality contamination, the siting and process of cultivation has documented ecological impacts, but trespass grow sites located on tribal and public lands often result in hazardous solid waste. Many trespass sites are abandoned, either to avoid detection during a raid or, following a profitable harvest, a mess is simply left behind. The quantity of waste left behind is truly astonishing and reminiscent of episodes of the popular television show *Hoarders*. Waste left behind ranges from household garbage to abandoned vehicles, open and closed barrels with unknown contents, batteries, plastics, spent irrigation lines, stripped trailers for starting cuttings, vegetative plants, and materials and equipment such as insulation, fiberglass, pressboard paneling, air conditioners, and refrigerators. In 2018, after four years of Operation Yurok, the Yurok Tribe (2018b) issued a press release:

> The tremendous amount of environmental damage left in the wake of the approximately 150, previously active grow sites on the reservation will require an extended and extremely expensive effort to clean up. In several cases, growers had used heavy machinery to carve deep benches into mountains, removing all of the vegetation and even the topsoil. Trash heaps containing toxic chemicals, such as petroleum products and pesticides, were left in the forest. Hundreds of miles of plastic PVC pipe are strewn across several drainages that flow into the Klamath River. These are just a few examples of the types of costly environmental issues that the Tribe will now have to figure out how to resolve. (*Times Standard*, para. 12)

Former YTEP interim director Micah Gibson recalls one particularly horrific site:

> We were walking down this road and we saw some garbage over the hillside and so we started looking at it and then the ground felt really spongy. We could bounce on it. And I dug about 3 inches down and we were standing on garbage. And so we looked back on the other side of the road and there was a large chunk of the hillside taken out, so what we figured out was they had just dug a large pit where all of this garbage went in and when they were done they took dirt from the opposite side of the road out of the mountain and just covered it so it kind of looked like a big turnout but really you were standing on this massive pile of garbage. And who knew how deep it went? We were looking thirty to forty feet down the hillside and still seeing garbage, so there was potential for it to be twenty to thirty feet deep of garbage that was over one hundred feet long. (Gibson interview)

While extreme, this is not an isolated case. The cumulative impact of a wide variety of pollutants is extremely concerning to the Yurok Tribe. Another site Gibson recalled contained approximately 130 refrigerators, 500 bicycles, 200 toilets, 200 cars in disarray, "and it just went on and on and on for like three quarters of a mile down the side of this road" (Gibson interview). Other waste includes generators, equipment, and petroleum products.

Plastic pollution—one of the most widespread and long-lasting contributors to anthropogenic change that poses growing hazards for fish and wildlife—is also a concern within the cannabis industry.[3] Because plastics are virtually nonbiodegradable, they are released into terrestrial and aquatic ecosystems. There have not been any formal studies on the use of plastics within cannabis cultivation specifically, but it is commonly known to be widespread. "At outdoor cannabis cultivation sites, cultivators may use, for example, plastic mulching to protect seedlings and shoots, polyvinyl chloride (PVC) pipes to transport water, plastic monofilament for plant support or erosion control, plastic netting to exclude birds and other wildlife, and an array of additional plastic products (e.g., fertilizer bags and pots)" (Rich et al. 2020, 122). Wildlife can ingest or become entangled in plastics. Over half of all plastics have chemical additives that, over time, can leach into surface water, groundwater, sediment, and soil.

Initially, enforcing environmental regulations on cannabis cultivation was a key argument for legalization in California. While the state of California is only a few years out from legalization and the emerging cannabis industry still has a lot of unanswered questions, what has legalization meant for pesticide use and cleaning up after cultivation sites? "California state regulations restrict the use of pesticides in or around permitted cannabis cultivation if they are a) California restricted materials, b) on the ground water protection list, or c) not registered for a food use in California" (Rich et al. 2020, 45). Cultivators must also abide by pesticide regulations imposed on other agricultural industries, such as containing leaks, cleaning up spills, preventing drift, avoiding contact with surface waters, and so on. The Bureau of Cannabis Control requires cultivators to have a pest management plan that includes names and ingredients of all pesticides used during the cultivation process and requires that a half gram of every cannabis batch be tested for pesticides. "At legal cultivation sites, for example, the toxic pesticide products that tend to result in acute and sublethal effects in non-target wildlife species cannot be legally applied. At illegal cultivation sites, alternatively, the use of these toxic pesticides and numerous ensuing environmental impacts have been well documented" (Rich et al. 2020, 48). While these regulations are certainly necessary for legal cultivation, they do not, unfortunately, negate the ongoing contamination of illicit cultivation.

Cleaning up abandoned cultivation sites remains an important priority for tribal nations in northwestern California; however, resources for tribal environmental departments—often completely reliant on external grants—are limited. Additionally, the magnitude and scope of the environmental damage is daunting. As Greta Wengert et al. (2018) state, it is "estimate[d] that law enforcement likely detects fewer than half of the active marijuana cultivation sites each year, and of those detected, fewer than 10 percent are reclaimed or restored to their natural state" (30). The problem is "Funding, funding, funding, always funding. There's no money out there to perform these cleanups" (Gibson interview). In 2017 the state of California earmarked $1.5 million to the California Department of Fish and Wildlife (CDFW) toward the cleanup of abandoned cultivation sites in Humboldt, Trinity, and Mendocino Counties ("Gov. Brown Earmarks" 2017). The CDFW awarded the Integral Ecology Research Center—which was working in collaboration with numerous government agencies, nonprofits, and the Hoopa Valley Tribal Forestry Division—over $1 million to reclaim 170 trespass cultivation sites on public lands at Six Rivers, Shasta-Trinity, and Klamath National Forests and the Hoopa Valley Indian Reservation (CDFW 2020). While this is an important start, many uncleaned cultivation sites remain and trespass cultivation continues.

Some counties have developed incentive programs for cultivators to move their operations to more ecologically suitable areas. In Humboldt County, for example, the Retirement, Remediation, and Relocation (RRR) program was created "to incentivize, promote, and encourage the retirement, remediation and relocation of pre-existing cannabis cultivation operations occurring in inappropriate, marginal, or environmentally sensitive sites to relocate to environmentally superior sites" (Humboldt County 2018b, 20). This program is designed for growers that were cultivating *prior to* legalization and provides an incentive to being able to cultivate four times the area of the preexisting grow, provided the site does not surpass a total 20,000 acres.

However, to be eligible to relocate the cultivator must also remediate the original site. According to Section 55.4.6.5.9(e) of the ordinance (Humboldt County 2018b), a full environmental remediation includes "removal of all cultivation related materials, equipment and improvements, regarding to preexisting contours, reseeding with native vegetation, reforestation, habitat restoration, and monitoring" (21). The ordinance specifies that the applicant must complete the tasks outlined within the remediation plan within twelve months following the retirement and relocation from the site. Additionally, the applicant must post a bond for the estimated cost of the remediation in the event the applicant abandons the site. After the cleanup a covenant is placed on the property for no further commercially cultivated cannabis. If the covenant is ever violated, all permits for operation in the relocation site are terminated. In theory, then, certain lands will be protected from cannabis cultivation in the future. However, for those opting to engage in the illicit market, such covenants will hardly serve as a deterrent—and environmental resources, as well as tribal cultural resources, will remain at risk.

Because many of the remediated sites are within Yurok ancestral territory, the Yurok Tribe Cannabis Task Force plays a key role in the RRR program. To go through the RRR process for a parcel within reservation boundaries, applicants must collaborate directly with the Yurok Tribe. Such collaborations, of course, require a great deal of resources from the Yurok Tribe, as the process requires site visits to remote locations and thorough reviews of the site. The tribe must create an estimate of how much it will cost to remediate the site, which has created tension for some growers, who often pay a consultant that estimates a lower amount. The assistant director of the Pollution Prevention Program, Koiya Tuttle, explains the discrepancy between cleanup estimates. First there is a moral obligation that the Yurok Tribe has to ensure that sites are cared for in responsible ways—taking the time and labor to separate out recyclable materials:

> Other people have these recommendations for something that I would estimate to be anywhere from sixty to eighty thousand dollars in cleanup time at most. Other people have estimated fifteen to twenty-five thousand because what they would do in order to make that cost special is to go in with the excavator and just crush every-

thing and stuff it into a bin and everything would go to a landfill. So that's that difference when we look at a cleanup and when everyone else looks at a cleanup.

As a tribal member first of all, I hope that people are respectful of where the trash is going on some other person's tribal land too. So, we want to make sure that we are not going to just pass the buck, so to speak. We'll accept the problem and then we'll remedy it so it's no longer a problem for us and a problem for someone else. The only way to do that is to properly dispose of things. (Koiya Tuttle, author interview, June 4, 2018)

The perspective that the Yurok Tribe takes in cleaning up abandoned sites is farsighted; it is not about completing a checklist of items to be removed from the site, but rather about ensuring the long-term ecological integrity of tribal lands for seven generations to come.

While programs like the RRR have led to site remediation, these processes, just like environmental regulations, are limited to folks that choose to navigate the legal industry. Trespass cultivation persists and many sites still need to be cleaned. The state of California and specifically the counties in Northern California not only need to claim responsibility for the ecological damage that has occurred because of the illegal industry; they also must account for the legacy impacts from previous cycles of resource rushing. For starters, revenue permit application fees and taxes should be used to rectify the damage that the cannabis industry has created thus far. But more is required. The crux of the issue is not necessarily cannabis cultivation in and of itself, but rather the cycles of resource extraction that enact relationships with the environment based on extraction rather than on mutual benefit. Settler-colonial natural resource management has been unable to move beyond a framework based on economic resources that is ultimately detrimental to Indigenous peoples and landscapes.

TOXICITY, ENVIRONMENTAL JUSTICE, AND SETTLER COLONIALISM

For many Indigenous communities, environmental justice struggles began with the invasion and colonization of our lands (Gilio-Whitaker 2019; Weaver

1996; Whyte 2016, 2018). But the contemporary environmental justice movement (EJM) that many of us are familiar with today arose out of the activism in the 1980s challenging environmental racism (Cole and Foster 2001; Foreman 1998; Turner and Wu 2002; Sze and London 2008). Specifically, resistance against a municipal landfill in Houston, Texas, and the disposal of soil contaminated with PCBs in Warren County, North Carolina—both located in predominantly African American communities—gave shape to what would become the environmental justice movement. Considered the "father of environmental justice," Robert D. Bullard's *Dumping in Dixie: Race, Class, and Environmental Quality*, published in 1990, chronicled environmental racism in the siting of landfills, hazardous waste sites, incinerators, refineries, and chemical plants (Bullard 2021). Resistance to toxic pollution, then, has been a central part of the American environmental justice movement since the 1980s.

For Native communities, however, notions of environmental justice are far older than the EJM born in the 1980s—and instead are rooted in the invasion and dispossession of Indigenous territories. As such, within Indigenous communities, environmental justice must be framed through colonization: "As Indian lands are assaulted, so are Indian peoples. . . . Environmental destruction is simply one manifestation of the colonialism and racism that have marked Indian/White relations since the arrival of Columbus in 1492" (Weaver 1996, 3). Native lands are the most targeted (for environmental injustice) in the world, and the United States is no exception (LaDuke 1999). Environmental abuses range from industrial pollution to toxic dumping to nuclear testing and mining (LaDuke 1999; LaDuke and Cruz 2012; Vickery and Hunter 2016; Weaver 1996; Whyte 2018, 2016). Felix Cohen—considered to be the father of modern federal Indian law—likened Native Americans to miners' canaries: "the multiple ills that are visited upon them are only a prelude and a harbinger of what is to be expected for society as a whole" (Weaver 1996, 17). For example, nearly a quarter of the thirteen hundred Superfund sites in the United States are located in Indian Country (Hansen 2014; Lambert 2020). Many of them have yet to be cleaned up. Scholars have referred to Indian Country as "sacrifice zones": places that are flooded, polluted, and/or extracted to allow capitalist settler industries to expand and profit (Middleton Manning 2018; Voyles 2015).

From a critical Indigenous perspective, environmental justice necessitates an understanding of and engagement with settler colonialism (Gilio-Whitaker 2019; Voyles 2015; Whyte 2018, 2016). Settler colonialism as a structure constitutes a form of environmental injustice because it eliminates the socio-ecological contexts required for Native peoples to observe commitments to their homelands and their more-than-human relatives (Whyte 2018, 2016). Two significant concepts come from Kyle Whyte (2018, 2016): "moral terrain" and "collective continuance." Moral terrain refers to the responsibilities that Indigenous peoples have regarding land: accountability to one's ancestors and responsibility to take care of the land for future generations. Environmental injustice occurs when Indigenous systems of responsibilities are erased or interfered with. Such responsibilities, however, are not solely affixed to other beings, but all elements of creation; these responsibilities are outlined within natural law. This differs markedly from a people-centered environmental justice approach. Tribal nations in Northern California, for example, hold relationships with Salmon relatives that extend beyond economic resources. As David Gensaw explains, "We've been told since the beginning of time, 'once those fish are gone, so are the Yurok people'" (David Gensaw, author interview, July 6, 2018). Collective continuance, then, refers to the ways in which Indigenous peoples can adapt to external forces, from environmental change to human-induced change, in order to maintain cultural lifeways. Ecological transformations through processes of ecocolonialism have altered—sometimes in irreversible ways—the places where Indigenous peoples have always lived. Sacred sites have been desecrated and traditional subsistence practices have been all but impossible to perform due to expanding capitalistic economies. In other words, settler ecologies must be inscribed on top of already existing Indigenous ecologies (Whyte 2016). The inability to maintain or continue cultural lifeways as a result of settler-colonial land dispossession is an environmental injustice to Indigenous peoples. If land enables Indigenous life, the dispossession or contamination of those lands threatens Indigenous life.

Native American studies scholars have linked settler colonialism, environmental justice, and toxics. Anne Spice (Tlingit) (2018) argues that "colonization is the foundation of environmental decline." Specifically, Spice uses the example of environmental toxins found in our lands, waters, and bodies to illustrate her connection between environmental spoliation and settler colonialism. As Spice points out, the discourse around "toxics"—stemming from the Greek word for bow and arrow—in the environment lacks intentionality or agency; in this reading they just happen to be there. But this is not true. Spice encourages us to rethink this passive understanding of toxics: "Our ways of sustaining ourselves, our local economies, our food provision, our medicine, are cleared for the expansion of an economy based primarily on oil and gas. Here, the pipeline spills and toxic emissions, while perhaps 'accidents,' are not without direction or intent. Trace the poison arrow back through its flight path, to the archer. Who is holding the bow?" (sec. 1, para. 5). Without settler colonialism our lands and our bodies would not have been poisoned. Gone are the days of child abduction and violent boarding school "educations," but deterrents from practicing our cultures remain. Basketweavers risk the ingestion of poisons as they run strands of grasses through their mouths.[4] As we gather materials in our forests we must wonder when the last time the US Forest Service sprayed atrazine. Blue-green algae, swelled by myriad pesticides and herbicides, choke once-clear Rivers and produce microcystin toxins that contaminate surface waters, fish, mussels, and people (Fluharty and Sloan 2014; Middleton et al. 2019).

I wish us to return to an argument made by Tony Barta, put forth in chapter 1. Barta (2000) argues that there needs to be a new conception of genocide, one that "embraces *relations* of destruction and removes from the word the emphasis on policy and intention which brought it into being. . . . We know that the destruction of many peoples, genocidal *outcomes*, have been the result of complex and only obscurely discerned causes, and in that respect genocide should properly lose its uniqueness of having intentionality as its defining characteristic" (238). Often, environmental harms lack the "intent" deemed necessary to qualify as genocide. For example, Daniel Brook (1998), in his article "Environmental Genocide: Native Americans and Toxic Waste," argues that genocide vis-à-vis environmental spoliation or "environmental genocide is perpetuated by the U.S. government and by private corporations alike" (105). Using the examples of hazardous waste citing and illegal dumping on reservations, Brook further argues that "this type of genocide is not (usually) the result of a systematic plan with malicious intent to exterminate Native Americans, it is the consequence of activities that are often carried out on and near the reservations with reckless disregard for the lives of Native Americans" (105–6). In Brook's analysis, Native peoples experience genocide as an unintended consequence of environmental extraction. This is why Spice's critique of the lack of agency and intentionality behind environmental destruction is necessary. We must ask "Who is holding the bow?" Who profits or benefits from such environmental spoliation? Who suffers the consequences? Rather than thinking about environmental genocide as a unique form of genocide, we can think about environmental destruction as the consequence of relations of genocide or as a genocidal outcome. However, Brook's argument that "toxic pollution is a *genocide through geocide*, that is, a killing of the people through a killing of the Earth" remains significant because it highlights the connections between violence against land and violence against Indigenous bodies (111, emphasis added). However, like Indigenous conceptions of environmental justice that are not human-centric but rather underscore the importance of environmental justice for more-than-human relatives, genocidal violence is also experienced by more-than-human relatives (e.g., nineteenth-century buffalo extermination, 2002 fish kill). Damien Short (2016) argues that "if we take the genos in genocide to be a social figuration which forms a comprehensive culture . . . then genocide is the forcible breaking down of such relationships—the destruction of the social figuration" (36). Conceptions of genocide must expand beyond intentionality and a human-centric worldview that does not consider other species or relations or the agency of the natural world. How is our notion of genocide—or the forcible breaking down of relationships—altered when our position of analysis considers a kinship-oriented relationship to and with other species and the land itself?

Settler colonialism has rendered Indigenous lands and bodies—as well as Indigenous worldviews, histories, cultures, and relations—inherently pollutable (Voyles 2015). In *Pollution Is Colonialism*, Max Liboiron (Red River Métis/Michif) (2021) argues that the structures that allow industrial pollution necessitate settler-colonial access to Indigenous territories. In other words, "pollution is not a manifestation or side effect of colonialism but is rather an enactment of ongoing colonial relations to Land. That is, pollution is best understood as the violence of colonial land relations rather than environmental damage, which is a symptom of violence" (6–7). Pollution occurs under the assumption of settler-colonial claims to land and that bodies (water, human, etc.) can withstand a certain quantity of contaminants without harm, indeed that the very purpose of some of these bodies is to hold and store said pollutants. In what Liboiron refers to as the "permission to pollute" system, "specific quantities of contaminants are allowed legally in bodies of water, human bodies, air, food, and environments" (39). Liboiron describes two sanitation engineers named H. W. Streeter and Earle B. Phelps, who did a study in the Ohio River Valley in the 1920s to determine the "conditions and rates under which water (or at least that bit of the Ohio River) could purify itself of organic pollutants" (4). Of course, this study was about a particular watershed and not all Rivers are the same.[5] Nevertheless, "the Streeter-Phelps equation, as it came to be known, not only became a hallmark of water pollution science and regulation but also contained within it their theory of pollution: that a moment existed when water could not purify itself and that moment could be measured, predicted, and properly called pollution. Self-purification became known as *assimilative capacity*, a term of art in both environmental science and policy making that refers to 'the amount of waste material that may be discharged into a receiving water without causing deleterious ecological effects'" (4–5). Liboiron refers to this as the threshold theory of pollution—the threshold being "that arbitrary line between pollution and nonpollution" (57). This idea—whether referred to as assimilative capacity, critical load, permissible dose, or maximum acceptable concentration—operates under the assumption that pollution is acceptable and certain places and bodies are pollutable. From a settler-colonial perspective, the question is not whether to pollute but rather *how much* the state is allowed to pollute. Settler-colonial solutions work to mitigate, rather than eliminate, pollution. And often, Indigenous folks are left to endure the "mitigation."[6]

Additionally, the ways in which Indigenous peoples are exposed to contaminants may often be overlooked by settler scientists. Indigenous peoples may have numerous exposure pathways and multiple sites of exposure that are overlooked or intentionally not considered. Potential sources of exposure "range from direct exposure to contaminants to casual indirect exposure through the uptake and bio-assimilation of contaminants in local waters, food sources, and culturally important plants that are ingested, inhaled, or handled" (Middleton et al. 2019, 7). Through cultural and ceremonial activities such as subsistence hunting, fishing, and gathering, Indigenous peoples may face additional and cumulative exposures from multiple contaminants. Despite this situation, environmental violence that occurs through destruction and contamination is not perceived as violence in the same way that spectacles of violence are, such as the Indian-killing militias during the California gold rush. Rob Nixon (2011) refers to environmental violence as slow violence: "Violence that occurs gradually and out of sight, a violence of delayed destruction that is dispersed across time and space, an attritional violence that is typically not viewed as violence at all" (2). Thom Davies (2022) adds to this analysis by challenging the notion that toxic landscapes are "out of sight" because peoples that interact with toxic landscapes see the violence they produce (e.g., via health disparities). Slow violence renders particular populations as pollutable and vulnerable to sacrifice. And within settler states, Indigenous populations, worldviews, and landscapes are also rendered pollutable or sacrificial (Voyles 2015). "Chemical toxicities from resource extraction and industrial and military development cause slow death for Indigenous peoples, either through the illnesses produced by environmental destruction or the generational elimination of Indigenous ways of life" (Spice 2018, sec. 1, para. 8).

In addition to such physical repercussions from ecological contamination, many Indigenous peoples experience psychological repercussions as well. Kari Norgaard and Ron Reed (2017) examine the emotions experienced by Karuk people in the face of environmental decline—namely, grief, anger, shame, and hopelessness—and how these emotions are part of the experience of ongoing settler colonialism:

> The most frequently expressed emotion in the face of the degraded water quality and diminished quantity of fish in the river was grief . . . experiences of grief were bound up with three other important social experiences: 1) disruptions to identity, 2) disruptions to social interactions, and 3) the association of environmental degradation with both cultural and physical genocide . . . in people's lived experience there is no clear line between the experience of grief on behalf of dead salmon, grief on behalf of one's son who cannot go fishing, or grief that the Karuk people may come to an end . . . these aspects are not only interconnected, they are *compounded* by one another. (475–76)

Karuk people also expressed anger and shame at the current state of the Klamath River: "When the river's degraded, and it's liquid poison in some ways . . . then of course that weighs on you. It's like, you want to be a proud person and if you draw your identity from the river and the river is degraded, that reflects on you" (481). Physical and psychological repercussions of ecological stress are multigenerational, rooted in legacy impacts that continue to impact Indigenous subsistence and cultural practices throughout California.

While settler colonialism has presented an onslaught of assaults to Indigenous lands, waters, bodies, and cultures, Native peoples continue to resist settler-colonial violence and they work to protect and reclaim their ancestral territories. This is done through direct action, legal action, participating in culture and ceremony, hunting and fishing, and traditional knowledge and language transmission (Norgaard and Reed 2017). As ecological crises continue to unfold in response to more than a century of settler-colonial land management, tribal nations are working to take matters into their own hands. The Wiyot Tribe, for example, has been working for decades to clean up and reclaim its sacred island, Tuluwat. The story of Tuluwat is a fitting conclusion, not because it was a significant site of land return but because the Wiyot Tribe asserted its ancestral connections to it through ecological remediation, care, and stewardship.

Tuluwat, the site of the annual World Renewal Ceremony, is sacred to the Wiyot peoples. It is also where the Wiyot massacre of 1860 took place (see chapter 1). After settlers stole the island, they constructed dikes and channels on it, which impacted tidal action along the shore and eroded the edges of shellmounds on the land. Between 1913 and 1985 an estimated 2,000 cubic yards of the shellmound were destroyed by erosion. During this time the island was also subjected to looting. One amateur archaeologist was said to have looted as many as five hundred gravesites on the island (Wiyot Tribe n.d.). From 1870 to 1990 Tuluwat was used by settlers as the location for a ship repair facility. Tons of scattered metal, wood debris, and hazardous materials littered the area, along with several dilapidated structures and contaminated soil (Wiyot Tribe n.d.). The Wiyot Tribe has been in the process of cleaning up the debris and pollutants left on the village site since its initial purchase of 1.5 acres of the island in 2000. Because of the Wiyot Tribe's leadership, the vast majority of the metal and wood debris has been removed and most of the contaminated soil has been excavated. Tuluwat was eventually returned by the Eureka City Council to the Wiyot Tribe in October 2019. While this is certainly a historic moment for celebration, if the island had not been subjected to settler-colonial contamination, would the story have ended in the same way? The restoration and reclamation of Tuluwat Island demonstrates the ways in which tribal nations are at the forefront of protecting their territories from continued settler-colonial violence and working to heal the wounds of this violence by restoring ecological balance.

As we continue to navigate the current wave (and what if the last wave?) of resource rushing, the green rush, we have amazing examples of leadership and healing to look to for inspiration—but we also have a history of violence to amend for:

> We're still dealing with the effects of the Gold Rush on our environment. It's been 150 years and they haven't been able to mitigate what happened during the Gold Rush to our environment. When they blew up mountains, they have never been able to figure out how to regrow a mountain . . . these effects are long term and I don't think that people approach the rush mentality with "What does that mean 150 years from now? How are we going to think about 150 years from now? What does that mean?" So that's what I think Rushing tells—the word is right there. "Just rush into it, don't worry about it, just go!" (Cutcha Risling Baldy, author interview, August 28, 2017)

According to the Sierra Fund (2008), in 2008 there were forty-seven thousand abandoned mining sites dating back to the gold rush. Approximately 87 percent of these mines present physical safety hazards and 11 percent represent environmental hazards. "The toxic chemicals that remain from the Gold Rush era also threaten salmon for ceremonies, medicinal plants, and ceremonial plants. The fish that have been the staple of the native diet have become a poison" (25). There are over four thousand registered mines in the Klamath River Basin alone (Fluharty and Sloan 2014). "Contaminated runoff from abandoned mines impacts land, groundwater, streams, rivers, and lakes. Principal environmental pollutants from abandoned mines are mercury from contaminated sediments, arsenic, lead, and other heavy metals associated with acid rock drainage" (Sierra Fund 2008, 19). These chemicals persist in the environmental and human bodies for generations and are passed on as a form of historical trauma. Additionally, ecological contamination prevents Indigenous peoples from passing on cultural experience and knowledge. Karuk Tribe members express sadness and anger over their inability to feed their children Salmon or take them fishing (Norgaard 2019).

In this way, legacy impacts perpetuate what some scholars refer to as cultural genocide, or the destruction of specific characteristics of a group. Cultural genocide should not be seen as distinct and separate from physical genocide, but rather a method of genocide that exists in relationship with physical genocide (Short 2016, 2010). Just as the impacts of the gold rush are still felt today, the impacts from the green rush will be felt far into the future. For Indigenous peoples, trespass cannabis cultivation represents a continuation of gold rush–era violence. Plastic bottles filled with various chemicals can take a decade or longer to degrade; when—not if—those bottles leak, they will create lasting contamination well into the future. Pesticides and fertilizers that seep into our River and soil systems will continue to harm our more-than-human relatives. The scars created by deforestation and soil erosion will be felt by future generations.

The environmental injustices experienced by Indigenous peoples are rooted in settler-colonial practices of violence and resource extraction and thus environmental justice for Indigenous communities must reckon with the disparities and oppressions facilitated and perpetuated by settler colonialism. Due to multiple waves of resource extraction, impacts from the cannabis industry cannot be viewed in isolation. Rather, they must be seen as cumulative impacts that began with invasion. If the state of California remains unequipped to deal with the ecological ramifications of the gold rush, what makes us think the state is equipped to deal with the ramifications of the green rush happening now and resource rushes yet to come?

CONCLUSION

Ecological Crisis and Land Back

We are in a crisis, a full-blown emergency, here on the Klamath River. We are losing our salmon. They are everything to us. Our children's future depends on it. . . . Our culture and economy have been impacted by the loss of fish. Our river is now poisoned with toxic algae. Fathers and mothers can't pass on their knowledge about fishing without fish. The Klamath River is who we are. It is our lifeline. It is our livelihood. —Yurok Tribe Chairman Joseph L. James, quoted in Elaine Weinreb, "'Witnessing the Collapse'"

We have entered an ecological crisis. As fires engulf the western United States and water shortages impair habitats, we will be forced to reckon with the unsustainable nature of settler-colonial orientations to land.

> Together, colonialism and capitalism then laid key parts of the groundwork for industrialization and militarization—or carbon-intensive economics—which produce the drivers of anthropogenic climate change, from massive deforestation for commodity agriculture to petrochemical technologies that burn fossil fuels for energy. The colonial invasion that began centuries ago caused anthropogenic environmental changes that rapidly disrupted many Indigenous peoples, including deforestation, pollution, modification of hydrological cycles, and the amplification of soil-use and terraforming for particular types of farming, grazing, transportation, and residential, commercial and government infrastructure. . . .
>
> Indigenous scholars discuss climate vulnerability as an intensification or intensified episode of colonialism. Wildcat claims that Indigenous climate relocation today is part of three removals occurring as part of U.S. colonial, capitalist, and industrial expansion. The first two removals were "geographic" (displacement, e.g., Trail of Tears and the forced occupation of reservations), and "social" and "psycho-cultural" (such as through removal of children to boarding schools). . . . For

Wildcat, the immediacy of climate refugees is like the experience of déjà vu given that relocation and displacement are part of the history of colonially-induced environmental changes that harmed Indigenous peoples. (Whyte 2017, 154–55)

The ecological crisis wrought by climate change will, whether by force or choice, change the way settler society engages with the environment. And while the damages of climate change become more visible every day through uncontrollable wildfires to fish die-offs, a "business as usual" approach to economic growth via resource extraction rages on.

Economic projections indicate that the cannabis industry will continue to grow. In 2020 cannabis sales in California hit $4.4 billion and increased to $5.2 billion in 2021 (Bartlett 2021; Lange 2022). Nationwide, some predict legal cannabis could potentially become a $40 billion industry (Silver 2016). However, if we have learned anything about resource rushing thus far, it is that resource rushes ultimately end—and the resultant ecological transformation lasts much longer. This is not merely a call to end the green rush; the green rush is but a symptom of a larger structure. Rather, it is a call to end the settler-colonial mentality and relationship to land that not only enables resource rushing as a possibility but constructs it as a good or profitable idea. Natchee Blu Barnd concludes *Native Space: Geographic Strategies to Unsettle Settler Colonialism* (2017) with a reflection on Water Protectors at Standing Rock. Given the Black Snake prophecy, it is fitting to return to this influential and precedent-setting movement. Brand reflects on how the stance taken by Water Protectors, using the phrase "Mni Wiconi" (Water is life), did not frame it as a political choice, but rather "signaled an ontological position that required consideration of a nonhuman world and reflected a cultural framework organizing the relationship between humans and water" (150). The stance implied in Mni Wiconi has allowed for Indigenous peoples and their allies to reframe relationships to water outside of settler-colonial relations that frame water as a lifeless and manipulable commodity. Barnd asks: "If we can reframe how we connect all to water, can we also extend Indigenous-centered responsibilities and relationships?" (152).

In his reflections on the UN's 2007 passage within the Declaration on the Rights of Indigenous Peoples (UNDRIP), Walter Echo-Hawk articulates urgent environmental reasons for honoring Indigenous rights: protecting the rights of Indigenous peoples goes hand in hand with protecting and sustaining healthy environments.[1] Echo-Hawk (2013) argues that because settler-colonial relations to land are framed in economic terms, wherein relatives become commodities, a new American land ethic is sorely needed.[2] "Decolonizing the way that we look at the land goes hand-in-hand with decolonizing the way we look at Native Americans, and the restoration of their rights opens a door to a new way of looking at the land" (135). The return to Indigenous stewardship is necessary to rectify historical injustices of settler-colonial dispossession and extraction, but it also is fast becoming an ecological necessity.

Decolonization means land return. In their seminal essay "Decolonization Is Not a Metaphor," Eve Tuck and K. Wayne Yang (2012) critique the appropriation of the language of decolonization to advocate for social justice issues broadly. Decolonization does not have a synonym: "Decolonization in the settler colonial context must involve the repatriation of land simultaneous to the recognition of how land and relations to land have always already been differently understood and enacted; that is, all of the land, and not just symbolically" (7). We are at an incredibly important moment regarding decolonial land returns. Powerful examples of healing are occurring throughout Indian Country. "Returning stolen land to Indigenous peoples is a growing movement with not only international and national examples, but a very important and groundbreaking local example in the recent return of 200 acres of Tuluwat Island (sometimes referred to as 'Indian Island') to the Wiyot Tribe in October 2019. The movements for decolonization in education, research and policy must necessarily include the return of land to Indigenous peoples" (Risling Baldy and Tully 2019, 7). On October 21, 2019, the city of Eureka returned Tuluwat Island—a site of both World Renewal Ceremonies and genocidal violence—to the Wiyot Tribe in northwestern California. This is "the first time in the history of our nation that a local municipality has voluntarily given back Native land absent an accompanying sale, lawsuit, or court order" (Greenson 2019, para. 4). A ceremony was held to celebrate the return. And Tuluwat is just one example of many—there have been numerous anticolonial land returns across California, including the Tásmam Koyóm (Humbug Valley) to the Maidu Summit; the Blue Creek (in Klamath) to the Yurok Tribe; the Sogorea Te' Land Trust (in Oakland) to the Ohlone Tribe; the Kuuchamaa Mountain and Ah-Ha Kwe-Ah-Mac' village (in Tecate) to the Kumeyaay-Diegueño Land Conservancy; and Old Woman Mountains (in San Bernardino) to the Twenty-Nine Palms Band of Mission Indians, among several others (Risling Baldy and Tully 2019).

Across the nation, more land is being returned—by universities, missions, governments, nonprofits, and even individuals (Risling Baldy and Tully 2019). Despite a financial loss from the transaction, a plumber in Colorado named Rich Synder returned his land to the Ute Tribe (Kenny 2019). Other entities across that nation that have returned land include Brown University and the Jesuit St. Francis Mission. The state of Oregon passed the Western Oregon Tribal Fairness Act in 2018 to return 17,000 acres to the Cow Creek Band of Umpqua Indians and 15,000 acres to the Confederated Tribes of Coos, Lower Umpqua, and Siuslaw Indians.

> What is most interesting about these cases, is that (1) the Native American Tribe never precluded people from interacting with the lands that they receive, except during a ceremony, and (2) *stronger* relationships were forged due to this process. Some of these cases were not easy decisions by the landowner(s), yet there is a clear sense of responsibility to do what is right: to return land to the peoples who were forcibly removed from the land hundreds of years ago. These processes have proven to be of teamwork and building a sense of community; something every human can relate to. At the end of the day nothing really changed, except the name on the title and the way the land is treated. (Risling Baldy and Tully 2019, 19)

The return of stolen land is possible. Healing is possible.

On June 18, 2019, Governor Gavin Newsom formally apologized to Native Americans on behalf of the state of California and issued Executive Order N-15-19 which, in addition to documenting his formal apology, requires the governor's tribal advisor to establish a Truth and Healing Council. Composed of California tribal representatives and delegates, the purpose of the council is "to provide Native Americans a platform to clarify the historical record and work collaboratively with the state to begin the healing process" (California Office of the Tribal Advisor n.d.). While we can remain hopeful that this council will prove useful to tribal communities in some capacity, frustration with the settler state persists. The genocide against California Indians is not "Native history"—it is California history. The state already has access to these historical records because the state compiled them in 2002 (Johnston-Dodds 2002). Moreover, California Indians have been clarifying the historical record for a very long time. Jack Norton's seminal text *When Our Worlds Cried: Genocide in Northwestern California* was published more than forty years ago. Today, books that meticulously detail the deaths of California Indians—without regard for how we survived—make national bestsellers lists. The truth is widely available, but what is the state of California going to do with our truth?

I implore the Truth and Healing Council to advocate for land return and ecological restoration. The dispossession and destruction of our lands was central to the California Indian genocide, and maintaining this dispossession is central to historic and contemporary waves of resource extraction. In other words, both people and the land must heal from genocide; after all, we are a part of the land and the land is us. The land—and the Trees, and the Rivers, and the Rocks—were witness to the genocide that occurred here. The land experienced great violence during the California genocide. The environmental destruction endured during the gold rush in California, but it left long-lasting impacts that continue to affect Native peoples and homelands and waters today. To begin healing from the genocide that tried to destroy us—our lands and our peoples—we must engage in community environmental restoration. We must begin to pick up the pieces that over a century of resource rushing has scattered about. This is not to devalue other critical methods of healing—such as language revitalization, cultural restoration, or mental health treatments to address what Lawrence Gross (2003) refers to as "post-apocalypse stress syndrome" (128). Rather, it is by engaging with community-centered environmental restoration projects that we can restore relationships with each other and with our environments. For example, Coleen Fox et al. (2017) demonstrate how River restoration "has the potential to not only restore ecosystem processes and services, but to repair and transform human relationships with rivers" (521). Settler colonialism has worked to sever these connections; we must work to rebuild them. The process of working together to rectify historical wrongs can have transformative powers.

Research shows that granting Indigenous groups formal rights to their lands is one of the most effective ways to conserve forests (Rosen 2019). One study tracked what happened in the Peruvian Amazon after Indigenous groups received official titles to their land. Using satellite imagery to estimate forest loss, researchers found the deforestation rates plummeted by 75 percent during the next two years (Blackman et al. 2017). Another wide-ranging analysis showed that securing land rights significantly correlated with forest preservation—even gain—in South America, Central America, and Africa (Robinson et al. 2014). Here in Northern California, Indigenous tribes have been at the forefront of all critical environmental movements, including dam removal (Orona 2013), Salmon habitat protection (Middleton Manning and Reed 2019; Sims 2018), and returning fire to the landscape (Marks-Block and Tripp 2021; Tripp 2020).

While working on this book about cannabis in California, I received several invitations to speak at various academic gatherings. I recall being asked what my sustainable vision of cannabis production in California looks like. This was an entirely reasonable question, but I was stumped. So I repeated what I always tell my students: here in California, our land was stolen only 170 years ago. Before that, our ecosystems thrived. The Salmon runs were so huge, our elders say you could walk across the River on their backs. To us, 170 years is not very long ago. For a people who have been here for tens of thousands of years—and, by the way, some believe over 100,000 years (see Holen et al. 2017)—170 years is a blink, a flash. So my sustainable vision, then, is not focused on preserving folks' ability to continue to cultivate for-profit cannabis. My sustainable vision is land return. Decolonization. Ecologically speaking, I argue this is the only path forward. We need to operate within a framework of radical relationality that rejects the commodification and control of nature for wealth accumulation.

The other thing I tell my students is that we are never taught to imagine anything beyond settler colonialism. As Cutcha Risling Baldy humorously phrases it, "We're Manifest Destinied our whole lives." We are told from our public education, if not before that, that this is the way it was always meant to be. But we have to imagine beyond settler-colonial orientations to land; we must think outside the prescribed "rush" pattern of the gold rush, the timber rush, the fish rush, and now the green rush. Many cannabis advocates proclaim dedication to social and environmental justice causes. But for Native people, social and environmental justice is impossible without land return. Real justice requires decolonization. This is why I had to write this book. California Indians did not have a seat at the table during the gold rush. There was no public forum or open comment period where we could submit our knowledge and research or perspectives. In fact, when we tried to sit at that table, we were jailed and auctioned off into slavery—thanks to the 1850 Act for the Government and "Protection" of Indians. This time around we insist on having our voices heard—until it reverberates throughout this place and our lands are returned to us.

> It will all come back.
> The languages.
> The cultures.
> The land.
> It will all come back.
> We never left. Our ancestors still find us,
>   and we still walk in their paths.
> This is not what you think. This time will be
>   but [a] blip in our timelines.
> It will all come back.
>
> —Jesse Wente (Ojibwe), Native Twitter, September 19, 2018

NOTES

INTRODUCTION

1. While on the subject of settler-colonial erasure of Indigenous governance and political structures, the US government structure was directly modeled after the Haudenosaunee Confederacy's Great Law of Peace (see Grinde 1977).

2. TEK is also sometimes referred to as Indigenous knowledge, tribal knowledge, tribal science, Native science, Indigenous environmental science, or Indigenous environmental studies.

3. Governor Peter Burnett, in his 1851 State of the State Address, describes California Indians as "all poor and savage tribes of men ... who are enabled to supply the simplest wants of Nature from the spontaneous productions of the earth, they are, from habit and prejudice, exceedingly adverse to manual labor" (Burnett 1851).

4. "The term *colonization* is derived from the Latin colere, 'to till, cultivate, farm (land).' Thus colonization can be thought of in terms of the steps involved in a process of cultivation: taking control the indigenous soil, uprooting the existing indigenous plants (peoples), overturning the soil (indigenous way of life), planting new colonial seeds (people) or transplanting colonial plants (people) from another environment, and harvesting the resulting crops (resources) or else picking the fruits (wealth) that result from the labor of cultivation (colonization). . . . However, another root metaphor of colonization is colo, 'to remove (solids) by filtering' and 'to wash (gold).' From a Christian European colonizing perspective, the indigenous peoples are considered as being among those solids (objects) that must be filtered out of (or expunged and washed from) the land in order to acquire that which is most valuable, such as gold" (Newcomb 2008, 14).

5. Firsting refers to the belief that Euro-American settlers were the first people to establish civilization in North America. This belief is reflected in local histories, monuments, and signage throughout the United States, documenting the "first" dwelling, the "first' school, etc., as though there had never been occupants thriving in those places before Euro-Americans arrived. Simultaneously, the national narrative tells of the "last" Indians (e.g., the last of the Mohicans, Ishi the last Indian, etc.) (O'Brien 2010).

6. By 1850 hemp was the third-largest crop in the United States, exceeded only by cotton and tobacco (Lee 2012).

7. The director of the Federal Bureau of Narcotics, Henry Anslinger, selected cannabis as the scapegoat for society's ills in the 1930s. In fact, Anslinger's boss, Andrew Mellon, was the chief financial backer of DuPont (at the time the fourth-largest chemical producer in the world) and his wife's uncle. Hemp enthusiast Jack Herer alleges that had hemp not been outlawed, as much as 80 percent of DuPont's business would not have materialized, "and the great majority of the pollution which has poisoned our rivers would not have happened" (quoted in Lee 2012, 197).

8. My use of the term "decolonization" deserves clarification. Drawing on Tuck and Yang's influential piece "Decolonization Is Not a Metaphor" (2012), decolonization is not synonymous with social, environmental, or economic justice. Rather, as they note, "decolonization eliminates settler property rights and settler sovereignty. It requires the abolition of land as property and upholds the sovereignty of Native land and people" (26).

1. GOLD, GREED, AND GENOCIDE

1. Lawrence Gross (Anishinaabe) (2003) developed the term "post-apocalypse stress syndrome," or PASS (20). PASS is similar to PTSD (post-traumatic stress disorder) but exists at the scale of a culture rather than an individual. Gross defines apocalypse not as the end of time but as the end of the world—although this does not imply the destruction of a worldview. Deborah Miranda (2013) offers the metaphor of a mosaic to illustrate the post-apocalypse revitalization of Indigenous culture: "If we allow the pieces of our culture to lie scattered in the dust of history, trampled on by racism and grief, then yes, we are irreparably damaged. But if we pick up the pieces and use them in new ways that honor their integrity, their colors, textures, stories—then we do those pieces justice, no matter how sharp they are, no matter how much handling them slices our fingers and makes us bleed."

2. Sara-Larus Tolley (2006) identifies three waves of genocide in California: Spanish missionization, the first wave, lasted from 1769 to 1820; the second wave, between the end of the missionization period and the Mexican-American War, was from 1821 to 1845; the third wave—coinciding with the infamous gold rush—spanned from 1846 to 1873.

3. In September 2015 student Chiitaanibah Johnson (Navajo/Maidu) was dismissed from Maury Wiseman's history course at California State University, Sacramento, after challenging Wiseman's comments that he "does not like to use the term 'genocide' because 'genocide' is something that is done on purpose" (Flaherty 2015).

4. The papal bull "Inter caetera"—also referred to as the Doctrine of Discovery—was issued by Pope Alexander VI in 1493. It allowed Christian nations to "discover," claim, and conquer non-Christian nations. The US Supreme Court relied on this declaration to justify the settler-colonial dispossession of Indigenous territories affirmed in *Johnson vs. McIntosh* in 1823 (Newcomb 2008; Barker 2005).

5. This section was repealed in 1872, but the law in its entirety was not repealed until 1937.

6. Additionally, the 1850 Act for the Government and Protection of Indians specifically outlawed Indian burning practices (Section 10), which prevented Native peoples from maintaining their land management practices. This led to a variety of harms for Native peoples—discussed at length in chapter 2.

7. The federal agents included George W. Barbour, Redick McKee, and O. M. Wozencraft. None of them had ever worked with Native people or negotiated a treaty before (Whiteley 2020).

8. To file a land claim one had to go to the Public Land Commission office in the nearest town. Remember, at this time in California history it was both *legal* and *profitable* to kill California Indians, and Indians "loitering in public" could be sold into slavery. Therefore, it is unlikely that the state ever thought California Indians would file their land claims.

9. This description is in sharp contrast to Jack Norton's (1979): "Northern California shuddered and, in some cases, broke under the plundering horde that raped her in the 1850s" (37).

10. The Environmental Protection Agency attempts to manage these health risks by advocating for a maximum fish consumption to reduce contamination risk. The maximum exposure standard is catered to the "average American" (read: white settler) and does not take the lived realities of Indigenous fishing communities into account (Hoover 2017; National Environmental Justice Advisory Council 2002).

2. FORESTS ON FIRE

1. The process of wastelanding and resource extraction, to be sure, occurred throughout Turtle Island—and virtually everywhere else invaders settled. However, California was unique in its abundance and biological diversity. Indeed, "the colonizers variously saw California as a foreboding wilderness, a place to do God's work, a giant untapped storehouse of wealth, and a place of raw, unspoiled beauty" (M. Anderson 2005, 62). Thus the temptation to extract and commodify its natural resources was considerable.

2. Maintaining cultural burns is important for more than just Indigenous

people. Elder Ron Goode (North Fork Mono) explains: "You should be able to smell every single different kind of smoke. The animals teach their young to do that, but if there's no fire, they can't teach them to do that. That's why we have to burn. That's why we have to keep the fires going so that all parts of life understand what it is that we're doing with fire" (quoted in Yuan 2016).

3. In fact, Pocahontas was a child when settlers invaded her homeland. Later she was forcibly taken from her husband and child and was the victim of rape and sexual abuse. She was allegedly murdered without ever seeing her family again (Gunn Allen 2004). See Rayna Green's (1975) essay "The Pocahontas Perplex" for a thorough discussion of Pocahontas as a symbolic representation for the "new world."

4. This is consistent with settler-colonial rejections of Indigenous foods, such as pine nuts, acorns, and other roots and tubers. Traditional foods were considered primitive and savage and backward by settlers—but today a bag of pine nuts will run you at least $20 from Trader Joe's.

5. As Lynn Huntsinger and Sarah McCaffrey (1995) state: "Studies in Asia, Africa, and Latin America have characterized 'scientific forestry' as a vehicle used by a centralized state to wrest control of forest resources from local people" (157).

6. The Forest History Society—a nonprofit archive—considers the Weeks Act to be one of the "most successful pieces of conservation legislation in U.S. history. To date, nearly 20 million acres of forestland have been protected by the Weeks Act" (Forest History Society, n.d.). This kind of statement is a prime example of how settler-colonial narratives erase and exclude Indigenous peoples, histories, and knowledge. Land acquisitions through the Weeks Act facilitated Indigenous land dispossession, while the fire suppression policies enacted on these lands criminalized Indigenous land management practices, all the while creating conditions ripe for catastrophic wildfires.

7. Wartime tools included aerial retardant drops, helitack crews, bulldozers, and smokejumpers (Norgaard 2019).

3. SALMON IS EVERYTHING

1. The Yurok Tribe Fisheries Program Final Report states the official estimate, as stated by the US Fish and Wildlife Service, is 34,925 dead salmonids (97 percent of which were adult Chinook). However, both the California Department of Fish and Game and the Fish and Wildlife Service have acknowledged that this estimate is conservative (Belchik, Hillemeier, and Pierce 2004).

2. This phrase comes from the work of Zoe Todd (Métis) (2016b).

3. Cultural keystone species can be defined as a "culturally salient species that shape in a major way the cultural identity of a people, as reflected in the fun-

damental roles these species have in diet, materials, medicine, and/or spiritual practices" (Garibaldi and Turner 2004).

4. The title of this chapter, "Salmon Is Everything," comes from the title of a 2014 play of the same name, created in collaboration with students and faculty of Humboldt State University, the University of Oregon, Klamath Watershed Community, and members of the Karuk, Yurok, Hoopa Valley, and Klamath Tribes (May et al. 2014).

5. Vine Deloria's (1994) use of the term "sacred geography" refers to the contrast between Christianity and spatially located Indigenous religions, "clearly illustrated when we understand the nature of sacred mountains, sacred hills, sacred rivers, and other geographical features sacred to Indian tribes" (122).

6. Settlers used this strategy in other regions as well; for example, the US military systematically slaughtered millions of bison to weaken the Oceti Sakowin Nation (Estes 2019; Hubbard 2014).

7. The tribes included in this study include the Yurok Tribe, the Karuk Tribe, and the Klamath Tribes.

8. Here, Risling Baldy is citing Chisa Oros (Zuni Pueblo/Yoeme) (2016).

9. Moreover, the baseline for studying "healthy" streams is, in fact, impaired. Nancy Langston (1995) argues: "All the streams that ecologists have ever studied have been streams that trappers had stripped of their prime shapers [beaver]. All the models of nature that ecologists have ever used to formulate their ideas about how 'normal' streams function are therefore not normal at all. They grow out of impoverished waters" (57).

10. However, white settlers in the area contested this. Following massive floods in December 1861 and February 1862, a group of white squatters who wanted to claim ownership of the mouth of the Klamath River petitioned for the reservation to be disbanded (Raphael and House 2007).

11. By "first" I am referring to the first commercial fishery, designed specifically for export, profit, and wealth accumulation. Yurok people, of course, have had established fisheries at the mouth of the River for thousands of years.

12. See Joshua Reid's *The Sea Is My Country* (2015) for an in-depth discussion of Makah fishing rights in Washington State, wherein he makes several significant parallels to fishing rights in Northern California. He argues that domestic regulations and international conservation efforts operate within colonial paradigms that favor settlers over Indigenous peoples, whose fishing rights get solely relegated to subsistence (despite the fact that vast trade networks existed between Indigenous nations engaged in commercial fisheries as well).

13. These eggs came from the US Fish and Wildlife Service's Livingston Stone National Fish Hatchery near Redding, California, not the Rakaia River in Aotearoa.

4. BACK TO WHOSE LAND?

1. "The traditional story of white flight centers around post–World War II federal housing and highway programs, deteriorating urban housing stocks, the application of mass manufacturing techniques to home construction, and the in-migration of populations of color to urban areas. These factors collectively made suburbanization attractive to and possible for white middle-class families, who consequently left cities and urban public schools" (Schneider 2008, 996).

2. For a California Indian perspective on the mission system, see Miranda (2013).

3. For a useful dissection of this myth, see Dunbar-Ortiz and Gilio-Whitaker (2016a).

4. This phrase is attributed to Richard Henry Pratt. Pratt founded the first boarding school, Carlisle Indian Industrial School, in Pennsylvania in 1879.

5. The Indian Citizenship Act of 1924 had already extended citizenship to Native peoples. Termination was not about citizenship, but rather aimed at eliminating the trust status of reservations as outlined and guaranteed through negotiated treaties.

6. For a detailed chronicle of events at Alcatraz, see Smith and Warrior (1996).

7. It is important to push back against language like this. Native peoples didn't lose anything—our lands, cultures, and lifeways were violently wrested from us. Such language of loss erases settler culpability, and shifts the focus to Native peoples' act of losing.

8. Ray Raphael is the author of numerous texts that provide detailed information on settler-colonial violence. However, like many historians, Raphael's violence is temporally bound (e.g., *Two People, One Place: Humboldt History*, coauthored with Freeman House).

9. Dominic Corva (2013) refers to the Emerald Triangle as "a geographical imagination likely introduced by law enforcement as part of a media campaign" to conjure images of the Golden Triangle—an opium production region in Southeast Asia (1).

5. WEED GREED

1. This claim relies on estimations of illicit cannabis production as well. As of 2021, regulated legal cannabis (which represents only a portion of the cannabis produced throughout the state) is the fifth-largest cash crop in California (Guilhem 2021).

2. Paraquat is a defoliant generally used for broadleaf weed control that typically destroys green plant tissue on contact. It is highly toxic for both animals and humans. In animals, a single large dose administered orally or via injection can lead to convulsions and respiratory failure. In humans, ingestion leads to heart, kidney, and liver failure. Numerous illnesses and deaths attributed to paraquat have been reported. Additionally, paraquat is considered to be moderately to highly toxic to many species of aquatic life (CDC 2018).

3. The result was the Cannabis Cultivation Policy, issued on October 17, 2017. The policy established principles and guidelines for cannabis cultivation activities to protect water quality and instream flows (State Water Resources Control Board 2017).

4. Formed in 2016, the Bureau of Cannabis Control is the lead agency regulating commercial cannabis for both medical and recreational use in California; it is responsible for licensing all retailers, distributors, testing laboratories, microbusinesses, and temporary cannabis events (https://bcc.ca.gov).

5. In 2021 these three entities merged to form the Department of Cannabis Control.

6. The basic principle of the doctrine of tribal sovereign immunity is that "federally recognized Indian tribes are immune from suit by any entity or individual, other than the United States, absent their consent or congressional abrogation" (quoted in Seelau 2014, 137).

7. "Known as the precautionary principle, this perspective seeks to mobilize environmental and public health policy making that otherwise can be paralyzed when implementation is too dependent on scientific certainty" (Morello-Frosch, Pastor, and Sadd 2022, 50). Due to the length of time it takes to scientifically verify contamination, vulnerable populations are in many cases already dealing with ill effects well before evidence of contamination is verified.

6. NO JUSTICE ON STOLEN LAND

1. This second dataset includes only grow sites located on private property and does not include trespass cultivation on tribal or public lands.

2. Additionally, the Yurok Tribe Wildlife Program's prairie restoration efforts, designed to increase habitat for grassland-dependent bird species, are also being counteracted by trespass cultivation. After the Yurok Tribe restored prairies through prescribed burning to create additional habitat for grass-dependent bird species, growers plowed and planted cannabis (Chris West, author interview, August 22, 2017).

3. For example, the Yurok Tribe purchased approximately fifty thousand acres

of ancestral territory in 2018. For additional information, see Middleton Manning and Reed (2019).

4. The Native American Church originated in Oklahoma Territory at the turn of the twentieth century. It combines elements of Indigenous religions and Christianity and employs the use of peyote. For additional information, see Maroukis (2010).

5. The Wilkinson Memorandum, issued on October 28, 2014, was a response to increasing requests on behalf of tribes for guidance on the enforcement of the federal Controlled Substances Act on tribal lands. Essentially the memo extends to Indian Country the eight enforcement priorities outlined in the Cole Memo.

6. Partners included the Humboldt County Sheriff's Office, the Humboldt County District Attorney's Office, the Marin County Sheriff's Office, the California Department of Fish and Wildlife, the California State Water Resources Control Board, the California National Guard Counterdrug Task Force, CalFire, the US Bureau of Land Management, and the US Bureau of Indian Affairs.

7. CANNABIS AND WATER

1. The name Gidughurralilh can also be spelled Girrughurralilh.

2. By comparison, Butsic et al. (2017) found an average of 180 plants per parcel from their dataset of 1,341 private property parcels in Humboldt County.

3. Noncompliant is not equivalent to unpermitted or trespass grows. To incentivize enrollment, existing cultivation sites are not required to comply with standard conditions for enrollment in the Cannabis Waste Discharge Regulatory Program. Cultivators unable to comply are required to indicate their noncompliance and develop a plan for achieving compliance. Twenty-eight percent of permitted sites analyzed in this study were noncompliant (Dillis et al. 2019).

4. Comparatively, water sources for Trinity County were wells (59.4 percent), surface (20 percent), spring (11.2 percent), rain (2.6 percent), and off-site (14.7 percent). Mendocino and Sonoma reported wells (73.1 percent), surface (12.1 percent), spring (14.1 percent), rain (10.3 percent), and off-site (5.8 percent) (Dillis et al. 2019).

8. TOXIC ENVIRONMENTS

1. Often "banned" chemicals are produced in the United States and exported to Third World countries—where somebody is poisoned by pesticides every minute (Weir and Schapiro 1981).

2. "The ARs are grouped into two classes: first-generation compounds, which

require several doses to cause intoxication, and second-generation ARs, which are more acutely toxic often requiring only a single dose to cause intoxication and persist in tissues and in the environment" (Gabriel et al. 2012, sec. 1, para. 1)

3. For a fascinating and insightful discussion of plastic pollution within the context of colonialism, see Liboiron (2021).

4. For additional information, check out the California Indian Basketweavers' Association website, specifically the page "Pesticides and Basketweavers."

5. For an excellent discussion of universalism in the dominant sciences, see Liboiron (2021).

6. For example, fish advisories imposed due to the presence of contaminants represent a devastating cultural loss for Indigenous peoples but also the loss of a primary protein source that has led to community health problems such as diabetes.

CONCLUSION

1. UNDRIP created a framework of human rights and fundamental freedoms for Indigenous peoples. It was adopted by the UN General Assembly in 2007. Only four nations voted against it: Australia, New Zealand, Canada, and the United States—the four largest settler states of the world. The United States eventually signed UNDRIP in 2010, but UNDRIP is a nonlegal binding document and the United States is not required to uphold its principles.

2. This land ethic must not reproduce the same settler-colonial erasure of Native peoples (e.g., wilderness) as the preservation/conservation movement critiqued by Gilio-Whitaker and others. Instead, it must respectfully engage Indigenous nationhood and cosmologies.

REFERENCES

Abinanti, Abby, Blythe George, and Annita Lucchesi. 2020. "To' Kee Skuy' Soo Ney-Wo-Chek'—I Will See You Again in a Good Way: MMIWG2 of Northern California." Eureka, CA: Sovereign Bodies Institute. https://www.sovereign-bodies.org/tokeeskuysooney-wo-chek.

Akers, Donna L. 2011. "Removing the Heart of the Choctaw People: Indian Removal from a Native Perspective." In *Native Historians Write Back: Decolonizing American Indian History*, edited by Susan A. Miller and James Riding In, 105–16. Lubbock: Texas Tech University Press.

Akins, Damon B., and William J. Bauer Jr. 2021. *We Are the Land: A History of Native California*. Oakland: University of California Press.

Anderson, Kim. 2011. "Native Women, the Body, Land, and Narratives of Contact and Arrival." In *Storied Communities: Narratives of Contact and Arrival in Constituting Political Community*, edited by Hester Lessard, Rebecca Johnson, and Jeremy Webber, 167–88. Toronto: University of British Columbia Press.

Anderson, M. Kat. 2005. *Tending the Wild: Native American Knowledge and the Management of California's Natural Resources*. Berkeley: University of California Press.

Armitage, Lynn. 2015. "Pot Raid Has Pit River Tribe Fuming; Rips BIA." *Indian Country Today*, July 17, 2015. http://indiancountrytodaymedianetwork.com/2015/07/17/pot-raid-has-pit-river-tribe-fuming-rips-bia-161119.

Bacher, Dan. 2014. "Karuk Tribal Members Thwart Pot Growers' Attempts to Desecrate Sacred Site." *San Francisco Bay Area Independent Media Center*, May 5, 2014. https://www.indybay.org/newsitems/2014/05/05/18755331.php.

Bacon, J. M. 2019. "Settler Colonialism as Eco-Social Structure and the Production of Colonial Ecological Violence." *Environmental Sociology* 5, no. 1: 59–69.

Barker, Joanne, ed. 2005. *Sovereignty Matters: Locations of Contestation and Possibility in Indigenous Struggles for Self-Determination*. Lincoln: University of Nebraska Press.

Barnd, Natchee Blu. 2017. *Native Space: Geographic Strategies to Unsettle Settler Colonialism*. First Peoples: New Directions in Indigenous Studies. Corvallis: Oregon State University Press.

Barta, Tony. 2000. "Relations of Genocide: Land and Lives in the Colonization of Australia." In *Genocide and the Modern Age: Etiology and Case Studies of*

Mass Death, edited by I. Walliman and N. M. Dobrowski, 237–51. Westport, CT: Greenwood.

Bartlett, Lindsey. 2021. "Cannabis Sales in California Reach $4.4 Billion in 2020: 'Essential,' Edibles, and the Election." *Forbes*, January 29, 2021. https://www.forbes.com/sites/lindseybartlett/2021/01/29/cannabis-sales-in-california-reach-44-billion-in-2020-essential-edibles-and-the-election.

Bauer, Scott, Jennifer Olson, Adam Cockrill, Michael van Hattem, Linda Miller, Margaret Tauzer, and Gordon Leppig. 2015. "Impacts of Surface Water Diversions for Marijuana Cultivation on Aquatic Habitat in Four Northwestern California Watersheds." *PLoS ONE* 10, no. 3: e0137935. https://doi.org/10.1371/journal.pone.0120016.

Bauer, William J., Jr. 2009. *We Were All Like Migrant Workers Here: Work, Community, and Memory on California's Round Valley Reservation, 1850–1941*. Chapel Hill: University of North Carolina Press.

———. 2016. *California through Native Eyes: Reclaiming History*. Seattle: University of Washington Press.

———. 2017. "Ghost Dances, Bears and the Legacies of Genocide in California." *Journal of Genocide Research* 18, no. 1: 137–42. https://doi.org/10.1080/14623528.2017.1265795.

Belchik, Michael, Dave Hillemeier, and Ronnie M. Pierce. 2004. "Final Report: The Klamath River Fish Kill of 2002; Analysis of Contributing Factors." Klamath, CA: Yurok Tribal Fisheries Program. https://www.waterboards.ca.gov/waterrights/water_issues/programs/bay_delta/california_waterfix/exhibits/docs/PCFFA&IGFR/part2/pcffa_155.pdf

Berkeley Cannabis Research Center (CRC). n.d. "Mission Statement." https://crc.berkeley.edu/about/.

Bettles, Gordon. 2014. "Forward: When Cultures Collide." In *Salmon Is Everything: Community-Based Theater in the Klamath Watershed*, edited by Theresa May, Suzanne Burcell, Kathleen McCovey, and Jean O'Hara, xi–xvi. First Peoples: New Directions in Indigenous Studies. Corvallis: Oregon State University Press.

Black, C. F. 2011. *The Land Is the Source of the Law*. London: Routledge.

Blackburn, Thomas C., and Kat Anderson, eds. 1993. *Before the Wilderness: Environmental Management by Native Californians*. Menlo Park, CA: Ballena.

Blackhawk, Ned. 2006. *Violence over the Land: Indians and Empires in the Early American West*. Cambridge, MA: Harvard University Press.

Blackman, Allen, Leonardo Corral, Eirivelthon Santos Lima, and Gregory P. Asner. 2017. "Titling Indigenous Communities Protects Forests in the Peruvian Amazon." *Proceedings of the National Academy of Sciences* 114, no. 16: 4123–28.

Boal, Iain, Janferie Stone, Michael Watts, and Carl Winslow, eds. 2012. *West of Eden: Communes and Utopia in Northern California*. Oakland, CA: PM.

Bodwitch, Hekia, Michael Polson, Eric Biber, Gordon M. Hickey, and Van Butsic. 2021. "Why Comply? Farmer Motivations and Barriers in Cannabis Agriculture." *Journal of Rural Studies* 86: 155–70. https://doi.org/10.1016/j.jrurstud.2021.05.006.

Bowcutt, Frederica. 1998. "Resistance to Logging." In *Green versus Gold: Sources in California's Environmental History*, edited by Carolyn Merchant, 166–71. Washington, DC: Island.

Bowers, Amy, and Kristen A. Carpenter. 2011. "Challenging the Narrative of Conquest: The Story of Lyng v. Northwest Indian Cemetery Protective Association." In *Indian Law Stories*, edited by Carole Goldberg, Kevin Washburn, and Philip Frickey, 489–533. New York: Foundation.

Brady, Emily. 2013. *Humboldt: Life on America's Marijuana Frontier*. New York: Grand Central.

Braithwaite, Tina. 2019. Letter to Governor Gavin Newsom. April 25, 2019. https://bcc.ca.gov/about_us/meetings/materials/20190628_tribal_ind.pdf.

Brook, Daniel. 1998. "Environmental Genocide: Native Americans and Toxic Waste." *American Journal of Economics and Sociology* 57, no. 1: 105–13.

Bullard, Robert D. 2021. "From Civil Rights to Black Lives Matter." In *Lessons in Environmental Justice: From Civil Rights to Black Lives Matter and Idle No More*, edited by Michael Mascarenhas, 2–18. Thousand Oaks, CA: Sage.

Bureau of Indian Affairs (BIA). n.d. "Mission Statement." Washington, DC. https://www.bia.gov/bia.

Burnett, Peter. 1851. "State of the [California] State Address." January 6, 1851. https://governors.library.ca.gov/addresses/s_01-Burnett2.html.

Burns, Ryan. 2017. "Real Estate Listings for Humboldt's Weed-Growing Properties Now Feature Transparent Advertising, Sky-High Prices." *Lost Coast Outpost*, April 4, 2017. https://lostcoastoutpost.com/2017/apr/4/weed-property-legalization-brings-open-advertising/.

Butsic, Van, and Jacob C. Brenner. 2016. "Cannabis (Cannabis Sativa or C. Indica) Agriculture and the Environment: A Systematic, Spatially-Explicit Survey and Potential Impacts." *Environmental Research Letters* 11: 1–10.

Butsic, Van, Benjamin Schwab, Matthias Baumann, and Jacob C. Brenner. 2017. "Inside the Emerald Triangle: Modeling the Placement and Size of Cannabis Production in Humboldt County, CA, USA." *Ecological Economics* 142: 70–80.

California Bureau of Cannabis Control (BCC). n.d. "California Code of Regulations, Title 16, Division 42, Section 5009." https://bcc.ca.gov/law_regs/readopt_text_final.pdf.

California Department of Fish and Wildlife (CDFW). 2020. "Trespass Cannabis Cultivation Research and Cleanup Projects." May 20, 2020. https://storymaps.arcgis.com/stories/10914273df5348459fab6acf6807f5ae.

California Growers Association. 2018. "An Emerging Crisis: Barriers to Entry in California Cannabis." Accessed June 19, 2020. https://www.jennifermcgrath.com/wp-content/uploads/Emerging-Crisis-Barriers-Entry-California-Cannabis-Cal-Growers-Report-2.15.18.pdf.

California Native American Cannabis Association (C-NACA). 2019. "Tribal Participation in the Legal Cannabis Industry." Paper presented at the California Bureau of Cannabis Control Cannabis Advisory Committee meeting, Los Angeles, June 28, 2019. https://bcc.ca.gov/about_us/meetings/materials/20190628_tribal_ind.pdf.

California NORML (Cal NORML). 2015. "Cal NORML Challenges Fish and Wildlife Figures on Marijuana Water Consumption." August 3, 2015. https://www.canorml.org/cal-norml-challenges-fish-wildlife-figures-on-marijuana-water-consumption/.

California Office of the Tribal Advisor. n.d. "California Truth and Healing Council." Accessed August 7, 2021. https://tribalaffairs.ca.gov/cthc/.

Canter, Adam N. 2017. Letter to John Ford, Steve Lazar, and Steve Werner, "Wiyot Terr. Cannabis Applicant GIS Layer and Ethnobotany." April 19, 2017. https://humboldtgov.org/DocumentCenter/View/59727/Public-Comments-Agencies-Districts-and-Tribes-PDF.

Carah, Jennifer K., Jeanette K. Howard, Salley E. Thompson, Anne G. Short Gianotti, Scott D. Bauer, Stephanie M. Carlson, David N. Dralle, et al. 2015. "High Time for Conservation: Adding the Environment to the Debate on Marijuana Liberalization." *BioScience* 20, no. 10 (June 19, 2015): 1–8.

Carroll, Clint. 2015. *Roots of Our Renewal: Ethnobotany and Cherokee Environmental Governance*. Minneapolis: University of Minnesota Press.

Cart, Julie. 2014. "Was Poisoning of Scientist's Dog a Warning from Humboldt Pot Growers?" *Los Angeles Times*, May 10, 2014. https://www.latimes.com/local/la-me-adv-dog-poisoning-20140511-story.html.

Carvill, Sarah Gardner. 2015. "Old Saws and New Laws: Regulatory Failure and Ownership Transformation in the North Coast Redwood Timber Industry." PhD diss., University of California, Santa Cruz.

Centers for Disease Control and Prevention (CDC). 2018. "Facts about Paraquat." Accessed June 19, 2020. https://emergency.cdc.gov/agent/paraquat/basics/facts.asp.

Child, Brenda J. 1998. *Boarding School Seasons: American Indian Families, 1900–1940*. Lincoln: University of Nebraska Press.

Clay, Karen, and Gavin Wright. 2005. "Order without Law? Property Rights during the California Gold Rush." *Explorations in Economic History* 42: 155–83.

Colby, Bonnie G., John E. Thorson, and Sarah Britton. 2005. *Negotiating Tribal Water Rights: Fulfilling Promises in the Arid West*. Tucson: University of Arizona Press.

Cole, Luke W., and Sheila R. Foster. 2001. *From the Ground Up: Environmental Racism and the Rise of the Environmental Justice Movement*. New York: New York University Press.

Colegrove Powell, Anna. 2019. "Climate Change and California Tribes: Stories of Resilience and Partnerships, Part 1." November 15, 2019. Panel discussion at California Indian Conference, Sonoma State University.

Cook, Sherburne F. 1978. "Historical Demography." *California*. Vol. 8 of *Handbook of North American Indians*, edited by Robert F. Heizer, 91–98. Washington, DC: Smithsonian Institution Press.

Corva, Dominic. 2013. "Requiem for a CAMP: The Life and Death of a Domestic U.S. Drug War Institution." *International Journal of Drug Policy* 24: 1–10.

Corva, Dominic, and Joshua S. Meisel, eds. 2022. *The Routledge Handbook of Post-Prohibition Cannabis Research*. New York: Routledge.

Costo, Rupert, and Jeanette H. Costo. 1987. *The Missions of California: A Legacy of Genocide*. San Francisco: Indian Historian Press.

Coulthard, Glen. 2014. *Red Skin, White Masks: Rejecting the Colonial Politics of Recognition*. Minneapolis: University of Minnesota Press.

Cronon, William. 1996. "The Trouble with Wilderness: Or, Getting Back to the Wrong Nature." *Environmental History* 1, no. 1: 7–28.

Curley, Andrew. 2019. "'Our Winters' Rights': Challenging Colonial Water Laws." *Global Environmental Politics* 19, no. 3: 57–76.

David, Aaron T., J. Eli Asarian, and Frank K. Lake. 2018. "Wildfire Smoke Cools Summer River and Stream Water Temperatures." *Water Resources Research* 54: 7273–90.

Davies, Thom. 2022. "Slow Violence and Toxic Geographies: 'Out of Sight' to Whom?" In "Spatial Politics of Slow Violence and Resistance," theme issue, *Politics and Space* 40, no. 2: 409–27.

Deer, Sarah. 2015. *The Beginning and End of Rape: Confronting Sexual Violence in Native America*. Minneapolis: University of Minnesota Press.

Deloria, Phillip. 1998. *Playing Indian*. New Haven, CT: Yale University Press.

Deloria, Vine, Jr. 1969. *Custer Died for Your Sins: An Indian Manifesto*. Norman: University of Oklahoma Press.

———. 1994. *God Is Red: A Native View of Religion*. Golden, CO: Fulcrum.

Dillis, Christopher, Eric Biber, Hekia Bodwitch, Van Butsic, Jennifer Carah, Phoebe Parker-Shames, Michael Polson, and Theodore Grantham. 2021. "Shifting Geographies of Legal Cannabis Production in California." *Land Use Policy* 105: 1–11.

Dillis, Christopher, Theodore E. Grantham, Connor McIntee, Bryan McFadin, and Kason Grady. 2019. "Watering the Emerald Triangle: Irrigation Sources Used by Cannabis Cultivators in Northern California." *California Agriculture* 73, no. 3: 146–53.

Dillis, Christopher, Connor McIntee, Van Butsic, Lance Le, Kason Grady, and Theodore Grantham. 2020. "Water Storage and Irrigation Practices for Cannabis Drive Seasonal Patterns of Water Extraction and Use in Northern California." *Journal of Environmental Management* 272: 1–15.

Doremus, Holly, and A. Dan Tarlock. 2003. "Fish, Farms, and the Clash of Cultures in the Klamath Basin." *Ecology Law Quarterly* 30: 279–350.

———. 2008. *Water Wars in the Klamath Basin*. Washington, DC: Island.

Drew, Jesse. 2012. "The Commune as Badlands as Utopia as Autonomous Zone." In *West of Eden: Communes and Utopia in Northern California*, edited by Iain Boal, Janferie Stone, Michael Watts, and Cal Winslow, 41–53. Oakland, CA: PM.

Dunbar-Ortiz, Roxanne. 2014. *An Indigenous Peoples' History of the United States*. Boston: Beacon.

Dunbar-Ortiz, Roxanne, and Dina Gilio Whitaker. 2016a. "Indians Were the First Immigrants to the Western Hemisphere." In *"All the Real Indians Died Off": And 20 Other Myths about Native Americans*, 14–22. Boston: Beacon.

———. 2016b. "Native American Culture Belongs to All Americans." In *"All the Real Indians Died Off": And 20 Other Myths about Native Americans*, 100–108. Boston: Beacon.

Echo-Hawk, Walter R. 2010. *In the Courts of the Conqueror: The 10 Worst Indian Law Cases Ever Decided*. Golden, CO: Fulcrum.

———. 2013. *In the Light of Justice: The Rise of Human Rights in Native America and the UN Declaration on the Rights of Indigenous Peoples*. Golden, CO: Fulcrum.

Eid, Troy A. 2015. "Federal Narcotics Laws Can Still Trump Tribal Sovereignty."

Law 360, July 20, 2015. http://www.law360.com/articles/680734/federal-narcotics-laws-can-still-trump-tribal-sovereignty.

Estes, Nick. 2019. *Our History Is the Future: Standing Rock versus the Dakota Access Pipeline, and the Long Tradition of Indigenous Resistance*. London: Verso.

Estrada, Natalya. 2018. "EPA Considers Hoopa Mine for Superfund Designation." *North Coast Journal*, September 27, 2018. https://www.northcoastjournal.com/humboldt/epa-considers-hoopa-mine-for-superfund-designation/Content?oid=11177136.

Extension Toxicology Network (EXTOXNET). 1996a. "Abamectin." Cornell University; Michigan State University; Oregon State University; University of California, Davis; University of Idaho. http://extoxnet.orst.edu/pips/abamecti.htm.

———. 1996b. "Methamidophos." Cornell University; Michigan State University; Oregon State University; University of California, Davis. http://extoxnet.orst.edu/pips/methamid.htm.

Farmer, Jared. 2017. *Trees in Paradise: The Botanical Conquest of California*. Berkeley, CA: Heyday.

Fenelon, James V., and Clifford E. Trafzer. 2014. "From Colonialism to Denial of California Genocide to Misrepresentations: Special Issue on Indigenous Struggles in the Americas." *American Behavioral Scientist* 58, no. 1: 3–29.

Ferrara, John Ross. 2017. "A Look at One of the Latest Operation Yurok Trespass Grow Busts: Numerous Environmental Violations Found." *Lost Coast Outpost*, October 19, 2017.

Fixico, Donald L. 1986. *Termination and Relocation: Federal Indian Policy, 1945–1960*. Albuquerque: University of New Mexico Press.

Flaherty, Colleen. 2015. "Academic Freedom and Compassion." *Insider Higher Ed*, October 9, 2015. https://www.insidehighered.com/news/2015/10/09/sacramento-state-ends-investigation-disagreement-over-what-professor-said-about.

Fluharty, Suzanne, and Kathleen Sloan. 2014. "Understanding the Cumulative Effects of Environmental and Psycho-Social Stressors That Threaten the Pohlik-Lah and Ner-Er-Ner Lifeway: The Yurok Tribe's Approach." Report no. RD-83370801-0. Klamath, CA: Yurok Tribe Environmental Program.

Forbes, Jack D. 1971. "The Native American Experience in California History." *California Historical Quarterly* 50, no. 3: 234–42.

Foreman, Christopher H., Jr. 1998. *The Promise and Peril of Environmental Justice*. Washington, DC: Brookings Institution Press.

Forest History Society. n.d. "The Weeks Act." https://foresthistory.org/research-explore/us-forest-service-history/policy-and-law/the-weeks-act/.

Fortmann, Louise P., and Sally K. Fairfax. 1989. "American Forestry Professionalism in the Third World: Some Preliminary Observations." *Economic and Political Weekly* 24, no. 32: 1839–44.

Fox, Coleen A., Nicholas James Reo, Dale A. Turner, JoAnne Cook, Frank Dituri, Brett Fessell, James Jenkins, Aimee Johnson, Terina M. Rakena, and Chris Riley. 2017. "'The River Is Us; the River Is in Our Veins': Re-Defining River Restoration in Three Indigenous Communities." *Sustainability Science* 12: 521–33.

Fried, Jeremy S., Margaret S. Tom, and Evan Mills. 2004. "The Impact of Climate Change on Wildfire Severity: A Regional Forecast for Northern California." *Climatic Change* 64, no. 1: 169–91.

Fuller, Michelle. 2017. Letter to Steve Lazar, "Re: Notice of Preparation—Cannabis EIR." May 9, 2017. https://humboldtgov.org/DocumentCenter/View/59727/Public-Comments-Agencies-Districts-and-Tribes-PDF.

Gabriel, Mourad. 2016. "The Green Rush: Marijuana Cultivation on California Public Lands and Its Ecological Impacts." January 5, 2016. Presentation "Explore It Science Talks," DMG Mori, Davis, CA.

Gabriel, Mourad W., and Greta M. Wengert. 2020. "Introduction." In "Impacts of Cannabis Cultivation on Fish and Wildlife Resources," special issue, *California Fish and Wildlife Journal* 106, no. 2: 10–11.

Gabriel, Mourad W., Leslie W. Woods, Robert Poppenga, Rick A. Sweitzer, Craig Thompson, Sean M. Matthews, J. Mark Higley, et al. 2012. "Anticoagulant Rodenticides on Our Public and Community Lands: Spatial Distribution of Exposure and Poisoning of a Rare Forest Carnivore." *PLoS ONE* 7, no. 7. https://doi.org/10.1371/journal.pone.0040163.

Gabriel, Mourad W., Leslie W. Woods, Greta M. Wengert, Nicole Stephenson, J. Mark Higley, Craig Thompson, Sean M. Matthew, et al. 2015. "Patterns of Natural and Human-Caused Mortality Factors of a Rare Forest Carnivore, the Fisher (*Pekania pennanti*) in California." *PLoS ONE* 10, no. 11: e0140640. https://doi.org/10.1371/journal.pone.0140640.

Galeano, Eduardo. 1973. *Open Veins of Latin America: Five Centuries of the Pillage of a Continent*. New York: Monthly Review.

Garibaldi, Ann, and Nancy Turner. 2004. "Cultural Keystone Species: Implications for Ecological Conservation and Restoration." *Ecology and Society* 9, no. 3. https://www.ecologyandsociety.org/vol9/iss3/art1/.

Gienger, Richard. 2018. "Timber Wars and Aftermath in Northwest Coastal California." *Humboldt Journal of Social Relations* 40: 15–22.

Gilio-Whitaker, Dina. 2016. "Decolonizing the Black Bear Ranch Hippie Commune." *Indian Country Today*, March 28, 2016. https://indiancountrytoday.com/archive/decolonizing-the-black-bear-ranch-hippie-commune.

———. 2017. "The Problem with the Ecological Indian Stereotype." *Tending the Wild*. https://www.kcet.org/shows/tending-the-wild/the-problem-with-the-ecological-indian-stereotype.

———. 2019. *As Long as Grass Grows: The Indigenous Fight for Environmental Justice, from Colonization to Standing Rock*. Boston: Beacon.

Goode, Ron, Shasta Gaughan, Marissa Fierro, Don Hankins, Keir Johnson-Reyes, Beth Rose Middleton, Teri Red Owl, and Randy Yonemura. 2018. "Summary Report from Tribal and Indigenous Communities within California." California's Fourth Climate Change Assessment, no. SUM-CCCA4-2018-010. Sacramento, CA: California Governor's Office of Planning and Research, California Natural Resources Agency, and the California Energy Commission. https://www.energy.ca.gov/sites/default/files/2019-11/Statewide_Reports-SUM-CCCA4-2018-010_TribalCommunitySummary_ADA.pdf.

"Gov. Brown Earmarks $1.5M for Cleanup of Emerald Triangle Marijuana Grow Sites." 2017. *Times-Standard* (Eureka, CA), May 10, 2017. https://www.times-standard.com/2017/05/10/gov-brown-earmarks-15m-for-cleanup-of-emerald-triangle-marijuana-grow-sites/.

Grantham, Theodore E., and Joshua H. Viers. 2014. "100 Years of California's Water Rights System: Patterns, Trends and Uncertainty." *Environmental Research Letters* 9, no. 8.

Green, Rayna. 1975. "The Pocahontas Perplex: The Image of Indian Women in American Culture." *Massachusetts Review* 16, no. 4: 698–714.

Greenson, Thadeus. 2019. "The Island's Return: The Unprecedented Repatriation of the Center of the Wiyot Universe." *North Coast Journal of Politics, People, and Art*, October 24, 2019.

Grinde, Donald A. 1977. *The Iroquois and the Founding of the American Nation*. San Francisco: Indian Historian Press.

Gross, Lawrence W. 2003. "Cultural Sovereignty and Native American Hermeneutics in the Interpretation of the Sacred Stories of the Anishinaabe." *Wicazo Sa Review* 18, no. 2: 127–34.

Guilhem, Matt. 2021. "Cannabis Is Now 5th Largest Crop from California, Ahead of Tomatoes and Wheat." KCRW. https://www.kcrw.com/news/shows/kcrw-features/this-week-in-weed-cannabis-crop-harvest.

Gunn Allen, Paula. 2004. *Pocahontas: Medicine Woman, Spy, Entrepreneur, Diplomat*. New York: HarperCollins.

Halvorsen, Emily. 2018. "Compact Compliance as a Beneficial Use: Increasing the Viability of an Interstate Water Bank Program in the Colorado." *University of Colorado Law Review* 89: 937–66.

Hamann, Emily. 2013. "Deputies Find Dead Animals at Marijuana Grow." *North

Coast Journal, August 1, 2013. https://www.northcoastjournal.com/News Blog/archives/2013/08/01/deputies-find-dead-animals-at-marijuana-grow.

Hansen, Terri. 2014. "Kill the Land, Kill the People: There Are 532 Superfund Sites in Indian Country!" *Indian Country Today*, June 18, 2014. https://indiancountrytoday.com/archive/kill-the-land-kill-the-people-there-are-532-superfund-sites-in-indian-country.

Harris, Cheryl I. 1993. "Whiteness as Property." *Harvard Law Review* 106, no. 8: 1707–91.

Hecht, Peter. 2014. *Weed Land: Inside America's Marijuana Epicenter and How Pot Went Legit*. Berkeley: University of California Press.

Hernandez, Jessica. 2022. *Fresh Banana Leaves: Healing Indigenous Landscapes through Indigenous Science*. Huichin (unceded Ohlone land, aka Berkeley, CA): North Atlantic Books.

Herrington, A. J. 2019. "CA's Tribal Nations Are Shut Out of the Legal Cannabis Industry." *High Times*, February 5, 2019. https://hightimes.com/news/what-about-social-equity-cas-tribal-nations-kept-out-of-legal-cannabis-market/.

Higley, Mark J., Greta M. Wengert, Dawn M. Blake, and Mourad W. Gabriel. 2018. "The Marijuana Green Rush Is Anything but Green: A Report from the Hoopa Tribal Lands." In *Where There's Smoke: The Environmental Science, Public Policy, and Politics of Marijuana*, edited by Char Miller, 58–68. Lawrence: University Press of Kansas.

Hilborn, Ray, and Carl J. Walters. 1981. "Pitfalls of Environmental Baseline and Process Studies." *Environmental Impact Assessment Review* 2, no. 3: 265–78.

Hillman, Leaf. 2017. Letter to Steve Lazar, "Notice of Preparation of a Draft Environmental Impact Report: Amendments to Humboldt County Code Regulating Commercial Cannabis Activities." May 2, 2017. https://humboldtgov.org/DocumentCenter/View/59727/Public-Comments-Agencies-Districts-and-Tribes-PDF.

Holen, Steven R., Thomas A. Deméré, Daniel C. Fisher, Richard Fullagar, James B. Paces, George T. Jefferson, Jared M. Beeton, et al. 2017. "A 130,000-Year-Old Archaeological Site in Southern California, USA." *Nature* 544, no. 7651: 479–83.

Hoover, Elizabeth. 2017. *The River Is in Us: Fighting Toxics in a Mohawk Community*. Minneapolis: University of Minnesota Press.

Hossack, Joanna. 2019. "Leading the Way in Sustainable Practices: How the Cannabis Cultivation Policy Is Rethinking Water Management in California." *Hastings Environmental Law Review* 25, no. 2: 281–300.

Houck, Darcie L. 2019. "Salmon Repatriation: One Tribe's Battle to Maintain Its

Culture and Spiritual Connection to Place." *Natural Resources and Environmental Change* 34, no. 1: 23–27.

Hubbard, Tasha. 2014. "Buffalo Genocide in Nineteenth-Century North America: 'Kill, Skin, and Sell.'" In *Colonial Genocide in Indigenous North America*, edited by Andrew Woolford, 292–305. Durham, NC: Duke University Press.

Humboldt County. 2017. "Amendments to Humboldt County Code Regulating Commercial Cannabis Activities." Eureka, CA: Humboldt County Planning and Building Department.

———. 2018a. "Final Environmental Impact Report: Amendments to Humboldt County Code Regulating Commercial Cannabis Activities." Eureka, CA: Humboldt County Planning and Building Department.

———. 2018b. "Ordinance Amending Provisions of Title III of the Humboldt County Code Relating to the Commercial Cultivation, Processing, Manufacturing, Distribution, Testing, and Sale of Cannabis for Medicinal or Adult Use." Ordinance 2599. Eureka, CA: Humboldt County Board of Supervisors.

Humboldt County Sheriff's Office. 2021. "Marijuana Enforcement Team Watershed Protection Operation." Press release, July 23, 2021. https://humboldtgov.org/CivicAlerts.aspx?AID=4110.

Huntsinger, Lynn, and Sarah McCaffrey. 1995. "A Forest for the Trees: Forest Management and the Yurok Environment, 1850–1994." *American Indian Culture and Research Journal* 19, no. 4: 155–92.

Huntsinger, Lynn, Sarah McCaffrey, Laura Watt, and Michele Lee. 1994. "A Yurok Forest History." Translated by Department of Environmental Science, Policy, and Management, University of California, Berkeley. Sacramento, CA: Bureau of Indian Affairs.

Hurwitz, Laura Sarah. 2017. "Settler Colonialism and White Settler Responsibility in the Karuk, Konomihu, Shasta, and New River Shasta Homelands: A White Unsettling Manifesto." Master's thesis, Humboldt State University.

Isenburg, Andrew C. 2005. *Mining California: An Ecological History*. New York: Hill and Wang.

Jacobs, Emma. 2021. "Communities Plan to Search for More Indigenous Children's Remains in Canada." NPR, October 5, 2021. https://www.npr.org/2021/10/05/1043156113/canada-indigenous-children-residential-school-burial-search.

Jacobs, Margaret D. 2009. *White Mother to a Dark Race: Settler Colonialism, Maternalism, and the Removal of Indigenous Children in the American West and Australia, 1880–1940*. Lincoln: University of Nebraska Press.

Johnson, Nick. 2017. *Grass Roots: A History of Cannabis in the American West.* Corvallis: Oregon State University Press.

Johnston, Andrew Scott. 2013. *Mercury and the Making of California: Mining, Landscape, and Race, 1840–1890.* Boulder: University Press of Colorado.

Johnston-Dodds, Kimberly. 2002. "Early California Laws and Policies Related to California Indians." Sacramento, CA: California Research Bureau.

Jones, Corbett. 2019. *History of Native California.* The Range. https://www.youtube.com/watch?v=T-azcPugmKQ.

Kanazawa, Mark. 2015. *Golden Rules: The Origins of California Water Law in the Gold Rush.* Chicago: University of Chicago Press.

Karuk Tribe. 2021. "Karuk Tribe Declares Climate Emergency: Massive Fish Kill Edges Salmon Runs Closer to Extinction." Press release, June 1, 2021. Happy Camp, CA: Karuk Tribe. https://www.karuk.us/images/docs/press/2021/01-06-21_Karuk_Tribe_Declares_Climate_Emergency_Final.pdf.

Kaufmann, Obi. 2019. *The State of Water: Understanding California's Most Precious Resource.* Berkeley, CA: Heyday.

Kelly, Erin Clover, and Marisa Lia Formosa. 2020. "The Economic and Cultural Significance of Cannabis Production to a Rural Place." *Journal of Rural Studies* 75: 1–8.

Kemp, Kym. 2018a. "As Humboldt County Supervisors Meet to Talk Cannabis, Karuk/Yurok Tribes Demand Stronger Regulations for the Industry." *Redheaded Blackbelt*, March 19, 2018. https://kymkemp.com/2018/03/19/as-humboldt-county-supervisors-meet-to-talk-cannabis-today-karuk-yurok-tribes-demand-stronger-regulations-for-the-industry/.

———. 2018b. "Tribe Suspends Operation Yurok: No Large Marijuana Grows." *Redheaded Blackbelt*, July 20, 2018. https://kymkemp.com/2018/07/20/tribe-suspends-operation-yurok-no-large-marijuana-grows/.

———. 2018c. "Potentially Dangerous Pesticides Spilled into Mill Creek Which Flows into the Trinity River." *Redheaded Blackbelt*, October 3, 2018. https://kymkemp.com/2018/10/03/potentially-dangerous-pesticides-spilled-into-mill-creek-which-flows-into-the-trinity-river/.

Kenny, Andrew. 2019. "A Nomadic Plumber Found Mysterious Stones on His Land—So He Became the First Person to Return Land to the Ute Indian Tribe." *Denver Post*, September 13, 2019. https://www.denverpost.com/2019/09/13/land-reparations-san-luis-ute-tribe/.

Kimmerer, Robin Wall. 2015. *Braiding Sweetgrass: Indigenous Wisdom, Scientific Knowledge and the Teachings of Plants.* Minneapolis: Milkweed.

Kimmerer, Robin Wall, and Frank Kanawha Lake. 2001. "The Role of Indigenous Burning in Land Management." *Journal of Forestry* 99, no. 11: 36–41.

Klassen, Mark, and Brandon P. Anthony. 2019. "The Effects of Recreational Cannabis Legalization on Forest Management and Conservation Efforts in U.S. National Forests in the Pacific Northwest." *Ecological Economics* 162: 39–48.

Knott's Berry Farm. n.d. "Pan for Gold." https://www.knotts.com/rides-experiences/pan-for-gold.

Korns, Kristan. 2013. "Drought and Expanding Marijuana Grows Paving Way for Repeat Fish Kill." *Two Rivers Tribune*, August 8, 2013. http://www.tworiverstribune.com/2013/08/drought-and-expanding-marijuana-grows-paving-way-for-repeat-fish-kill/.

LaDuke, Winona. 1999. *All Our Relations: Native Struggles for Land and Life*. Cambridge, MA: South End.

———. 2005. *Recovering the Sacred: The Power of Naming and Claiming*. Cambridge, MA: South End Press.

LaDuke, Winona, and Sean Aaron Cruz. 2012. *The Militarization of Indian Country*. East Lansing: Michigan State University Press.

Lake, Frank K. 2007. "Traditional Ecological Knowledge to Develop and Maintain Fire Regimes in Northwestern California, Klamath-Siskiyou Bioregion: Management and Restoration of Culturally Significant Habitats." PhD diss., Oregon State University. https://www.proquest.com/openview/42d0405eb504444a76327698bedd2ae6/1?pq-origsite=gscholar&cbl=18750.

Lambert, Amber. 2020. "Hidden in Plain Sight: The US Government's Use of the Choctaw Nation as an Environmental Toxics Dumping Ground." *American Indian Culture and Research Journal* 44, no. 1: 97–111.

Lange, Tony. 2022. "California Cannabis Banks $5.2 Billion in 2021 Sales." *Cannabis Business Times*, February 23, 2022. https://www.cannabisbusinesstimes.com/article/california-cannabis-banks-5-point-2-milion-in-2021-sales/.

Langston, Nancy. 1995. *Forest Dreams, Forest Nightmares: The Paradox of Old Growth in the Inland West*. Seattle: University of Washington Press.

Lazar, Steve. 2016. "Mitigated Negative Declaration: Medical Marijuana Land Use Ordinance—Phase IV: Commercial Cultivation of Cannabis for Medical Use." Translated by Humboldt County Planning and Building Department. Eureka, CA: Humboldt County Planning and Building Department.

Lee, Martin A. 2012. *Smoke Signals: A Social History of Marijuana—Medical, Recreational, and Scientific*. New York: Scribner.

Levitan, Mark. 2019. "Tribal Participation in the California Cannabis Market." June 28, 2019. Bureau of Cannabis Control Meeting. Los Angeles, CA. https://www.youtube.com/watch?time_continue=636&v=VnAEMjDIfg0.

Levy, Sharon. 2014. "Pot Poisons Public Lands." *BioScience* 64, no. 4: 265–71.

Lewis, Amanda Chicago. 2016. "How Black People Are Being Shut Out of America's Weed Boom: Whitewashing the Green Rush." *Buzzfeed News*, March 16, 2016. https://www.buzzfeednews.com/article/amandachicagolewis/americas-white-only-weed-boom.

Liboiron, Max. 2021. *Pollution Is Colonialism*. Durham, NC: Duke University Press.

Lichatowich, Jim. 1999. *Salmon Without Rivers: A History of the Pacific Salmon Crisis*. Washington, DC: Island.

Lichatowich, Jim, Rick Williams, Bill Bakke, Jim Myron, David Bella, Bill McMillan, Jack Stanford, David Montgomery, Kurt Beardslee, and Nick Gayeski. 2018. "Wild Pacific Salmon: A Threatened Legacy." St. Helens, OR: Bemis.

Lightfoot, Kent G., and Otis Parrish. 2009. *California Indians and Their Environment: An Introduction*. California Natural History Guides. Berkeley: University of California Press.

Lindsay, Brendan C. 2012. *Murder State: California's Native American Genocide, 1846–1873*. Lincoln: University of Nebraska Press.

Lindström, Susan. 2000. "A Contextual Overview of Human Land Use and Environmental Conditions." In *Lake Tahoe Watershed Assessment, Vol. 1*, edited by D. D. Murphy and C. M. Knopp, 23–127. Pacific Southwest Research Station: US Forest Service.

Lomawaima, K. Tsianina. 2002. "American Indian Education: By Indians versus for Indians." In *A Companion to American Indian History*, edited by Philip J. Deloria and Neal Salisbury, 422–40. Oxford: Blackwell.

Lowry, Chag, Kate Droz-Handwerker, Rain Marshall, Ron Griffith, Fawn White, and Lonyx Landry. 1999. *Northwest Indigenous Gold Rush History: The Indian Survivors of California's Holocaust*. Center for Indian Community Development.

Lumsden, Stephanie. 2014. "Native Americans and the Prison-Industrial Complex in California." Master's thesis, University of California, Davis.

———. 2018. "American Genocide: Historical Methodologies of Settler Disavowal." May 19, 2018. Paper presented at Native American and Indigenous Studies Association Conference, Los Angeles.

Lyons, Oren. 2005. "Fall 2005 Commencement Address by Chief Oren Lyons." University of California, Berkeley, May 22, 2005. https://nature.berkeley.edu/news/2005/05/fall-2005-commencement-address-chief-oren-lyons.

"Marijuana Market Spikes Land Prices in Humboldt." 2017. *Cannifornian*, March 27, 2017. https://www.thecannifornian.com/cannabis-business/cultivation/marijuana-market-spikes-land-prices-humboldt/.

Marks-Block, Tony, Frank Kanawha Lake, Rebecca Bliege Bird, and Lisa M.

Curran. 2021. "Revitalized Karuk and Yurok Cultural Burning to Enhance California Hazelnut for Basketweaving in Northwestern California, USA." *Fire Ecology* 17, no. 6: 1–20.

Marks-Block, Tony, and William Tripp. 2021. "Facilitating Prescribed Fire in Northern California through Indigenous Governance and Interagency Partnerships." *Fire* 4, no. 37: 1–23.

Maroukis, Thomas C. 2010. *The Peyote Road: Religious Freedom and the Native American Church*. Norman: University of Oklahoma Press.

Matsui, Kenichi. 2009. *Native Peoples and Water Rights: Irrigation, Dams, and the Law in Western Canada*. McGill-Queen's Native and Northern Series. Montreal: McGill-Queen's University Press.

Mattei, Ugo, and Laura Nader. 2008. *Plunder: When the Rule of Law Is Illegal*. Malden, MA: Blackwell.

May, Theresa, Suzanne Burcell, Kathleen McCovey, and Jean O'Hara. 2014. *Salmon Is Everything: Community-Based Theater in the Klamath Watershed*. First Peoples: New Directions in Indigenous Studies. Corvallis: Oregon State University Press.

McAuliffe, Barbara A. 2018. "Stolen or Lawful: A Case Review of an Indian Tribe's Claim to Aboriginal Land in California." *California Western International Law Journal* 49, no. 1: 1–25.

McCool, Daniel. 2002. *Native Waters: Contemporary Indian Water Settlements and the Second Treaty Era*. Tucson: University of Arizona Press.

McEvoy, Arthur F. 1986. *The Fisherman's Problem: Ecology and Law in California Fisheries, 1850–1980*. Cambridge: Cambridge University Press.

McLeod, Christopher, dir. 2001. *In Light of Reverence*. Bullfrog Films.

Merchant, Carolyn, ed. 1998. *Green versus Gold: Sources in California's Environmental History*. Washington, DC: Island.

Middleton, Beth Rose, Sabine Talaugon, Thomas Young, Luann Wong, Suzanne Fluharty, Kaitlin Reed, Christine Cosby, and Richard Myers II. 2019. "Bi-Directional Learning: Identifying Contaminants on the Yurok Indian Reservation." *International Journal of Environmental Research and Public Health* 16: 1–18.

Middleton Manning, Beth Rose. 2018. *Upstream: Trust Lands and Power on the Feather River*. Tucson: University of Arizona Press.

Middleton Manning, Beth Rose, and Kaitlin Reed. 2019. "Returning the Yurok Forest to the Yurok Tribe: California's First Tribal Carbon Credit Project." *Stanford Environmental Law Journal* 38, no. 1.

Mihesuah, Devon A., and Elizabeth Hoover. 2019. *Indigenous Food Sovereignty in* the United States: Restoring Cultural Knowledge, Protecting Environments, and Regaining Health. Norman: University of Oklahoma Press.

Miller, Char, ed. 2018. *Where There's Smoke: The Environmental Science, Public Policy, and Politics of Marijuana*. Lawrence: University Press of Kansas.

Miller, Timothy. 2002. "The Historical Communal Roots of Ultraconservative Groups." In *The Cultic Milieu: Oppositional Subcultures in an Age of Globalization*, edited by Jeffrey Kaplan and Heléne Lööw, 75–109. Walnut Creek, CA: AltaMira.

Mills, Evan. 2012. "The Carbon Footprint of Indoor Cannabis Production." *Energy Policy* 46: 58–67.

———. 2021. "Comment on 'Cannabis and the Environment: What Science Tells Us and What We Still Need to Know.'" *Environmental Science and Technology Letters* 8, no. 6: 483–85.

Miranda, Deborah A. 2010. "Extermination of the Joyas: Gendercide in Spanish California." *GLQ: A Journal of Lesbian and Gay Studies* 16, no. 1–2: 253–84.

———. 2013. *Bad Indians: A Tribal Memoir*. Berkeley, CA: Heyday.

Monkerud, Don, Malcolm Terence, and Susan Keese, eds. 2000. *Free Land, Free Love: Tales of a Wilderness Commune*. Aptos, CA: Black Bear.

Morello-Frosch, Rachel, Manuel Pastor Jr., and James Sadd. 2002. "Integrating Environmental Justice and the Precautionary Principle in Research and Policy Making: The Case of Ambient Air Toxics Exposures and Health Risks Among Schoolchildren in Los Angeles." *Annals of the American Academy of Political and Social Science* 584, no. 1: 47–68.

Moreton-Robinson, Aileen. 2015. *The White Possessive: Property, Power, and Indigenous Sovereignty*. Indigenous Americas Series. Minneapolis: University of Minnesota Press.

Morgan, Betsy, Kaitlyn Spangler, Jacob Stuivenvolt Allen, Christina N. Morrisett, Mark W. Brunson, Shih-Yu Simon Wang, and Nancy Huntly. 2021. "Water Availability for Cannabis in Northern California: Intersections of Climate, Policy, and Public Discourse." *Water* 13, no. 1: 1–18.

Most, Stephen. 2006. *River of Renewal: Myth and History in the Klamath Basin*. Portland: Oregon Historical Society Press.

Moyle, Peter B., Jacob V. E. Katz, and Rebecca M. Quiñones. 2011. "Rapid Decline of California's Native Inland Fishes: A Status Assessment." *Biological Conservation* 144: 2414–23.

Moyle, Peter B., Rob Lusardi, and Patrick Samuel. 2017. "State of the Salmonids II: Fish in Hot Water: Status, Threats and Solutions for California Salmon, Steelhead, and Trout." San Francisco: Center for Watershed Sciences, University of California, Davis, and California Trout.

Moyle, Peter B., and Robert D. Nichols. 1974. "Decline of the Native Fish Fauna of the Sierra Nevada Foothills, Central California." *American Midland Naturalist* 92, no. 1: 72–83.

Nagle, Mary Kathryn, and Gloria Steinem. 2016. "Sexual Assault on the Pipeline." *Boston Globe*, September 29, 2016. https://www.bostonglobe.com/opinion/2016/09/29/sexual-assault-pipeline/3jQscLWRcmD12cfefQTNsL/story.html.

Napoleon, Val. 2007. "Thinking about Indigenous Legal Orders." National Centre for First Nations Governance. https://www.law.utoronto.ca/sites/default/files/documents/hewitt-napoleon_on_thinking_about_indigenous_legal_orders.pdf.

National Environmental Justice Advisory Council. 2002. "Fish Consumption and Environmental Justice: A Report Developed from the National Environmental Justice Advisory Council Meeting of December 3–6, 2001." Seattle: Environmental Protection Agency. https://www.epa.gov/environmentaljustice/epa-fish-consumption-and-environmental-justice.

National Organization for the Reform of Marijuana Laws (NORML). 2021. "Study: Legal Marijuana Farms Are Not a Drain on Water Resources." July 8, 2021. https://norml.org/news/2021/07/08/study-legal-marijuana-farms-are-not-a-drain-on-water-resources/.

Nelson, Melissa K., ed. 2008. *Original Instructions: Indigenous Teachings for a Sustainable Future*. Rochester, VT: Bear and Company.

New Frontier Data, Berkeley Cannabis Research Center and Resource Innovation Institute. 2021. "Cannabis H2O: Water Use and Sustainability in Cultivation." https://newfrontierdata.com/product/cannabis-h2o-water-use-and-sustainability-in-cultivation/.

Newcomb, Steven T. 2008. *Pagans in the Promised Land: Decoding the Doctrine of Christian Discovery*. Golden, CO: Fulcrum.

Ngai, Mae. 2021. *The Chinese Question: The Gold Rushes and Global Politics*. New York: W. W. Norton.

Nichols, Robert. 2020. *Theft Is Property! Dispossession and Critical Theory*. Durham, NC: Duke University Press.

Nixon, Rob. 2011. *Slow Violence and the Environmentalism of the Poor*. Cambridge, MA: Harvard University Press.

NoiseCat, Julian Brave. 2015. "Native Tribes Want Pot Business, but Financial Gain May Cost Their Sovereignty." *The Guardian*, October 9, 2015. https://www.theguardian.com/commentisfree/2015/oct/09/native-tribes-want-pot-marijuana-business-financial-gain-may-cost-sovereignty.

Norgaard, Kari Marie. 2005. "The Effects of Altered Diet on the Health of the

Karuk People." Submitted to Federal Energy Regulatory Commission Docket #P-2082 on Behalf of the Karuk Tribe. https://pages.uoregon.edu/norgaard/pdf/Effects-Altered-Diet-Karuk-Norgaard-2005.pdf.

———. 2019. *Salmon and Acorns Feed Our People: Colonialism, Nature, and Social Action.* Nature, Society, and Culture Series. New Brunswick, NJ: Rutgers University Press.

Norgaard, Kari Marie, and Ron Reed. 2017. "Environmental Impacts of Environmental Decline: What Can Native Cosmologies Teach Sociology about Emotions and Environmental Justice?" *Theory and Society* 46: 463–95.

Norton, Jack. 1979. *When Our Worlds Cried: Genocide in Northwestern California.* San Francisco: Indian Historical Press.

———. 2019. "The Past Is Our Future: Thought on Identity, Tradition and Change." In *Ka'm-t'em: A Journey toward Healing*, edited by Kishan Lara-Cooper and Walter J. Lara Sr., 115–33. Pechanga, CA: Great Oak.

Noss, Reed F., ed. 2000. *The Redwood Forest: History, Ecology, and Conservation of Coast Redwoods.* Washington, DC: Island.

Nunn, Neil. 2018. "Toxic Encounters, Settler Logics of Elimination, and the Future of a Continent." *Antipode* 50, no. 5: 1330–48.

O'Brien, Jean. 2010. *Firsting and Lasting: Writing Indians Out of Existence in New England.* Minneapolis: University of Minnesota Press.

Orona, Brittani. 2013. *Stories of the River, Stories of the People.* Video in exhibit. Seven 30 Seconds. https://www.nativewomenscollective.org/storiesoftheriver.html.

Oros, Chisa. 2016. "The Role of Fort Humboldt during the California Gold Rush: A Focus on Local Indigenous Women's Struggle, Resistance and Resilience." Master's thesis, Humboldt State University.

Paley, Dawn. 2014. *Drug War Capitalism.* Oakland, CA: AK.

Parr, Delia, and Jedd Parr. 2009. "California Tribal Water Rights." Paper presented at the California Tribal Water Summit.

Pesticide Action Network. 2010. "Undue Influence." https://www.panna.org/resources/undue-influence.

Pierce, Ronnie. 1998. "Klamath Salmon: Understanding Allocation." Klamath River Basin Fisheries Task Force, US Fish and Wildlife Service, Yreka, CA.

Pierotti, Raymond, and Daniel Wildcat. 2000. "Traditional Ecological Knowledge: The Third Alternative." *Ecological Applications* 10, no. 5: 1333–40.

Pit River Tribe. 2015. "Federal Government Fails to Respect Tribal Self Governance: Pit River Tribe Disappointed in Enforcement Action against the Tribe's Lawful Medical Marijuana Project." July 9, 2015. Burney, CA: Pit River Tribe..

Platt, Tony. 2011. *Grave Matters: Excavating California's Buried Past*. Berkeley, CA: Heyday.

Powell, Tori B. 2021. "$1.19 Billion Worth of Marijuana Seized in Massive Drug Bust in California." *CBS News*, July 9, 2021. https://www.cbsnews.com/news/marijuana-seized-california-billion-drug-bust-illegal-cultivation/.

Prestemon, Jeffrey P., Frank H. Koch, Geoffrey H. Donovan, and Mary T. Lihou. 2019. "Cannabis Legalization by States Reduces Illegal Growing on US National Forests." *Ecological Economics* 164: 106366.

Price, Jennifer. 2019. "The Great California Cannabis Experiment—Is It Working? Regulatory and Industry Perspectives on the Success and Challenges of 2018." Paper presented at the North American Cannabis Summit, Los Angeles. http://northamericancannabissummit.org/wp-content/uploads/2019/03/B6-194_PRICEslides.pdf (website discontinued).

Pyne, Stephen J. 2001. *Fire: A Brief History*. Seattle: University of Washington Press.

Ramirez, Renya K. 2007. *Native Hubs: Culture, Community, and Belonging in Silicon Valley*. Durham, NC: Duke University Press.

Ramos, Seafha. 2019. "Sustaining Hlkelonah Ue Meygeytohl in an Ever-Changing World." In *Ka'm-t'em: A Journey toward Healing*, edited by Kishan Lara-Cooper and Walter J. Lara Sr., 85–93. Pechanga, CA: Great Oak.

Raphael, Ray. 1985. *Cash Crop: An American Dream*. Mendocino, CA: Ridge Times.

Raphael, Ray, and Freeman House. 2007. *Two People, One Place*. Vol. 1. Humboldt History Series. Eureka, CA: Humboldt County Historical Society.

Red Road Project. n.d. "The Winnemem Wintu's Cry to Restore Their Salmon." https://redroadproject.com/winnemem-wintu/.

Reed, Kaitlin. 2022. "Cannabis, Settler Colonialism, and Tribal Sovereignty in California." In *The Routledge Handbook of Post-Prohibition Cannabis Research*, edited by Dominic Corva and Joshua S. Meisel, 53–62. London: Routledge.

Reed, Kaitlin, Beth Rose Middleton Manning, and Deniss Josefina Martinez. 2021. "Becoming Storms: Indigenous Water Protectors Fight for the Future." In *Lessons in Environmental Justice: From Civil Rights to Black Lives Matter and Idle No More*, edited by Michael Mascarenhas, 233–47. Los Angeles: Sage.

Reid, Joshua L. 2015. *The Sea Is My Country: The Maritime World of the Makahs, an Indigenous Borderlands People*. New Haven, CT: Yale University Press.

Reiman, Amanda. 2018. "Cannabis Legalization in California: A Long and Winding Road." In *Where There's Smoke: The Environmental Science, Public Policy, and Politics of Marijuana*, edited by Char Miller, 199–212. Lawrence: University Press of Kansas.

Reo, Nicholas James, and Angela K. Parker. 2013. "Re-Thinking Colonialism to

Prepare for the Impacts of Rapid Environmental Change." *Climatic Change* 120: 671–82.

Reséndez, Andrés. 2016. *The Other Slavery: The Uncovered Story of Indian Enslavement in America*. New York: Houghton Mifflin Harcourt.

Rich, Lindsey N., Margaret Mantor, Erin Ferguson, Ange Darnell Baker, and Erin Chappell. 2020. "Potential Impacts of Plastic from Cannabis Cultivation on Fish and Wildlife Resources." Cannabis special issue, *Journal for the Conservation and Management of California's Species and Ecosystems* 106: 121–31.

Rich, Lindsey N., Stella McMillin, Ange Darnell Baker, and Erin Chappell. 2020. "Pesticides in California: Their Potential Impacts on Wildlife and Their Use in Permitted Cannabis Cultivation." Cannabis special issue, *Journal for the Conservation and Management of California's Species and Ecosystems* 106 : 31–53.

Risling Baldy, Cutcha. 2013. "Why We Gather: Traditional Gathering in Native Northwest California and the Future of Bio-Cultural Sovereignty." *Ecological Processes* 2, no. 17: 1–10.

———. 2015. "Coyote Is Not a Metaphor: On Decolonizing, (Re)Claiming and (Re)Naming Coyote." *Decolonization: Indigeneity, Education and Society* 4, no. 1: 1–20.

———. 2018. *We Are Dancing for You: Native Feminisms and the Revitalization of Women's Coming-of-Age Ceremonies*. Seattle: University of Washington Press.

———. 2020. *Humboldt State University Food Sovereignty Lab and Cultural Workspace: History and Vision*. Arcata, CA: Humboldt State University. https://www.youtube.com/watch?v=hgQQQ3E1Xb8.

———. 2021. "Why We Fish: Decolonizing Salmon Rhetorics and Governance." In *Native American Rhetoric*, edited by Lawrence W. Gross, 165–93. Albuquerque: University of New Mexico Press.

Risling Baldy, Cutcha, and Kayla Begay. 2019. "Xo'ch Na: Nahsde'tɬ-Te: Survivance, Resilience and Unbroken Traditions in Northwest California." In *Ka'm-t'em: A Journey toward Healing*, edited by Kishan Lara-Cooper and Walter J. Lara Sr., 39–61. Pechanga, CA: Great Oak.

Risling Baldy, Cutcha, and Carrie Tully. 2019. "Working for and toward Land Return of Goukdi'n (Jacoby Creek Forest)." https://www.cutcharislingbaldy.com/uploads/2/8/7/3/2873888/working_for_and_toward_land_return_of_goukdi%E2%80%99n___jacoby_creek_forest___1_.pdf

Robbins, William G. 1997. *Landscapes of Promise: The Oregon Story, 1800–1940*. Seattle: University of Washington Press.

Roberts, Anthony. 2019. Letter to Honorable Members of the Board of Supervisors, Yolo County, "Re: Yolo County Cannabis Land Use Ordinance Draft." June 4, 2019.

———. 2021. Letter to Jim Provenza, "Re: Yolo County's Cannabis Land Use Ordinance." March 2, 2021.

Robinson, Brian E., Margaret B. Holland, and Lisa Naughton-Treves. 2014. "Does Secure Land Tenure Save Forests? A Meta-Analysis of the Relationship between Land Tenure and Tropical Deforestation." *Global Environmental Change* 29: 281–93.

Robinson Bosk, Beth, ed. 2000. *The New Settler Interviews, Vol. 1: Boogie at the Brink*. White River Junction, VT: Chelsea Green.

Robison, Jason, Barbara Cosens, Sue Jackson, Kelsey Leonard, and Daniel McCool. 2018. "Indigenous Water Justice." *Lewis and Clark Law Review* 22: 841–921.

Romney, Lee. 2014. "Massive Raid to Help Yurok Tribe Combat Illegal Pot Grows." *Los Angeles Times*, July 21, 2014. https://www.latimes.com/local/lanow/la-me-ln-tribal-drug-bust-20140720-story.html.

Rose, Jeff, Matthew T. J. Brownlee, and Kelly S. Bricker. 2018. "Managers' Perceptions of Illegal Marijuana Cultivation on US Federal Lands." In *Where There's Smoke: The Environmental Science, Public Policy, and Politics of Marijuana*, edited by Char Miller, 69–85. Lawrence: University Press of Kansas.

Rosen, Julia. 2019. "They've Managed the Forest Forever, It's Why They're Key to the Climate Change Fight." *Los Angeles Times*, November 5, 2019. https://www.latimes.com/environment/story/2019-11-05/climate-change-forests-indigenous-peoples.

Saito, Natsu Taylor. 2020. *Settler Colonialism, Race, and the Law*. New York: New York University Press.

Santa Ysabel Tribal Cannabis Regulatory Agency. 2019. "Mountain Source Cannabis Dispensary." Press release. Iipay Nation of Santa Ysabel.

Schneider, Jack. 2008. "Escape from Los Angeles: White Flight from Los Angeles and Its Schools, 1960–1980." *Journal of Urban History* 34, no. 6: 995–1012.

Schneider, Tsim D. 2017. "Coastal Lives and Resilient Histories in Gold Rush–Era Native California." *News from Native California*, Summer 2017.

Schwab, Benjamin, and Van Butsic. 2016. "Estimating the Impact of Cannabis Production on Rural Land Prices in Humboldt County, CA." Paper presented at the Coast Redwood Science Symposium, Eureka, CA.

———. 2017. "Green Acres? Cannabis Agriculture and Rural Land Values in Northern California." Paper presented at the Agricultural and Applied Economics Association Annual Meeting, Chicago.

Scott, James. 1998. *Seeing Like a State: How Certain Schemes to Improve the Human Condition Have Failed*. New Haven, CT: Yale University Press.

Secrest, William B. 2003. *When the Great Spirit Died: The Destruction of the California Indians, 1850–1860*. Sanger, CA: Word Dancer.

Seelau, Ryan. 2014. "In Defense of Tribal Sovereign Immunity: A Pragmatic Look at the Doctrine as a Tool for Strengthening Tribal Courts." *North Dakota Law Review* 90, no. 1: 121–69.

Shiva, Vandana. 1992. "Resources." In *The Development Dictionary: A Guide to Knowledge as Power*, edited by Wolfgang Sachs, 206–18. London: Zed.

Shogren, Elizabeth. 2014. "Illegal, Remote Pot Farms in California Poisoning Rare Wildlife." NPR, February 14, 2014. https://www.npr.org/2014/02/14/275351164/illegal-remote-pot-farms-in-california-poisoning-rare-wildlife.

Short, Damien. 2010. "Cultural Genocide and Indigenous Peoples: A Sociological Approach." *International Journal of Human Rights* 14, no. 6: 833–48.

———. 2016. *Redefining Genocide: Settler Colonialism, Social Death*. London: Zed.

Short Gianotti, Anne G., Jennifer Harrower, Graeme Baird, and Stephen Sepaniak. 2017. "The Quasi-Legal Challenge: Assessing and Governing the Environmental Impacts of Cannabis Cultivation in the North Coastal Basin of California." *Land Use Policy* 61: 124–34.

Sierra Fund. 2008. "Mining's Toxic Legacy: An Initiative to Address Mining Toxins in the Sierra Nevada." Sacramento, CA: Sierra Fund.

Silvaggio, Anthony. 2018. "Cannabis Agriculture in California: The Environmental Consequences of Prohibition." In *Where There's Smoke: The Environmental Science, Public Policy, and Politics of Marijuana*, edited by Char Miller, 13–28. Lawrence: University Press of Kansas.

Silver, Curtis. 2016. "Marijuana's $40 Billion Dollar Green Rush." *Forbes*, June 2, 2016. https://www.forbes.com/sites/curtissilver/2016/06/02/marijuanas-40-billion-dollar-green-rush/#28f627a93097.

Simpson, Leanne Betasamosake. 2017. *As We Have Always Done: Indigenous Freedom through Radical Resistance*. Minneapolis: University of Minnesota Press.

Sims, Hank. 2018. "Yurok Tribe Acquires Thousands of Acres of Blue Creek Watershed from Green Diamond; Will Manage Land to Restore Ecosystem." *Lost Coast Outpost*, February 28, 2018. https://lostcoastoutpost.com/2018/feb/28/yurok-tribe-acquires-thousands-acres-blue-creek-wa/.

Smith, Andrea. 2005. *Conquest: Sexual Violence and American Indian Genocide*. Cambridge, MA: South End.

Smith, Linda Tuhiwai. 2012. *Decolonizing Methodologies: Research and Indigenous Peoples*. 2nd ed. London: Zed.

Smith, Neil. 1996. "The Production of Nature." In *FutureNatural: Nature, Science, Culture*, edited by George Robertson, Melinda Mash, Lisa Tickner, Jon Bird, Barry Curtis, and Tim Putnam. London: Routledge.

Smith, Paul Chaat, and Robert Allen Warrior. 1996. *Like a Hurricane: The Indian Movement from Alcatraz to Wounded Knee*. New York: New Press.

Smith, Sherry L. 2012. *Hippies, Indians and the Fight for Red Power*. New York: Oxford University Press.

Solnit, Rebecca. 2006. "Winged Mercury and the Golden Calf." *Orion*, October 2006. https://orionmagazine.org/article/winged-mercury-and-the-golden-calf/.

Sowerwine, Jennifer, Lisa Hillman, Megan Mucioki, Daniel Sarna-Wojcicki, and Edith Friedman. 2019. "Food Security Assessment of Native American Communities in the Klamath Basin with the Karuk Tribe, Klamath Tribes, Yurok Tribe, and Hoopa Tribe." Berkeley: Karuk–UC Berkeley Collaborative, University of California. https://nature.berkeley.edu/karuk-collaborative/wp-content/uploads/2019/05/Food-Security-Assessment-Web-5.20.pdf.

Spence, Mark David. 1999. *Dispossessing the Wilderness: Indian Removal and the Making of the National Parks*. New York: Oxford University Press.

Spice, Anne. 2018. "Processing Settler Toxicities: Part 2." *Footnotes* (blog), June 23, 2018. https://footnotesblog.com/2018/06/23/processing-settler-toxicities-part-ii/.

State Water Resources Control Board (SWRCB). 2017. "Cannabis Cultivation Policy—Principles and Guidelines (Requirements) for Cannabis Cultivation." Res. No. 2017-0063. https://www.waterboards.ca.gov/board/final_cannabis_policy_with_att_a.pdf.

———. 2021. "Cannabis Cultivation Water Rights." https://www.waterboards.ca.gov/water_issues/programs/cannabis/cannabis_water_rights.html.

———. n.d. "Beneficial Uses: Definitions." https://www.waterboards.ca.gov/about_us/performance_report_1314/plan_assess/docs/bu_definitions_012114.pdf.

Steel, Zachary L., Hugh D. Safford, and Joshua H. Viers. 2015. "The Fire Frequency-Severity Relationship and the Legacy of Fire Suppression in California Forests." *Ecosphere* 6, no. 1: 1–23.

Stephens, Scott L., and Neil G. Sugihara. 2006. "Fire Management and Policy since European Settlement." In *Fire in California's Ecosystems*, edited by Neil G. Sugihara, 431–43. Berkeley: University of California Press.

Stevenson, E. A. 1998. "A Federal Agent Assesses Mining's Impact on the Indians, 1853." In *Green versus Gold: Sources in California's Environmental History*, edited by Carolyn Merchant, 109–10. Washington, DC: Island.

Stoa, Ryan B. 2016. "Weed and Water Law: Regulating Legal Marijuana." *Hastings Law Journal* 67: 565–622.

Stone, Janferie. 2012. "Occupied Alcatraz: Native American Community and Activism." In *West of Eden: Communes and Utopia in Northern California*, edited by Iain Boal et al., 81–91. Oakland, CA: PM.

Strong, Douglas. 1998. "Cutting the Sierra Forests." In *Green versus Gold: Sources in California's Environmental History*, edited by Carolyn Merchant, 162–65. Washington, DC: Island.

Sze, Julie, and Jonathan K. London. 2008. "Environmental Justice at the Crossroads." *Sociology Compass* 2, no. 4: 1331–54.

Teves, Stephanie Nohelani, Andrea Smith, and Michelle H. Raheja, eds. 2015. *Native Studies Keywords. Critical Issues in Indigenous Studies*. Tucson: University of Arizona Press.

Thiesen, Stan, and Orrin Plocher. 2016. "Water Demand Estimate for Marijuana Cultivation within the Yurok Indian Reservation." Translated by Yurok Tribe Environmental Program. Arcata, CA: Freshwater Environmental Services. https://aa66d7ad-ce17-4f18-b261-e08464f615b8.filesusr.com/ugd/23c897_26ab747919ca4e31ad1fbdc1c54f7f56.pdf.

Thompson, Craig, Mourad W. Gabriel, Greta M. Wengert, and J. Mark Higley. 2018. "Effects of Illegal Marijuana Cultivation on Wildlife: Pesticide Exposure in a Native Carnivore and Consequences for the Species' Survival." In *Where There's Smoke: The Environmental Science, Public Policy, and Politics of Marijuana*, edited by Char Miller, 40–57. Lawrence: University Press of Kansas.

Thompson, Lucy. 1916. *To the American Indian: Reminiscences of a Yurok Woman*. Berkeley, CA: Heyday.

Thornton, Russell. 1987. *American Indian Holocaust and Survival: A Population History since 1492*. Norman: University of Oklahoma Press.

Thorson, John E., Sarah Britton, and Bonnie G. Colby, eds. 2006. *Tribal Water Rights: Essays in Contemporary Law, Policy, and Economics*. Tucson: University of Arizona Press.

Todd, Zoe. 2014. "Fish Pluralities: Human-Animal Relations and Sites of Engagement in Paulatuuq, Arctic Canada." *Études/Inuit/Studies* 38, no. 1–2: 217–38.

———. 2016a. "Fish Pluralities, Refraction and Decolonization in Amiskwaciwâskahikan." Paper presented at the Master of Visual Studies Proseminar Series, University of Toronto, March 14, 2016. https://www.youtube.com/watch?v=tO-WvCQ3PJU&t.

———. 2016b. "An Indigenous Feminist's Take on the Ontological Turn: 'Ontology' Is Just Another Word for Colonialism." *Journal of Historical Sociology* 29, no. 1: 4–22.

Tolley, Sara-Larus. 2006. *Quest for Tribal Acknowledgment: California's Honey Lake Maidus*. Norman: University of Oklahoma Press.

Trafzer, Clifford E., and Joel R. Hyer, eds. 1999. *"Exterminate Them": Written Accounts of the Murder, Rape, and Slavery of Native Americans during the California Gold Rush, 1848–1868*. East Lansing: Michigan State University Press.

Trafzer, Clifford E., Jean A. Keller, and Lorene Sisquoc, eds. 2006. *Boarding*

School Blues: Revisiting American Indian Educational Experiences. Indigenous Education Series. Lincoln: University of Nebraska Press.

Tripp, Bill. 2020. "Our Land Was Taken, but We Still Hold the Knowledge of How to Stop Mega-Fires." *The Guardian*, September 16, 2020. https://www.theguardian.com/commentisfree/2020/sep/16/california-wildfires-cultural-burns-indigenous-people.

Tuck, Eve, and K. Wayne Yang. 2012. "Decolonization Is Not a Metaphor." *Decolonization: Indigeneity, Education and Society* 1, no. 1: 1–40.

Turner, Robin L., and Diana Pei Wu. 2002. "Environmental Justice and Environmental Racism: An Annotated Bibliography and General Overview, Focusing on U.S. Literature, 1996–2002." Berkeley Workshop on Environmental Politics, Institute of International Studies. https://digitalcommons.butler.edu/facsch_papers/575.

Unsettling Klamath River. 2016. "An Open Letter to the Black Bear Ranch Family." https://unsettlingklamathriver.files.wordpress.com/2016/03/black-bear-open-letter-from-unsettling.pdf.

US Environmental Protection Agency (EPA). 2007. "Tulare Lake Basin Hydrology and Hydrography: A Summary of the Movement of Water and Aquatic Species." Document no. 909R07002. https://www.epa.gov/sites/default/files/2018-05/documents/tulare-fullreport.pdf.

———. 2021. "Basic Information about Nonpoint Source (NPS) Pollution." United States Environmental Protection Agency. 2021. https://www.epa.gov/nps/basic-information-about-nonpoint-source-nps-pollution.

US Forest Service (USFS). n.d. "History and Culture." United States Department of Agriculture. https://www.fs.usda.gov/main/lpnf/learning/history-culture.

Vanderheiden, Isabella. 2021. "Cannabis Farms Not as Thirsty as Previously Thought." *Times-Standard*, July 6, 2021. https://www.times-standard.com/2021/07/06/study-cannabis-farms-not-as-thirsty-as-previously-thought/.

Vickery, Jamie, and Lori M. Hunter. 2016. "Native Americans: Where in Environmental Justice." *Society and Natural Resources* 29, no. 1: 36–52.

Vinyeta, Kirsten. 2022. "Under the Guise of Science: How the US Forest Service Deployed Settler Colonial and Racist Logics to Advance an Unsubstantiated Fire Suppression Agenda." *Environmental Sociology* 8, no. 2: 134–48. https://doi.org/10.1080/23251042.2021.1987608.

Visit California. n.d. "Discover Gold Country: Jamestown." https://www.visitcalifornia.com/in/node/38831.

Voyles, Traci Brynne. 2015. *Wastelanding: Legacies of Uranium Mining in Navajo Country*. Minneapolis: University of Minnesota Press.

Walter, Shoshana. 2016. "In Secretive Marijuana Industry, Whispers of Abuse and Trafficking." *Reveal News from the Center for Investigative Reporting*, September 8, 2016. https://revealnews.org/article/in-secretive-marijuana-industry-whispers-of-abuse-and-trafficking/.

Wang, Ian J., Jacob C. Brenner, and Van Butsic. 2017. "Cannabis, an Emerging Agricultural Crop, Leads to Deforestation and Fragmentation." *Frontiers in Ecology and the Environment* 15, no. 9: 495–501.

Warren, Karen J., and Nisvan Erkal, eds. 1997. *Ecofeminism: Women, Culture, Nature*. Bloomington: Indiana University Press.

Wartenberg, Ariani C., Patricia A. Holden, Hekia Bodwitch, Phoebe Parker-Shames, Thomas Novotny, Thomas C. Harmon, Stephen C. Hart, et al. 2021. "Cannabis and the Environment: What Science Tells Us and What We Still Need to Know." *Environmental Science and Technology Letters* 8, no. 2: 98–107.

Weaver, Jace, ed. 1996. *Defending Mother Earth: Native American Perspectives on Environmental Justice*. Maryknoll, NY: Orbis.

Weinreb, Elaine. 2021. "'Witnessing the Collapse': Officials Warn of Cascading Crises Facing Pacific Salmon." *North Coast Journal*, August 5, 2021. https://www.northcoastjournal.com/humboldt/witnessing-the-collapse/Content?oid=21162729.

Weir, David, and Mark Schapiro. 1981. *Circle of Poison: Pesticides and People in a Hungry World*. Oakland, CA: Institute for Food and Development Policy.

Wengert, Greta M., Mourad W. Gabriel, J. Mark Higley, and Craig Thompson. 2018. "Ecological Impacts across the Landscape: Trespass Marijuana Cultivation on Western Public Lands." In *Where There's Smoke: The Environmental Science, Public Policy, and Politics of Marijuana*, edited by Char Miller, 29–39. Lawrence: University Press of Kansas.

Westerling, Anthony L., and B. P. Bryant. 2008. "Climate Change and Wildfire in California." *Climatic Change* 87, no. 1: 231–49.

White, Kenneth Michael, and Mirya R. Holman. 2012. "Marijuana Prohibition in California: Racial Prejudice and Selective-Arrests." *Race, Gender and Class* 19, no. 3–4: 75–92.

Whited, Tamara. 1998. "Myth and Reality of the Humboldt Forests." In *Green versus Gold: Sources in California's Environmental History*, edited by Carolyn Merchant, 155–61. Washington, DC: Island.

Whiteley, Kathleen. 2020. "The Indians of California versus the United States of America: California Dreaming in the Land of Lost Treaties, 1900–1975." PhD diss., University of Michigan.

Whyte, Kyle Powys. 2015. "Indigenous Food Systems, Environmental Justice, and Settler-Industrial States." In *Global Food, Global Justice: Essays on Eating under*

Globalization, edited by M. Rawlinson and C. Ward, 143–56. Cambridge: Cambridge Scholars.

———. 2016. "Indigenous Experience, Environmental Justice and Settler Colonialism." In *Nature and Experience: Phenomenology and the Environment*, edited by Bryan E. Bannon. London: Rowman and Littlefield.

———. 2017. "Indigenous Climate Change Studies: Indigenizing Futures, Decolonizing the Anthropocene." *English Language Notes* 55, no. 1–2: 153–62.

———. 2018. "Settler Colonialism, Ecology, and Environmental Injustice." *Environment and Society: Advances in Research* 9: 125–44.

Whyte, Kyle, Chris Caldwell, and Marie Schaefer. 2018. "Indigenous Lessons about Sustainability Are Not Just for 'All Humanity.'" In *Sustainability: Approaches to Environmental Justice and Social Power*, edited by Julie Sze. New York: New York University Press. https://kylewhyte.marcom.cal.msu.edu/wp-content/uploads/sites/12/2018/07/IndigenousInsightsintoSustainabilityarenotforAllHumanity.pdf.

Widick, Richard. 2009. *Trouble in the Forest: California's Redwood Timber Wars*. Minneapolis: University of Minnesota Press.

Wildcat, Daniel R. 2009. *Red Alert! Saving the Planet with Indigenous Knowledge*. Golden, CO: Fulcrum.

Wilkinson, Charles. 2005. *Blood Struggle: The Rise of Modern Indian Nations*. New York: W. W. Norton.

Williams, Robert A., Jr. 2005. *Like a Loaded Weapon: The Rehnquist Court, Indian Rights, and the Legal History of Racism in America*. Indigenous Americas Series. Minneapolis: University of Minnesota Press.

Winnemem Wintu Band. n.d. "Salmon Return: The Story of the New Zealand McCloud Salmon." https://www.winnememwintu.us/mccloud-salmon-restoration/.

Wiyot Tribe. 2021. "Wiyot Tribe Declares State of Emergency Regarding Local Rivers." Press release, June 16, 2021. Loleta, CA: Wiyot Tribe. http://www.wiyot.us/CivicAlerts.aspx?AID=55&ARC=102.

———. n.d. "Tuluwat Project." Loleta, CA: Wiyot Tribe. http://www.wiyot.us/186/Tuluwat-Project.

Wolfe, Patrick. 2006. "Settler Colonialism and the Elimination of the Native." *Journal of Genocide Research* 8, no. 4: 387–409.

Yakowicz, Will. 2021. "U.S. Cannabis Sales Hit Record $17.5 Billion as Americans Consume More Marijuana than Ever Before." *Forbes*, March 3, 2021. https://www.forbes.com/sites/willyakowicz/2021/03/03/us-cannabis-sales-hit-record-175-billion-as-americans-consume-more-marijuana-than-ever-before/?sh=6198ad292bcf.

Yazzie, Melanie K., and Cutcha Risling Baldy. 2018. "Introduction: Indigenous Peoples and the Politics of Water." *Decolonization: Indigeneity, Education and Society* 7, no. 1: 1–18.

Yellowhorse Kesler, Sam. 2021. "Indian Boarding Schools' Traumatic Legacy, and the Fight to Get Native Ancestors Back." NPR, August 28, 2021. https://www.npr.org/sections/codeswitch/2021/08/28/1031398120/native-boarding-schools-repatriation-remains-carlisle.

Yoshiyama, Ronald M., and Frank W. Fisher. 2001. "Long Time Past: Baird Station and the McCloud Wintu." *Fisheries* 26, no. 3: 6–22.

Yoshiyama, Ronald M., Frank W. Fisher, and Peter B. Moyle. 1998. "Historical Abundance and Decline of Chinook Salmon in the Central Valley Region of California." *North American Journal of Fisheries Management* 18: 487–521.

Yuan, Christine, dir. 2016. *Tending the Wild*. KCETLink Media Group. https://www.kcet.org/shows/tending-the-wild/episodes/tending-the-wild.

Yurok Tribe. 2006. "Zero Tolerance Ordinance." Resolution 06-65. Klamath, CA: Yurok Tribe. https://yurok.tribal.codes/YTC/AppC.

———. 2012. "Prop 215 Is Not Recognized on Reservation." *Yurok Today*, November 2012.

———. 2013a. "Controlled Substances Ordinance." Klamath, CA: Yurok Tribal Code.

———. 2013b. "Pot Growers Not Welcome on Yurok Land: Tribal Cops Team Up with BIA, Hoopa Tribe to Eradicate Large Grows." *Yurok Today*, October 2013.

———. 2014. "Operation Yurok Takes Down Big Grows: Multi-Agency Raids Help Drought-Stricken Klamath River." *Yurok Today*, August 2014.

———. 2015. "Tribal Operation Nets 55,000 Illegal Plants: Operation Yurok Halts Major Water Diversions, Sends Message to Growers." *Yurok Today*, August 2015.

———. 2016. "Public Safety Removes Big Pot Plantations: Humboldt Sheriffs, CA National Guard, BIA Involved in Eradication Effort." *Yurok Today*, August 2016.

———. 2018a. "Ke'wet Ceremonial District." Resolution 18–87. Klamath, CA: Yurok Tribe.

———. 2018b. "Operation Yurok Considered a Success as No Major Illegal Grows Found on Tribal Lands." Press release, *Times-Standard*, July 20, 2018. https://www.times-standard.com/2018/07/20/operation-yurok-considered-a-success-as-no-major-illegal-grows-found-on-tribal-lands/.

———. 2018c. "Yurok Tribe Cannabis Task Force." https://www.yuroktribe

.org/departments/planning/YurokCannabisTaskForce.htm (website discontinued).

———. 2019. "Yurok Tribe Says Humboldt Planning Commission 'Made the Right Call' Denying Commercial Cannabis Grow Permit in Meeting Thursday." *Redheaded Blackbelt*, February 16, 2019. https://kymkemp.com/2019/02/16/yurok-tribe-says-humboldt-planning-commission-made-the-right-call-denying-commercial-cannabis-grow-permit-in-meeting-thursday/.

Yurok Tribe Environmental Program (YTEP). 2018. "Environmental Impacts of Illegal Cannabis Cultivation on Yurok Territory." Paper presented at the Yurok Tribe Annual Meeting, Klamath, CA, August 4.

Yurok Tribe GIS Program. 2015. "Yurok Reservation and Surrounding Area." Klamath, CA: Yurok Tribe. https://aa66d7ad-ce17-4f18-b261-e08464f615b8.filesusr.com/ugd/23c897_dabe47690bd64ae9bded650879132a76.pdf.

Zipper, Samuel C., Jennifer K. Carah, Christopher Dillis, Tom Gleeson, Ben Kerr, Melissa M. Rohde, Jeanette K. Howard, and Julie K. H. Zimmerman. 2019. "Cannabis and Residential Groundwater Pumping Impacts on Streamflow and Ecosystems in Northern California." *Environmental Research Communications* 1, no. 12: 1–15.

INDEX

Adult Use of Marijuana Act (AUMA), 130
aerial imagery, 145
Agustinez, Anecita, 176
Akers, Donna, 97
Akins, Damon, 27–28, 35
Allen, Hezekiah, 136
ancestors, 153–54
Anderson, M. Kat, 3, 30, 53, 55, 56, 183
Arneil, Barbara, 188
As Long as the Grass Grows: The Indigenous Fight for Environmental Justice, from Colonization to Standing Rock (Gilio-Whitaker), 19

back-to-the-land movement, 99–100, 107, 109, 110, 112–13, 116–18, 125
Bacon, J. M., 14, 16, 73
Baird, Spencer, 92, 93
Baird Hatchery, 93–94, 135
Barnd, Natchee Blu, 235
Barta, Tony, 33, 34, 227
Bauer, Scott, 149, 160
Bauer, William, Jr., 27–28, 33, 35, 63, 128
Blake, Dawn, 167
Blue Lake Rancheria Tribe, 163, 207
Boal, Iain, 100
boarding schools, 102–3, 218
Brady, Emily, 118, 119
Brenner, Jacob C., 157–58, 159
Brook, Daniel, 227–28
Brown, Edmond, 191
Bullard, Robert D., 225

Bureau of Indian Affairs (BIA), 65, 67–68, 133–34
Burnett, Peter, 37–38
Bustic, Van, 157–58, 159

California (state of), 12, 27–28, 29–30, 35–36, 43, 63, 153
California Environmental Quality Act (CEQA), 146, 163
California Indians: and ecological disaster of settlement, 46; enslavement of, 35, 36; and environmental justice, 225–26; and exposure to contaminants, 229–30; extermination of, 38–40; food insecurity of, 47; genocide, 15, 27, 31–34, 38, 41, 238; Indigenous ecological management practices of, 1, 71; land, 7, 42–43, 54–55, 63; and land return, 236–37; population, 1; and psychological repercussions, 230–31; racist rhetoric, 2–3; relocation of, 104–5; removal of, 33; and settler colonialism, 24; shut out of cannabis industry, 136–37; stewardship, 53, 183–85; traditional ecological knowledge (TEK), 3–6; treaties, 41–42, 103; violence against, 35–36; and Western scientists, 6
California Native American Cannabis Association (C-NACA), 136–38
"California Story," 27, 32, 128
Campaign Against Marijuana Planting (CAMP), 126–27

cannabis: cultivation of, 120–21, 122–24, 125, 132, 139, 153, 161–62, 221–23; cultivation of, and California Indians, 20, 22–23; ecological impacts of, 131, 139–41, 158–59; and inaccessible sacred sites, 169–71; legalization of, 17–18, 130–31; medicinal, 128–30; and plastic pollution, 221; prohibition, 17, 18, 126–27; and white supremacy, 18
Capay Valley, 131–32
Carroll, Clint, 134–35
Cash Crop (Raphael), 65, 117
Central Valley Water Project, 14, 122
Che-Na-Wah Weitch-Ah-Wah (Lucy Thompson), 59
Clay, Karen, 34, 45
Colegrove-Powell, Anna, 56
colonization, 241n4
conservation, 115
Coulthard, Glen, 15
cultural burns, 70, 74, 243n2
Curley, Andrew, 44
Custer Died for Your Sins (V. Deloria), 103

Davies, Thom, 230
Dawes General Allotment Act, 63, 109, 110
decolonization, 236, 242n8
"Decolonization Is Not a Metaphor" (Tuck and Yang), 236
de Corti, Espera Oscar, 116
Deloria, Phillip, 110–11
Deloria, Vine, Jr., 103
Dispossessing the Wilderness: Indian Removal and the Making of the National Parks (Spence), 114

dispossession, 15, 16–17, 22, 34, 50, 63–64, 97–98, 155–56
Drew, Jesse, 108
Drug War Capitalism (Paley), 127
Dumping in Dixie: Race, Class, and Environmental Quality (Bullard), 225

Echo-Hawk, Walter, 235–36
ecocolonialism, 14
Emerald Triangle, 99, 119
Emerson, Ralph Waldo, 4, 113
environmental contamination, 212
environmental justice movement (EJM), 225

fire management, 53, 56–57, 60, 69–74
firsting, 241n5
Forbes, Jack D., 2–3, 31
forestry, scientific, 68
Fox, Coleen, 238

Gabriel, Mourad, 209–10, 214, 216–17
Galeano, Eduardo, 29
Gemmill, Mickey, Jr., 133–34
Genocide in Northwestern California: When Our Worlds Cried (Norton), 25
Gensaw, David, 175, 178, 226
Gibson, Micah, 161, 165, 221
Gilio-Whitaker, Dina, 19, 99, 107, 110, 113, 134, 135
Golden Rules: The Origins of California Water Law in the Gold Rush (Kanazawa), 44
gold rush, 16, 23, 26–29, 31, 34–35, 48–49, 60, 232–33
Goode, Ron, 57
green rush: birth of, 66, 126; cannabis cultivation, 15, 118, 121, 123–24, 129, 131; contamination, 212; and

dispossession, 128; end of, 20, 235; environmental harms of, 120, 141, 185, 207; and genocide, 17, 21; and land, 21, 160–62; and Native peoples, 123–24; negative impacts on Native peoples, 138, 153, 207, 208, 233; origin story, 98; profits, 18, 208; and real estate prices, 160–61; and self-determination, 135; and settler-colonial land dispossession, 13, 17, 172; and settler-colonial resource rushing, 131; and settler cultivation, 12; systemically benefits settler populations, 138, 207, 210; and tribal nations, 23; violence of, 117, 135, 164, 232
Gross, Lawrence, 238

Hanson, G. M., 36
Haozous, Bob, 166
Harris, Cheryl, 12
hazardous solid waste, 219–20
Henley, Thomas J., 47
Hernandez, Jessica, 3, 14, 19, 46
Higley, Mark, 130–31, 143
Hillman, Leaf, 153, 171, 207
Hoopa Valley Tribe, 130, 167, 216
Humboldt Bay 26, 62
Humboldt County, 25–26, 30, 35, 62, 64, 118, 120, 147; cannabis, 20; region 83, 86
Humboldt: Life on America's Frontier (Brady), 118
Hupa peoples, 111, 117
Hurwitz, Laura, 22, 99, 101–2, 107, 162

Iipay Nation, 137–38
Indian Island Massacre, 25–26
Indigenous peoples: burning practices of, 56–57, 69, 71–72; and the California story, 27; and cannabis, 22; and cannabis cultivation, 124, 154, 172; cannabis industry inaccessible to, 121; and climate, 234–35; cultural appropriation of, 110, 115, 116; displacement of, 187, 190, 207; and dispossession, 15, 19, 22, 34, 50, 63, 98–99, 155–56; and ecological management, 1, 4; ecologies 54, 62, 73, 226; environmental governance, 134–35; and environmental justice, 225–26, 233; and environment movements, 115; eradicating, 38–39; erasure of, 27, 28, 62, 108, 109, 113, 183, 226; fishermen, 87–88, 90, 210; and food sovereignty, 81, 83, 95; and forest management, 69–70, 71–72; genocide, 128; knowledge, 5–6, 21, 23, 46, 71, 72, 74, 101; land and water stewardship, 3, 45, 53, 55, 78, 97, 236; lands of, 46, 67, 107, 152–53, 156–57, 181, 228; and the law, 35–36; living in settler states, 8, 11; racism toward, 60; relationships to land, 7, 9–14, 18–19, 21, 28, 102, 177; relationships to Salmon, 76, 77–78, 79–84, 226; relationships to water, 183–84, 188; relocation of, 42, 104; rhetoric of, 61–62; rights of, 235–36, 238; sacred sites of, 112, 171; and toxins, 213, 229–30, 232; and traditional ecological knowledge (TEK), 55–56, 95, 208; treaties, 42–43; violence against, 15–16, 26, 29, 31, 48–49, 52–53, 78, 117. *See also* California Indians
Iron Eyes Cody, 115–16

Johnson, Nick, 128
Johnston, Scott, 48

Kanazawa, Mark, 44–45
Karuk peoples, 57, 107, 108, 117, 162, 170, 181, 207; territory confiscation, 65
Kelsey, Charles E., 43
Kimmerer, Robin Wall, 6–7
Klamath River Basin, 3–4

LaDuke, Winona, 97
LaPena, Sage, 5
Leeper, Joseph, 119
Liboiron, Max, 228–29
Lichatowich, Jim, 86, 91, 92, 95
Lindsay, Brendan, 37
Lindsay, Jeff, 217
loggers, 57–58
lumber, 64
Lumsden, Stephanie, 32, 33, 37
Lynn, Daniel D., 26
Lyons, Chief Oren, 6

manifest destiny, 118
Marks-Block, Tony, 56
Marshall, John, 95
Matsui, Kenichi, 188
McCovey, Louisa, 164
McCovey, Richard, 87
McEvoy, Arthur, 89–90, 95
Medicinal and Adult-Use Cannabis Regulation and Safety Act (MAUCRSA), 130
Mexican-American War, 15
Middleton Manning, Beth Rose, 42–43, 186, 190, 191
militias, 38–39, 53, 124
Miller, Timothy, 100, 146

mining, 47–49
Miranda, Deborah A., 2, 242n1
Miwok Indians, 55, 108
Modoc Indians, 108
Morehead, Janet, 164
Moreton-Robinson, Aileen, 12
Morgan, Thomas J., 112, 201
Muir, John, 4, 55, 113, 184
Myers, Richard, 165

National Organization for the Reform of Marijuana Laws (NORML), 198–99, 201, 205
Native Space: Geographic Strategies to Unsettle Settler Colonialism (Barnd), 235
Nelson, Melissa, 7
Newsom, Gavin, 237
Ngai, Mae, 28
Nixon, Rob, 230
Norgaard, Kari M., 13, 16, 46, 73, 162, 184, 230
Norton, Jack, 25, 32, 33, 36, 53, 238

O'Brien, Jean, 10
Oceti Sakowin nation, 105
Operation Yurok, 23, 142, 168, 173–74, 175, 176–80, 194–95, 201

Paley, Dawn, 127
paraquat, 125–26, 247n2
Phelps, Earle B., 229
Pinchot, Gifford, 4, 67, 71
Pit River Tribe, 133
Pole, Aaron, 167–68
Pollution Is Colonialism (Liboiron), 228
post-apocalypse stress syndrome (PASS), 242n1

Ramos, Seafha, 55–56, 208
Raphael, Ray, 65–66, 117, 119
Redefining Genocide: Settler Colonialism, Social Death and Ecocide (Short), 33
Reed, Ron, 230
residential schools, 102–3, 218
Risling Baldy, Cutcha, 6, 27, 184, 239
Roosevelt, Theodore, 4
Roots of Our Renewal: Ethnobotany and Cherokee Environmental Governance (Carroll), 134

Saito, Natsu Taylor, 10
Salmon: canneries, 86–87; decline, 79, 88–89, 91–92, 198; fisheries, 60; and gold rush, 85–86; habitats, 82, 90, 200, 239; hatcheries, 92–96; Indigenous relationships to, 76, 77–78, 79–84, 226; kill, 76–77, 130; marine nutrients of, 8, 78; mining impacting, 212; as Native relatives, 135; and natural resources, 90; parasites, 75; pathogens, 207; populations, 193, 199; runs, 57, 181–82, 239; rush, 16; people, 194; settler management of, 90–91; spawning, 92, 94–95, 97, 123, 142, 147, 157–58, 187; species, 66–67; and timber rush, 86; and toxins, 219, 232; Yurok relationships to, 77–78
Salmon and Acorns Feed Our People (Norgaard), 73
Scott, James, 50, 199
Seeing Like a State (Scott), 199
settler colonialism: and California Indians, 24; definition of, 8–9; dispossession, 15, 16–17, 34; and ecological violence, 53; ecology of, 13, 14, 15, 16, 62; and environmental justice, 19, 226–27; and exploitation of Indigenous lands, 49; and land, 10, 11–14; mitigation, 229; and natural resource management, 224; and orientations to land, 234–35, 239; violence, 9, 12–13, 14, 15–16, 18, 231, 233
Shasta Dam, 14
Shiva, Vandana, 51
Short, Damien, 33, 228
Short Gianotti, Anne, 144
Sierra Fund, 48
Silvaggio, Anthony, 125, 127
Sisk, Chief Caleen, 112–13
Spence, Mark David, 114
Spice, Anne, 226–27, 228
State Water Project (SWP), 190, 191
State Water Resources Control Board (SWRCB), 129–30, 195–96, 201
Stevenson, E. A., 47
Stone, Janferie, 106
Stone, Livingston, 92–93, 96
Streeter, H. W., 229
sugarpine trees, 60
Synder, Rich, 237

Teller, Henry, 112
Tending the Wild (Anderson), 53
termination, 103
Thoreau, Henry David, 4, 113
timber rush, 22, 50–53, 60–61
toxins, 210, 211–13, 214, 216, 218–19
traditional ecological knowledge (TEK), 3–6, 55–56, 208
treaties, 41–42, 103, 105, 153
trespass cultivation, 138, 141–42, 147–50, 180, 210–11, 213, 216–17, 222
Tripp, Bill, 70, 74

Trouble in the Forest: California's Redwood Timber Wars (Widick), 62
Tuck, Eve, 9, 102, 106, 185, 236
Tuluwat, 231–32, 236
Turtle Island, 2, 5, 100, 112, 183, 243n1
Tuttle, Koiya, 166, 168–69, 223–24

US Forest Service (USFS), 67, 72

Voyles, Traci Brynne, 19

Walter, Shoshana, 165
Wang, Ian, 159
Wartenberg, Ariani, 146
Washoe peoples, 61
water: and cannabis production, 192; diversion, 195–97, 199; forbearance period, 204–5; and genocidal violence and displacement of Indigenous peoples, 207; Indigenous relationships to, 183–84; Operation Yurok and, 194–95, 201; quantifying, usage, 197–202, 206; rights, 44–46, 185–87, 188–92; sources for cannabis production, 202–4; State Water Resources Act, 191; Tribal perspectives of, 193–94; and Wiyot Tribe, 181–83
We Are the Land: A History of Native California (Akins and W. Bauer), 27
Weeks Act, 71
Wengert, Greta, 222
West of Eden: Communes and Utopia in Northern California (Boal et al.), 100
We Were All Like Migrant Workers Here (W. Bauer), 63

When Our Worlds Cried: Genocide in Northwestern California (Norton), 53, 238
Where There's Smoke: The Environmental Science, Public Policy, and Politics of Marijuana (Miller), 146
Whiteley, Kathleen, 43
Whiteness as Property (Harris), 12
The White Possessive: Property, Power, and Indigenous Sovereignty (Moreton-Robinson), 12
Whyte, Kyle Powys, 7, 14, 16, 19, 46, 156, 226
Widick, Richard, 62
Wildcat, Daniel, 5, 6
wildfires, 69
Winnemem Wintu Tribe, 88, 93–94, 112, 135
Wiseman, Maury, 32
Wiyot peoples, 25, 117, 162, 181–83, 231, 236
Wolfe, Patrick, 10, 13, 33
Wright, Gavin, 34, 45

Yang, K. Wayne, 9, 102, 106, 185, 236
Yazzie, Melanie, 184
Yocha Dehe Wintun Nation, 131
Yurok ancestral territory, 65, 122–23
Yurok elders, 8
Yurok fishing rights, 87
Yurok tribal lands, 20, 23
Yurok Tribe, 20, 55, 56, 111, 117, 123, 167, 171–72, 173
Yurok Tribe Environmental Program (YTEP), 142, 161, 164, 166, 168, 178–79, 200, 219–20

CHARLOTTE COTÉ AND COLL THRUSH *Series Editors*

Indigenous Confluences publishes innovative works that use decolonizing perspectives and transnational approaches to explore the experiences of Indigenous peoples across North America, with a special emphasis on the Pacific coast.

Settler Cannabis: From Gold Rush to Green Rush in Indigenous Northern California, by Kaitlin Reed

A Drum in One Hand, a Sockeye in the Other: Stories of Indigenous Food Sovereignty from the Northwest Coast, by Charlotte Coté

A Chemehuevi Song: The Resilience of a Southern Paiute Tribe, by Clifford E. Trafzer

Education at the Edge of Empire: Negotiating Pueblo Identity in New Mexico's Indian Boarding Schools, by John R. Gram

Indian Blood: HIV and Colonial Trauma in San Francisco's Two-Spirit Community, by Andrew J. Jolivette

Native Students at Work: American Indian Labor and Sherman Institute's Outing Program, 1900–1945, by Kevin Whalen

California through Native Eyes: Reclaiming History, by William J. Bauer Jr.

Unlikely Alliances: Native Nations and White Communities Join to Defend Rural Lands, by Zoltán Grossman

Dismembered: Native Disenrollment and the Battle for Human Rights, by David E. Wilkins and Shelly Hulse Wilkins

Network Sovereignty: Building the Internet across Indian Country, by Marisa Elena Duarte

Chinook Resilience: Heritage and Cultural Revitalization on the Lower Columbia River, by Jon Daehnke

Power in the Telling: Grand Ronde, Warm Springs, and Intertribal Relations in the Casino Era, by Brook Colley

We Are Dancing for You: Native Feminisms and the Revitalization of Women's Coming-of-Age Ceremonies, by Cutcha Risling Baldy

www.ingramcontent.com/pod-product-compliance
Lightning Source LLC
Chambersburg PA
CBHW030525230426
43665CB00010B/767